SENATOR BENTON AND THE PEOPLE

 Early American Places is a collaborative project of the University of Georgia Press, New York University Press, Northern Illinois University Press, and the University of Nebraska Press. The series is supported by the Andrew W. Mellon Foundation. For more information, please visit www.earlyamericanplaces.org.

ADVISORY BOARD
Vincent Brown, *Duke University*
Stephanie M. H. Camp, *University of Washington*
Andrew Cayton, *Miami University*
Cornelia Hughes Dayton, *University of Connecticut*
Nicole Eustace, *New York University*
Amy S. Greenberg, *Pennsylvania State University*
Ramón A. Gutiérrez, *University of Chicago*
Peter Charles Hoffer, *University of Georgia*
Karen Ordahl Kupperman, *New York University*
Joshua Piker, *University of Oklahoma*
Mark M. Smith, *University of South Carolina*
Rosemarie Zagarri, *George Mason University*

Senator Benton and the People

Master Race Democracy
on the Early American Frontiers

KEN S. MUELLER

NIU Press
DEKALB

© 2014 by Northern Illinois University Press

Published by the Northern Illinois University Press
DeKalb, Illinois 60115

All Rights Reserved

Library of Congress Cataloging-in-Publication-Data

Mueller, Ken.
  Senator Benton and the people: master race democracy on the early American frontiers / Ken Mueller.
     pages cm
  Includes bibliographical references and index.
  ISBN 978-0-87580-479-8 (cloth)
  ISBN 978-0-87580-700-3 (pbk.)
  ISBN 978-1-60909-151-4 (e-book)
  1. Benton, Thomas Hart, 1782–1858. 2. Legislators—United States—Biography. 3. United States—Politics and government—1815–1861. 4. United States. Congress. Senate—Biography. 5. Missouri—Biography. I. Title.
  E340.B4M84 2014
  328.73'092—dc23
  [B]

2013041733

Contents

	Acknowledgments	ix
	Introduction	1
1	Honor and Country: Bloody Island	14
2	The Transformation of Frontier Missouri: Frontiers of Inclusion, Frontiers of Exclusion	54
3	The Triumph of Master Race Democracy: The Racialization of American Politics	95
4	"The Land Belongs to the People": Public Lands, States' Rights, and the "Indian Problem"	135
5	Old Bullion and the Borderlands: Mexican Dollars	177
6	The Destiny of the Races: The Free Soil Schism	226
	Notes	261
	Bibliography	293
	Index	307

ACKNOWLEDGMENTS

This work originated as my doctoral dissertation at Saint Louis University. The career of Thomas Hart Benton seemed to me an ideal subject for research as I wanted to write about a political figure of national importance and many of the surviving primary sources on Benton were close at hand in the archives of the Missouri Historical Society.

In the course of the ten-year journey from proposal to dissertation to book, a number of people have helped to make this project a reality. First and foremost I wish to thank my advisor, Lewis C. Perry, professor emeritus and former John Francis Bannon Chair at Saint Louis University. Lew Perry advised me early on to steer away from a straightforward biography of Senator Benton as it would be very difficult to write a better one than William N. Chambers already had. Rather, he encouraged me to develop an interpretive framework within which to reveal Benton's importance to a new generation of scholars of the early American republic. Thanks as well to Professor Michal J. Rozbicki, also of SLU, who not only served on my dissertation committee but as a mentor for my teaching endeavors, and to Professor Louis S. Gerteis, from the University of Missouri–St. Louis, an accomplished historian of Senator Benton's adopted home city, whose suggestions improved the quality of my final dissertation significantly.

More recently, I am in debt to the editors and staff at Northern Illinois University Press for their interest in publishing my manuscript. Editors Sara Hoerdeman, Mark Heineke, Kenton Clymer, Susan Bean, and Linda

Manning, in turn, guided me through the process from peer review to proofing and demonstrated considerable understanding with the questions and impatience of a novice author. Thanks also to Shaun Allshouse who completed the jacket design and to the reviewers whose suggestions helped clarify some of the ambiguities in the text.

Appreciation is also due to the Andrew W. Mellon Foundation for funding the Early American Places series, particularly to Tim Roberts, managing editor of that initiative, and copy editor Gary von Euer for their help in the final stages of getting the book to press. My thanks go as well to Enid Zafron and Indexing Partners LLC for their services.

To the degree that *Senator Benton and the People* is successful as a piece of historical research and interesting to the reader, everyone mentioned above had a hand in making it so. Whatever flaws or shortcomings this book possesses are solely the responsibility of the author.

Finally, thanks to Kami, without whose love and support neither this nor anything else worthwhile in my life would be possible. The adventure continues.

SENATOR BENTON AND THE PEOPLE

Introduction

Nineteenth-century Missourians liked to recount the story of a party held in honor of Senator Thomas Hart Benton. As the famous man was introduced, the guests tried to outdo one another in superlatives. One referred to Benton as "the greatest senator in the United States." Another as "not only the greatest senator in the United States; he is the greatest man in the United States." A third asserted that Benton was "the greatest man not only in the United States, but in the world." Still another . . . "not only the greatest man in the world, but he is the greatest man who ever lived." The final toast was proposed to "not only the greatest man who ever lived, but he is the greatest man who ever will live." At this point, the story goes, Benton rose, bowed, and replied, "My friends, you do me but simple justice."

Benton's national career spanned over three decades of American territorial expansion and political democratization. The conclusion of a generation of foreign crises that had consumed the young republic's attention prior to 1815 now allowed the people of the United States to turn to settling the nation's interior and developing its economy. As the growing American population pushed westward, an epic debate commenced over the shape of the country in years to come. Would it develop, as Thomas Jefferson had hoped, along the lines of a rural Arcadia, with land as the true measure of wealth and the vehicle of a rough equality for white men? Or would the vision of the Hamiltonian Federalists and of economic nationalists within Jefferson's own party prevail—one that encouraged the growth of cities and manufacturing? Never far from these debates were questions that threatened the very existence of the Union: the relationship of the states to the central government; the arrival of immigrants from different ethnic and religious backgrounds than most native-born citizens; the status of the Indians; the growing disagreement over slavery and *its* expansion into new territories; and the overwhelming desire for land and still more land.

During those crucial decades, the "Great Triumvirate" of Henry Clay, Daniel Webster, and John C. Calhoun dominated the national political scene. While different in many respects, the three were united in their opposition to the policies of Andrew Jackson and his supporters in the Democratic Party. Numerous works have examined the careers and relationships of the three great opposition leaders. Less attention has been devoted to Benton of Missouri, the greatest Jacksonian lawmaker of the era. No Democratic legislator of the period can compare, in terms of either influence or longevity, with Benton. While "Old Bullion" (as he was known for his hard-money stance) has been the focus of comparatively little scholarly attention in recent decades, in his own day Benton was every bit as celebrated as Webster, Clay, and Calhoun. Indeed the Missourian's foremost twentieth-century biographer placed Benton alongside his famous adversaries to form a "great Senatorial quadrumvirate."[1]

Like Clay, and like Jackson himself, Benton hailed from the West. Leader of the "radical" Democrats in the Senate, he claimed to represent the rights of "the common man"—the frontier farmers and urban laboring classes—against the "monied interests" of the eastern cities. "Benton and the people," Missouri's senator was fond of saying, "are one and the same, Sir; synonymous terms." This bit of bombast tells us a good deal about the man who represented his state in Congress for over thirty years. Benton was possessed of enormous ego and a touchy sense of personal honor. He was prone, in his early years, to pick fights over real or imagined insults. In his maturity, he became the apostle of the Democracy in the trans-Mississippi West, so wholly identifying himself with the radical agrarian principles of cheap land and hard money that, to many of his constituents, he seemed what he claimed himself to be—a sort of walking Leviathan dominating the Senate chamber, stumping his home state, and fending off the challenges of lesser politicians as he championed the cause of "the people." Ever an ardent nationalist, Benton supported war with Britain in 1812, both to defend the young country's honor and to expand its territory. He fought for Missouri's entrance into the Union and for American claims to Oregon and Texas. And as sectional issues arose, he stood with Jackson, Van Buren, and other Unionists against the nullifiers and secessionists—ultimately his most hated enemies—who would divide the people with whom he so fully identified himself.²

Yet this conflation of "the people" and their tribune raises questions that have not been addressed in earlier biographies of Benton, the most recent of which appeared more than a half-century ago. If we are to understand the career of Thomas Hart Benton today, it must be evaluated within the context of an evolving historical literature on western expansion, Jacksonian politics, slavery controversies, and a host of other areas that his lengthy public service influenced in one way or another. The nature of Jacksonian democracy, for instance, has been an issue of controversy among historians for well over a century. Only the broad outlines of these debates need be discussed here, but it will be helpful to bear in mind the major trends in twentieth-century American historiography as we examine studies in which Benton has figured prominently.

Late-nineteenth-century historians of the United States tended to view the Civil War as the climactic event in the American story and interpreted all national history in terms of the controversies that had brought on the war. Although influenced to some degree by the idea of "scientific" or critical history, they continued to view their work as a forum for moral judgments. Thus when dealing with questions relating to the Revolution, the adoption of the Constitution, the political controversies between Jeffersonians and Hamiltonians, or Jackson and the Whigs, they were deeply concerned with questions of who was right and what principles were correct. For the most part, history continued to be written from a northeastern standpoint. Southern accounts enshrining the nobility of the "Lost Cause" had yet to make their influence felt in American historiography. "Objectivity" was still largely defined by historians in opposition to a narrowly sectional (usually meaning southern) perspective.³

This "Whig" or nationalist interpretation of American history was evident in the first attempt at a formal biography of Thomas Hart Benton to fall outside the category of eulogies or memoirs. It was written in 1886 by a young Theodore Roosevelt during his stint as a Dakota rancher and published the following year as part of the American Statesmen Series. The author was much concerned over the quality of the work, completed in a period of three months between March and June 1886 without the benefit of adequate research materials. Roosevelt's *Benton* is therefore a flawed effort, its scholarship so haphazard as to now be irrelevant to historians of the Early Republic. Nonetheless, the book rewards examination as much for what it tells us about the author and the historical viewpoint of his times, as about the subject.⁴

Roosevelt approaches the events leading up to the Civil War from a perspective typical of northern historians of his day. Jefferson was "the father of nullification, and therefore of secession." Benton, however, though a southerner and a slaveholder, is the courageous nationalist who understands the dangers posed by Calhoun and his followers. Roosevelt asserts, "The United States has the same right to protect itself from death by nullification, secession, or rebellion that a man has to protect himself from death by assassination." Calhoun's disquisitions on the constitutionality of nullification were of no more interest to subsequent generations than "the extraordinary arguments and discussions of the schoolmen of the Middle Ages."⁵

Roosevelt finds his most authentic voice when discussing western expansion. "Benton was deeply imbued with the masterful, overbearing spirit of the West ... a spirit whose manifestations are not always agreeable, but the possession of which is certainly a most healthy sign of the virile strength of a young community." The statesman reflected the attitude of his constituents, "especially in regard to our encroachments upon the territory of neighboring powers ... which, reduced to its simplest terms was: that it was our manifest destiny to swallow up the land of all adjoining nations who were too weak to withstand us." Roosevelt disapproves of this theory as having "obtained immense popularity among all statesmen of easy international morality." Yet, a virulent sense of the Darwinian terms in which the author himself viewed the world comes through in his assessment of the war with Mexico as unavoidable. "As a matter of fact it was inevitable, as well as in the highest degree desirable for the good of humanity at large, that the American people should ultimately crowd out the Mexicans from their sparsely populated Northern provinces." In commenting on the Manifest Destiny of the 1840s, Roosevelt hints at his own role as an imperialist in the 1890s and after. Although one reviewer objected to a "stain [sic] of blood and iron, muscular Christianity minus the Christian part, in the author's philosophy of civilization," Roosevelt's *Benton* remained the standard, indeed the only, biography of the Missourian for nearly two decades.⁶

The next *Life of Thomas Hart Benton* was published in 1904. William M. Meigs produced a study that was better researched than Roosevelt's, but retained much the same emphasis. Meigs interviewed a number of surviving acquaintances who had known Benton personally and uncritically related anecdotes that had grown over the years with the telling.

Although aware of the 1855 fire that had destroyed Benton's Washington residence as well as "many valuable papers," Meigs curiously posits that his subject "was not, I think, much given to epistolary correspondence," as "I have not secured any large mass of his letters." Failure to consult relevant sources in North Carolina led Meigs to mistakenly identify Thomas Hart Benton's father Jesse as the English-born secretary to Governor William Tryon and to attribute Benton's expulsion from Chapel Hill to a practical joke gone wrong. These misconceptions would persist for decades and would even be included in a number of encyclopedia articles on Benton. Within a year, a second full-length biography, this one by Joseph M. Rogers, appeared. Rogers produced a narrative that was becoming the pattern for Benton studies—long on florid prose, riddled with factual errors or distortions, and almost devoid of source documentation.[7]

It would be a half-century before the publication of another comprehensive study of Benton. During the intervening decades, the senator was the focus of several articles and unpublished dissertations, the majority completed at institutions within Missouri. In 1926 Clarence H. McClure of Central Missouri State Teachers College published *Opposition in Missouri to Thomas Hart Benton*. McClure sought to identify the sources of political opposition that culminated in Benton's 1851 defeat for reelection to the Senate. He argued that Benton had difficulty being reelected as early as 1844. Long before that date the Democratic Party in Missouri had begun to break into factions over the questions of banking and currency policy. These disputes, in turn, led to the injection of constitutional problems into the contest and the eventual seizure of the Texas issue by the already well-organized opposition to Benton during the 1844 campaign. McClure's study, concentrating on the dynamics of politics at the state level, reveals the transition to the new "scientific" historiography during the early years of the twentieth century, which emphasized a critical reading of primary sources. He eschewed well-worn anecdotes about Benton's character or patriotism and focused on the topic of his study, which is the schism within the dominant state party between proponents of hard and soft money and how those divisions affected support for Benton.[8]

In 1953 Perry McCandless of the University of Missouri completed a dissertation on "Thomas Hart Benton, His Sources of Political Strength in Missouri from 1815 to 1838." Like McClure, McCandless focused on state politics, but began his inquiry with Benton's arrival in St. Louis following the War of 1812. McCandless made the former Tennessean's ties to the powerful "junto" faction much more explicit than in previous biographies. Although Benton had resumed his law practice in 1815, it was clear that his real interest was in territorial politics. Once elected as senator, Benton embraced programs favored by his growing Missouri constituency, such as national aid in developing the Santa Fe trade, while abandoning others that he had advocated earlier, such as broad federal support for internal improvements. All the while, the key to Benton's political rise was his appeal to western voters through his proposal to graduate the price of public lands. After 1825, Benton's shift to the Jackson camp made him unbeatable.

McCandless sees 1838 as a turning point; after that date the Democratic Party in Missouri split into the overt factions described by McClure. McCandless argues that "Benton did not want any party organization that stood between the people and the object of their choice. He feared that party organization and party machinery might be controlled by a few political leaders and hamper the free expression of the popular will, and he expressed his great opposition to the nominating caucus and convention." When a regular party apparatus did develop in Missouri after 1838, Benton was not a part of it—though McCandless speculates that this may have been because of his established position of power and his personal techniques.[9]

Perhaps McCandless did not want to acknowledge Benton's need to rely on anything so mundane as a party organization, but the ties between the senator and the "Central" or "Fayette" Clique (named for the central Missouri River counties) who controlled the Democratic Party in his state were indispensable. Although Benton eventually made direct appeals to the voters in opposition to the Central Missouri Clique, this break would occur more than ten years later and over differences concerning slavery in the territories. In the years that McCandless deals with, the hard-money Democrats who dominated the Boonslick counties were Benton's strongest supporters and he was their representative to the national government.

In 1956 William Nisbet Chambers of Washington University in St. Louis published *Old Bullion Benton: Senator from the New West*. Over a half-century later, Chambers's *Benton* remains the definitive biography. The book was exhaustively researched and corrects a number of errors found in the earlier works by Roosevelt, Meigs, and Rogers. We learn, for instance, that Jesse Benton Sr. was neither the first of his line in America nor was he a Loyalist during the Revolution. Chambers corrected the impression that the Benton family was reduced to grinding poverty following Jesse's death in 1790. (He dismissed these accounts as "twaddle" based on "the alleged egalitarian character of the Piedmont.") And it was Chambers who at last revealed the truth concerning the hundred-and-fifty-year-old rumors about Thomas Hart Benton's expulsion from the University of North Carolina. By consulting the faculty records at Chapel Hill, Chambers found that his subject, as an adolescent, did indeed repeatedly steal from his college roommates and that he confessed to the crime when confronted with incontrovertible evidence.[10]

Chambers's account of Benton's political career is developed in three fairly distinct phases. During the first, from Benton's arrival in St. Louis in 1815 to Jackson's election as president in 1828, his subject is undergoing "The Education of a Democrat." Still tied to St. Louis mercantile interests, Benton has yet to come down decisively on the side of the yeoman farmers who will constitute the base of Jacksonian democracy in the West. In Chambers's words, his rising politico is still "Roman-riding" (referring to an equestrian style in which the rider controls two horses at once with a foot on the back of each). The horses in this colorful image are the competing socioeconomic ideals of *Enterprise* and *Arcadia*—the Hamiltonian and Jeffersonian visions of America's future, respectively. The second stage of Benton's career lasts from Jackson's inauguration to the election of 1840. This phase is dominated by the "war" against the Bank of the United States and the legislative struggle for hard money. Benton is "Democracy's Advocate" against the "monied interests" of the East. Finally, during the 1840s and 1850s, Benton is portrayed as the mature statesman, fighting to save the country from the growing threat of disunion.

How are we to evaluate Chambers's biography, a book that remains the most widely cited source on its subject? One contemporary reviewer observed that, for all Chambers's attention to detail, "as regards the conflict of ideas and the confusion of objectives within the Jacksonian movement, still a matter for fruitful debate, [*Old Bullion*] is almost silent." This is far from true. Within the parameters that defined the political history of his day, Chambers did an admirable job of analyzing Benton's role. On one hand, it is tempting to look at this work as one more product of the Cold War consensus school. Benton's career, Chambers informs us, "makes a revealing case study not only in the politics of his era, but in American democratic politics in general . . . because what he stood for is part of the American democratic heritage on which we draw *as we face the problems of today.*"[11]

On the other hand, *Old Bullion Benton*, at least in its central chapters, describes the Jacksonian movement in tones reminiscent of Schlesinger and even Beard. Chambers justifies a study of Benton by arguing that "More than any other leader except Jackson himself, he was the distinctive advocate and representative of the democratic movement of his age." The Great Triumvirate of Clay, Calhoun, and Webster all acted in the Senate as the representatives of "some narrow, limited class or interest group combination—whether Northern or Eastern commerce, manufacturing, and capital, or Southern plantation slaveholders. In Benton, however, the nation's freeholding farmers, together with urban small traders and workingmen, found their great champion.... Despite some confusions and contradictions, Old Bullion Benton became in his maturity the most consistent, persuasive national spokesman for the emergent popular democracy of his day." As we shall see, Benton's response to the emerging political economy of antebellum Missouri was rather more complex than Chambers's stirring introduction would have us believe. To some degree he continued Roman-riding the twin horses of Enterprise and Arcadia right down to the end of his career. Nonetheless, Chambers defines the importance of his subject for all who would attempt to follow him in his task. "We can achieve no adequate appreciation of the Jackson era and its long-range significance," he writes, "unless we understand the role that Thomas Benton played in the portentous events of his times."[12]

In 1958 Elbert B. Smith of Iowa State College published *Magnificent Missourian: The Life of Thomas Hart Benton*. Compared to Chambers's study, Smith's biography may be characterized as less meticulous in the citation of primary sources (Smith relies on some of Chambers's earlier articles on Benton which had been published in regional journals). It is more topical and less rigidly chronological, and Smith is less prone to attempt cramming every personal fact about Benton between the covers of his book, though he is more willing to relate a colorful anecdote concerning Benton without the carefully footnoted caveats that fill Chambers's work. This being the case, *Magnificent Missourian* is more welcoming to the reader. It seems to have been published by the J.B. Lippincott Company with a more general audience in mind. The other noticeable difference in Smith's biography is the greater emphasis on western expansion. Smith spends more time discussing the fur trade and the Santa Fe Trail, and at least alludes to Benton's attitudes toward Indian removal (which Chambers fails to confront at all). *Magnificent Missourian* and *Old Bullion Benton* apparently did such an impressive job of providing biographical information on their subject that historians who have written about Benton since the 1960s have, for the most part, referred to these works rather than consult primary sources themselves.[13]

No book-length biographical studies of Benton have appeared since those of Chambers and Smith, though a number of articles—primarily in the *Missouri Historical Review* and the old *Bulletin of the Missouri Historical Society*—have dealt with various aspects of his career. These have added to the depth of our understanding of Benton's role in the context of Missouri politics. However, their scope of inquiry remained limited to an understanding of American political culture that informed both Chambers and Smith. In the article literature, Benton's policies and rhetoric are still interpreted within a paradigm that is not only defined by the concerns and values of white male voters, but that fails to even recognize other categories of Americans (and foreigners) who were directly impacted by these very controversies.[14]

A more truly modern interpretation of Benton is to be found in a handful of works appearing since the 1970s, which view Jacksonian democracy within the context of the overall racialization of American society and politics during the early nineteenth century. According to this view, Benton is less a hero of the common man or martyr for the cause of the Union than a racist demagogue, exemplary of the white male supremacy that was the foundation for the vaunted egalitarianism of the Age of Jackson. In *Race and Manifest Destiny* (1981), Reginald Horsman presented a portrait of Benton sharply at odds with traditional accounts. Horsman argued that, during the first half of the nineteenth century, American intellectuals developed a racist ideology that assumed an American national character derived from Anglo-Saxon and Teutonic ancestry. White Anglo-Saxons, according to this account, were inherently superior to blacks, Indians, Mexicans, and even non-English white immigrants, and allegedly benefited mankind by civilizing, exploiting, or exterminating the lesser races. Thus, Indian removal, black slavery, annexation of Mexican lands, and anti-immigrant nativism could all be justified by a racialist view that derived both from current scientific theories and the unique American experience of westward expansion and conquest.

Horsman introduced Benton as an example of this very Anglo-Saxon racism. He acknowledged, though, that Benton did not view racial categories in the same way throughout his career and at no point considered citizens of Anglo-Saxon heritage superior to other whites of European descent. Benton "clearly revealed in his writings and speeches the changing perceptions of the meaning of American expansion and the manner in which racial exclusiveness ultimately replaced hopes for the whole of humanity." In his editorials for the *St. Louis Enquirer* (1818–1819) and early Senate speeches, Benton emphasized the limitless benefits to be gained by trade with Asia and expansion into Latin America. He envisioned the United States bringing republicanism to the whole world and "seeking connections with Asiatic powers against their common enemies of freedom in Europe." As a senator, says Horsman, Benton never abandoned the dream either of trade with Asia or of America bringing hope to its peoples, "but never again after the 1820s was he able to conceive of cooperation with non-white peoples in the same sanguine terms."[15]

Even as the process that several recent historians have dubbed the "emergence of racial modernity" redefined America socially and politically during the Jacksonian era, Benton remained "willing to accept a variety of European white races while completely rejecting the races of the rest of the world. Benton wanted American Anglo-Saxonism to be tempered with a sense of its Celtic components, and he was unwilling to simply consign the Mexicans to the realm of the colored inferior races." Horsman goes on to quote an 1846 speech in which Benton describes his conception of the hierarchy of the world's races with the "Celtic-Anglo-Saxon division of the Caucasian race" at the apex, followed by the Mongolian, or "Yellow," race which was in turn superior to the Malay, or "Brown," the American Indian, or "Red," and the Ethiopian, or "Black" races. "The white race alone had followed the divine command to subdue and replenish the earth.... The principle is founded in nature and in God's command; and it will continue to be obeyed."[16]

Alexander Saxton's *Rise and Fall of the White Republic* (1990) also explored the links between racial attitudes and political ideology in nineteenth-century America. Saxton conceived a three-stage dialectic during which race played an essential role in the development of the American capitalist political economy. The earliest phase witnessed a National Republican or Whig "thesis" in which mercantile and planter elites provided a national agenda based upon hierarchies of both race and class. The Jacksonians provided an "antithesis," which adopted racism in support of egalitarianism for whites. Where the National Republican politics of deference had utilized a "soft" racism, with race as simply one more variant of class subordination, the *herrenvolk* democracy of Jackson's supporters asserted class equality for whites on the basis of racial exclusion. By mid-century, the Republican Party provided a "synthesis" by adopting the Jacksonian rhetoric of equal opportunity through such vehicles as free land, while retaining the Whig economic program of protective tariffs, internal improvements, and a national banking system. The "hard" racism of the Jacksonians became an element of Free Soil ideology as well as a bulwark of the post–Civil War settlement, setting the conditions under which racially exclusive organized labor became a stabilizing element of industrial capitalism.[17]

Benton figures prominently in the middle phase of Saxton's dialectic. Typical of "agrarian radicals," his rejection of efforts to reserve public lands for either special interests or federal revenues makes him a favorite of fellow westerners like David Crockett. The "people," in Saxton's account of Jacksonian legitimation, are the *producers*—defined by Benton as "planters, farmers, mechanics (with a slight infusion from the commercial and professional classes)"—the "productive and burthen-bearing classes of the nation." The Democrats, says Saxton, were so successful in propagating their populist vision "that farmers and workingmen for generations to come would look back on Jacksonian America as a classless society in which the fraternity of citizen producers had directly controlled governmental power."[18]

This interpretation necessarily overlooks the exclusion of blacks and Indians from the egalitarian agenda of the Jacksonians. Such an omission would likewise be essential in the transition to industrial capitalism under the Republican synthesis during the second half of the nineteenth century. "Thus," writes Saxton, "the legitimizing construct of the Jacksonian coalition in the 1830s and early 1840s ended by legitimizing the defection of its northern and western constituencies. Thomas Hart Benton—prince of expansionists, egalitarian defender of squatters' rights, indefatigable racist—became, appropriately, father-in-law to the first Republican candidate for president." Saxton links the breakup of the Jacksonian coalition by the 1850s to racial attitudes among northern farmers, frontiersmen, and urban workers who supported the Democracy. Just as they had earlier accepted southern arguments in favor of plantation slavery on the grounds that slavery provided the only effective means for quarantining Africans in America, they now concluded that the entry of Africans, slave or free, into the western territories had to be prevented. For former Democrats like Walt Whitman, allegiance to the white nation was transferred, at length, from the party of Jackson to the party of Frémont and Lincoln.[19]

In his 2005 synthesis, *The Rise of American Democracy: From Jefferson to Lincoln*, Sean Wilentz traced the lineage of popular government from Jacksonianism to the modern Republican Party. Most significant in his treatment of Benton is the author's linking of the Missourian to the "country" form of democracy that Wilentz traces from the Carolina Regulation of the 1760s, through the Whiskey Rebellion of the Federalist

Era, to the movements for cheap land and hard money during the Age of Jackson. A supporter of Henry Clay's American System prior to the 1824 presidential contest, Benton was by that date "in political transition." The outcry of his rural constituents against eastern creditors and the Second Bank of the United States after the Panic of 1819, coupled with the influence of Virginia's John Randolph, led Benton to back Jackson rather than Clay's ally John Quincy Adams when the election went to the House of Representatives. Combining his attacks on paper money with his advocacy for reduction in the price of public lands, Benton transformed himself into the spokesman for Missouri's small-farm settlers—and of western opposition to the National Republicanism of Clay and Adams.[20]

Throughout the central chapters of *The Rise of American Democracy*, which deal with Jackson's presidency, Benton appears in the familiar role of spokesman for a radical, hard-money, western democracy and always the steadfast supporter of Old Hickory's policies. He is often paired with Jackson's other loyal retainer, Martin Van Buren. Indeed, there are curious parallels in the attitudes of both men toward their party and the manner in which those views change over the years. "The Democracy," as contemporaries called it, goes from being the authentic voice of the common man to the vehicle of the Slave Power by the late 1840s. However, while Van Buren chose to lead an independent political movement against the expansion of slavery, Benton remained loyal to the party of Jackson to his dying day.

Students of nineteenth-century America found Wilentz's approach a welcome change from the extremes represented by earlier interpretive frameworks. While he views the Democrats of the 1830s in much the same positive terms that Arthur Schlesinger Jr. did in his *Age of Jackson*, Wilentz acknowledges the racist aspects of Jacksonians' ideology. He devotes a good bit of attention to the issue of Indian removal (which Schlesinger ignored), as well as taking on the contradictions of slavery. The fact that the peculiar institution was expanding at the same time that democracy was expanding was a paradox central to the story of American politics during these decades. Wilentz has provided an account of the rise—and decline—of Jacksonian democracy that is both sympathetic in its analysis and honest in the consideration of its drawbacks. It thus serves as a better starting point than any work of comparable scope for reexamining the career of Thomas Hart Benton in greater detail.[21]

It is impossible to understand Benton's political career without conceding that it was possible for him to be *both* the courageous nationalist portrayed in early biographies and an unquestioning believer in the racial superiority of white Americans. The contradiction inherent in this statement for the twenty-first-century reader was largely ignored by historians who published through the 1950s. Since that time scholars have emphasized that ideologies based on the concept of racial hierarchy were, in fact, at the heart of American democracy during the Age of Jackson. They correctly assert that the economic and political egalitarianism of the Jacksonians was exclusively for white men. The majority of the citizenry, thus narrowly defined, viewed blacks as fit only for enslavement or exclusion and Native Americans for removal or extermination. To read earlier biographies is to be made only remotely aware of Benton's status as a slaveholder. Neither, in these accounts, does Old Bullion's self-proclaimed hostility toward Indians warrant even the most perfunctory treatment. I have tried to present an account of antebellum politics that addresses some of the racial issues neglected by older biographies of Benton. At the same time, I hope to relate those aspects of Benton's devotion to the Union that have been ignored by his modern detractors, yet were worthy of admiration from earlier writers. The debates that took place during Benton's public career concerning slavery, territorial expansion, public lands, and the relation of the states to the federal government went to the heart of the issue of just who "the people" were and what rights various groups might expect in the developing American republic.

Any comprehensive portrait must reconcile recent interpretations, which place Benton's racial attitudes front and center, with older portrayals that reveal a heroic—if flawed—figure often absent from later accounts. In attempting to do so, it was necessary to resist the temptation to either praise or condemn my subject to excess. I try to show that Benton, while possessing many qualities repugnant to modern readers, retained a certain integrity within the terms understood by himself and his peers. However much he might compromise for political advantage over the course of his career—and he did this often—Benton's actions were always guided by an unconditional devotion to his peculiar vision of a united and expansive American republic. By evaluating Benton's career in light of his attitudes toward slavery, Indian removal, and the Mexican borderlands, amidst the other topics, I hope not only to reveal his importance to a new generation of readers, but also to offer a more authentic portrait of the man than has heretofore been presented by either his admirers or detractors.

1 / Honor and Country: Bloody Island

The morning was unusually hot for late September. In the first hour of light, before the town of St. Louis had fully awakened, the waters of the Mississippi were disturbed by the oars of two boats being rowed toward a sandbar near the far side of the river. One contained prominent St. Louis lawyer Thomas Hart Benton, along with his second, attorney Luke Lawless, and surgeon Dr. Bernard Farrar. In the other was U.S. District Attorney Charles Lucas, along with his seconds and surgeon. As the two small craft came up to the sandbar the men disembarked and began to complete the final preparations for conducting an "affair of honor."[1]

In 1817 Benton was thirty-five years old; Lucas ten years younger. The two had met at the same spot six weeks earlier following a public exchange of insults at the recent territorial election. Neither gentleman felt the incident could be allowed to go unanswered. The first "interview" on August 12, conducted with pistols at a distance of thirty feet had been inconclusive. Benton had shot his opponent in the neck, causing him to bleed profusely. Lucas, who had issued the initial challenge, agreed that honor had been satisfied and that he would not ask for another meeting. Benton, however, was not satisfied and announced that he wanted the young attorney to fight again as soon as his wound should be in a state to permit him. Lucas agreed to do so just before he fainted from loss of blood.

The second duel occurred on the oppressively warm and humid morning of September 27. Both of the principals were nervous and on edge. This time the two men were to stand only ten feet apart. Colonel Eli

Clemson, one of Lucas's seconds, was to give the preparatory command "Fire," followed by the count "One, two, three." The parties were not to fire before the count of "one" or after "three." Benton removed his coat and rolled up his shirtsleeves, exposing his red flannel undershirt. He complained of the heat as he went to a basin of water to rinse his neck and arms.

"Gentlemen are you ready," asked Colonel Clemson.

"Don't you *see* I'm not ready," snapped Benton.

He dried off and took his place as Lawless handed him his pistol.

"Now I am ready."

Clemson, shaken by his blunder and by Benton's anger, forgot now to give first the command "Fire," as he began counting, "One, two, three." Benton was startled. At the count of two, both he and Lucas pulled their triggers. The pistols fired so nearly together that the seconds and the surgeons later reported that they heard only a single shot.

Such affairs of honor punctuate the history of the early American republic. Benton and Lucas saw themselves as members of a class in which personal honor was an indispensable aspect of a man's public career. Both lived in an age where political and personal differences were often indistinguishable and were often settled through ritual violence. The youth and early career of Thomas Benton are best understood in light of those concepts of personal honor that caused gentlemen of his time to view dueling as not only a reasonable, but a necessary option for settling public disagreements. The idea of personal reputations redeemed through violence was all the more urgent because these affairs of honor occurred at a time when both the institutions and the physical boundaries of the United States were still very much in the process of being defined.

Antecedents and Upbringing

In September of 1817, Thomas Hart Benton had been in Missouri for about two years. Acquired from France as part of Louisiana in 1804, it was still considered the far West by Americans living in older, more settled parts of the country and would be for decades. Though the notion of an advancing frontier has fallen from favor among students of early American history, Benton's early life may be understood as a narrative of migration from one American "West" to another. His childhood in the Piedmont region of North Carolina and the experience of young manhood in Tennessee—a frontier of Anglo-American settlement in the midst of hostile natives and foreign powers—would have a profound effect on the development of Benton's political philosophy as it came to maturity in yet another "West" that was territorial Missouri. The son of slaveholders, Benton inherited both his early attitudes toward the peculiar institution and a kind of primal attachment to the idea of the national Union during his childhood in North Carolina. It was there also that he first seems to have developed his intense ambition as well as his hypersensitivity concerning matters of personal honor. The belief that settlers should have preemption rights to the land that they cleared no doubt took hold of Benton during his early years in Tennessee, along with certain notions concerning the savagery of the American Indians. During those years, the future statesman embraced the principles of agrarian republicanism that would later be identified with his Tennessee patron Andrew Jackson. Benton, the westerner, was to become the hero of the "common man." But Benton never considered himself common. Unlike most of the men who came to view him as the representative of their interests—unlike even Jackson—he came from a background of some wealth and status.

His roots lay well to the east and among the gentry of central North Carolina. This was part of the region once characterized by Frederick Jackson Turner as the Old West—an area intermediate between the coastal colonial settlements of the seventeenth century and the frontier of the late eighteenth century that lay beyond the Appalachians. It included the interior or upland portion of the South, known as the Piedmont, which lay between the mountains and the head of navigation of the Atlantic rivers marked by the "fall line." In these southern uplands of Virginia and the Carolinas there developed, after about 1730, a new kind of frontier society, "differing in essentials from the colonial society of the coast. It was a democratic, self-sufficing, primitive agricultural society, in which individualism was more pronounced than the community life of the lowlands."[2]

The degree of democracy in the Carolina Piedmont is debatable, but by the early 1780's, Hillsborough in Orange County was typical of the kind of society that Turner was describing. A village of about three hundred people, of whom about a quarter were slaves, it had been established thirty years earlier and was the southwestern terminus of a long road that ran down from Boston, through Baltimore and Richmond. Despite its status the commercial center of North Carolina's central region, the streets of Hillsborough were still unpaved until the British army of Lord

Cornwallis passed through in 1781 and provided cobblestones to support the weight of their wagons and artillery. It was at his family's plantation on the Eno River three miles west of Hillsborough that Thomas Hart Benton was born on March 14, 1782.[3]

The infant's grandfather, Samuel Benton, had been an early settler in the Piedmont. He came, we are assured, "not from the rich Tidewater plantation country to the east, but down from Virginia to the north, part of the current of vigorous English and Scotch-Irish settlers that swept into the province in the middle 1700s." Intelligent, energetic, and "not too scrupulous" as to how he utilized the perquisites of office, Samuel Benton is of interest not only as the grandfather of our subject but as a colonial official who figured prominently as a target of that eighteenth century movement known as "the Regulation." In North Carolina, the Regulator movement was an early instance of farmers in the western backcountry rebelling against an eastern "establishment" whose interests were contrary to their own. It may be regarded as a quasi-separatist movement as well, for the rebels demanded among other things the right to "regulate" their local affairs, free from the interference of outsiders.[4]

One source of discontent among the westerners was lack of representation in the colonial legislature. As population increased in the Piedmont, easterners in the assembly retained their majority by dividing many of the older eastern counties into new jurisdictions. The disparities thus created would not be addressed until North Carolina's constitutional convention of 1835.[5]

Of much more immediate concern to backcountry farmers was the character of local government and the conduct of local officials, none of whom were chosen by popular vote. Justices of the peace, who constituted the county courts, were appointed by the royal governor and they, in turn, appointed the sheriffs, constables, and most other local officials. Since about two-thirds of the members of the assembly were also justices of the peace, there was an alliance between the political leaders of the colony and appointed local officials who were fellow members of the local gentry, like Samuel Benton. These elites upheld the social order through the punishment of moral transgressions. They shaped economic development by the raising of taxes for public works and by the collection or forgiveness of debts. Elections were held at the courthouse and freeholders in possession of at least fifty acres or a half-acre in town were entitled to vote there. Stepping before the sheriff, the justices of the court, and the candidates, each man voiced his vote aloud. Under such circumstances, opportunities for various forms of intimidation or bribery were numerous. The holding of multiple offices by members of the gentry was a recurrent source of irritation and protest. Men who were appointed to positions of authority in the western counties were often outsiders who regarded their offices as private property and possessed ill-concealed contempt for the common people. The small farmers of the Piedmont, increasingly in debt financially to these same officials, became more and more resentful.[6]

Samuel Benton was apparently among the worst offenders. In 1752 he had been appointed justice of the peace for Granville County. From this post he not only exercised judicial powers, but also controlled the sheriff, the clerk of the court, the local militia, and the vestrymen through his patronage, as well as managing roads, ferries, and the construction of public buildings, and having a say in the local tax rates. Aided by the political influence of his multiple offices, he accumulated over 9,000 acres. By 1764 Benton was serving as both clerk of the superior court and register of deeds, at the same time establishing himself as the squire of a large plantation in the western part of Granville County, which he named "Oxford". The same year, he introduced a bill in the colonial assembly to divide the county and establish a new county seat in his own section. He then managed to have himself selected as head of the commission for creating a new county seat, which was inevitably located on his own plantation at Oxford. Holding several of the important county offices, Samuel Benton now directed both legal business and elections from his own private courthouse. Henceforth eligible voters for the colonial assembly had to attend a public meeting on Benton's land where they were required to state their choices *viva voce*.[7]

The yeomen of the backcountry were outraged over such "arrogance of power." In 1765, George Sims, a Granville County farmer and schoolmaster, addressed his his fellow freeholders in a political manifesto exhorting them to action. Citing the "malpractices" of Granville County's court officers, Sims asserted that there were few farmers who had not been forced to borrow money to pay for necessities. Creditors often sued for reimbursement before farmers could raise the money to pay their debts and in order to satisfy court costs, the debtors were forced to work for the sheriffs and judges. Samuel Benton charged whatever fees he chose to defendants appearing before his court. When the poor men who appeared before him were unable to pay their fees, Benton gave them the opportunity to work off the costs by performing a month's labor on his Oxford plantation. As a further example of the "misery which we groan under," Sims described the seizure and sale of property by the court. "Are not your lands executed, your negroes, horses, cattle, hogs, corn, beds, and household furniture.... taken and sold for one tenth of their value? Not to satisfy the just debts which you have contracted; but to satisfy the cursed exorbitant demands of the Clerks, Lawyers, and Sheriffs.... And who buys? Why the same villains who have taken your negroes and other personal estate, and have the County's money in their hands." Sims concluded ominously, "It would be enough to make us turn rebels."[8]

1768 marked the formal organization of the Regulators, who issued a series of "advertisements" stating their objectives and grievances. In April several dozen Regulators rode into Hillsborough and fired their guns at the house of Colonel Edmund Fanning to signify their dissatisfaction. Governor William Tryon responded by ordering the Regulators to disperse and by riding into Hillsborough at the head of three regiments of militia, including one of which Samuel Benton, among his multiplicity of offices, was Lieutenant Colonel. The purpose of this show of force was to ensure that the county court was able to hold session without further disturbance. Three of the Regulator leaders were tried and found guilty (though the governor, eager to find a peaceful resolution to the growing unrest, pardoned them). Before departing, the troops attended a sermon preached by the Reverend George Micklejohn of Orange County wherein the Regulators were admonished, on pains of "destruction here and damnation hereafter," to "be subject unto higher powers." Thus assured that he was on the side of righteousness, Samuel Benton died of natural causes in 1770.[9]

Samuel Benton's creative use of public office allowed him to leave his wife Frances and sons Jesse, Samuel Junior, and Augustine a considerable estate. Most of the land and slaves went to young Samuel, but Jesse was honored by the gift of his father's case of pistols and ten pounds to buy a sword—the accoutrements of a gentleman. He also inherited the office of register for Granville County and served as clerk of Surry County as well. Jesse worked steadily at the legal profession and showed little interest in resorting to either pistols or sword as means of settling his personal or political controversies. When the Regulator movement revived in 1771, he joined other men of property and position in forming an opposition group of "Redressors" who issued a stern, but otherwise ineffectual statement to the disaffected common folk of the Piedmont. According to the Redressors, the Regulation was subversive and showed "a spirit of licentiousness, sedition, and Riot," abhorrent to all "true and faithful subjects of our sovereign Lord King George the Third." In addition to Fanning and fifty-eight others, the group included Thomas Hart and Richard Henderson, officers of the court who had recently been roughly handled by the Regulators' in Hillsborough and whom Jesse Benton would shortly join in land speculation ventures far to the west. As to the Regulators, their demands for greater democracy and local autonomy were not to be "redressed" by the lecturing of local nabobs. The threat to men of property continued to grow until the Governor Tryon's cannons crushed the movement at Alamance Creek in May of 1771.[10]

Samuel Benton identified his own interests with those of that social system which, in his day, was headed by the royal governor of the colony. His son Jesse, like many of his station, would eventually side with the revolutionary cause as a means of defending his own relatively privileged status. In the fullness of time, grandson Thomas Hart Benton would identify his own political future, and his status in the nation Jesse's generation had founded, with those very "wretched and unthinking" commoners condemned by Reverend Micklejohn. Grandson Thomas would come to believe that the majority will of these ordinary yeoman farmers was sovereign. For him, it would be the suggestion of revolt by a later generation of southern gentlemen-planters against the government of the sovereign people that threatened to constitute an illegitimate rebellion.[11]

When the American Revolution began, Jesse Benton remained noncommittal, tending to his law business and land speculations. Not until 1781, when the fighting arrived in North Carolina's Piedmont, did he declare his allegiance to the revolutionary cause. In July, he was elected to the state assembly where he served on a committee to raise militia and where he characteristically voted against a bill to protect debtors against creditors by allowing for the depreciation of Continental currency. Among Jesse Benton's fellow legislators during his brief service was a young man named Nathaniel Macon, who later became a prominent member of the United States Senate. Jesse also played a minor role in the fighting. Bands of Loyalists had been plundering the Hillsborough area. Jesse joined a group of volunteers who located the Tories and made possible their defeat by local Whig forces.[12]

The confusion of loyalties that affected Jesse Benton, like so many caught up in the war who wanted only to pursue their affairs in peace, led a number of later historians to characterize him as a "Tory" or "Loyalist." There is no evidence to support this claim. Jesse "was never quite a Tory, though his conservative outlook inclined him in that direction. But he was no flaming patriot either, though his sympathies finally fell with the new American cause." It is certainly possible that some of his neighbors, who had chosen sides earlier and made greater sacrifices for the cause of American nationhood, made charges to the effect that Jesse Benton was a closet Loyalist after the fighting had moved on. It is also possible that echoes of these charges dogged his son Thomas into his teenage years in North Carolina, causing him to compensate by feeling required to become a kind of "super-patriot" and may also have been a factor in his early identification with the Federalist Party.[13]

The conservative nature of his politics notwithstanding, Jesse Benton was capable of vision and daring where speculation in western lands was concerned. With Richard Henderson and Thomas Hart he was one of the original partners in the Transylvania Company, a land speculation with interests on the far side of the Cumberland Gap. In March of 1775 a group from the Transylvania Company, including Jesse Benton and a hunter from the Yadkin Valley named Daniel Boone, met with Cherokee leaders to buy for 2000 pounds worth of goods a vast tract known as the Watauga Purchase. It included the entire Cumberland River valley west of the Cumberland Gap in what later became Tennessee, and about two thirds of what became Kentucky. By 1788, Jesse held claims—the legality of which were questionable—to some twenty-four thousand acres west of the mountains.[14]

The young woman Jesse Benton married came from a distinguished Virginia family. Ann Gooch Benton was the only child of James Gooch, the younger brother of Sir William Gooch, the former royal governor of Virginia. Orphaned in early childhood, she was raised thereafter by her mother's brother, Thomas Hart, who brought her to North Carolina sometime in the 1760s. Wealthy and prominent, Hart had served as sheriff of Orange County (from which post, he, like Samuel Benton became a target of the Regulators' wrath), had been a delegate to the first North Carolina revolutionary convention in 1774, and served as a colonel in the Continental Army in addition to his association with the Transylvania Company's land speculations. His business interests were so extensive that, when Hart left North Carolina to live in Kentucky, he named Jesse Benton his agent. Jesse, in turn, named his first son after his distinguished partner and his wife's former guardian.[15]

According to family tradition Ann was both attractive and a good companion to her husband, who called her "Nancy." A devout member of the Episcopal Church, she passed along her distaste for drinking, smoking, and gambling to her oldest son. Nancy Benton was aided in her household chores by Milly, a house slave, and as Thomas grew, his first playmate was most likely a slave named Betsy, who was eighteen months his senior. When the boy was old enough to walk he was accompanied about the plantation either by one of his older sisters or by one of the slaves. From such meager evidence as exists, it is fair to conclude that Thomas Benton's character was initially shaped by his family's status as local aristocrats. Piedmont gentry of "quality," if somewhat precarious material assets, the Bentons, no doubt took slaveholding for granted and the oldest male heir, like most plantation scions, first grew accustomed to command by giving orders to his black playmates.[16]

When the Thomas was somewhat older, Jesse arranged for the same Reverend Micklejohn who had preached on the duty of subjection to the civil powers during the Regulation to tutor his son. Perhaps some of the old Anglican message of deference to appointed authority influenced young Benton's later beliefs about government and those who would rebel against it. By the time that he was six, the citizens of the Piedmont were debating the merits of the new Federal Constitution that had been produced by the convention in Philadelphia the previous fall. Prewar social and economic divisions remained strong. The majority in the region, favoring stay laws and other debt-relief measures, took the side of the Antifederalists. Jesse Benton wrote to Thomas Hart that the lower classes would never allow themselves to be prevented the means of cheating their creditors with fraudulent paper currency and "suchlike dishonorable advantages." Opposition to the new government was intense, but when the state ratifying convention finally met late in 1789, Jesse's brother Samuel Benton was among the majority voting in favor of North Carolina's entry into the Union.[17]

Jesse had gone heavily into debt in order to acquire title to the great tracts of western lands which he believed the key to his family's fortune. Although the largest single landholder and slaveholder in the Hillsborough district, he was constantly short of money. Shortly after Thomas Hart Benton was born, Jesse bought a 215-acre plantation which he named "Hartford" on the far side of the Eno River on installment from Thomas Hart. Payments were a constant problem. That year brought drought, and Jesse was compelled to sell some of his slaves to augment his income as clerk of Orange County.[18]

In the midst of these tribulations, Jesse Benton's health began to fail and it eventually became clear that he was dying of consumption. He continued to pursue his land speculations in the West, but before the winter of 1790–1791 was out, Jesse Benton was dead. He left his family an estate that was large, though heavily in debt. Nancy was to have the Hartford plantation in Orange County to live on and was to retain the three house slaves Jack, Milley, and Rose. The children were to have the rest of the slaves and most of the western lands, to be divided equally whenever one of them came of age. Jesse authorized his executors to dispose of large tracts of his Carolina property to pay his debts and to collect any debts due him. He hoped thereby to secure the family's title to his western land speculations.[19]

Only thirty-two when her husband died, Nancy Benton was deeply afflicted. She became ill and was confined to her room for some months during which time the children were not allowed to see her. When, at length, eight-year-old Thomas and his siblings were allowed into her presence they were shocked. In place of their youthful mother they saw a thin, white-faced, white-haired woman. As they approached, Nancy took Thomas's hand and placed it on the hand of his baby sister. As the eldest son, she told him, he was now head of the family and must be her help in caring for the others.

"When I came out," he recalled, "I rushed into the grove, and there, with cries and tears, I made war on myself until I could accept that ghost in place of my mother." The next Sunday, a chaplain who was a friend of the family, took him by the hand and led him back to the grove, reading to him a verse in the New Testament and making Thomas repeat it until the chaplain was sure the boy understood the meaning of the words: "Blessed are they that mourn for they shall be comforted." Though there is no reason to doubt the sincerity of the Christian gloss placed on the story years later by Benton's daughter Jessie, it is the *cri de coeur*, "I made war on myself," that arrests the reader's attention and provides some clue to the chronic insecurity and compulsive need to vindicate himself, as well as the making and breaking of personal and political relationships that characterized Benton as an adult.[20]

Ill and prematurely aged or not, Nancy Benton was determined not only to meet her late husband's financial obligations, but also to raise her eight children in a manner befitting their social status. She was resolved to stay in the family home at Hartford on the Eno, although the achievement of this objective required selling a large part of the estate and putting herself in bond to her uncle Thomas Hart who agreed to buy much of the remaining land and hold it in trust for the family. She was also determined to instill in her children a respect for learning as well as her own religious faith and moral virtue. Jesse had left an excellent library and before Thomas was ten his mother launched him on a program of reading, including editions of the British state trials, British history, and Plutarch's Lives, with the goal of becoming a lawyer like his father. In his early teens Thomas was sent to the private academy in Hillsborough. There he was taught by Richard Sanford, who later served in Congress with John Randolph and Nathaniel Macon.[21]

In December 1798, sixteen-year-old Thomas Benton left home for the University of North Carolina. Established only four years earlier, the University attracted sons of the Tidewater aristocracy, as well as a handful of youths from the upper tier of Piedmont society. There were only about forty students at the college. The curriculum offered Latin, Greek, and, later, algebra, astronomy, DeLolme on the English constitution, trigonometry, Millot's *Elements of History*, Paley's *Moral Philosophy*, and Blair's *Lectures*. Benton was unable to complete the entire curriculum, but its strong classical bent, typical of the day, influenced his ostentatious, if self-taught, learning later in life and his tendency to play the schoolmaster even among colleagues in the U.S. Senate. Each member of the student body joined either the Philanthropic Society or the Dialectical Society. In his second month at the University, Thomas was elected to the former and attended their weekly meetings, which included reading aloud, declamation, and the delivery of original compositions. The "Phi" and "Di," as they were known, were largely responsible for discipline at the University, and to be dropped from one or the other was tantamount to expulsion.[22]

Early on, Thomas Benton became involved in a near-violent dispute with a fellow student. A grammar school was adjacent to the college, and one day Thomas undertook to reprimand a small boy named John Lytle for some act of indiscretion. The boy's older brother, Archibald, soon intervened calling Benton "a damned scoundrel" and a liar, whereupon Benton produced a loaded pistol. Archibald retreated in search of weapon for himself, but before the confrontation could escalate any further, a professor had taken away Thomas's gun. Later, Benton assured his teacher that he had not intended to kill Lytle, but only to wound him under the shoulder.[23]

More serious trouble soon followed and ended Thomas Benton's academic career with humiliating finality. He shared a dormitory room in the University's East Building with three other boys who came from well-to-do Tidewater families. Accustomed to a lifestyle of easy spending that reflected their status, they thought their roommate parsimonious when he chose to remain on campus. Nancy Benton apparently did not supply her son with sufficient funds and he lacked ready cash. Perhaps the three made comments to this effect that stung Benton's pride and caused him to claim his background was something other than the genteel poverty that it was. Academic bills came due, but he waited in vain for the money he needed. Locked in Benton's trunk was a purse his roommate Fleming Saunders had given him for safe-keeping. One night when he was alone, Thomas unlocked the trunk and took nine dollars from the purse. When Saunders asked for his money Benton expressed surprise that some of it was missing and nothing came of the matter. When the others also discovered themselves missing money left in Benton's safekeeping, however, they confronted him, searched him, and forced a verbal confession to all three thefts.[24]

On March 19, 1799, Thomas Benton was expelled by unanimous vote of Philanthropic Society and hence from the university. We can only speculate about the effects of this episode. The humiliation surely prodded Benton's determination to redeem himself in the eyes of his mother and to prove himself to the rest of the world as well. There is a bit of Chapel Hill folklore that one who knew something of Benton's later character might wish to believe. As he rode away from the university, so the story goes, amid the jeers of fellow students, Benton turned in the saddle and shouted at his tormentors, "I am leaving here now, but damn you, you will hear from me again!"[25]

For gentlemen of Benton's generation, honor and a reputation for integrity were not only central to personal identity but were the currency of career and status as well. Benton's honor was seemingly compromised beyond repair by this youthful transgression. So disgraced, how could he ever vindicate himself? A hint is revealed in his instinctive response to Archibald Lytle's insult. Only by risking physical danger could a young man gain a reputation for courage upon which the esteem of his peers and his community depended. For the revolutionary generation, the war had provided a chance to gain such a reputation (although Jesse Benton, apparently, had cared little for either its dangers or opportunities for glory). In the absence of war, a gentleman of the post-revolutionary era defended his "good name" by resort to the ritualized violence of the *code duello*. Gentlemen protected their reputations—their honor—by dueling. To challenge a member of the gentry and have the invitation to an "interview" accepted implied membership among the upper ranks of society who were the presumed leaders of the American republic. To refuse a challenge from an inferior implied no shame, merely aloofness to the sensibilities of the common "herd." Honor, however, was the reflection of what an individual's community judged him to be and although dueling, as such, was confined to elites it served essentially the same purposes as less exclusive forms of combat with fists and knives among the lower classes. Because of this, dueling was not by nature undemocratic. On the contrary, it enabled lower-class men to enter the ranks of the leadership through ritualized violence, as well as to manipulate leaders for their own ends. This was particularly true on the frontier where the lines of demarcation between the classes were less distinct. In addition, dueling apparently often served as an outlet for unresolved personal or psychological problems. This seemed to be the case for Thomas Hart Benton well into adulthood.[26]

He was no doubt anxious to put the past behind him. The Bentons remained in North Carolina for a time, but within a year-and-a-half Nancy Benton had decided to take her children across the mountains to the wilderness holdings left by Jesse's speculations in the Cumberland River valley. Thomas was just turning nineteen. In the spring of 1801, once the late snows melted, Nancy, with her eight children and some "twenty odd slaves," joined the westward migration through the Blue Ridge to the Cumberland Valley of Tennessee.[27]

Nationalism and Separatism in the Old Southwest

Two days before Christmas of 1806 Thomas Hart Benton attended an extraordinary meeting. The local citizens were in a state of great excitement over the activities of former vice president Aaron Burr. During the past eighteen months Burr had repeatedly visited the Nashville area. He had been the guest of Andrew Jackson and the object of both curiosity and acclaim among the region's inhabitants. There had been talk of war with Spain, and Jackson had been swept up by Burr's intimations of Spanish designs against the American Southwest. Now, the news confirmed that the real purpose of Burr's visits had been to recruit supporters for his scheme to separate the Southwest from the United States and establish a new nation with himself at its head.

The meeting that Benton attended at Franklin was held in the wake of these revelations. The twenty-four year old attorney served as secretary for an ad hoc committee which adopted a number of resolutions. They stated that the citizens of Tennessee lived under the freest government in the world and would defend "that government by whose fostering care they have so rapidly grown and prospered." They resolved "that the general government sustains the most endearing relations with this section of the Union" and "that Thomas Jefferson ought to be rewarded with the affections of a grateful people, for his distinguished services." The people of Tennessee, stated the resolutions, "would view a separation from the

Federal Head as productive of incalculable evils" and to prevent such a calamity, "there ought to be an annual interchange of the laws of the State Legislatures, as a means to assimilate the habits of the people, to bring them to a nearer state of brotherhood, as well as to afford help to the younger states." Benton's foremost biographer, having related this incident, laconically concludes, "Thus was Aaron Burr summarily disposed of."[28]

By his own summary dismissal of the Burr episode, William Chambers passed over an opportunity to examine an incident that profoundly affected his subject. More than forty years after the Franklin meeting Benton would refer to it on the floor of the U.S. Senate. The Burr Conspiracy, the exact nature of which remains controversial down to the present day, presents in microcosm some of the great questions that would define Benton's career: What was the proper relation of the various sections of the new American republic to the central government? What obligations did Americans in the South or the West owe to a government situated in the East—and vice versa? Although Benton played a negligible role in the Burr drama, his awareness of it would shape his own views on these questions. Therefore, an examination of both Aaron Burr's activities and earlier secessionist movements may serve as an introduction to the problems of nationalism and separatism in the early American republic as well as the responses of gentlemen like Alexander Hamilton, Andrew Jackson, and Thomas Hart Benton when confronted with the dilemmas that they posed.[29]

In the decades following the American Revolution, the potential for a part of the new nation or its western territories to separate from the Union was a persistent danger. During the Confederation period in particular—the years of Thomas Benton's childhood—the threat of foreign-induced secession appeared quite real in the trans-Appalachian West. American settlements in what would become Kentucky and Tennessee were the focus of a "Spanish Conspiracy" that had its beginnings in the concern of Spain to halt the tide of American immigration into the Southwest. The provisions of the 1783 Treaty of Paris, which set the southern boundary of the United States at the thirty-first parallel, were unacceptable to the Spanish, who still claimed large areas that had been awarded by the treaty to the Americans. Spain also refused to recognize treaty provisions that guaranteed free navigation of the Mississippi and in 1784 closed the port of New Orleans to American trade, hoping by this policy to choke off the American settlements economically.

To western farmers, free navigation of the Mississippi was essential. Only with access to the great river and the port of New Orleans could their crops reach national and international markets. In response, foreign minister John Jay of New York negotiated a treaty with Spanish ambassador Don Diego Gardoqui that abandoned the claim to navigation of the Mississippi in return for the opening of Spanish markets to American exports—a deal that favored coastal merchants. When terms of the Jay-Gardoqui agreement became public, the anger of western and southern inhabitants, who saw their own interests being sacrificed to those of the Northeast, was intense. Opposition from southern representatives in Congress caused the treaty to be defeated by a vote along sectional lines.

The Spanish also recruited the Indians into alliances against the American settlers. The Creeks, led by their mixed race chief Alexander McGillivray, launched a series of raids along the southwestern frontier that the Confederation was powerless to stop. Feeling doubly abandoned by their eastern government, the settlers of the Southwest began to talk openly of a separate western confederation under Spanish protection. The West was in ferment and the Spanish sought to take advantage of the Americans' divided loyalties, employing certain of them as spies and informants. In Kentucky, General James Wilkinson attempted to convince fellow settlers to secede from the United States. He failed—a majority of Kentuckians were opposed to separation—but the flirtations with Spain continued in hopes of securing Spanish intercession with the Creeks and free navigation of the Mississippi. Early in 1789, several leaders of the Tennessee settlements, including a twenty-one-year-old lawyer named Andrew Jackson, opened negotiations with a Spanish agent to discuss his government's intervention with the Creeks and hinted at possible secession from North Carolina.[30]

Secession, of course, never took place. The irate westerners were just as inclined to seize New Orleans by force as to make deals with the hated Spanish. James Wilkinson, his plans to separate Kentucky from the United States having failed, now suggested that the Spanish colonial government liberalize immigration policy in the Louisiana territory. The Spanish had always assumed that an increase in the population there would provide the best defense for their North American possessions. Wilkinson's suggestion had the added attractiveness of promising to depopulate Kentucky and Tennessee. Encouraging American settlers to enter Spanish territory by offering generous land grants and requiring them to swear allegiance to the Spanish crown in order to gain access to New Orleans was a risky proposition. In the end it contributed to weakening rather than strengthening the grip of Spain on her territories northeast of Mexico. At length, the policy also resulted in many inhabitants of Upper Louisiana holding Spanish land grants of dubious legality—an issue that would loom large in Thomas Hart Benton's later career in Missouri.

Land grants were a source of contention everywhere on the frontier. Upon their arrival in Tennessee, the Bentons claimed a homestead about 25 miles south of Nashville on the Leiper's Fork of the West Harpeth River. The chaotic state of land law in the region, however, posed difficulties for the family. At the time that Jesse Benton and his partners had negotiated their agreement with the Cherokees, the Treaty of Sycamore Shoals had been in direct violation of the British government's Proclamation of 1763 which forbade further purchases of Indian land west of the Appalachians. The Transylvania purchase was denounced by the royal governors of both Virginia and North Carolina, but the partners had been willing to take their chances on the long-range prospect that their western claims might be recognized in the troubled political climate of the mid-1770s. The proprietors lost their bid for the Kentucky part of the claim when neither the Continental Congress nor the revolutionary government of the state of Virginia would recognize its legitimacy. Turning their attention to that part of the purchase that remained in the Cumberland basin of what became Middle Tennessee, the proprietors or their heirs saw their land holdings dwindle further as the result of conflicting claims made after the war by a group of speculators that included future Tennessee governors William Blount and John Sevier. Hence, of the twenty thousand acres that Jesse had originally claimed, the family could only prove twenty-five hundred and sixty.[31]

The Benton's cabin bordered the hunting grounds left to the Cherokee and other tribes by recent peace treaties. It was only a few hundred yards from the Natchez Trace, an ancient trail running southwest from Nashville to Natchez on the Mississippi. The route had long been used by war parties and was still utilized both by Indians coming to the settlements to trade and whites returning overland from flatboat journeys to New Orleans. Threatened by the proximity of so many transients of uncertain intentions, Nancy Benton established a small white settlement by offering leases without rent for seven years and moderate rents thereafter. This practice of establishing a fortified "station"—sometimes no more than a blockhouse, as the Benton's cabin apparently was—for mutual protection was commonly the first stage of white settlement in the Old Southwest. Nashville had only recently become populous enough to abandon its stockade, and security could not yet be taken for granted in the outer settlements. The little community that resulted was known as Benton Town and soon included a log school-and-meeting-house and a mill.[32]

Around the fortress-like two-story wood and stone structure that was their home, the Bentons cleared the land and planted crops. Cotton prices were on the rise, and at the end of 1802 the family had a harvest of three to four hundred pounds per acre. But when Thomas took the harvest to Nashville, he was informed that Spanish authorities had again revoked the right of Americans to deposit their goods at the port of New Orleans so that the crop could not get to market. Once more, the importance of the Mississippi was driven home to farmers on the southwestern frontier. Angry congressmen from Tennessee and Kentucky made saber-rattling speeches about seizing New Orleans and funds were appropriated in the event an American army was required to do so. Young Benton's views of the momentary crisis are unrecorded, but he was no doubt caught up in the excitement and joined in the celebration when the successful purchase of the Louisiana territory was subsequently announced.[33]

In 1804, Thomas Benton left the farm for the isolated settlement of Duck River about forty miles west of Leiper's Fork. There he taught school for a time while studying to become a lawyer. Unlike many of his contemporaries, including Andrew Jackson, Benton does not appear to have "read" law with an established attorney. Rather, by his own account, Benton read with "system and regularity," first from his father's extensive library and later books he purchased on his own. His ability to complete his preparations for legal practice untutored probably reflects the greater degree of formal education he had received prior to arriving in Tennessee, as well as the strict self-discipline he imbibed from his mother. He considered history and geography his light reading; "national law, the civil law, the common law—and finally the law itself, as was usually read by law students—constituted his studies."[34]

Always short of cash, Benton lacked the money to buy his law books during the winter of 1804. The proprietors of the general store in Franklin offered to buy the books for him and accept payment later. Nicholas Perkins Hardeman and John Hardeman were the sons of Thomas Hardeman, one of Middle Tennessee's first settlers who had fought at the Battle of Kings Mountain in 1781 and who, earlier still, had helped to blaze the trail into the Cumberland Valley during a "long hunt" through Cherokee lands in the 1760s. Thomas Hardeman had also served with Andrew Jackson, James Robertson, and other Tennessee notables in drafting the state's first constitution in 1796. In December 1804 Thomas

Benton wrote to the Hardeman brothers: "I am now at Duck River, where I shall remain for the winter. Those books I spoke of when with you, I request you will now send me. They are Millot's General History; Legars Frederic William; Cookes Voyages; Goldsmiths Natural History; Grays Fables and Sheridan's Dictionary."

Benton made other book purchases from the Hardemans on credit, including Tucker's Blackstone, Homer's *Iliad*, Montesquieu's *Spirit of the Laws*, and Locke on Understanding. He also added more mundane requests: "Further, I want you to send me an almanac, not a last year's one, a pen knife, best double bladed, a comb to straighten out my hair with, a pair of black cotton stockings, half a dozen quires of common writing paper, and one pair of strong coarse shoes."

He teasingly encouraged the store owners "in an idle hour, to prevent the evaporation" of younger brother Peter's "industry" by having him "... to transcribe my account, and when he has finished, I desire that Peter will remind you from time to time of sending it to me, as knowledge of its amount will interest me in the regulation of my financial concerns."

Benton closed gratefully, "I am, dearest sirs, more thine than mine own."[35]

The paths of Benton and the Hardemans would intersect years later in Missouri. Upon the death of John Hardeman in 1829, Senator Benton wrote to the family's eighty-year-old patriarch.

> I will do all I can for you and the family of my deceased
> friend ... without fee or reward, and through gratitude for past services and friendship from you both. I can never forget that when I mentioned to your son, then a merchant at Franklin, that I wanted law books and intended to sell land to buy them, he answered that I should not, that he would buy the books for me and wait for reimbursement till I made the money, which was done: and out of those books I studied law, and it was several years before he was repaid. This is a favor not to be repaid in money: my friendship is still to you and to his children in his place, and I shall omit no opportunity to show it.[36]

Over the ensuing decades, the children and grandchildren of this remarkable family would take part in the Santa Fe trade, the Texas Revolution, and the U.S.-Mexican War, as well as the settlement of Oregon and California. In short, the Hardemans participated in nearly every phase of the westward expansion that was shaped so significantly by the senator whose career they helped to launch.[37]

By the spring of 1806, the twenty-four-year-old Benton appeared before the Superior Court of Mero District in Nashville, which certified him as an attorney qualified to practice law in Tennessee. On July 15th, 1806, he was admitted to the Bar of Williamson County. At first people were naturally reluctant to trust an untested attorney and few cases came his way, but Benton soon demonstrated a knack for making influential friends among expectant capitalists like the Hardeman family who could help him acquire clients. He set up his law office near the courthouse in Franklin and started representing residents in the most routine legal procedures. In addition he rode the lawyer's circuit, following the Williamson County court as it held its quarterly sessions and was soon dealing with cases from neighboring counties as well.[38]

Although the exact date of their initial meeting is not certain, it was in the course of his early legal practice that Benton first had the opportunity to observe Judge Andrew Jackson of the Superior Court in Nashville. Benton's recollection of the occasion conveys something of Jackson's presence in the courtroom. "He was a remarkable man and had his ascendant over all who approached him, not the effect of his high judicial station, nor of the senatorial rank which he had held and resigned ... but the effect of his personal qualities." In charging the jury, Jackson committed some grammatical errors which grated upon Benton's more sophisticated ear and lodged in his memory, "without derogating in the least from the respect that he inspired; and without awakening the slightest suspicion that I was ever to be engaged in smoothing his diction." This was probably a smart call for the novice attorney; as he would learn, the Judge was a man of unpredictable temper who would not have taken kindly to having his grammar corrected by a young stranger.[39]

Several years after the session that prompted this initial observation, the two met face-to-face at a frontier town to which Jackson, now major general of the state militia, was returning from a "Southern visit" through Indian country. As the General removed his overcoat, Benton noticed a dark speck "which had life and motion" on the white lining of the sleeve. He brushed it off and crushed the insect under his heel. Jackson smiled in thanks and struck up a conversation "in which he quickly revealed a leading trait of his character—that of encouraging young men in their laudable pursuits." Learning Benton's name and parentage, Jackson recalled staying at his father's house in North Carolina. Jackson must have recalled Jesse Benton as a gentleman of influence back East whose speculations had helped to shape the settlement of Tennessee. He invited Thomas to visit him at the Hermitage "and expressed a belief that I would do well at the bar—generous words which had the effect of promoting what they undertook to foretell."[40]

At the time of their meeting, Jackson was trying to emerge from the shadow of twin controversies in which he had been involved during the previous year. One concerned a fatal duel over a question of personal honor, curiously similar to Benton's later dispute with Lucas, in which Jackson had killed a popular young lawyer named Charles Dickinson. Although he was himself badly wounded in the affair, Jackson had come away with the image of a vengeful and violent bully who had pursued the dispute with Dickinson beyond all reason. Nor did Jackson help his own case, for months after the death of Dickinson, by carrying on his vendetta against those who mourned or had a favorable word to say about the lately deceased young lawyer. His early biographer James Parton asserted "at no time between the years 1806 and 1812, could Jackson have been elected to any office in Tennessee that required a majority of the voters of the whole state." For the time being, he was a social and political outcast.[41]

The Dickinson duel occurred in the midst of Jackson's involvement with another pariah, an old acquaintance from his time in Congress. Former vice president Aaron Burr was fleeing not only ostracism, but also an indictment for the murder of Alexander Hamilton when he arrived in Nashville in the spring of 1805. The scion of a distinguished bloodline, revolutionary war hero, and United States senator from New York, Burr had been chosen by the Republican caucus as Thomas Jefferson's running mate in 1800. The understanding was that Jefferson was to become president and Burr vice president, but when the Electoral College deadlocked at 73 votes for each, Burr refused to graciously step aside. With the ultimate prize within his reach, Burr's hopes were dashed when Hamilton, the de facto leader of the vanquished Federalists, convinced party members in the House of Representatives to vote for Jefferson for president. Many years after the controversial events of 1800, Benton commented on the passing of Aaron Burr in his memoir *Thirty Years' View*:

> He was one of the few who, entering the war of independence with ardor and brilliant prospects, disappointed the expectations he had created, dishonored the cause he had espoused, and ended in shame the career which he had opened with splendor . . . [In] 1800 he stood equal with Mr. Jefferson in the vote which he received, and

his undoubted successor at the end of Mr. Jefferson's term. But there his honors came to a stand, and took a downward turn, nor ceased descending until he was landed in the abyss of shame, misery, and desolation.[42]

Attempting to recoup his political influence, Burr aligned himself with another of the numerous separatist plots that plagued the young nation, this one located in the Northeast. The New England Federalists who comprised the so-called Essex Junto saw both their party and their region loosing political influence to the Jeffersonians and the West. Their solution was to lead New England out of the Union, and they believed an independent confederation would be viable if New York could be enticed to join. To this end, the Essex plotters turned to Aaron Burr, who indicated his support by allowing his name to be put in nomination for the governorship of New York in 1804. Once again Hamilton stepped in to scuttle Burr's plans, publicly referring to his long-standing rival as an unprincipled American Cataline (the ambitious Roman senator whose machinations threatened to destroy that ancient republic). When Burr pushed for clarification, Hamilton explained that his charges were political, not personal.[43]

This should have been sufficient to avert a challenge, but it was not. In the early years of the American republic, the distinction between the personal and the political criticism was continuously blurred. Character counted because the temptations to advance one's own interests at the expense of the public good were so numerous. Under the circumstances, the moral fiber of national leaders like Hamilton and Burr was repeatedly put to the test.[44]

Although Thomas Hart Benton was a generation younger than the duelists at Weehawken, he understood perfectly what Joanne Freeman described as "the grammar of political combat"—the symbolic rituals ranging from verbal exchanges to actual violence in which personal/political contests were resolved—and he utilized it throughout his career to battle those he perceived to be enemies of "the people" as he chose to define that term. What had occurred that July morning in 1804 was no simple clash of personalities. For Hamilton, honor and country were one and the same. Whether he would have consented to participate in the duel had he seen it as involving anything less than the fate of the country has been a matter of conjecture from that day to this, but no doubt both men were aware of the stakes involved. Benton wrote in 1852 that the affair had "on the part of Burr the spirit of an assassination—cold-blooded, revengeful, and falsely-pretexted." Overlooking the significance of the duel's proximate causes, Benton went on to claim that "[Burr] alleged some trivial and recent matter for the challenge, such as would not justify it in any code of honor; and went to the ground to kill upon an old grudge which he was ashamed to avow."[45]

This passage from Benton's memoirs had originally been intended as an obituary of Aaron Burr, but it instead becomes a paean to Burr's long-dead adversary. "This chapter commenced to write a notice of the character of Colonel Burr; but that subject will not remain under the pen. At the appearance of that name, the spirit of Hamilton starts up to rebuke the intrusion—to drive back the foul apparition to its gloomy abode—and to concentrate all generous feeling on itself." In the narrative of the ambitious separatist and the fallen martyr to national unity, Benton seems to have found an ideal metaphor to represent his own struggle against the self-serving disunionists of his own day.[46]

At the time, feeling was much the same in the highest circles of the government. The duel by which Burr sought to retrieve his reputation and revive his political fortunes had ruined both, in the East at any rate. He now focused his prodigious energies on the trans-Appalachian West where few mourned the passing of Alexander Hamilton. In May of 1805 Burr arrived in Nashville, leaving in his wake rumors concerning his intention to lead an expedition into Mexico should hostilities break out between the United States and Spain. The stately home that was to become the "Hermitage" had not yet been erected, but General and Mrs. Jackson lived in a plain wooden house where the mansion would shortly be built, some ten miles outside of Nashville. The famous visitor stayed there for five days, apparently taking Jackson's measure for whatever role he had assigned the Tennessee militia or its commander in his plans.

Three months later, Burr returned from a journey that had taken him to New Orleans and back. The citizens of Nashville held a splendid ball in his honor, Jackson attending in his military attire. If he was aware of the growing suspicions in some quarters concerning Burr's designs, Jackson chose to ignore them. Burr, for his part, played on Jackson's saber-rattling nationalism and his hatred of the Spanish to draw the general into his schemes. He asked for a list of officers who could be trusted in the event of war and paid Jackson $3,500 in Kentucky banknotes to build five large boats and secure a large quantity of provisions. Jackson never revealed the substance of his conversations with Burr, other than to insist that they were in no way treasonous, but he clearly believed that officers, boats, and provisions were all intended for an invasion of Spanish possessions, either in Florida or beyond the Louisiana territory in Mexico.[47]

Not until the 10th of November did the scales fall from Jackson's eyes. A Captain John Fort called at the Hermitage and disclosed the true nature of Burr's plans, including the seizure of New Orleans. When Jackson pressed him for details, Fort revealed that federal troops, under the command of General James Wilkinson, were to close the port and take part in the conquest of Mexico. The western part of the United States would then be joined to the conquered territory to form a new southwestern empire under Burr. Jackson was incredulous. Writing to the governor of Louisiana, Jackson warned him to "put your Town in a state of defense, organize your militia, and defend your City as well against internal enemies as external." Seeking to distance himself from whatever Burr was up to, Jackson concluded, "I love my Country and Government, I hate the Dons—I would delight to see Mexico reduced, but I will die in the last ditch before I would yield a part of it to the Dons, or see the Union disunited."[48]

Burr was arrested in Kentucky and called before a grand jury on charges of raising troops for the illegal purpose of leading a filibustering expedition against Mexico and possibly plotting to dismember the Union. Henry Clay, who in 1799 had married Thomas Benton's cousin Lucretia Hart, represented Burr in the proceedings. The charges were dismissed for lack of evidence. James Wilkinson, however, was a more serious problem for Burr. A double agent in the pay of the Spanish government even while he commanded American forces in the Mississippi Valley, Wilkinson had become increasingly pessimistic about the chances for Burr's success and the possible consequences for himself. He informed President Jefferson, who issued a call for the arrest of his former vice president. In the last week of December 1806 word of Jefferson's proclamation reached Nashville, prompting the citizens of Tennessee to hold meetings affirming their loyalty to the national government, and a demonstration at which an effigy of Aaron Burr was set aflame.

Thomas Benton was not yet a public figure, having just that year been admitted to the Tennessee bar, and he was still struggling to establish his law practice. Yet his presence at the Franklin gathering on December 26 and his modest contribution as recording secretary indicates that he wished to ensure there was no mistake about either his own sympathies or those of his neighbors. "At that time," Benton told congressional colleagues in 1848, there was not a neighborhood in the West in which Burr would disclose his project." Had he done so, "the women and children would have tied him down and sent him to the nearest place of justice, dragged by a dog chain." This was certainly an overstatement of the unity among Tennesseans at that time, or any other. Nonetheless, forty-five years after Aaron Burr's conspiracy, his "foul apparition" would still symbolize for Benton the unprincipled ambition that he associated with secession. All "generous feeling" in the seventy-year-old former senator was reserved for Hamilton, the ultra-nationalist, who had given his life to foil Burr's separatist schemes.[49]

Wars for Independence

There is no evidence that Benton was aware of the extent of Jackson's involvement with Aaron Burr at the time the two were introduced and perhaps not for many years after. The ambitious young attorney, desirous of making a name in politics, no doubt welcomed the acquaintance of the commander of Tennessee's militia. Their relationship grew warmer after Benton assisted in prosecuting the accused killer of another friend of Jackson's named Patton Anderson. On October 24, 1810, David Magness shot and killed Anderson in front of the Shelbyville courthouse. Magness was apprehended and brought to trial in Franklin. The trial attracted considerable public attention. Counsel included U.S. senator Jenkin Whiteside and Jackson's nephew Stockley Donelson Hays, as well as Benton. Felix Grundy was chief attorney for the defense. As the trial progressed, Grundy called Jackson to the witness stand, seeking to bait him into testifying that Anderson was a man of violent temper who frequently engaged in fights. Was not Anderson, he asked, hot-tempered and given to fighting? "Sir," replied the General, "Patton Anderson was the natural enemy of scoundrels." Grundy made much of this statement in his summation to the jury and Jackson complained to Benton that these tactics were unfair. "When you sum up for the prosecution, I want you to skin Grundy alive on that point."

"I'm afraid, General," replied Benton, "that he has got us down on that point—flat on our backs. I reckon we had better let it alone." The court found Magness guilty of the lesser charge of manslaughter, rather than murder, and sentenced him to eleven months in prison and the branding of the letter "M" on the hand. "As a junior counsel," remembered Benton, "I had to precede my elders, and did my best; and it being on the side of

[Jackson's] feelings, he found my effort to be better than it was. He complimented me greatly, and from that time our intimacy began."[50]

Benton thereafter became part of a circle of young men, including John Coffee, William Carroll, and William B. Lewis, who served as both friends and political lieutenants to Jackson. Viewed by their chief as a sort of extended family—a "band of brothers"—they would accompany their general into the field as his officers during the ensuing conflicts with Britain and the southern Indians. Many would also rely on the General to advance their postwar careers. Where Benton was concerned, the relationship would be long, stormy, and characterized by violent swings from loyalty to violent animosity and back again. In its earliest stage, Jackson seems to have taken on the role of a kind of surrogate father to replace Jesse Benton Sr. This kind of familial relationship among most of Jackson's officers persisted through the War of 1812 and the First Seminole War that followed. But it was in keeping with Benton's comment upon the death of his father—"I made war on myself"—that the decades-long friendship between the two men would be characterized by extremes.[51]

The causes for the War of 1812 were numerous. Some historians have viewed the conflict as primarily a dispute over neutral rights on the high seas. They argue that the United States went to war in response to the Orders in Council and the British impressment of American sailors. Others have emphasized the desire of westerners to conquer Canada and to end British aid to the Indians. Another school of thought focuses on political issues, claiming that Jeffersonian Republicans viewed foreign conflict as a means of uniting their party, retaining control of government, and marginalizing the Federalists. Still another group of scholars stress the imperatives of upholding national honor and ending the "neocolonial" status of the young republic in a world of aggressive and powerful rivals. The war was by no means unavoidable, and peace between the belligerents might have been concluded at almost any point once the fighting had commenced. Witness the fact that the British government withdrew its objectionable Orders in Council, authorizing the seizure of American merchant vessels, almost simultaneously with the American declaration of war. Why then were Americans, particularly residents of the southern and western states, so eager for a military showdown?[52]

Many Americans of the early nineteenth century viewed the war as a matter of national honor. If gentlemen of the day were willing to face each other at a few dozen paces with loaded pistols and risk death over personal insult, militant nationalists such as Hamilton, Jackson, and Benton would be willing and even eager to avenge any perceived insult to their country's honor by resort to arms. This had been the case in 1798 when Federalists had coined the battle cry, "Millions for defense, but not a penny for tribute!" in response to the s demands of the French agents later identified as X, Y, and Z for American bribes and a loan as the price for peace negotiations. By the time James Madison occupied the presidency, it was the British who seemed intent on challenging the honor of the United States with their seizures of American ships, impressments of American sailors, and support to the Indian tribes who were attempting to resist the tide of white settlement.

"War in this sense," wrote historian Robert Wiebe, "was quite literally a duel, and gentlemen of all ages from all parts of the United States understood it as such." The nation had been "insulted" by the actions of the British government and men of the day equated honor with independence. "Would the new United States, still undergoing an initial test of honor, take its place as a gentleman among the nations or declare itself a cringing menial? The gentry could not even consider the alternative.... Under such persistent, intolerable bullying, a gentleman had the right to demand a formal settling of accounts."[53]

As guardian of the nation's honor, it was up to President Madison to decide when the accumulation of insults demanded a challenge. "There could be no crude rush for pistols, however. Just as gentlemen moved in perfect control through their final negotiations, Madison carefully went through the motions of offering Britain a last chance to retract and waited out the months of diplomatic protocol with no unseemly show of haste."[54]

For the men who had come of age after the Revolution, there were other factors that were to make the conflict with Britain a "second war for independence" in a very personal sense. These Americans had grown up in the shadow of the founding generation and imbibed the heroic narrative of the Revolutionary War from their earliest memories. For the first generation of nineteenth-century Americans, nothing was more to be desired than the opportunity to emerge from that shadow by participating in a new war to defend the country their fathers had created.[55]

The congressional elections of 1810 brought to Washington many new members from the southern and the western states who became known collectively as the "War Hawks." This faction demanded vindication against Britain for her insults to American honor both at sea and on the frontier. For them, the resort to combat could not come soon enough. Their leader was Henry Clay, the new Speaker of the House, who was married Benton's cousin. Felix Grundy, counsel for the defense in the Magness trial, was among their number, as was a brilliant new member from South Carolina, born the same month as Thomas Benton, named John C. Calhoun.

In Tennessee Benton followed international developments with interest. For the twenty-nine-year-old lawyer, the possibility of war offered the opportunity for both political advancement and personal vindication. Suffering temporarily from symptoms of tuberculosis—the same illness that had killed not only his father but three of his sisters—Benton also viewed combat as an opportunity to end his life in a blaze of glory rather than from a wasting disease. In January 1812, as war looked increasingly likely, he sent Jackson a letter offering his services as an aide-de-camp and as a military chronicler. The letter reveals something of Benton's desire for glory—and perhaps political advancement—as the war began: "If there should be an expedition to the Canadas I shall make an experiment of my capacity to use the pen as well as the sword.... I think with Tacitus, that every man should aim at doing something worthy of being written, or at writing something worthy of being done."[56]

For the moment it seemed that Benton and the other members of Jackson's circle might well have to sit out any impending conflict, as Jackson was not trusted by the administration. The reasons for this reached back to his entanglement with Aaron Burr. In the aftermath of Jefferson's proclamation, Burr had been captured in Mississippi and was taken to Richmond, Virginia, in the spring of 1807 to stand trial for treason. Summoned to testify, Jackson had told a grand jury that he believed Burr to be innocent and that James Wilkinson was the true villain in this muddled tale. "I am more convinced than ever," Jackson wrote, "that treason was not intended by Burr, but if ever it was, you know my wish is and has always been, that he may be hung."[57]

John Randolph of Roanoke, the grand jury foreman, wrote to James Monroe that Jackson "does not scruple to say that W[ilkinson] is a pensioner of Spain, to his knowledge and that he will not dare to show his face here."[58]

Two weeks later prosecutor George Hay reported to President Jefferson that, "Gen. Jackson of Tennessee has been here ever since the 22nd denouncing Wilkinson in the coarsest terms in every company. The latter showed me a paper which at once explained the motive of this incessant hostility. His own character depends on the prostration of Wilkinson's."[59]

While Jackson had no doubt been eager to portray his own relationship to Burr in a more innocent light by tarring Wilkinson, there was more to his hostility than raw self-interest. Jackson had despised Wilkinson and regarded him as a petty tyrant ever since Wilkinson had court-martialed Jackson's friend, Colonel Thomas Butler, for refusing to cut his hair, which Butler still wore in a revolutionary-style queue. For Jackson, who saw the world in terms of right and wrong, friends and enemies, it was not a far leap to conclude that the despotic Wilkinson was a traitor as well. Jackson was so unable to control his rage that Burr's defense attorney decided against placing him on the witness stand during the jury trial.

In the aftermath, Jackson "harangued the crowd in Richmond's Capitol Square, defending Burr, and angrily denouncing Jefferson as a persecutor. There are those living who heard him do this," wrote biographer Parton. "He made himself so conspicuous as Burr's champion at Richmond, that Mr. Madison, the Secretary of State, took deep offense at it, and remembered it to Jackson's disadvantage five years later when he was President of the United States, with a war on his hands." Jackson's break with Jefferson had been coming for some time. Shortly after the Louisiana Purchase became public knowledge in 1804, Jackson had sought appointment as governor of the new territory, only to be passed over by the president—a humiliation that probably influenced his performance at Richmond. The estrangement from Jefferson became complete as a result of the Burr affair. In 1808 Jackson opposed the nomination of Madison as the Republican candidate, gravitating to the extreme states' rights or "Tertium Quid" faction of the party, and supported the nomination of James Monroe.[60]

Observing the political controversies of that year from Nashville, Benton had written a series of articles supporting Madison for the presidency. Monroe, he said, was the man of a "little knot of protesters, the opposition band of republicans, Johnny Randolph & Co., the candidate of factious radicals." Monroe was a friend of the "atheist Tom Paine" and of the Jacobins, who molested American commerce and tried to involve America in a war with Britain. Monroe, indeed, had "fraternized with the Sans Culottes Bloodhounds so cordially, and entered into their mad projects so enthusiastically that General Washington was under the necessity of recalling and disgracing him." This is the voice of a young, as yet politically immature, Benton who supported the incumbent Republican administration against all challengers. His ties to the North Carolina Piedmont aristocracy and the Federalist Party of his father had only recently been forsaken and those changes were no small matter. It would take some time, and many shifts of political fortune to bring an older, more seasoned, Thomas Hart Benton to friendship with "Johnny Randolph & Co."[61]

In 1812 these differences faded to insignificance in the face of the common enemy. Benton came to the aid of his mentor, originating a plan (we have only Benton's account in this instance) by which Jackson could get into the war. In January Congress had passed a bill authorizing the states to raise up to fifty thousand volunteers in the event of war. When the news reached Benton he immediately drew up a plan to raise three regiments, then saddled his horse and rode thirty miles through rain, sleet, and hail to the Hermitage. The major general was impressed with the plan and, though the Congress was maddeningly slow in appropriating funds for implementation, by spring Jackson was able to issue a call to arms.[62]

Under the heading "For what are we going to fight," Jackson appealed to the popular ideals and aspirations of fellow westerners. "We are going to fight," he proclaimed, "for the re-establishment of our national character, misunderstood, and vilified at home and abroad; for the protection of our maritime citizens, impressed on board British ships of war and compelled to fight the battles of our enemies against ourselves; to vindicate our right to free trade, and to open a market for the productions of our soil, now perishing on our hands because the mistress of the ocean has forbid us to carry them to any foreign nation; in fine, to seek some indemnity for past injuries, some security against future aggressions, by the conquest of all the British dominions upon the continent of North America."[63]

On April 29 Thomas Benton was commissioned a captain of volunteers. War was declared on June 18, and the news reached middle Tennessee just in time for Fourth of July celebrations. At a meeting in Franklin, martial music was played, volleys fired, and numerous toasts "were drank with enthusiasm," including one by Thomas Benton: "The war against England: Honor and life to its friends; confusion to its enemies." Initially, however, all of the confusion seemed to be on the side of the Americans. Throughout the summer and into the fall, news of defeat upon humiliating defeat—Hull's surrender at Detroit, Van Rensselaer's debacle at Queenston Heights—arrived from the northern front. But for the time being, that was where the fighting was; Jackson's force in Tennessee did nothing but drill. Benton wrote to Henry Clay that he was resolved to go to Washington and ask for service on the Canadian border.[64]

This proved to be unnecessary. Orders shortly arrived for the Tennessee volunteers to go down the Mississippi and defend New Orleans against possible attack by the British on that front. Jackson issued a new proclamation. "Every man of the western country turns his eyes intuitively upon the mouth of the Mississippi," his general orders stated. "He there beholds the only outlet by which his produce can reach the market of foreign or the Atlantic States: Blocked up, all the fruits of his industry rots upon his hand—open and he carries on a trade with all the nations of the earth. To the people of the western Country is then peculiarly committed by nature herself the defense of the lower Mississippi and the city of New Orleans."[65]

The volunteers were to be raised from the standing militia companies. Benton dashed from one militia muster to another in the Franklin area, making speeches to raise volunteers for the expedition. In late November the ninety officers of the Tennessee militia met in Nashville. The proposed division of 1,500 was to be organized as one regiment of cavalry and two regiments of infantry. When field officers were elected, Benton was rewarded for his efforts by being named colonel of the Second Regiment of Infantry.[66]

For Jackson the long-awaited call to action from the secretary of war was not without its personal frustrations. Upon the arrival of his volunteer army at the mouth of the Mississippi, Jackson was to become subordinate to the despised General James Wilkinson. Writing to Tennessee governor Willie Blount, he commented, "There appears something in this thing that carries with it a sting to my feelings that I will for the present suppress—The place of destination, and the officer under which [the volunteers] are to be placed when they reach that destination, cannot be mistaken."[67]

Benton harbored no such reservations. On January 8, 1813, Jackson ordered him to supervise the embarkation of the First Regiment of Infantry on flatboats for the trip down the Cumberland to the Ohio and Mississippi rivers. Benton's own Second Regiment was to march overland until enough boats could be impressed to put them afloat. Benton kept a journal of the voyage that he and other officers made downstream by boat. The installments, which he sent to the Nashville *Democratic Clarion*, revealed his penchant for the melodramatic.

> The group had embarked at midnight.
> The moon had not yet gone down, and her pale beams were glistening upon the surface of the water. The night was, but still, and nothing was heard to interrupt the silence that reigned save the hollow murmuring of the water which broke upon the rocky

shore.... Col. Anderson placed himself at the helm; the other officers stood by him. No one said he was afraid, but the question of Caesar to the pilot, *Quid times?* repeatedly and involuntarily occurred. Finally, recollecting that they were fatalists, they gave the boat to the stream; surrendered themselves to their destiny, and went below to the cabin.[68]

The articles were also quite critical of the performance of Jackson's quartermasters who—Benton alleged—had allowed businessmen to keep their boats to get their goods to market, causing his regiment to fall ten days behind the rest of the force. Benton informed the public, by way of his journal, that the delay would cost the United States twenty thousand dollars. He argued that quartermasters should be under the direct control of the commanding general in the field. "As things stand at present," wrote Benton, "if an army is stopped on its march for want of bread, or stuck in the mud for want of transportation, all that the general can do is to send a complaint to the president, perhaps a thousand miles off; the delinquent commissary or Quarter-Masters, at the same time sends his counter-affidavit... while the reason for action passes entirely away.[69]

By January 23 sufficient boats had been found for the regiment to continue. Three days later Benton's troops reached the confluence of the Cumberland and Ohio Rivers. The freezing weather had left the Ohio filled with dangerous ice floes capable of smashing a boat. Locals advised against trying to navigate the river under these circumstances:

> It rested with Col. Benton to decide. He had never before felt the responsibility of command; and his anxiety became painful as he reflected that upon a word which he was to speak it might depend whether a multitude of fine men should perish in the ice, or live to see their friends again. Benton ordered the boats into the river. The men obeyed with alacrity and, using long poles spiked with iron to fend off the ice, the regiment made rapid progress downstream.[70]

By February 13 Benton and his regiment arrived at Natchez to join Jackson. Making camp, the volunteers now waited week after week for instructions from the War Department. On March 15 orders finally arrived stating that the British were no longer expected at New Orleans. Jackson was to dismiss his troops immediately, delivering all public property to General Wilkinson. "Accept for yourself and the Corps the thanks of the President of the United States," the dispatch concluded. Jackson was enraged. He was not about to leave his men to their own resources in the midst of the wilderness and five hundred miles from home. He determined to lead them back to Nashville as a unit and discharge them there—paying the cost of transportation and care for the sick out of his own pocket.[71]

The army completed the long march back up the Natchez Trace, arriving in Nashville, weary and footsore, some weeks later. Upon their return, Jackson's officers held a dinner in his honor praising him for the concern he had shown for his men and his leadership throughout the episode, joining officers and men on foot while the ailing rode the horses. Benton came in for a share of the praise as well. According to the *Clarion*, "he shared every fatigue with the most common soldier, and in no case shunned the mire his men had to wade through."[72]

Still anxious to see action against the British, Benton prepared to go to Washington to pursue assignment to an active theater of operations. While there, he would also work for Jackson's financial reimbursement for the expenses of the Natchez expedition. First, however, there was an unfinished matter from the expedition that remained to be dealt with. Major William B. Lewis, the deputy quartermaster for Jackson's troops, had read Benton's journal in the press and had taken offense at his remarks. Convinced the criticism of quartermasters was aimed at him, Lewis sent the newspaper an insulting letter mocking the florid language of the journal and questioning both the motives and the courage of its author: "Most inimitable Journalist!—'He mounts stilts, and at every step kicks out a star!'" When Benton returned to Nashville and read Lewis's letter in the *Clarion*, he immediately dispatched a messenger, Ensign Lyttleton Johnston, to Lewis with a note demanding satisfaction: "I shall neither give nor take explanations; my mind is made up, and you must fight me sir. . . . I lay before you the pistol, the sword, and the dagger: take which you like."[73]

Lewis refused to take up the gauntlet. He was unable to fight just now, he wrote back, because he was too busy disposing of public property left over from the expedition; he would not indulge himself in an affair of honor while the public welfare required his attention. Benton was not about to accept such an excuse. Major Lewis was as much in the public service when he penned his insults as he was now. "You must fight me sir," he wrote, "or you must flinch openly. . . . to demand indefinite time now, is to say, that as you attacked me with lies when I was 500 miles to the south, so you will be ready to fight me when I have gone 500 miles to the north."

When Lewis again refused to set a date, Benton denounced him as a coward and had their correspondence printed and distributed as a handbill. Benton was responding to Lewis's refusal to meet him on the field of honor by the customary practice of "posting" their correspondence. This was the prescribed way to obtain satisfaction from an offender who was too cowardly to duel. The wounded party, with no other way to redeem his reputation, was entitled to "post" his offender with broadsides tacked up in public places, declaring him a liar, rascal, scoundrel, and coward. These were all ritualistic insults to the honor of the other party.[74]

The angry Lewis tried to have the last word by letting it be known that he would fight Benton sometime and that by publishing his leaflet Benton had taken an easy, safe way out. Not to be outdone, the colonel assured Lewis that he would postpone his trip to Washington if the major would name the date, hour, and place—any day, any hour, any place would be acceptable. Lewis again refused to be definite or to receive any further communication from Benton who turned the whole correspondence over to the newspaper with a personal statement. He apologized to the "People of Tennessee" for staying to settle a personal matter when the republic needed his services, but honor had required it. As he prepared to leave Nashville, he concluded, "if the chances of war prevent me from returning, suffer me not to be lied out of your friendship by men without honor, without shame, without public character, who under the pretext of serving their country, have been laboring to destroy me in my absence!"[75]

This seemingly ridiculous exchange underscores Benton's extreme sensitivity where his public image was concerned. In light of his behavior over the next few years, it is somewhat surprising that no record exists of his challenging anyone prior to this point. Benton's ordinarily short fuse was no doubt cut shorter still by the frustrating conclusion of the Natchez expedition. His quarrel with Lewis indicates that all was not selfless camaraderie among the fellowship surrounding Jackson, and that real rivalries for the favor of the Chief existed among the younger members. Despite being "posted" by Benton, Major Lewis remained in the good graces of Jackson, who needed his talents and—especially at this juncture—his money. Lewis remained Jackson's loyal subordinate for thirty-five years, and in 1845 he carried the Old Hero's last message to another trusted lieutenant—Thomas Hart Benton.[76]

In the spring of 1813, Benton likewise retained Jackson's confidence as he prepared to depart for Washington with the twin purposes of trying to get the General reimbursed for expenses related to the Natchez expedition and of seeking reassignment to an active war front. On his way to the capital, Benton stopped at the Hermitage for a letter of introduction. Jackson's letter to the secretary of war warmly praised his aide. "Did I think anything was necessary to be said on the fitness of Col. Benton to command it would be here added. His uniform good conduct, his industry and attention to the discipline and police of his regiment, speak more for his fitness than words. And a personal acquaintance with Col. Benton will soon decide on the capacity of his mind."[77] If anything was yet amiss in their relationship, it is not apparent from the surviving documents.

Arriving in Washington on May 26, Benton found the capital a town of muddy streets and unfinished buildings. Nonetheless, for Benton, who had never seen a larger place, it was impressive. He was able to observe Congress in session for the first time, and wrote his impressions to Henry Clay upon his departure several weeks later. He begins by revealing his unabashed hope for military glory. "I am now a soldier for the war, and have an unbounded desire to make some figure in it. My younger brothers have also entered: they will do something or they will perish." Benton goes on to express his concern, even at this early stage of his career, that the nation might be divided as a result of the war with Britain.

> I am apprehensive this conflict will last several years. The enemy will keep it alive to make it an instrument of dividing the Union, and pulling down those who are now in power; and the heads of the opposition will secretly encourage its continuance with the last of those views. Shall I give you my opinion? Then press on vigorously. Spare neither men nor money: make the war successful and glorious, and the people will bear with pride the burdens it imposes.

Finally, in a passage that seems to foreshadow the activities of the Hartford Convention the following year, he has some words regarding the dubious loyalty of the opposition party in the Northeast. "There are many honest Federalists in our state. They will be filled with horror when I tell them what I have seen here; for they have no idea of treason and of civil war. And my testimony will go far, because I have been of that soil, but not of the New England school."[78]

In Benton's view, so long as the war with Britain continued, anything but full support for the policies of the administration was tantamount to treason. Meanwhile, he haunted the offices of the War Department, pressing both his own case and Jackson's. He finally met with President Madison himself, who inquired after Jackson's health "on terms of particular kindness." Although complaining to his commander that "things go but slowly here," Benton was successful in securing Jackson's claims before Secretary of War Armstrong. He worked out a scheme of payment that the secretary was willing to adopt. As for himself, Benton was not assigned to Canada, but was commissioned as Lieutenant Colonel of the Thirty-ninth Infantry Regiment, Regular Army, that was to be recruited in Tennessee.[79]

Upon returning from his mission to the capital, Benton heard disturbing news. His younger brother Jesse had become involved in a dispute between Ensign Lyttleton Johnston and Major William Carroll, brigade inspector in Jackson's army. Jesse had carried a duel challenge from Johnston to Carroll, returning the service Johnston had performed for Thomas Benton in his dispute with Major Lewis. When Carroll refused to honor the challenge on the grounds that Johnston was no gentleman, Jesse Benton suggested that he himself might stand in Johnston's place. Jesse's social standing was such that Carroll could not refuse without being posted as a coward. Carroll conferred with Jackson, and the general tried to dissuade Jesse Benton by arguing that Jesse had no quarrel with Carroll and that the matter should be dropped. But Jesse, with all of his brother's hot temper and hypersensitivity concerning questions of honor, refused to be pacified.

Yet to see real combat, Jackson and his subordinates vented their aggression over petty slights and personal jealousies. Carroll was a favorite of the General's and Jesse was egged on by his fellow junior officers. The duel was set for June 14 and Jackson, apparently seeing no conflict posed by his personal friendship with Thomas Benton, agreed to serve as Carroll's second. As the major was a "remarkably defective" shot, he and Jackson surprised Jesse the morning of the duel with rules designed to compensate for Carroll's poor marksmanship. The adversaries would stand back to back only ten feet apart and wheel and fire on signal. Jesse protested, but he was now bound to finish what he had started. At the signal he wheeled, fired, and missed. Turning his back to Carroll he assumed a squatting position to reduce the target he presented. Carroll's bullet inflicted a long, raking wound across Jesse's buttocks that was not lethal, but did prove both painful and embarrassing.[80]

When Thomas Benton heard all this he was furious. While he had been in Washington, pleading Jackson's case, the General had been participating in the shooting of his brother. Benton stayed home at Franklin, avoiding Jackson, but not hesitating to speak his mind to friends about the affair. Rumors reached the Hermitage that Benton had been speaking ill of his patron. Jackson wrote Benton an ominous note. Hadn't Benton left Tennessee as a friend? Why had he not come with information? Did Benton speak disrespectfully of him? Had any of Jackson's own acts been "inconsistent with the strictest principles of friendship" and if so how? Finally, did Benton threaten to challenge him to a duel?[81]

Benton replied, by letter, that it was poor business for a man of Jackson's age to conduct a duel between two young men, that Jackson had meanly drawn the challenge out of Jesse, "that if you could not have prevented a duel you ought at least have conducted it in the usual mode and on terms equal to both parties." On the contrary, Jackson had conducted it in "a savage, unequal, unfair, and base manner." He had not challenged Jackson, but he would continue to speak his mind.[82]

Jackson sent an immediate answer: "It is the character of the man of honor, and particularly of the soldier not to quarrel and brawl like the fish woman." So it went. For the next six weeks Jackson and Benton avoided each other while town gossip continued to poison the atmosphere. One rumor had Jackson announcing that he would horsewhip Benton on sight. On September 4 Thomas and Jesse Benton arrived in Nashville on business, putting up at a tavern they knew Jackson did not frequent. Word was carried to the Hermitage and shortly Jackson, John Coffee, and Mrs. Jackson's nephew, Stockley Hays, arrived and took rooms at the Nashville Inn. They walked to the post office, passing near the hotel where the Bentons were staying. Seeing Jesse step from the street into the hotel, Jackson and Coffee followed him inside. In the hallway that led to the back porch of the inn, Jackson came face-to-face with Thomas Benton.

"Now defend yourself you damned rascal," shouted Jackson. Thomas reached for his pistols, but Jackson beat him to the draw. Thomas Benton stepped backward, looking down the barrel of the General's gun. Suddenly, Jesse appeared in a side doorway and fired at Jackson. At the same moment Jackson fired at Thomas, who fired both of his own pistols in return. Jackson fell to the floor, wounded in his left arm, while the muzzle flash from his pistol burned a hole in Thomas's coat sleeve. John Coffee also fired at Thomas, but his bullet whizzed past Benton's head and smacked into the wall. By now three other men were wrestling, hitting, and stabbing in the black powder smoke. His pistols emptied, Thomas now was attacked by Coffee and Alexander Donelson, who managed to wound him with their daggers. In the barroom Jesse desperately defended himself against Charles Hammond, who attacked him with a dagger, and Stockley Hays, who was armed with a sword cane.

Jesse thrust his pistol into Hays's midsection and pulled the trigger, but the gun misfired. He was saved only by the intervention of James Sumner, who rushed in to help drive off his attackers. The battle concluded as Thomas, fending off the daggers and clubbed pistols of Coffee and Donelson, fell backwards down a flight of stairs at the rear of the hotel.[83]

The combatants finally noticed Jackson lying in the hallway. Friends carried him back to the Nashville Inn, where the town's doctors took turns trying to stop the flow of his blood, which soaked through two mattresses. The General lost consciousness after giving orders that his shattered arm was not to be amputated. It was not and Jesse Benton's bullet remained lodged there until 1831.[84]

In the meantime, Thomas Benton publicly denounced Jackson as an assassin and challenged the wounded man to come out and renew the battle. Benton then symbolically crowned his victory, and ended the relationship with his erstwhile patron, by breaking a sword belonging to the General across his knee in the town square.[85]

"I Am Literally in Hell"

The War Hawks of 1812 sought not only to conquer British Canada and Spanish Florida, but to eliminate the Indian threat and make the frontiers safe for white settlement. At the outset of the war, the southern Indian tribes still occupied two-thirds of Georgia, most of Alabama and Mississippi, and western sections of both Tennessee and Kentucky. The harassment of Alexander McGillivray and the Creeks had eventually been brought to a halt by an agreement between the United States and Spain in 1795, and an uneasy truce descended upon the southern frontier that lasted for nearly a generation. By 1812, however, a faction of the Creeks, under the leadership of William Weatherford, a mixed-blood kinsman of McGillivray, began to embrace the message of the Shawnee chieftain Tecumseh. Envisioning a pan-Indian confederacy from Canada to the Gulf of Mexico that would be capable of resisting the insatiable demand of whites for Indian land, Tecumseh visited the Creeks in 1811 and again in 1812, seeking recruits. Weatherford's group, known as the Red Sticks (because they painted their war clubs bright red), accepted Tecumseh's message and welcomed his promises of support from Britain and Spain. During the summer of 1813 a Red Stick party journeyed to Pensacola to receive arms from the Spanish. On their return trip they were ambushed by whites at a place called Burnt Corn in the Alabama territory. The leaders of the Burnt Corn attack repaired to Fort Mims, a stockade about forty miles north of Mobile. There, on August 30, Weatherford and the Red Sticks launched an onslaught against the poorly prepared garrison and killed over five hundred whites, mixed-race settlers, and peaceful Creek Indians, including many women and children.[86]

Still recovering after his fight with the Benton brothers, Jackson now rose from his sick bed and issued a new call for volunteers to head south in a campaign to punish the Creeks. Benton, during the fall of 1813, was occupied with organizing the 39th United States Infantry Regiment. He hoped that when the regiment was ready it might be sent to the main battlefront on the Canadian border. But events brought only disappointment and frustration. Despite publishing a circular giving his and Jesse's version of events, it was Benton who had emerged from the affair as a pariah. "I am literally in Hell here," he wrote soon after the brawl. "It is a settled plan to turn out puppy after puppy to bully me, and when I have got into a scrape, to have me killed somehow in the scuffle." His only alternatives were to kill or be killed because he would not "crouch" to Jackson. Only a decisive duel could clear the air and vindicate him. When William Carroll published a statement of his position that Benton interpreted as a challenge, he immediately wrote Carroll a note of acceptance. Benton was disappointed. Carroll replied that he challenged no one, though he would fight if Benton challenged him. That was the end of the matter, and ill feelings were left to fester between the feuding parties for years to come.[87]

In the meantime Jackson, his left arm still in a sling, led his volunteers southward to victories over the Creeks. Had Benton remained with the volunteers, he might have shared in the glory of this campaign of retaliation and conquest. As it was, he remained in Nashville training his regulars while Carroll, Coffee, and the other "puppies of the General" became heroes. In March 1814 the decisive battle of the Creek War was fought at Horseshoe Bend on the Tallapoosa River, but Benton was not there. He rejoined Jackson's army in the field in July 1814, but again and again his hopes for vindication on the field of battle were dashed.[88]

By this time Napoleon had been defeated in Europe and the British could turn their full might toward concluding the war in America. In September, Washington was burned and Baltimore attacked. Another invasion was coming from the north by way of Lake Champlain. New England Federalists, never enthusiastic about the war, met in Hartford that fall and hinted at secession if their demands were not met. With peace negotiations underway in the Belgian town of Ghent, the success or failure of American forces in the southern theater became all-important.

In October Jackson prepared to launch an assault against Pensacola with all available forces.

Benton, however, was to be frustrated yet again. He and six other officers were ordered back to Tennessee for recruiting. Upon hearing the news, they protested to the adjutant general that "Finding ourselves unexpectedly ordered upon recruiting service at a moment when active operations were about to commence, unwilling to be seen creeping home at such a period, desirous of being employed in some way . . . we respectfully request that we be permitted to serve in the rank and file." It was to no avail. Although the order was sent for legitimate reasons, Jackson could not resist inserting a statement into the adjutant general's reply: "Not only the wishes of some, but the public services would be promoted by the order given."[89]

Determined to see action before the war ended, Benton got his regimental commander to order him to Washington, and he set off carrying a petition from the officers of the 39th asking to be sent where the fighting was. In the capital city, blackened from fires of the British, Benton waited for still more weeks. Finally, he received orders to proceed to Canada, but before he could leave the news arrived that peace had been concluded at Ghent on Christmas Eve. A week earlier had come the sensational news that Jackson's troops had defeated the British at New Orleans on January 8. Had General Edward Packenham's force succeeded in capturing the Crescent City they would have controlled the mouth of the Mississippi. The British quite likely would have nullified the Louisiana Purchase by returning that territory to their Spanish allies. As it was, the threat of a European sphere of influence in the West was eliminated once and for all. Jackson had won the greatest American victory of the war. Ironically, due to the slowness of trans-Atlantic communications, the battle had been fought after the war had already ended.[90]

Benton's chances for martial glory vanished once and for all. The "Second War of Independence," as Americans subsequently viewed it, had served to vindicate the nation's honor in the face of British violations. Further, the country was now united behind the Republican administration of James Madison, as the Federalists faded to irrelevance in the aftermath of the Hartford Convention. The defeats of Tecumseh's Indian confederacy in the North and of the Red Stick Creeks in the South now opened the trans-Appalachian West for white settlement. After a generation of struggling to remain out of Europe's conflicts, Americans could now turn their attention to developing the continent's vast interior.

Benton left Washington in the spring of 1815. Returning to Tennessee held little promise for him. His only combat during the last three years had resulted in his nearly killing the man who was now the country's greatest hero. His prospects in Jackson's home state had been ruined by the Nashville fight and the military ostracism that followed. Rather, the desire to leave behind a checkered past and make a new start led Benton, like thousands of others after the war, to move westward again. By the fall of 1815, the former colonel of Tennessee volunteers was once more practicing law, sizing up the political landscape, and warily guarding his public reputation—this time in the frontier town of St. Louis in the Missouri territory.

2 / The Transformation of Frontier Missouri: Frontiers of Inclusion, Frontiers of Exclusion

Benton's arrival in Missouri coincided with the transformation of that territory from a "cosmopolitan" or "expeditionary" frontier, in which the political economy was dominated by the fur trade and mineral mining, to a "sedentary" and self-sufficient farming frontier. The years after 1815 also witnessed Missouri's change from a relatively multicultural colonial society to the kind of racialized society more characteristic of the antebellum United States. That is to say, it was transformed from a "frontier of inclusion," in which Anglo-Americans, French Creoles, and Indians had cooperated more or less peacefully in pursuit of mutual economic benefit, and in which black slaves labored under the relatively mild constraints of the colonial *code noir*, to a frontier of racial "exclusion." After the War of 1812, a tide of white immigrants from the Upper South and their black slaves accelerated the "racial modernization" of Missouri. Benton's career as lawyer, editor, and politician during the decade between his arrival in St. Louis and his declaration of support for the presidential candidacy of Andrew Jackson reflected Missouri's transition from territory to statehood and from an expeditionary/inclusive frontier to a sedentary frontier of exclusion.[1]

In the course of Missouri's transition from territory to statehood, interest groups that had coalesced over the issue of land grants issued during Spanish rule, matured into factions that would shape Missouri's political landscape for years to come. Although Benton was initially linked to the fur trading and land grant interests of St. Louis's elite Creole families, he was astute enough to sense the direction that political winds were blowing as early as 1820. As a southerner and a slaveholder, he embraced these changes and played a prominent local role in opposing restrictions on slavery as a condition for Missouri's entry into the Union. After the Compromise of 1820, Benton would lead the state's planter-slaveholders and yeoman farmers into the emerging coalition that eventually became the Democratic Party. By the time he entered the U.S. Senate, he was already shifting from his role as delegate for the old cosmopolitan interests to spokesman for the farmers and expectant capitalists who would later support Jackson.

Benton and the Spanish Land Grants

Following his discharge from the army, in the spring of 1815, Benton traveled to Smithfield plantation in western Virginia to visit Colonel James Preston, an acquaintance from his mother's side of his family. The Preston family produced an unusual number of political leaders and opinion makers. Thomas L. Preston was a coeditor with Thomas Ritchie of the Richmond *Enquirer*, the leading Democratic-Republican newspaper in the state. Laetitia Preston married John Floyd, future governor of Virginia, and James Preston himself later served as governor. Francis Preston, another brother, was a friend to Thomas Benton's second cousin Nathaniel Hart, and another sister, Susan, had married this same Nathaniel Hart, thus providing a link to the Benton family. Through Colonel Preston, Thomas Benton had met Colonel James McDowell who was married to James Preston's sister, Sarah. James and Sarah McDowell lived at a modest plantation called Cherry Grove, near Lexington, Virginia, with their three children James Jr., Susan, and Elizabeth. Benton visited the McDowells and was smitten with twenty-one year old Elizabeth. Impressed by her beauty, intellect, and "exalted moral tone," he had proposed to her, but was rejected. Nonetheless, Benton apparently considered Elizabeth McDowell an ideal mate and never forgot her during the years when he was establishing his fortune in Missouri.[2]

Ties of blood and affiliation to the Virginia gentry, stretching back to Colonel Thomas Hart, helped to shape Benton's essential ambivalence toward many of the crucial issues of his day, especially, as time went on, the slavery question. They would also influence his choice of companions during his early Senate career and solidify his essentially Jeffersonian attitudes toward race and democracy. It is likely that Benton decided to go to Missouri while visiting the Prestons and McDowells. "You know what I told you when I parted from you," Benton wrote Governor Preston some years later, "... that I was going forth as an adventurer to begin a new theater and to endeavor to lay with my own hands some foundation of character and fortune." Among others already in Missouri with strong ties to the Old Dominion was the territorial governor, William Clark, whose wife Julia was also related to the Preston family through marriage.[3]

Benton arrived in St. Louis in the fall of 1815. "I crossed the Mississippi on a Sunday evening," he later wrote to James Preston, "four hundred dollars in my pocket, and nobody ahead I had ever seen before, my law reading to revise and the French language to learn." The town on the west bank of the river consisted of whitewashed wood and mud or stone buildings and gradually rose from the shore to the summit of a bluff, giving it the appearance of an amphitheater. St. Louis contained many handsome buildings and a few splendid ones in the midst of a native "meanness" that became apparent only upon closer inspection. Only three streets deep from the shore of the river, the town straggled along its banks for nearly twenty square blocks.[4]

Arriving on the western shore, Benton sought to inquire after lodgings where he might eat and sleep. Walking toward the center of the village, asking directions as he went, Benton was finally approached by "a most respectable old gentleman" who invited the Colonel into his own home. Benton's first friend in St. Louis was Charles Gratiot. Sixty-three at the time of their meeting, Gratiot had been born in Switzerland and at seventeen accompanied an uncle to Montreal, where he became involved in the fur trade. His business ventures had led him, by the 1770s, to the Illinois Country, where he opened a store and, shortly, joined George Rogers Clark's campaign against the British. Moving to St. Louis in 1781, Gratiot had married Victoire Chouteau, sister of the village's cofounder, and became a successful investor, fur trader, and land agent. Gratiot's daughters had married other leading members of the French community—Jean P. Cabanne, Sylvestre Labadie, and Pierre Chouteau *fils*. Benton lived in the Gratiot house for the next six weeks. There, he had the opportunity to meet these local magnates and others, including Auguste Chouteau—the town's aging founder—and Governor William Clark. The new arrival from Tennessee was introduced to the most influential men in the territory. The Chouteaus, Gratiots, and Clarks were members of the territorial gentry, and Benton sought to establish himself as one of their number. "How precious are the rights of hospitality!" he later wrote. "It has been my happiness everywhere to meet with good people whose remembrance is dear to me."[5]

Although Benton's account of his meeting with Gratiot conveys the impression that the episode was completely fortuitous, in all likelihood the Tennessean's reputation had preceded him. Territorial jurisprudence was, at this time, in a state of uncertainty. Early French and Spanish rule had bequeathed a system of Latin civil law to the region. American immigrants brought with them a version of English common law that augmented, but did not entirely supplant, the existing system. Benton spoke no French (he would later be tutored by Bishop William Dubourg), but his talents as both a lawyer and a fighter were probably known to the Creoles before he ever set foot upon the levee at St. Louis. Gratiot and other members of the small group, related by family and interest, would have been impressed not only with Benton's legal talents, but also with his ambition and aggressiveness. "It was therefore no coincidence," wrote Missouri historian Dick Steward, "that Gratiot met the thirty-five-year old belligerent that autumn day at the river's edge. Benton's job as apparatchik of the ruling class, was to popularize their cause, to defend their grants in court, and, if need be, to intimidate and silence their adversaries." William Chambers stated more ambiguously, "Undoubtedly Gratiot and his associates saw in Benton a promising addition to their circle."[6]

Promptly after arriving in Missouri, Benton's law practice was, as he put it, "ardently recommenced." On October 2, 1815, he went to the courthouse in St. Louis, paid his fee, and enrolled as an attorney at the local bar. He set up an office and walked there daily from the Gratiot house to meet clients, prepare briefs, and handle routine business. Unlike many other new attorneys at the territorial bar, Benton found it unnecessary to either advertise in Joseph Charless's *Missouri Gazette* or to hang about the territorial courts to solicit cases. His personal relationship with Charles Gratiot and, through him, to the Chouteaus, Governor Clark, and others, gave him all the business he needed. Benton developed a particularly close relationship with Edward Hempstead, another Anglo-American lawyer who had tied his fortunes to the Creole elite. Two years Benton's senior, Hempstead was a former territorial delegate to the national Congress and possessed the foremost reputation in St. Louis as a courtroom lawyer. He had a notable manner of barking out his assertions in the courtroom, which overawed jury members, and his fierce style was imitated by other young lawyers in Missouri, including Benton.[7]

The new arrival not only became Hempstead's protégé, but a friend to his brothers as well, serving as second to Thomas Hempstead in a duel with Joshua Barton. Thomas Benton and Edward Bates drew up the rules for this particular gentlemen's "interview" on August 10, 1816, on the Mississippi sandbar shortly to be known as "Bloody Island." The meeting ended without bloodshed; both parties, acting in "a firm, cool, and collected manner," fired simultaneously, missed each other, and declared that honor had been satisfied. "No explanation, concession, or even mention of the cause of the difference was made upon the ground; but the gentlemen shook hands as friends, upon mutual declaration that they owed each other no ill will, and upon the unanimous declaration of the friends and surgeons present that the affair ought not to proceed any further." A public statement was issued to the effect that the affair had been honorably settled among gentlemen.[8]

The Barton-Hempstead duel underscores the fact that, in the elaborate rituals enacted upon the "field of honor," not every confrontation was followed by a funeral. Indeed, in the older, more cultured regions of the Deep South, affairs of honor were usually bloodless encounters in which decorum and punctilio were more highly valued than homicide. Men in frontier Missouri, by contrast, considered dueling a deadly serious business, and a much higher number of fatalities resulted. For Benton, whose only consummated affair of honor thus far had been his ungentlemanly shoot-out with Jackson, participation as Hempstead's second in a formal duel signaled his acceptance into the ranks of genteel society. For Joshua Barton's friends and allies, however, Benton's role in the affair would become a source of lasting enmity.[9]

Most of Benton's work as a lawyer had to do with uncertain land titles held under grants from the former Spanish regime. Benton quickly became an expert in this field and an advocate for recognition of the old, if doubtful, Spanish titles. It was in this capacity that he provided his most valuable services as council to the Creole "junto." As we have seen, from 1763 to 1800, the Spanish regime in the Mississippi River valley had displayed a strong interest in immigration and settlement in order to create a buffer colony between Spain's provinces to the south and her enemies to the north and east. In 1778, to bolster the precarious defenses of Upper Louisiana, Spanish officials announced special inducements, including grants of land in tracts five arpents in width (one arpent is equal to about .84 acre) for every immigrant over the age of twelve.

After the American Revolution, Spanish colonization activities accelerated in an attempt to check American expansion in the Tennessee and

Ohio valleys. By the 1790s Spanish officials, convinced that American immigration was the key to strengthening their colony while weakening the grip of the United States on the territories to the east, offered free land to attract settlers to Upper Louisiana. Under Spanish rule, however, the process of having land claims confirmed was so burdensome that few settlers went through the entire procedure, which included a trip to the seat of government at New Orleans. With a great deal of land and a small population, Spanish officials were generous in awarding land grants to those who requested them and became increasingly so during the last days of their regime. Many of the concessions were made in a questionable manner, and no effort was made to encourage settlers to secure full title. Local commandants accepted incomplete concessions as authorizations to hold the lands, and the situation could be further complicated when the tracts were sold or inherited.

This confused state of affairs became one of the major issues confronting the new government when Louisiana became part of the United States in 1803. Speculators grabbed up every available title, however questionable, in confidence that all would be speedily confirmed by the American government. Property values increased somewhere between 200 and 500 percent during the first months of American government. Anglo-American speculators like Rufus Easton and John Rice Jones joined Creoles in the race to acquire titles. Taking advantage of the legal chaos in Upper Louisiana, some individuals obtained, through influence or bribery, antedated petitions from Spanish officials confirming large land grants to them. The holders of the counterfeit titles believed that the American government would be unable or unwilling to separate the bona fide from the fraudulent grants since neither had been registered or recorded in New Orleans. Competition to win the favor of newly appointed territorial officers intensified the growing conflict between the established and mostly French claimants of extensive land holdings and the growing number of American newcomers who challenged the legitimacy of those claims.[10]

The U.S. Congress was committed to stopping speculation and fraud in Louisiana land titles. An act of March 2, 1805, sought to establish regular procedures for the confirmation of land claims. The new legislation contained strict guidelines for approving titles by creating a three-man board of land commissioners empowered to consider and rule upon grants presented for confirmation. The act did not provide for the wholesale confirmation of all land grants sought by local residents. As a result, the measure failed to eliminate the growing factionalism and bitterness between rival groups of large claimants seeking approval for their grants.[11]

This contentious situation confronted the newly appointed governor for Upper Louisiana upon his arrival in St. Louis early in 1805. He was none other than the ubiquitous James Wilkinson, who was greeted warmly by the St. Louis gentry. A dinner and gala ball held on the Fourth of July to honor Wilkinson's arrival helped win him over to the cause of the longtime residents. Reconciling the conflicting interests of the territory would have been a daunting task for the most skilled and fair-minded of governors. Wilkinson was neither. His determination to exercise complete control over the territory; his attempt to develop a clique of subordinates loyal only to him; his efforts to remove any officials who disagreed with him; as well as his inability to judge fairly between the rival factions—all added to an already volatile political situation.

By the fall of 1805, two identifiable factions had emerged, with loyalty or opposition to the new governor determined largely by rivalry over the Spanish land grants. The party supporting Wilkinson included not only most of the territory's French inhabitants, who feared the growing influence of American newcomers and hoped for the governor to protect their interests, but also the largest Spanish land claimants, who believed Wilkinson favored the confirmation of their grants, as well as an assortment of adventurers and supporters of Aaron Burr's western schemes, in which Wilkinson was by now secretly involved. Members of the pro-Wilkinson faction included Gratiot, Auguste Chouteau, Jacques Clamorgen, Bernard Pratte, and mining entrepreneur John Smith T.[12]

The opposing group was composed almost entirely of Americans who had arrived in the territory since the United States had taken control, including a group of ambitious young lawyers who sought advancement through land speculation as well as politics. They were to play an important role in the introduction of American law and government in Louisiana and hence became a powerful force in territorial politics. Wilkinson's position and power was undermined by their influence, and they became targets of his enmity. Rufus Easton, William C. Carr, and Edward Hempstead were early leaders of this group (Hempstead would later go over to the Creole opposition). They gathered support from among other potential land speculators interested in blocking confirmation of Spanish claims in order to enhance their own chances for success.[13]

The board of commissioners created by Congress to review land claims in Louisiana soon became part of the factional disputes. In May 1805 James Donaldson, Clement B. Penrose, and John B.C. Lucas were selected to serve on the board. None could speak or read Spanish, which one might have presumed a useful skill given the nature of the task ahead. Donaldson, an Irish-born lawyer, had been active in Maryland politics. Penrose was descended from the prominent Biddle family of Philadelphia and was a nephew of Governor Wilkinson as well. Lucas, descended from an aristocratic Norman family, had come to the United States in 1784 bearing a letter of introduction from Benjamin Franklin. He became active in Pennsylvania politics and succeeded Albert Gallatin as representative to Congress from western Pennsylvania when the latter became treasury secretary. Upon Lucas's arrival in Missouri, President Jefferson had appointed him a territorial judge of the superior court as well as a member of the board of land commissioners.[14]

Within days of its first hearings the board found itself badly split. Penrose and Donaldson supported the policies of Governor Wilkinson. Hence, the initial decisions handed down by the Penrose-Donaldson majority tended to favor those with Spanish land claims. Lucas, hoping to enhance his family's shaky finances through land speculation, sided with the opposition. He suspected bias on the part of Penrose and Donaldson when, by majority vote, they appointed Gratiot as clerk of the board and employed Philip Marie Leduc as translator. Both men were close associates of the Spanish land claimants and themselves possessed sizable claims. Reports of the questionable activities of the board of commissioners at length reached Washington. Even after Secretary Gallatin instructed the commissioners to adhere to the letter of the law and leave policy making to Congress, relations between Lucas and the other members of the board remained troubled. When Penrose and Donaldson continued to demonstrate bias in favor of the land claimants, the latter was removed from the board and replaced by Frederick Bates, formerly a justice of the Michigan territory's supreme court.[15]

By the time Wilkinson departed the territory in the summer of 1806, little had changed in the status of the Spanish land claims. The governor's meddling in the land claims issue had only exacerbated tensions. The situation improved for a time under Wilkinson's successor, Merriwether Lewis, who steered clear of involvement in factional disputes during his tenure. A realignment of those factions occurred around this time as well. Recognizing that continued opposition to the growing American majority was futile, influential Creoles began to adjust to their new circumstances by seeking acceptance among the more influential Americans in the territory. The lure of the handsome retainers for litigation of the land titles also led several American attorneys like Edward Hempstead, who had opposed Wilkinson, to join forces with the Spanish land claimants in what they hoped would be a mutually profitable relationship. Gradually, an elite coalition of leaders emerged that would dominate Missouri socially, politically, and economically for the remainder of the territorial period. Editor Joseph Charless of the *Missouri Gazette* referred to this circle, which Benton joined upon his arrival, as the "little junto."[16]

The board of land commissioners issued their final report in January 1812. They had examined a total of 3,300 claims, and confirmed 1,340 of them, the majority containing less than 500 acres. Frederick Bates, now the recorder of land titles, spent four more years reexamining unsettled claims before presenting his final report to the General Land Office on February 2, 1816. Although Bates had approved confirmation of many additional Spanish titles, he rejected a large number of others. Therefore, following the conclusion of Bates's investigation (shortly after Benton's arrival in St. Louis), the remaining claimants—nearly half of the original number—were still unsatisfied.[17]

Benton's enemies accused him, as pleader for recognition of the unconfirmed Spanish grants, of serving "the interests of the tiny French aristocracy" in St. Louis. The holders of the largest grants, ranging up to 25,000 arpents, were men like the Chouteaus, Moses Austin, Francois Vallé, and Charles Gratiot. It is also clear that at least some of the grants were made after the 1803 treaty of purchase in circumstances suggesting fraud. Benton's earlier biographers claimed that hundreds of small holders, both French and American, were also involved. If the members of the junto were interested in validating their Spanish grants, they argued, the issue also had popular appeal among the farmers of the backcountry, and Benton, as an aspiring political leader, was smart enough to be aware of this.[18]

This argument may be consistent with Benton's populist land policies as they were presented after 1823, but it is reading events backwards to use those policies to justify his actions prior to that date. During his early years in Missouri, deference to the ruling class was still the order of the day and neither the junto nor anti-junto factions were much concerned with serving the interests of the "lower orders." They *were* very much concerned with protecting their own interests—which in this context meant land claims—and they were willing to use any means necessary to do so. Immigration to Missouri, which had slowed to a trickle during the War of 1812, increased many times over with the return of peace. Benton was one of an estimated forty thousand new arrivals—the overwhelming majority without land claims—who entered the territory between 1814 and 1820. Like him, the majority of the newcomers came from the Upper South—Virginia, Kentucky, Tennessee, and North Carolina. The absence of antislavery restrictions west of the Mississippi made the territory especially inviting to prospective white settlers from that region. With the flood of humanity arriving daily in the Mississippi River towns, land prices rose so rapidly that even speculators wished for a temporary halt to the boom so that they could acquire additional lands and take full advantage of the situation. In these circumstances, a greater degree of both political and economic democratization was coming to Missouri, but it would still take several years for the "will of the people" to make itself felt.[19]

The Benton-Lucas Duel

In this atmosphere of frontier conflict and Old World gentility, the attorney from Tennessee made plans to resume his career in politics. Benton waited a year-and-a-half from the time he crossed the Mississippi until he entered the political arena. Even a character as talented and driven as Benton found it necessary to establish himself in the community before seeking electoral office. In 1816 Congress elevated Missouri to the status of a third-class territory. The governor, the secretary of the territory, judges, and several other officials were still appointed by the president, but Missourians were now able to elect members of the Legislative Council as well as members of the lower House and Missouri's nonvoting delegate to Congress. Elevation to this highest grade of territory also represented the last steps generally taken prior to admission by Congress as a state.

Politics in Missouri was often a matter of personalities. Reflecting the Democratic-Republican consensus of the national Era of Good Feelings, nearly every voter in Missouri counted himself a Jeffersonian. Still, definite factions had emerged with cleavages largely determined by the land-claims issue. The "little junto," as Joseph Charless styled them, now consisted not only of the French families who had long dominated the economic affairs of St. Louis, but Governor Clark, Edward Hempstead and his brothers, John Scott of St. Genevieve, and certain others who represented the interests of this circle in territorial politics. Opponents of the junto looked to land speculators William Russell and Rufus Easton, and banker Samuel Hammond, for leadership. Leading opposition figures also included Judge John B.C. Lucas—late of the Board of Land Commissioners—and his son Charles, Alexander McNair, the popular David Barton, and editor Charless.

Neither of these groups represented "the people" of the territory. Politics remained a genteel affair in which men of position and property made policy with the assistance of lawyers and publishers. The masses were largely omitted from the process, save at election time. Both "junto" and "anti-junto" candidates couched their appeals in Jeffersonian rhetoric, but the real issue remained whether the established families or the newcomers would get the lion's share of the territory's unsettled lands.

In the spring of 1817, Thomas Benton was appointed by Governor Clark to his first public office in Missouri, the newly established Board of Trustees for Schools in St. Louis. By the summer of 1817, rumor had it that he might be a candidate for delegate to Congress. In point of fact, a special election was to be held to address certain controversies arising from the previous biennial election for territorial delegate the previous year. In the 1816 contest the junto candidate, John Scott, an attorney from Ste. Genevieve, challenged the incumbent delegate, Rufus Easton. Scott campaigned on a platform similar to Easton's. He pledged to end government monopoly of mineral lands, to dismantle the federal system of fur-trading factories, to work for the speedy admission of Missouri to statehood, to oppose removal of squatters, and to work for internal improvements. All of these planks represented the clear demands of Missouri voters, and it would have been foolhardy for any candidate to oppose them.[20]

Since there was little to choose between the factions on policy, attention focused on the candidates themselves and on their backers. Scott's supporters claimed that Easton's land speculation and his large holdings were behind his efforts to increase the amount of public land up for sale. They also attributed Easton's attempt to block the confirmation of Spanish land claims as protection for his own holdings. Easton's supporters portrayed Scott as part of a faction of Missouri lawyers and government officials seeking to dominate the territory against the public interest. They pointed to Scott's large holdings of Spanish land grants as proof of their own charges.[21]

In the voting on September 19, 1816, the junto candidate had been behind in the vote, with all the ballots counted except those from Cote Sans Dessein in the district of St. Charles. Scott rode to Cote Sans Dessein to obtain the uncounted ballots on his own, whereupon Governor Clark declared him the victor by a margin of 15 votes. Clark, whose preference for Scott was common knowledge, was accused of intervening to award the victory to his favorite. Although Scott was known to be popular in Cote Sans Dessein, the anti-junto charges set off a battle that carried the disputed election all the way to Washington, D.C. In January 1817 Congress voided the result and ordered a new election.

As the special election approached, William Russell penned a lengthy epistle to Easton, his political ally and fellow land speculator. Identifying himself as among those who believed that "Governor Clark *cheated* you out of the last election," Russell made it clear that Scott, Hempstead, and Benton should be "*kept out*" and either Bates, Easton, or Barton "put in—This I say is *my wish*, and I am ready and willing to spend some of my money and time to effect it." Russell believed that chances of victory for the anti-junto faction were good, though it would depend greatly on which candidate had the most active, and warmly attached personal friends. "Governor Clark is *now* about as unpopular as he *can be*, with Hempstead, Scott, & Benton for his friends—It will be well for the public to believe them all so closely united as they are; so that each of them may partake of the Governor's popularity." Benton had no plans to stand for office in the upcoming election, but his advocacy in and out of court had apparently won enough popular support for liberal recognition of land grants to make that cause a factor in the outcome. Russell therefore advised Easton, in his public addresses, to acknowledge "that there are a number of very fair claims to lands in this Territory not yet confirmed which ought to be immediately provided for by law."[22]

Carefully weighing the situation, both the junto and the anti-junto factions chose to renominate the candidates they had supported in the original race. Both sides trotted out their well-worn attacks on the opposition, as well as their usual appeals to the electorate. In this second contest on August 4, 1817, Scott again defeated Easton. The margin this time was considerably larger: 2,406 to 2,014 (less than 4,500 total votes were cast out of a population of over 40,000), but once again the losing side angrily questioned the conduct of the polling. "MILITARY ELECTION!" ran the headline of the *Missouri Gazette*. "On Monday last, an election for delegate to Congress took place in the several election districts of this territory. In this town the election was conducted in the most violent, turbulent and savage manner." The night preceding the election the members of the militia and soldiers and musicians of a military recruiting party had paraded the streets and early on election day the soldiers, with tickets in their caps bearing the name "JOHN SCOTT," occupied the polling place with two stands of colors on which the words "TRUE REPUBLICAN NOMINATION, *John Scott*" were painted. A large shed, covered with boat sails, was erected near the door of the election area, under which was spread tables covered with whiskey.[23]

Much of what Charless decried in his article was not at all unusual for the conduct of a nineteenth-century American election. Nonetheless he succeeded in securing a court of inquiry, which investigated his charges against the militia but found them to be false and dismissed the affair. Voting in St. Louis on election day *was* accompanied by fistfights, and a few men were stabbed or beaten with cudgels. Captain John O'Fallon, Governor Clark's nephew, engaged anti-junto voter Dr. Robert Simpson in an exchange of insults, which led O'Fallon to administer a beating to Simpson in the streets several days later.[24]

Another such exchange, involving Benton and Charles Lucas, set in motion the series of events that ended in their fatal meeting at Bloody Island. There had been ill feelings between Benton and the son of Judge Lucas for some time. Partly it was political animosity. Partly it was the clash of two strong and ambitious personalities. Ten years younger than Benton, Lucas had read law with Rufus Easton, had developed a wide practice, and was a member of the Territorial Legislature. Industrious, sober, and mild-mannered, young Lucas despised frontier brawlers like Benton. The two met as counselors for opposing sides in the St. Louis Circuit Court in October 1816. When the time came for summation, Benton asserted to the jury that since the evidence *was* as he had presented it, they *must* decide in his favor. Lucas sprang to his feet to correct his adversary; there was no such evidence. "I contradict you sir," barked Benton.

"I contradict *you* sir," answered Lucas.

"If you deny that," shouted Benton, "you deny the truth."

"If you assert that," Lucas answered firmly, "you assert what is not true."

The jury found for Lucas's client. Before the month was out, Benton was demanding satisfaction for the insult Lucas had inflicted on his personal honor. To Lucas's question, What kind of satisfaction?, Benton responded, a duel with whatever weapons Lucas chose. Lucas would not allow his actions at the bar to be called to account privately. He refused Benton's challenge.[25]

But the ill feeling between the two men persisted. On the day of the territorial elections, when Benton approached the clerks to vote, Charles Lucas challenged his right to do so, asking if he had paid his taxes on property that included his slaves. The Colonel gave young Lucas a withering look. "Gentlemen," he said, turning to the election judges, "if *you* have any questions to ask, I am prepared to answer, but I do not propose to answer charges made by any *puppy* who may happen to run across my path."[26]

By his use of the term "puppy," Benton had used one of those words that was bound to bring forth a challenge from another gentleman; "liar," "scoundrel," "rascal," and "coward" were others. At the time, however, Lucas was either unaware of the insult or unsure of his response. Five days later he addressed a letter to Benton which read, "Sir: I am informed that you applied to me on the day of the election the epithet of 'puppy.' If so I shall expect that satisfaction which is due from one gentleman to another for such an indignity."[27]

The challenge reached Benton at a bad time. He had just been up through the night attending the wake of Edward Hempstead, who had been thrown from his horse, collapsed in court a few days later, and died at the age of 38. Benton had returned to his office to refresh himself before going to the funeral at the Hempstead plantation outside of town. He was there when the challenge from Lucas arrived. "Sir," he immediately replied, "I accept, but I must go now and bury a dead friend; that is my first duty, after that is discharged I will fight, tonight if possible; if not, tomorrow morning at daybreak."[28]

The articles were drawn up that day. Smoothbore pistols "not over 11 inches long" were to be used and the principals were to stand thirty feet apart. At the command, either might present and fire. If either fired before the command was given, the other's second was to shoot him immediately. The following morning at dawn the men were rowed across to Bloody Island with Joshua Barton serving as second to Lucas and Colonel Luke Lawless, an Irish soldier of fortune who had fought under Napoleon, serving his friend Benton. Both men appeared cool and confident as they stripped to their shirtsleeves. At the command they fired almost simultaneously. Benton's well-aimed shot went through Lucas's neck to the left of his windpipe and opened his jugular. Blood spurted from the left side of Lucas's throat. Benton received a slight wound to the knee. Lucas's surgeon refused to allow another fire. When Lawless asked Lucas if he was satisfied, he said that he was and would not ask for another meeting. "But I am not satisfied." declared Benton loudly, "and I require that Mr. Lucas should continue to fight, or pledge himself to come out again as soon as his wound should be in a state to permit him." Lucas agreed to fight again as soon as his wound permitted.[29]

Talk about the duel soon divided St. Louis into pro-Benton and pro-Lucas factions. Benton's friends now insisted that his demand for a second meeting and his oversensitivity regarding his honor would look like vengeance. They urged him to withdraw his demand. Despite rumors that Lucas was willing to fight again and had told friends that at the next meeting he would insist on a shorter distance to make the contest more even, by the end of August Lawless wrote Charles Lucas that Benton authorized him to say he no longer demanded a second meeting. But gossip still ran the streets. Word soon reached Benton that Lucas's friends and especially his father, the Judge, were charging that Benton was a common criminal who had fled Tennessee to escape prosecution and that he declined to fight again because of his fears of a duel at a shorter distance. Benton dispatched Lawless with a new challenge on September 23. He was determined now to finish his vendetta against Lucas.[30]

Why, one might ask, was Benton thus driven, not only in this instance but in his previous scrapes with Jackson, with William Lewis, even with schoolmate Archibald Lytle, to vindicate himself with violence? Michael Paul Rogin, in his intriguing psychological history of Andrew Jackson, informed readers that while dueling was common in the early American republic, in the South and among lawyers and military men it enjoyed special popularity. Benton included himself within all of these categories. "Dueling enforced a code of honor which held men accountable for their conduct in the absence of stable, routinized, standards of professional behavior." This was especially true in frontier communities like Missouri. Benton, like Jackson, chose the legal profession: "a source of mobility important in early America, most lawyers were among the nation's elite. But the law was also looked on with suspicion, and there was mistrust of lawyers who used the fine points of land litigation to acquire acreage for themselves." There is no evidence that Benton manipulated the law to enrich himself, but his clients certainly benefited from his litigation on behalf of their land claims, and his power and prestige grew accordingly.[31]

Yet there was more still to the tendency to violence among some men, Benton included. Dueling, writes Rogin, "reflected preoccupation with family, reputation, and honor under circumstances in which personal and clan loyalties were intense but fragile." Family ties provided the major social bonds of the eighteenth and early nineteenth centuries. Bertram Wyatt-Brown concedes that, in the Old South, courage was a personal attribute, "but it could not be wholly separated from the familial context. Therefore it was important to have kinsfolk who needed valorous protection and who would undertake justifiable revenge when the hero was himself slain. Without relatives one was helpless and shorn of a major reason to exist." Behind the readiness of men like Alexander Hamilton and Andrew Jackson to kill over questions of personal honor was an acute awareness of their vulnerability and solitariness in the world. "These men, noted for their high-strung sensibilities, hot tempers, and depressed spirits, had forbearers little respected in the community, or else had lost parents early in their lives. Though each posed different psychological complexities, kinlessness and the stigma attached to it affected the attitudes of all of them toward the world."[32]

Benton was not kinless. In fact, it was the opprobrium of his brother Jesse's duel with William Carroll that led to the falling out with Jackson, a man who had created his own kinship network out of nothing over his years in Tennessee. John Coffee and the Donelsons were as close as blood relatives to the General, and Benton, too, had been chosen to be part of the "band of brothers," the officers under Jackson's command. But Benton's ambition, Jackson's perpetual suspicions of disloyalty, and the temperament of both men contributed to their violent confrontation instead.

Andrew Jackson was an orphan from the age of fourteen. Benton lost his father when he was only eight. Insecurity haunted both men throughout their lives. Both men were dominated by the presence (in Benton's case) or the memory (in Jackson's) of strong mothers. Rogin's descriptions of Elizabeth Jackson and the influence she exercised over Andrew, even after her death, are paralleled by the influence of Nancy Benton over her sons. Here was the archetypical "Spartan mother" of the American frontier who both empowered and controlled her son with the admonition to fight. In the absence of a living father figure, the effect of such a strong female must have been profound for Thomas Hart Benton. "I made war on myself," he supposedly told his daughter, after he had suddenly been thrust into the premature role of *pater familias*. The gaze of his white-haired mother and her high expectations would never really go away. Benton would make war on the rest of the world for the next sixty years to please the shade of this domineering woman. Imagine his mortification and her disapproval when he was expelled for theft from Chapel Hill—and that apparently motivated by the desire to live according to the standards expected among the other young gentlemen. The humiliation was then compounded by the mother's decision to "rescue" her son's future by taking the family west into Tennessee. No wonder Benton swaggered and bullied, just as Jackson choked with rage. These two men were as volatile a combination as ever met in the Old Southwest, and the shoot-out in Nashville was unexpected only insofar as it took so long to occur. When Benton moved west again, his violence took on a new form, linked to his political and legal career in the little junto but still, perhaps, reflecting his resentment against the genteel, well-connected, young Lucas. Benton arrived in St. Louis without kin or connections, more determined than ever to make his mark. Already thirty-five in 1817, he would let nothing, least of all a spoiled "puppy" like Charles Lucas, stand in his way.

Fatherless since childhood, dishonored, dominated by a strong mother, and thwarted in martial ambition, Benton had attained such reputation as he possessed by intelligence and unwillingness to back down from a fight. Young Charles, on the other hand, appears to have been goaded into the fight by his father's sense of family honor, as well as the desire of other anti-junto politicians to have Benton out of the picture. It is worth mentioning, however, that Nancy Benton and her surviving children had finally relocated to St. Louis in the spring of 1817. The eyes of his family were on him once again. The kind of loose talk circulating about him in the town could not go unanswered. "When I released you from your engagement to return to the island," he wrote Lucas, "I yielded to a feeling of generosity in my own bosom and to a sentiment of deference to the judgment of others. From the reports which now fill the country, it would seem that yourself and some of your friends have placed my conduct to very different motives. The object of this is to bring these calumnies to an end, and to give you an opportunity of justifying the great expectation which has been excited." Once again Luke Lawless was to receive Lucas's terms for the meeting. Benton informed his opponent that he expected the duel to be conducted at the lethal distance of nine feet or less.[33]

Lucas was out of town attending the Superior Court for the Southern District. When he returned to St. Louis on the morning of September 26, he was stunned by the challenge and at the local excitement over the whole matter. Nonetheless he made one more attempt to restore the peace in a meeting with Lawless, insisting verbally that he had nothing to do with the slanderous rumors in town. With this Lawless went back to Benton. Lucas's verbal denial was unsatisfactory. Nothing but a written declaration would suffice. At last Lucas accepted. "I shall give you an opportunity of gratifying your wishes and the wishes of your news carriers."[34]

The second duel occurred on the morning of September 27. It was hot and humid. Both of the principals appear to have been nervous and on edge. Benton was attended by Lawless and by his surgeon Dr. Bernard Farrar. Charles Lucas was accompanied by Joshua Barton, Colonel Eli Clemson, and Dr. Quarles. The two men were to stand only ten feet apart. Clemson was to give the preparatory command, "Fire," followed by the count "One, two, three."

Clemson, rattled by Benton's anger in response to his query as to the opponents' readiness to begin, forgot to give the command "Fire" before he began counting, "One, two, three." Apparently both combatants were startled—at the count of "two," both fired simultaneously. Lucas missed Benton. Benton's ball passed through Lucas's arm and lodged near his heart. The young man fell to the ground. Benton's demeanor now changed completely. He stood for a moment, still holding his empty pistol, then approached the small group kneeling over the dying Lucas. Seemingly shocked by the outcome, he stammered, "I trust he forgives me the cruel necessity under which I acted."

"Colonel Benton," Lucas groaned, turning away, "you have persecuted me and murdered me. I don't, or cannot, forgive you."

This was a breach of dueling etiquette. A dying man was expected to absolve his opponent before passing from the world. Lucas's seconds urged him to do so. Benton dropped the pistol he had been holding and knelt beside Lucas, taking his hand. Finally Lucas turned toward Benton and said, "I can forgive you—I do forgive you." A moment later he was dead.

Lawless now interrupted to break up the tableau. He had been watching the river and saw a boat coming from the direction of the town. "Come Benton," he called, "That boat may have the sheriff in it. It will not do for them to find us here." He led Benton to their boat and together they left the island.[35]

Charles Lucas may have observed the fine points of the *code duello* in his final moments by forgiving his opponent, but Judge Lucas was not about to forgive the man who killed his son. He insisted that Benton, an adept duelist and superior marksman, had murdered Charles to remove a potential political opponent. Supporters of the Lucas faction made much of Benton's red undershirt, which could be seen from the west bank of the river when Benton rolled up his shirtsleeves. In genteel society this was evidence of Benton's uncouth background—the equivalent of a modern-day American male wearing a tie with a short-sleeved shirt. Benton, claimed the anti-junto forces including Joseph Charless, was a ruffian, a hired gun for the Creole faction, who had goaded young Charles into sacrificing the remainder of his blood.[36]

These charges were not entirely fair. On the contrary, one could very well make the case that it was Judge Lucas, Rufus Easton, and others who had pushed Charles Lucas into the quarrel with Benton to remove *him* from the scene. At any rate, at least in the near term, the affair hurt Benton's professional and political prospects in Missouri in much the same way that the killing of Charles Dickinson had temporarily damaged Jackson's career in Tennessee. Despite Clemson's mistake in neglecting to give the preparatory command to fire, Benton's behavior throughout the affair made him appear intent on killing young Lucas from the outset. Among his enemies, he would henceforth be known as "Bully" Benton wherever he went. For the moment, the already deep divisions in territorial politics were further embittered by the affair. But Benton did not leave Missouri, as he had quit Tennessee after the fight with Jackson. He eventually overcame the blow to his popularity resulting from the death of Lucas, but he never again challenged a man to a duel. From this point on, the legislative arena rather than the dueling ground would become his field of honor.[37]

In an "autobiographical sketch" written decades later for his political memoir *Thirty Years' View*, the author, speaking of himself in the third person, relates the following:

> a duel in St. Louis ended fatally, of which Colonel Benton has not been heard to speak except among intimate friends, and to tell of the pang which went through his heart when he saw the young man fall, and would have given the world to see restored to life. As proof of the manner in which he looks on all these scenes, and his desire to bury all remembrance of them forever, he had all the papers burnt which relates to them, that no future industry should bring to light what he wishes had never happened.[38]

Slavery in the Missouri Territory

The political culture that took shape in Missouri after the War of 1812 recognized white masters and black slaves as the only racial categories to hold a legitimate place in American society. This had not always been the case. Until quite recently, the settlements that the French had called *Pays des Illinois*, regardless of which bank of the Mississippi they occupied, had been representative of what a number of geographers and historians of the American West have dubbed "frontiers of inclusion." These were multiracial communities in which red, white, and black inhabitants lived together, worked together, and in some cases married and procreated without the strict regard to racial categories. Characteristic of the Spanish provinces of northern Mexico and French settlements of the Great

Lakes region and the Mississippi River valley, ethno-cultural relations were markedly different from those found in the British colonies that became the United States. Partly because they lacked the numerical superiority enjoyed by Anglo-Americans over the Indians, partly as a result of different religious and political imperatives, Spanish and French colonists tried to assimilate Native Americans rather than remove or annihilate them—processes that characterized "frontiers of exclusion." Similar differences were to be found in patterns of slaveholding in French and Spanish colonies in North America, as opposed to the English plantation colonies and the American South.[39]

Slavery had come to Missouri with the first Europeans. Initial attempts by the French to use Indians as slaves proved unsuccessful, but black slaves of African descent, transported up the Mississippi from New Orleans by Philippe Renault, were present in the lead mining camps of the western Illinois Country by 1723. It is likely that the Jesuits at Kaskaskia purchased blacks from lower Louisiana even earlier to serve as agricultural laborers at that mission settlement. By the time that St. Louis, Ste. Genevieve, and the other white settlements on the west bank came under Spanish rule in 1763, 198 black slaves lived among 399 white *habitants* in the region's farming villages, constituting about one-third of the total population.

The legal status of slaves in both Lower Louisiana and the Illinois Country was regulated by the *Code Noir* or Black Code of 1724. Adopted from rules pertaining to French plantations in the West Indies, the Louisiana Black Code contained 55 articles that required slaves to be properly housed, clothed, and fed, and forbade selling slave children away from their parents before the age of puberty. Masters might whip their slaves, but the slaves could not be imprisoned, mutilated, or put to death without due process of law. Slaves could not be worked before sunrise or after sundown, and the old and infirm among them were to be cared for. They were to be baptized and instructed in the Catholic faith, were allowed to marry with their masters' consent, and masters were forbidden from sexually exploiting slave women. The code also provided slaves with the right to take their masters to court at no cost if they believed their masters were abusing them in violation of other provisions.[40]

While it is difficult to imagine black slaves in French Louisiana bringing suit against their masters for mistreatment, in parts of the colony at least, the slave-holding regime was lax enough to compel Governor-General Vaudreuil to amend the *Code Noir* in 1751 in an attempt to keep

African-American slaves from engaging in forbidden activities such as drinking alcohol, racing horses, and visiting establishments of ill repute (run by free blacks). Concerned to strike a balance between humanity and severity in the discipline of slaves, Vaudreuil encouraged masters to act the part of "en bon père de famille"—a good father of the family. In light of such rhetoric, one should not succumb to the temptation to romanticize the paternal nature of slavery in French and Spanish Louisiana. Bondage, however benevolent in theory, retained its brutal aspect. Vaudreuil's decree provided that any black or Indian slave who "is insolent or forgets he is a slave and does not show appropriate submissiveness" was to be punished by 50 lashes and branding on the buttocks with the fleur-de-lis.[41]

Still, there were significant differences between slavery as it was practiced in Louisiana and slavery in the Anglo-American colonies. For one thing, while the Black Code defined slaves as chattels that could be bought and sold like other property, it also recognized them as human beings with certain legal rights. The French made no attempt, as did their contemporary English counterparts, to justify slavery on racial grounds. There was no need to. Slavery had been an aspect of human society since ancient times and required no rationalization. Slave deaths, or for that matter serious physical mistreatment of slaves, appear to have been the exception rather than the rule in Upper Louisiana. Critics often complained, in fact, that the region's slave owners were too lenient. In 1781 Lieutenant Governor Francisco Cruzat found it necessary to promulgate new ordinances in response to many of the same "abuses" that Vaudreuil had attempted to curb, "which are daily creeping in through the unruly conduct of the slaves at this post of St. Louis, owing to the criminal indulgence of some masters who are too little solicitous for their authority and for the public welfare."[42]

Edmund Flagg, a widely traveled journalist, visited the French villages of Illinois in the early 1800s and reported that he had never seen a "sleeker, fleshier, happier-looking set of mortals" than the blacks he found there. Flagg's observation may have been prompted because he had seen black slaves in the Anglo-American Southeast whose material conditions of life were poorer than those of the slaves in the mid-Mississippi Valley. "At the turn of the nineteenth century," writes Illinois Country historian Carl Ekberg, "it was accepted knowledge that slaves in Upper Louisiana were better treated than elsewhere in North America.... The fact that there was never a hint of slave rebellion in the Illinois Country, and that slaves there often carried firearms, suggests that French slaves in Upper Louisiana were living about as well as any slaves in the world during the eighteenth century."[43]

The comparatively easy relations between masters and slaves would be transformed by the transfer of Louisiana to American sovereignty. During the later years of Spanish rule American slaveholders had crossed the Mississippi to settle there, motivated in part by the ban on the introduction of slaves north of the Ohio River contained in the Northwest Ordinance of 1787. Spain, as previously noted, welcomed the Americans with low taxes and generous grants of land. When the United States took control of Upper Louisiana in 1803, over half of the population was comprised of Americans; slaves constituted almost 13 percent of the 10,340 inhabitants. Like Benton, the majority of the newcomers came from the Upper South—Virginia, Kentucky, Tennessee, and North Carolina.[44]

The American immigrants pushed into the territory's hills and backwoods beyond the settled bottomlands along the rivers to clear new areas for cultivation. Many of the immigrants were small freeholders who produced corn, wheat, rye, and oats, which flowed into St. Louis from the surrounding countryside. Southeastern Missouri and the Boon's Lick region along the Missouri River were coveted for their potential to grow cotton, tobacco, and hemp, all of which were crops whose production relied on slave labor. After the War of 1812 more and more plantation families from the Upper South arrived in the territory bringing their slaves with them. As a southerner and slaveholder himself, Benton welcomed this influx, the majority of whom tended to settle in the Boon's Lick.

It was apparent from the time the American government assumed control of the region that Upper Louisiana was proslavery. White Missourians, temporarily placed under the administrative jurisdiction of the Indiana territory, feared that the antislavery provisions of the Northwest Ordinance might be extended to Upper Louisiana. Among the remonstrances framed by a committee headed by Charles Gratiot in April 1804 was the demand to be able to continue the importation of slaves (which Missourians erroneously thought had been denied them) and the demand for the protection of slave owners' rights.[45]

Once in place, Upper Louisiana's territorial government responded by enacting an elaborate slave code which, one historian noted, "would have answered for a much larger slave society." The new code was very different in both tone and detail from the old Creole *Code Noir*. Based largely on the Virginia and Kentucky codes, it was considerably less protective of slave rights than the French and Spanish codes. Both slaves and free blacks were denied the right to testify in court against whites. Slaves could not leave their owners' plantation without permission or bear arms. Rioting, striking a white person, conspiring to rebel or foment insurrection, and "going at large and trading" were offenses for which severe penalties were prescribed. The new code lacked provisions concerning food and clothing for slaves, care of aged slaves, and safeguards against physical abuse. Under Spanish rule, slaves had been able to use free time on Sundays and holidays to work for wages that could be applied toward self-purchase and freedom. No free time was provided for in the new code, though emancipation was still possible. It remained lawful for any person, by his or her last will and testament, to set free his or her slave or slaves. But in Missouri, as elsewhere in the American South, slavery as a hereditary and lifelong condition was fixed by race. Slaves were placed on the level of cattle, horses, and other property; in all courts they were to "be held, taken, and adjudged to be personal estate."[46]

With such a legal environment, slaveholders could feel secure in bringing their human chattel into the Missouri territory. Baptist minister John Mason Peck was part of the great westward movement into Missouri after the war. He wrote that some families had come in the spring of 1815, "but in the winter, spring, summer, and autumn of 1816, they came like an avalanche. It seemed as though Kentucky and Tennessee were breaking up and moving to the 'Far West.'" Caravans of wagons passed over the prairies of Illinois, crossing the Mississippi at St. Louis, all bound to the Boon's Lick in central Missouri.[47]

This immense folk movement, one of several in American history to be dubbed "The Great Migration," transformed Missouri in the space of three or four years from a virtually unknown frontier outpost to a populous territory clamoring for statehood and the center of the first great national controversy over the slavery issue. For some members of the clergy, like Peck, the slavery question posed a particularly painful dilemma. Some of the territory's fastest-growing denominations, including the Baptists and Methodists, originally opposed slavery in principle. Gradually, however, members of these churches in slaveholding areas modified their stance in order to win more white converts. Peck conducted special services for blacks in St. Louis and St. Charles. He promoted education for blacks and accepted black children into his school. But when the slavery issue threatened statehood for Missouri, he denied that he had ever spoken out on slavery from his pulpit: "Whatever my private sentiments on the subject of slavery itself or the policy or the expediency of its limitation, I have too much regard for the cause of religion, the interests of the country, and my own public and private character, to preach on slavery or on any other subject of party politics." Such prudent silence on the slavery question would form the basis of sectional cooperation during the period of the Second Party System.[48]

The *St. Louis Enquirer*

The issue of slavery in Missouri was to breathe new life into the political aspirations of Thomas Hart Benton. Notwithstanding the opprobrium that had resulted from his killing Charles Lucas, Benton still desired a career in Missouri politics. He found a new medium to influence public opinion in August 1818 when Sergeant Hall, proprietor-editor of the St. Louis *Western Emigrant*, sold out. Hall was succeeded as owner and business manager by Isaac N. Henry, formerly of Nashville, and as editor by Benton. They changed the name of the paper to the *St. Louis Enquirer* and for the next few years provided a rival voice to Joseph Charless's *Missouri Gazette*. "Newspapers," declared Benton in typically exalted prose, "are the school of public instruction. They are in America what the Forum was in Greece and Rome, with the advantage of speaking to a *nation* instead of an *assembly*; and when conducted with talent and directed to objects of public utility, they are justly deemed the most powerful lever which can be applied to the human mind." Benton's terminology is revealing. He sees the role of the press as more democratic than the elitist assemblies of antiquity, possessing the ability to speak to the politically qualified "nation." Throughout his career, Benton would have his most important speeches printed and distributed in pursuit of similar goals. Yet, this begs the question both as to who was included in his definition of the nation and just what degree of influence the newspapers could be expected to apply. The role played by the *Enquirer* in the upcoming controversy over Missouri's admission to the Union was to clarify his views.[49]

During his career as editor, Benton continually addressed the issue of western development, which he viewed as vital to the prosperity of both Missouri and the nation. In late 1818 and early 1819, the *Enquirer* carried a series of editorials on this topic. Missouri was still a Federal territory with a population of less than 70,000 and large tracts of underdeveloped wilderness. To the west, the vague boundaries of the Louisiana Purchase marked the limits of the United States. Yet Benton demanded a still greater domain. "The magnificent valley of the Mississippi" was now American, and to many southerners like Benton this included Texas up to the edge of the Rio Grande watershed. "Woe to the statesman that undertakes to surrender one drop of its water, one inch of its soil." He also asserted American claims to the Pacific Northwest or the "Oregon country" against Great Britain.⁵⁰

Wanting to keep his name before the voters as a potential political leader once statehood was achieved, Benton wrote an editorial published in the *Enquirer* on June 16, 1819, entitled "Objects of Public Interest with the People of Missouri; the Accomplishment of which requires the aid of the National Government." In the article, Benton summed up everything his paper had been advocating in a 13-point program, and he emphasized the need for federal action to achieve those ends.

He called on Congress to act quickly to admit Missouri to the Union, urged Congress to expedite "the adjustment of the land titles derived from the late Spanish Government in Upper Louisiana," and demanded better "protection of the Missouri frontier" through more military posts and the "protection of Missouri fur traders" as well. The editor of the *Enquirer* also enthusiastically promoted a system of transportation improvements to facilitate western development. He called on the national government to build a national road to Washington City, a post road to New Orleans, post routes throughout the Missouri territory, and another between St. Louis and Louisville by way of Vincennes. He argued that the national government should establish St. Louis as an official port of entry with its own customs house, and build a canal between Lake Michigan and the Illinois River and a canal to unite the Mississippi with Lake Superior.⁵¹

Two points bear mentioning. At this stage of his career, as evidenced by more than half his agenda, Benton advocated federally sponsored internal improvements with all the enthusiasm of fervent nationalists such as Clay and Calhoun. Second, he revealed a shrewd ability to promote the interests he represented—the fur trade, lead mining, the land junto—while presenting his program in popular terms—western expansion and private enterprise—that had broad appeal to the electorate. In any event, the continued economic growth of Missouri depended on continued increase of the population. That most of the new arrivals in Missouri during the territorial period were from the five slave states of Virginia, Kentucky, North Carolina, South Carolina, and Tennessee had the effect of making public opinion in Missouri distinctly proslavery when the time came to enter the Union.⁵²

The territorial government was ill equipped to deal with the rapid growth of Missouri's population and economy after the War of 1812. The qualified voters could elect members of the territorial legislature and a nonvoting delegate to sit in the U.S. House of Representatives, but the president still appointed the governor of the territory and Missourians still lacked voting representation in Congress. Until statehood was accomplished, the "aid of the National Government" that Benton viewed as necessary to the economic development of Missouri and the West would be much more difficult to achieve. The territorial legislature took up the issue in November of 1818 and formally requested admission to the Union a month later. Territorial government, the petition asserted, denied the residents of Missouri their full rights as citizens of the United States. As territorial residents they were subject to congressional decisions in which they had no voice. With statehood, the people of Missouri would increase their sovereignty over internal affairs, limit congressional control over the state, and gain representation in the making of national policy. Economic interest was thus framed in terms of republican self-government. Speaker Henry Clay laid Missouri's memorial requesting statehood before the House of Representatives on December 18, 1818. The memorial stated that the population of the territory was "little short of one hundred thousand souls," outlined the proposed boundaries of the state, and expressed confidence that Congress would act "from the spirit of a generous and enlightened policy by granting the rights, privileges and immunities belonging to citizens of the United States that the people of Missouri aspired to."[53]

To move the process along more quickly, on February 13, 1819, John Scott, Missouri's territorial delegate, successfully moved that the House resolve itself into the Committee of the Whole to perfect enabling legislation for the people of Missouri and Alabama to form state governments. Almost immediately Representative James Tallmadge of New York proposed an amendment to the Missouri bill providing that "the further introduction of slavery or involuntary servitude be prohibited" and that "all children of slaves, born within the said state, after the admission thereof into the Union, shall be free, but may be held to service until the age of twenty-five years." Voting separately on the two clauses after lengthy debate, the House passed the first by a vote of 87–76 and the second 82–78. The division in each case was sectional, with southerners almost unanimous against both clauses.[54]

The Missouri bill, as amended, went on to the Senate, where the balance of representation between slave and free states was equal. There, the Tallmadge amendment was struck from the Missouri bill, with all senators from slaveholding states voting against both parts of the amendment, as did Senators Ninian Edwards and Jesse B. Thomas of Illinois (much of which maintained de facto slavery in violation of the

Northwest Ordinance of 1787). The bill, without the Tallmadge amendment, was passed and returned to the House, but that body twice refused to approve the Senate version, and Congress adjourned on March 3, 1819, without passing the enabling legislation.⁵⁵

Caught by surprise, most white Missourians were dismayed and angered by the turn of events in Washington. The *Enquirer* noted that territorial delegate John Scott only learned of Tallmadge's plans to introduce his antislavery proviso "at a late period, at second hand, through the medium of a foreigner, the Portuguese ambassador."⁵⁶ Debate has continued since that time as to whether the supporters of the restriction of slavery were motivated by humanitarian impulse, by purely political considerations, or by some combination of the two. Slavery had existed in Missouri since the earliest days of white settlement and a majority of white Missourians, born and raised in the South, retained southern ideas about slavery. Many feared that attempts to restrict slavery in Missouri would have a negative effect on future immigration from the older slave states. To the extent we can judge from speeches, resolutions, grand jury remonstrances, toasts, and newspaper editorials, Missourians preferred not to discuss slavery itself, but rather what they viewed as northern attempts to meddle in their affairs. The "antirestrictionists," as the overwhelming majority came to be called, insisted that Congress had no power under the Constitution to place any conditions on a new state, other than that it should have a republican form of government. Benton maintained early on that the proper role for Congress in the admission of new states was merely that of a master of ceremonies.⁵⁷

He was in natural agreement with the proslavery majority as a result of his background and status. Benton also saw an opportunity to revive his political fortunes by making the cause of antirestriction his own. On May 15 he addressed a large crowd in St. Louis, exhorting them to "make a fair and regular stand against the encroachment of Congress upon the Sovereignty of the States." Slavery, he argued, was not the issue in this controversy. Rather, it was a question of freedom versus coercion. Benton laid before the meeting six resolutions that were unanimously adopted by the assemblage. The first resolution declared "That the Congress of the United States have no right to control the provisions of a state constitution, except to preserve its republican character." The second stated that to prohibit slavery in Missouri would be "equally contrary to the rights of the states and the welfare of the slaves themselves."⁵⁸ The third resolution declared that Missouri's population so much exceeded that of other territories when admitted that the majority's action of the House of Representatives "was an outrage on the principles of the American Constitution and a direct infraction of the third article of the [Louisiana] treaty of cession." The fourth stated "That the right of the Missouri territory to be admitted into the union of the states, depends not upon the will of Congress, but upon the treaty of cession, and the principle of the federal constitution." The fifth declared "that the people of this territory have a right to meet in conventions by their own authority and to form a constitution and a state government whenever they shall deem it expedient to do so, and that a second determination on the part of Congress to refuse them admittance upon an equal footing with the original states, will make it expedient to exercise that right." The sixth resolution continued on this point, stating "that a constitution so formed cannot be disapproved by Congress for any other cause than for anti-republican features; and if disapproved upon any other pretext, it will be equivalent to an attempt to exclude the territory of Missouri from the federation of the states."[59]

By petitions, memorials, editorials, grand jury remonstrances, and resolutions such as those adopted by the mass meeting in St. Louis, Missourians denounced Congress for delaying statehood and attempting to dictate the status of slavery. At a Fourth of July celebration in Marthasville, toasts were drunk in honor of John Scott, Henry Clay, and other congressmen "who supported the Constitution of the United States and their treaty with France, in the discussion of the Missouri State Bill." Another toast derided "Messrs. Tallmadge and [John] Taylor—Politically Insane. May the next Congress appoint them a dark room, a strait waistcoat, and a thin gruel diet." A third saluted "The Territory of Missouri—May she be admitted to the union on an equal footing with the original states, or not be received in any other way."[60]

Throughout the spring of 1819 the *Enquirer* blasted the "disorganizers or emissaries of [Rufus] King and [Dewitt] Clinton," the restrictionist leaders in New York, or "the busy spirits of anarchy." In addition Benton's paper printed several letters charging Joseph Charless of the *Gazette* and John B.C. Lucas with restrictionism. Though the charges were greatly exaggerated and genuine restrictionists were hard to find within Missouri, the issue was an effective one for Benton, providing a means for him to identify himself not just with particular interests, but with the sectional patriotism of Missourians in general. Regarding the slavery restriction clause, the *Gazette* objected to congressional interference in terms as strong as Benton's *Enquirer*. Nonetheless, the bitter rivalry between the two editors, predating the Benton-Lucas duel continued over these new grounds. At one point Isaac Henry, the co-proprietor of the St. Louis *Enquirer* physically assaulted Charless; neither was seriously hurt, though the incident enhanced Missouri's already violent reputation among easterners.[61]

Charless, whose motto was "Truth without Fear," was determined to give as good as he got. He accused Benton and his friends of composing a lawyers' "junto"—a depraved and debauched group of bachelors who advocated freehold suffrage and *viva voce* voting. There was some substance to these curious charges. Charless had coined the term "little junto" to describe the wealthy Creoles and their Anglo-American cronies who had dominated territorial politics since the Louisiana Purchase. That he was once more slinging that imprecise term with all of its conspiratorial implications is no surprise. It also seems likely that Benton and his copartisans indeed favored both a freehold qualification for voting (albeit with the assumption of widespread property ownership in the new West) and the traditional spoken declaration of one's vote that allowed for maximum influence to be exercised by the wealthy and powerful men with whom he allied himself. Charless, the reformer, supported both universal suffrage for white males and the secret ballot even at this early date.[62]

What, however, of the "bachelor" charge and its association with debauchery and depravity? A clue to the meaning of these words is offered in a footnote in William Chambers's 1956 biography, *Old Bullion Benton*. Around the end of 1814 "according to one authority," Benton acquired "Mary," a quadroon girl, as his mistress. Chambers dismissed the tale as improbable and charged that it was incorporated by nineteenth-century Memphis historian James D. Davis as "second or third hand information." Davis had asserted that Benton picked up Mary while serving in New Orleans under Jackson and kept her "presumably in Tennessee" for two or three years. "The fact that Benton was not at New Orleans under Jackson, but in Washington, and the fact that he moved to St. Louis in the late summer or fall of 1815, makes it hard to understand how he acquired the girl, or how he could have kept her in Tennessee for two or three years." Chambers is being disingenuous on two counts. His biography is silent as to Benton's activities and whereabouts from the time of his discharge from the army in June 1815 until his arrival in St. Louis, which Chambers himself places "on a Sunday evening in the early fall of 1815." There is indeed the possibility that Benton passed through New Orleans on his way from the East to Missouri and might have met Mary under those circumstances rather than while serving with Jackson.

Further, there is no reason to assume that Benton and Mary maintained their relationship in Tennessee for the "two or three years" after the war ended. They could just as easily have gone upriver to St. Louis.[63]

Bertram Wyatt-Brown found the tale sufficiently credible to use it as an example of the "acceptable variety" of miscegenation that was widely practiced in the Old South. He relates that Mary was beautiful and well educated as well as a native of Louisiana, and that Benton was so careful in concealing the relationship "that even his most recent biographers have not mentioned the liaison." Several years later, Benton married Elizabeth McDowell, daughter of a prosperous and well-connected Virginia planter, and a suitable match for a newly elected United States Senator. At that time Benton "relinquished Mary to fellow militia officer Major Marcus Winchester." Winchester, we are told, made the unforgivable mistake of marrying the beautiful mulatto, leading to social ostracism and the end of a promising political career in Memphis.[64]

Thomas Hart Benton was too socially and politically attuned to the mores of the Upper South to have made the same mistake as Winchester. Nonetheless, keeping a mulatto mistress would not have been considered unacceptable among the majority of white males in frontier St. Louis. Miscegenation between a white male and black female posed few ethical problems for the antebellum southern community, as long as the appropriate etiquette governing such liaisons was observed. Relationships, even if long-standing, had to appear casual in nature. The concubine should appear sexually attractive by white male standards—the lighter the skin, the more comely the shape, the better. The interracial pairing should also not be part of a general pattern of dissoluteness, such as alcoholism and dereliction of civic duty on the part of the white male. If, in fact, Benton and Mary were lovers, they followed these rules conscientiously. The penalties for failure to do so are apparent in the career of Marcus Winchester. Likewise, finding another mate for his erstwhile lover when the time came to make his own personal transition from racial inclusiveness to respectable exclusivity was equally within the acceptable boundaries of behavior for a southern gentleman. Was Joseph Charless, with his veiled references to debauchery among bachelor lawyers, playing the role of a latter-day James Callender to Benton's Jefferson? The evidence is inconclusive, but the idea is far from implausible. If there is any truth to the charges, then Benton's repeated praise for Elizabeth McDowell's "exalted moral tone" contrasts sharply with his silence concerning the mixed-race "Mary," a woman who could be the object of a gentleman's sexual desire as well as his social scorn.[65]

While Missourians toasted their liberties and resolved to defend them, antislavery forces in the Northeast were organizing around the controversies generated by Missouri's quest for admission. By the summer of 1819 an "Anti-Missouri Crusade," originating in New Jersey, was launched by reformers opposed to Missouri's admission as a slave state. Opposition was fueled by northeastern resentment of southern voting strength in Congress and the Electoral College, based on the provision for counting three-fifths of the slaves in southern states for representation in the House. This compromise, necessary to secure the support of southern states for the Constitution of 1787, had never been popular in the Northeast. Anger over the three-fifths clause burst into the open when Jefferson won the presidential election of 1800 with an electoral majority of nine votes over John Adams, the result—alleged northern Federalists—of "slave representation."[66]

During the first half-century or more of its history, the federal government of the United States was disproportionately controlled by southerners. In the 62 years between George Washington's election and the Compromise of 1850, for example, slaveholders controlled the presidency for 50 years, the Speaker's chair for 41 years, and the chairmanship of House Ways and Means (the most important committee) for 42 years. Further, the only men to be reelected president—Washington, Jefferson, Madison, Monroe, and Jackson—were all slaveholders. More important than these impressive realities were the perceptions of northerners who felt increasingly marginalized in national politics by the time Missouri petitioned to enter the Union. Two decades of the federal executive being monopolized by Virginians had only heightened the frustration of northern leaders. At this level, at least, the Missouri controversy involved a struggle for sectional supremacy in the national government that had little to do with slavery as a moral issue.[67]

In the Sixteenth Congress, the House once more passed a restrictive bill excluding slavery or involuntary servitude as a condition for Missouri statehood. A new development, however, promised a way out of the deadlock. The Senate, seeking to expedite the admission of Missouri, tied her statehood to Maine's request for entrance into the Union. Massachusetts had agreed to a division that allowed the Maine area to seek admission as a state, if Congress approved by March 4, 1820. The burden was now on congressmen from the northern states to compromise on Missouri if Maine was to be admitted before the deadline. When the Senate considered a bill already passed by the House admitting Maine without any restrictions, two amendments were added before the measure was passed. One enabled Missouri to draft a constitution without any restriction of slavery; the second, offered by Jesse B. Thomas of Illinois, prohibited slavery elsewhere in the Louisiana Purchase north of 36°30' north latitude. After lengthy negotiations, a joint conference committee recommended that the House accept the proposed amendments. These recommendations were followed and President Monroe signed the Missouri Enabling Act on March 6, 1820, formally authorizing the people of Missouri to frame a state constitution and organize a government, the only condition being that the constitution be republican in nature and that it contain no provisions contrary to the Constitution of the United States. Significantly, there was no vote on the whole compromise package in the House of Representatives, where antislavery forces had held up the admission of Missouri for over a year. In a maneuver presaging later sectional confrontations, Speaker Henry Clay brought the constituent parts of the compromise before the House, enabling a majority of southern members to vote in favor of admitting Missouri without restrictions on slavery, while a majority of northern members voted to admit Maine. As for the Thomas Proviso, outlawing slavery in the northern territorial latitudes, the crucial margin of support came from the states of the Lower South, including South Carolina.[68]

The willingness of the Deep South to compromise in 1820 stands in marked contrast to its aggressive leadership of the states' rights cause a few decades later. "It seems strange," wrote Glover Moore in his history of the controversy, "that Thomas Ritchie [of the Richmond *Enquirer*] and Thomas Hart Benton should ever have heaped fuel on the fires of sectionalism, while Calhoun sought to quench them.... Because of their announced intention of refusing to submit to congressional restriction, Missourians were accused of being advocates of disunion. Actually they were primarily concerned with fighting their way into the Union rather than out of it." As the primary organ of these early "fire-eaters," Benton's *Enquirer* "was intensely pro-American" and devoted as much ink to nationalist outlines for developing the West as to defying the power of Congress to restrict slavery, which it regarded as unconstitutional.[69]

The *Enquirer* was able to announce the "happy intelligence," carried from Washington by Thomas Hempstead on March 25, of the final passage of the Missouri State Bill without restrictions. The *Gazette* related that "The town was generally and splendidly illuminated; several transparencies were displayed. Among others a very handsome one displaying the American Eagle surmounting the Irish Harp. We were diverted by another, representing a slave in great spirits, rejoicing at the permission granted by Congress to bring slaves into so fine a country as Missouri." The enabling legislation authorized all free, white, male citizens of the United States who had reached the age of twenty-one and who had resided in the Missouri Territory for three months prior to the election to vote for members of the constitutional convention. Campaigns for the election of delegates from each of the fifteen existing counties in the territory quickly got under way. About the only questions to generate any controversy in the election of delegates were whether suffrage should be limited to freeholders, whether voting should be conducted by voice or ballot, and whether the further introduction of slaves into Missouri should be prohibited. Some Missourians who had opposed congressional interference with slavery now urged that the state itself stop the importation of slaves after a "reasonable time" was allowed for slave owners east of the Mississippi to enter Missouri with their property. Supporters of the proposal such as Charless and Lucas disavowed advocating immediate emancipation, espousing rather a peaceful and constitutional opposition to slavery as a permanent institution.[70]

This "gradualist" approach to ending the institution of slavery was safely within the Jeffersonian tradition—Benton himself would eventually come around to something like the same philosophy where other western territories were concerned. In 1820, however, the *Enquirer* attacked such proposals as abolitionist and editorialized as if the restrictionists were on the verge of dominating the state. Nothing could have been further from the truth. A majority of the new arrivals in Missouri since the War of 1812 were from slave states and the number of slaves had tripled during the last decade of the territorial period, while the total capital investment in slave property had probably quadrupled. Avowed restrictionists ran for seats only in St. Louis, Jefferson, Lincoln, Washington, and Cape Girardeau counties and were soundly defeated in all. The restrictionists were hopelessly in the minority, being outnumbered at least seven to one, perhaps more. Nonetheless, slaveholders could hardly be expected to agree with critics of the institution, even if men like Charless denied any intention of interfering with slaves already in the state. While slaves comprised only 15 percent of the territory's population in 1820 and fewer than 10 percent of white families owned slaves, a majority of non-slaveholders opposed restrictions as well. One reason for this overwhelming solidarity among white Missourians was the desire of non-slaveholding whites to eventually own blacks themselves. The major reason for the huge antirestrictionist sentiment, however, was that the leaders to whom the majority deferred—the prosperous merchants, traders, professionals, and politicians—were slave owners without exception. There was also concern among citizens with no personal stake in slaveholding that restriction would shut out potential settlers who owned slaves. Non-slaveholders identified their own economic interests with those of the slave owners, and the attempt by congressional opponents of slavery to delay Missouri's admission to the Union was met with almost universal hostility among the territory's white majority.[71]

The convention elected to frame Missouri's first constitution was composed of 41 members, mostly wealthy and conservative men of financial means, a majority of whom were businessmen and lawyers. Benton was an early candidate for delegate but withdrew in favor of a consolidated anti-restriction ticket for St. Louis County. Whether wary of defeat at the hands of his numerous political enemies, or concluding that he could exert more influence outside the convention, he chose to bide his time and focus his efforts instead on the *Enquirer's* editorial war against the *Gazette*. Nonetheless, the influence of the St. Louis mercantile elite was apparent in the convention's work. "Democracy"—the widespread participation of white male voters, regardless of socioeconomic status—had not yet arrived in Missouri and played little part in the election of delegates. As a result, the constitution itself provided for a governmental structure that was essentially conservative in nature.

The document provided for the usual three branches of government with a bicameral legislature. Senate members were elected to four-year terms; House members served two years, with each county being guaranteed at least one representative. The governor and lieutenant governor were elected for four-year terms—this at a time when most states still held elections for executive office every one or two years. The secretary of state, attorney general, and auditor were all appointed by the governor with the consent of the Senate and served for four years. The General Assembly was empowered to elect a state treasurer every two years. The judicial branch was to consist of a supreme court, a series of circuit courts, and a chancery court with jurisdiction in cases of equity and probate affairs. The General Assembly could establish additional lower courts as it deemed necessary. The question of judicial appointment was one of the few matters of controversy at the convention and revealed divisions that would persist into early state politics. The majority, led by Edward Bates and David Barton, wanted a strong, independent judiciary and pushed through their proposal that judges be appointed by the governor with the consent of the Senate to serve during "good behavior" (that is, for life). Alexander McNair led the minority opposition who sought to make judges subject to popular election. The court question carried over into the first state elections, with public opinion coming down on the side of McNair.

The constitution, adopted on July 19, 1820, continued the national trend—especially in the West—toward greater liberalization of the franchise by granting the right to vote to every free, white male citizen of the United States who was at least twenty-one years old and who had resided in the state one year before the election. The written ballot was provided for and the legislature was authorized to charter a single bank. The government was restricted in the areas of personal and property rights by a state bill of rights. No law could be passed for the emancipation of slaves without the consent of their masters, or without full compensation. Nor could the General Assembly prevent immigrants from bringing their slaves with them as long as slavery was legal in Missouri. In addition, the constitution required the first General Assembly to pass a law preventing free blacks and mulattoes from entering or settling in the state. This measure was to prove problematic in the final stages of Missouri's admission to the Union.

Though democratic by standards that still prevailed in many of the eastern states, in its restriction of elective officials to members of the General Assembly, the governor, and the lieutenant governor, the first Missouri Constitution was not the populist instrument that many voters might have desired. Ratification of the constitution itself, as well as of proposed amendments, was to take place not by referendum to the voters but by two-thirds vote in each house of the legislature for both proposal and ratification.[72]

The first elections held under the constitution in August 1820 resulted in a reaction against its undemocratic features. The political cleavages along "junto" and "anti-junto" lines that had divided Missourians for a decade-and-a-half remained in place, although the lines were not always clear. Neither group had what would later be recognized as a party organization; alliances were continuously in a state of flux. Attorney David Barton was probably closer to the anti-junto faction but remained popular with both groups. Both represented the upper-class, conservative citizens of the state; neither made any attempt to appeal to the interests of the majority of Missourians. Charless was certain that the members of the little junto had already determined the allocation of offices in the new government: William Clark was to retain the governorship; Benton and John Rice Jones were to be the two U.S. senators. Superior judges would be David Barton, William Harper, and John B. Cook.[73]

The editor of the *Gazette* was giving the junto credit for more power and discipline than it really had. As the elections approached, there was growing evidence of opposition in the rural areas to the domination of the "St. Louis Clique." In the contest for governor, Alexander McNair, attacking the undemocratic features of the Constitution, was elected by a substantial majority over Clark. The territorial governor had been absent because of the illness of his wife in Virginia and made no effort to campaign on his own behalf. In a letter to Benton's *Enquirer* less than a month before the election, Clark demonstrated his lack of awareness of the changing political mood in Missouri by citing his friendship with the unpopular junto as a qualification for office. "My long residence," he wrote, "has given me a personal acquaintance which time has ripened into friendship, with most of the old inhabitants and early settlers; and to them I refer for answer to any inquiries which may concern my individual and private character."[74]

In attempting to state his qualifications for governor, Clark emphasized his efforts during the War of 1812 to keep the territory safe; he made no reference to the controversies of the day. In the meantime, the Missouri *Gazette* carried on a persistent campaign of attacks on Clark. It appealed to the landowning aspirations of white settlers, censuring the governor for his friendliness to Indians at the expense of his own race, for his frequent absences from the territory, and for his arbitrary manner of conducting the territorial delegate elections of 1816 and 1817. Unable to identify with the interests that were creating a new order in Missouri, Clark was by 1820 an anachronism—a colonial administrator with nothing but disdain for democratic society.[75]

William H. Ashley, a wealthy landowner and gunpowder manufacturer, became Missouri's first lieutenant governor, defeating Nathaniel Cook, a southeast Missouri political leader and favorite of the junto who had served as a member of the constitutional convention. Of the 41 framers of the Constitution, only 7 were elected to the 51-seat General Assembly. Territorial delegate John Scott managed to escape the ire of the electorate and was returned to Congress as Missouri's first voting representative.[76]

"All of our calculations have failed," wrote Benton to Scott at the end of August. Clark had been defeated by "the reports that poured in from every quarter that he had no chance.... Many of his friends gave way under it." Benton's own election to the Senate would be more difficult than he had anticipated; he would have to make the best of a "doubtful" situation in the Assembly. He inventoried the legislators elected from the various counties: St. Charles, Jefferson, Montgomery, St. Louis, and the Boon's Lick, concluding with David Barton who has "great zeal for me."[77]

Shocked by their losses in the August elections, Benton and other members of the St. Louis junto were now spurred into a flurry of activity. They had been caught flatfooted in the popular election, apparently assuming that the General Assembly, like the constitutional convention, would be composed of men representing the old territorial elite and committed to policies they favored. The popular elections cast these assumptions to the wind. Benton and Scott now struggled to keep their friends unified while seeking out allies in the General Assembly. The legislature met in joint session on October 2, 1820, to elect Missouri's first two U.S. senators. On the first ballot, with each legislator voting for two candidates, David Barton received 34 votes, Thomas Hart Benton 27, John B.C. Lucas 16, Henry Elliot 11, Nathaniel Cook 8, and John Rice Jones 8. Barton and Benton were each duly elected with the required majority.

Barton's election had been virtually assured. He had the support of the St. Louis junto without being too strongly identified with them, yet he retained popularity in the rural areas of the state as well. Benton's election was a different matter. He had the support of the fur traders and Spanish land claimants who comprised the junto, but in the shifting political landscape of 1820, that alone would not have been sufficient to secure his election. Even among the legislators from St. Louis, Benton only got three of seven votes. According to undocumented historical lore, two men—Daniel Ralls, who was carried into the Assembly to cast his vote from his deathbed, and Marie P. Leduc, who hated Benton but was persuaded by his fellow Creoles to vote for him instead of Lucas—finally decided the election.[78]

As it was, Benton won not because of his identification with the little junto, but because of his editorial advocacy for a program of western development and his opposition to antislavery and restriction. A successful candidate needed a statewide reputation to win the support of a majority in the legislature, and there was no one else of that stature to oppose Benton. Cook, Elliot, and Jones were little known throughout the state. Judge Lucas had made powerful political enemies and had failed to cultivate new allies. Benton's political program for Missouri, publicized in the *Enquirer*, had won him a statewide reputation. Further, he was not directly associated with the unpopular features of the 1820 constitution as he had not been a member of the constitutional convention. His close relationship to the special interests of the St. Louis junto was probably not well known throughout the state, while measures beneficial to those interests had been stated in his editorials in such a way as to possess broad popular appeal. The support of Barton, at some risk to his own political prospects, was likewise crucial in securing the votes necessary to elevate his colleague to the Senate. Missouri historian Floyd Shoemaker asserted that Benton "could never have won victory in 1820 without the unselfish support of his friend." Shoemaker pointed out that the popular condemnation of Benton's "brutal murder" of the talented son of Judge Lucas had not subsided, and he was frequently referred to as "the man of blood, the assassin." For Barton to have thus jeopardized his position for Benton and for Benton to have "so perfidiously betrayed" Barton later on was, according to Shoemaker, "one of the tragedies in the political history of the State."[79]

This account may be overly dramatic, but the narrow margin of his election must surely have given Benton pause. As his first term progressed, the senator and the interests he represented would have to accommodate themselves to calls for greater democracy in the political process. The possibilities and limits of this movement would define Benton's first term in the Senate and would lead to his eventual break with former political allies like Barton.

A Second Missouri Compromise

Senators-elect Benton and Barton journeyed to Washington by way of Kentucky and Virginia. Along the way they observed the growing distress resulting from the previous year's financial panic. They stopped in Lexington to visit Henry Clay. At this juncture, both Missourians were substantially in agreement with the Speaker on questions of tariffs and internal improvements to promote western development, though Benton was already developing the distaste for banks and paper money that would characterize his Senate career. Clay loaned his wife's cousin one $150 to get established in Washington. In 1820 the two slaveholding nationalists from the Upper South still considered each other both personal and political intimates.[80]

Benton had not been to the capital since the end of the war over five years earlier, but he made another detour to pursue an unfinished errand from his previous visit. On the way to his newly won seat in the United States Senate, Benton stopped at Cherry Grove to see Elizabeth McDowell once again. He again proposed to her, and this time she accepted. They were married the following March, and shortly thereafter moved into the home Thomas had bought for his mother some years earlier in

St. Louis. Whatever questions remain unresolved concerning Benton's private life prior to 1820, his family life from then on was praised even by his political enemies as a model of warmth and marital fidelity.[81]

Benton proceeded in the meantime to Washington, where he arrived in mid-November. The city was not greatly changed in the past five years. Livestock still freely roamed the muddy streets, and brickyards were everywhere to be found producing material for the unfinished Capitol building. During the session Benton stayed at Brown's hotel on Pennsylvania Avenue. Other names on the register that year included David Barton and John Scott from Missouri; John Williams, who had commanded the Thirty-ninth Regiment, of which Thomas Hart Benton had been lieutenant colonel, and who was now a senator from Tennessee; and Representative John Floyd of Virginia, Elizabeth McDowell's uncle.[82]

Congress convened on December 13, but Benton and Barton were temporarily denied full membership. The admission of Missouri had hit another snag, this time over the clause in the state's constitution that required the General Assembly to pass legislation barring free blacks and mulattoes from settling in Missouri. Opposition was once again centered in the House, where northerners argued that the right to enter and settle in any state was guaranteed by the provision of the national Constitution that "the Citizens of each State shall be entitled to all Privileges and Immunities of Citizens of the Several States." Since blacks were granted citizenship rights in several northern states, opponents argued that Missouri's constitution was in conflict with the federal Constitution and therefore unacceptable.

Dedicated opponents of Missouri's admission as a slave state had yet to accept the original compromise as final. Less than a month after its passage, antislavery members of the Pennsylvania legislature introduced a resolution condemning the Missouri Compromise and asking the state's congressional delegation to make the gradual abolition of slavery in Missouri a prerequisite for acceptance of that state's constitution. Similar resolutions were introduced in Indiana, New York, and Vermont. Antislavery newspapers and spokesmen continued to voice opposition to the admission of Missouri as a slave state. In February 1821 a member of the House of Representatives introduced a resolution requiring Missouri to provide for the gradual abolition of slavery before being admitted. A substantial majority of northern representatives voted to support this measure, which was ultimately unsuccessful.[83]

As a new deadlock over the Missouri issue seemed immanent, David Barton wrote home to the *St. Louis Enquirer* on December 3rd, charging that New York was leading the restrictionists and that most of the northern and northwestern Congress members "chime in," as well as members of President Monroe's cabinet who "aid and abet the enemies of our rights." Playing on the racial fears of white Missourians that were inseparable from their notions of republican government, Barton warned, "We should (not) be surprised after four years to see our next President riding into the City of Washington, not on a white horse, or on an ass's colt, but on a free negro or mulatto.... But if we should be rejected, I hope Missouri has spirit and energy enough to adhere to her constitution in respect to the disputed point, and if it must go down, to go down with it."[84]

Benton, observing the debates, sent an article off to the *Enquirer*. The question, he argued, was no longer one of admission, but of exclusion. Missouri must stand firm. "What shall Missouri do, if rejected?" he asked. "Fall back into the territorial grade? We hope not. Set up for herself? We hope not. The former would be to succumb to the Catalines of the north; the latter would be to promote their views." Benton was once again associating disunion and disloyalty with the northerners who would deny the full political rights for proslavery Missourians that statehood implied. To "promote their views" and "set up for herself" harkened back to the secessionism of the Essex Junto and the Hartford convention. Support for republican government meant acceptance of the constitution that a majority of qualified Missourians had voted for.[85]

Most Missourians were pleased that statehood was at last accomplished, if chagrined at the conditions under which it was imposed. Without debate the General Assembly passed the required act on June 26, 1821, but so phrased the preamble as to make clear the state's defiance of congressional power. It declared that Missouri had already assented to abide by all provisions of the national Constitution and that the General Assembly had no power to change the state's constitution other than by the procedure prescribed therein; but, as Congress desired the legislature to declare its assent to the stipulated conditions, it would do so, for "such declaration will neither restrain, or enlarge, limit or extend the operations of the Constitution of the United States, or of this state, but the said constitutions will remain in all respects as if the said resolution had never passed, and the desired declaration never made."[87]

On August 10, 1821, President Monroe proclaimed the admission of Missouri into the Union as the twenty-fourth state. The transition from inclusive colonial frontier to an American frontier of exclusion had been accomplished. The General Assembly would later violate the second Missouri Compromise by enacting laws in 1825 and 1847 that excluded free blacks and mulattoes from entering the state. The subsequent legislation sparked little controversy, however, as it was neither challenged by the national government nor rigorously enforced within the state.[88]

By the time Benton took his seat in the U.S. Senate, Missouri's transformation from colonial "frontier of inclusion" to an Anglo-American frontier of racial "exclusion"—a border state at the confluence of the nation's North and South as well as its East and West—was largely accomplished. Tens of thousands of new settlers, some bringing their human property to the newly admitted state, would further accelerate Missouri's process of "racial modernization" in the coming decade. Along with statehood, the door had also been flung open to greater democratic participation for white males. The "Era of the Common Man" was at hand for the growing American republic. Over the next half-dozen years, Benton would continually shift his political posture to accommodate himself to the changing political landscape. In the course of doing so, he manifested some of the less admirable characteristics of the new order's beliefs about Indians and blacks, even as he grew into the role of tribune for the common white man.

3 / The Triumph of Master Race Democracy: The Racialization of American Politics

Benton's career in the Senate during the 1820s and 1830s demonstrates the centrality of race in the movement toward greater political and economic equality for white men. Although he was initially identified with St. Louis's elite land-owning and fur-trading "junto," by 1825 Benton sensed the changing political winds, and transformed himself into the foremost spokesman for the Jacksonian party in Missouri. He did not blanch to utilize the rhetoric of white racial supremacy to cement his following either in his home state or in the Senate, where he shortly emerged as a leader of the opposition to President John Quincy Adams. Benton's references to African racial inferiority did not at this time present any conflict of principles for the bellicose frontier colonel who continued to trumpet American westward expansion and who was a leading advocate for the removal of another racially "inferior" group—the Indian tribes of the Old Southwest—as well. By 1830 Benton was a staunch advocate for the ethnic cleansing of Native Americans from the rich cotton-growing lands of Alabama and Mississippi. Indian removal, in turn, would make possible the large-scale practice of plantation slavery in those territories that would become so problematic for the nation by mid-century. During the 1820s and 1830s, however, most Americans considered the slavery question settled. Those decades witnessed a broad consensus on the part of white men in favor of the racial exclusion that accompanied the promise of greater equality for themselves.

Agreement over what direction white supremacy should take in shaping the nation's future was, however, to be short-lived. By 1832 the rift between Jackson and the followers of John C. Calhoun over tariffs and the right of states to nullify federal law would present a dilemma for Benton, which the Missourian characteristically sought to straddle. Not until the late 1830s did he begin to view the slavery issue and the demands of his fellow slaveholders from the Deep South as a threat to both the liberty of white citizens and to the unity of the nation. Benton's early alliance with John Randolph and other proponents of extreme states' rights, while persisting into the 1830s, would be supplanted over time by an ever closer relationship with Martin Van Buren and the northern pro-Union—and eventually free soil—wing of the Democratic Party.

The Old Republicans

In December 1821 Benton was sworn into the U.S. Senate as a full voting member. As a freshman senator, Benton was eager to learn the fine points of the upper house from senior members. He began taking his meals at Dawson's Number Two, one of the celebrated Capitol Hill "messes" and the favorite of those members from the southern states popularly known as Old Republicans or "Tertium Quids." To some extent these agrarian ideologues, who believed themselves the true keepers of the Jeffersonian flame, were no more than vestiges of a quickly passing era when Tidewater planters had dominated national politics. By 1821 they comprised an odd assortment of strict constructionists and states' rights aristocrats seemingly out of step with the current enthusiasm for a vigorous national government. Benton nonetheless viewed them as both valuable political allies and sources for the parliamentary knowledge he would need to succeed in the Senate. He also shared elements of their political philosophy, much of which would later become identified with the tenets of Jacksonian democracy.

Nathaniel Macon, the senior senator from North Carolina, had known Samuel Benton in the colonial days and served with Jesse Benton in the State Assembly in 1781. First elected to Congress in 1791, Macon had served as Speaker of the House under Jefferson. The decline of tobacco markets transformed Macon into the champion of the small farmers celebrated in Jeffersonian lore and made him a fierce opponent of protection at the time when a majority of postwar congressmen were touting higher tariffs as the answer to British dumping on American markets. Macon wore homespun clothes, lived in a two-room house on his Buck Spring plantation, and worked in the fields beside his slaves. His land—"poor and stony" he asserted—would "not raise much for sale, and buy less," but what it did produce "is honestly made, enough to have full bellies and warm clothes for any time of year."[1]

Macon's distrust of paper money and credit was very much in harmony with Benton's own costly experiences. The Missourian had witnessed two St. Louis banks with which he was associated collapse in as many years, leaving him deeply in debt. Macon characterized banks as "gaming shops" and argued that "every kind of negotiable paper adds to the evil." Credit allowed unscrupulous "projectors"—entrepreneurs—"to live off the labor of others." He recoiled from the ambitious schemes of the economic nationalists in his party and regarded Secretary of War Calhoun's "fashionable and favorite expression to conquer Space" (through internal improvements) with contempt. He advised a younger colleague against being "led astray" by "love of improvements or a thirst for glory ... grand notions or magnificent opinions.... You belong to a meek state and just people, who want nothing but to enjoy the fruits of their labor honestly and lay out their profits in their own way." While Benton shared the Old Republican's views on banking by the early 1820s, time would reveal him unwilling to eschew either internal improvements or glory.[2]

The Missourian shared an even closer relationship with John Randolph of Roanoke, whom Benton, in the guise of "Sir John Oldcastle," had once characterized as the leader of a group of "factious radicals," and who likewise opposed the Jeffersonian drift toward the apostasy of activist government. Fierce in his attacks on political opponents, Randolph could be exuberant, witty, and morose by turns. He was plagued throughout his life by ill health. A youthful illness had left him emasculated, with a shrill voice that enhanced his sarcasm—fearsome to those who were its targets. Benton later speculated that physical suffering must have had its effect on Randolph's temper and on his mind. The eccentric Randolph's sanity was questioned more than once. Benton, however, asserted that, while his friend experienced "temporary aberrations of mind," during which "he would do and say strange things," Randolph possessed "always in his own way—not only method but genius in his fantasies.... The most brilliant talk that I ever heard from him came forth on such occasions." Randolph and Benton stayed at the same lodgings and, both chronic insomniacs, would often talk late into the night about politics and the great issues of the day.[3]

Benton became something of an understudy to Randolph in the Senate chamber as well as a close personal friend, though historians have sometimes overstated the degree of the younger senator's political identification with the Virginian. One of Randolph's anachronisms was his habit of inveighing against the rule of "King Numbers." While he opposed the growing power of banks, commercial interests, and an activist federal government, Randolph declared that "I have never flattered the people, and so help me God I never will." Benton, on the other hand, having been chosen for the Senate by only the narrowest of margins, was just beginning to appreciate the white male majoritarianism that characterized western states like Missouri.[4]

Benton and the Special Interests

During his first session, however, Benton was still very much legislative point man for the interests in Missouri that had supported his election to the Senate. He had certain political debts to repay and his record during the 1822 and 1823 term reflects his attempts to do so. Three major areas demanded his attention—the Spanish land titles, the fur trade, and the lead mines.

In March 1822 Benton proposed a bill to authorize the Federal District Court in Missouri to dispose of land claims, and to settle them on the basis of Spanish or French legal procedures rather than English or American. Reviewing Spanish colonial decrees, Benton argued that the land grants in the former Louisiana territory had been issued for services to the crown and for the goal of populating the region rather than for revenue. Under this policy, the Spanish government had given refugees from the French and Irish revolutions great tracts to which the titles were incomplete until confirmed by the Spanish governor in New Orleans. As we have seen, the United States government confirmed only those grants that had been surveyed prior to the transfer of Louisiana to American control; the majority had not yet been surveyed. Such claims had been registered in 1805 and withheld from sale pending the decision of Congress as to their disposition. Having represented the interests of the claimants in the courtroom and upon the dueling field, Benton now argued before the U.S. Senate that further withholding of the Spanish claims was in violation of treaties and international law. All holders of incomplete Spanish and French titles should therefore be authorized to institute proceedings for validation in the U.S. District Court in St. Louis. Though Benton's characteristically exhaustive preparation for the speech that accompanied his bill secured passage in the Senate, it was tabled in the House. He was required to reintroduce it in the next legislative session and again in the one after that. By January 1824 Benton could write to Bernard Pratte, a St. Louis claim-holder, and assure him not only of his willingness "to oblige . . . my individual friends" but also that appropriate legislation was progressing in both the House and the Senate. In May 1824 a bill referring the Spanish claims to the District Court was finally enacted, but a series of lawsuits were to keep the Spanish grants from resolution for another five years.[5]

Next Benton turned to matters of interest for his friends in the fur trade. Since the 1790s the Federal government had operated "factories," or trading posts, licensed to provide trade goods for the Indians. For some time spokesmen for the fur trade, from St. Louis and elsewhere, had demanded an end to the government-operated Indian factory system. The depressed conditions in the trade after the War of 1812 had lent new urgency to calls for an end to government competition. When Benton arrived in Washington in December 1820, three fellow residents at the hotel where he lodged were Ramsay Crooks and Russell Farnham of the American Fur Company, and Elizabeth Benton's uncle, Congressman John Floyd of Virginia. The four discussed issues related to the fur trade at length. Floyd would serve as representative of the Company's interests in the House; Benton would do so in the Senate.

Crooks, Farnham, and other traders wanted government protection in their competition with the British Hudson's Bay Company, but they wanted the government out of the business of trading with—and protecting—the Indians. Government factories were an obstacle to effective exploitation of the fur trade by St. Louis traders like William H. Ashley, Henry Andrews, and Manuel Lisa as well as John Jacob Astor's American Fur Company. Among other things, the Federal government prohibited the sale of whiskey to Indians at its factories; private traders considered this practice essential to getting the best bargains when dealing with the tribes. Benton's views were in harmony with those of private companies and on March 25, 1822, he launched his campaign against the factory system in the Senate. He began with a detailed summary of the institution's history and shortcomings. Over the years, he said, six hundred thousand dollars had been spent, yet the system had not Christianized the Indians, had not kept them at peace, had not created respect for the government among them, had not prevented the Indians from trading with the British, nor had it protected them from extortion.

With sarcasm that Randolph himself might have admired, Benton examined the conduct of the government-run factories. He was particularly critical of Indian Superintendent Thomas McKenney in regards to purchasing trade goods "of a kind not suitable to the Indians," including men's and women's shoes, worsted and cotton hose, tea, and various medicines that Benton doubted "necessary to promote the comfort or restore the health of the aborigines." He attacked the requisition of "8 gross of Jewsharps" for trade at the factories. Despite his intimacy with the Missouri fur trade, said Benton, he was unfamiliar with the uses to which such items might be applied. Neither could he perceive in what manner they might be used to effect the removal of British traders from the Northwestern Territories. However, in light of the superintendent's "schemes for the amendment of the heads and hearts of the Indians; to improve their moral and intellectual faculties; to draw them from the savage and hunter state, and to induct them into the innocent pursuit of civilized life . . . the Jewsharps might have their use." They were, after all, a musical instrument, and music, intoned Benton, "hath charms to sooth the savage heart."[6]

The factory system had its defenders in the Senate, who answered Benton's charges and emphasized the role of the private companies in the proposed legislation. Among those in opposition to the bill were New York senators Rufus King, with whom Benton was close personally if not politically, and Martin Van Buren, with whom he was to have a long and complex relationship. In the end, Congress nonetheless voted to do away with the factory system. An ecstatic Ramsay Crooks informed Benton that "You deserve the unqualified thanks of the community for destroying the pious monster." Crooks had reason to be grateful; the fur trade now became the domain of the private fur companies without the threat of government competition.[7]

Benton biographer Elbert Smith defended the actions of those who pushed to abolish the factory system, claiming that by the 1820s it was "stagnant, while men like Crooks, Farnham, and the Chouteaus were dynamic adventurers in search of an empire." This is far from the whole truth. In fact, the system of Indian trading houses failed because it had received only half-hearted support from the federal government from the outset. Francis Paul Prucha noted that the government was unable to admit that it might be required to maintain a monopoly over the fur trade in order to end abuses and to supply the Indians fairly with the goods they needed. Instead a dual system was allowed, with private traders operating under a less rigorous licensing system. After the War of 1812, the factory system was squeezed out by the private traders and, despite arguments on its behalf by Superintendent McKinney, Secretary of War Calhoun, and others, the system never enjoyed more than lukewarm support in Congress. Smith asserts that Benton, since his arrival in St. Louis, "had been well aware of the evils of the system." Instead of working to correct those shortcomings, however, he worked with his allies in the fur trade to abolish the system altogether. The only effective defense of the factory system "yet mustered," wrote Smith, "has been the speculation that with needed reforms the government could have served the Indians better than the greedy private traders." But, he correctly admitted, "To the Westerner of 1822 this was no argument at all."[8]

When the factories remained in operation in order to dispose of trade goods still left on hand, Robert Stuart, another agent of the American Fur Company, wrote to Crooks that "the young man ... who has been sent to close the factory concern [at Prairie du Chien], in place of doing so has opened it with as much éclat as ever." Would it not be well, asked Crooks, for Mr. Astor to communicate with the appropriate officials on the matter, and if they did not order the factory closed, "Benton ought to give them another *rap*." Crooks accordingly wrote to Benton in December, objecting to the government's policy of continuing the factories in order to close them out and demanding that their trade goods be sent to the trading posts of the American Fur Company![9]

Benton not only served as both lobbyist and legislator for the company, but as attorney too. He sued the commanding officer at Prairie du Chien on behalf of the American Fur Company, and won a $5,000 judgment for time and profits lost. Later, Senator Benton would serve the interests of the company by working to get tariffs imposed on British furs.[10]

Benton's activities on behalf of the fur trade were undoubtedly beyond the pale by modern-day standards of congressional ethics. In the early nineteenth century, however—and for some time thereafter—this simply appears to be the way things were done. The line between public and private interests was much less distinct than it is today. In addition, Benton, who was always short of cash, was in particularly dire financial straits at this point in his career. The Bank of Missouri, of which he had served as a director, had just failed, leaving him deeply in debt. He had a large family to support; and senatorial pay was low. In 1824 Benton lost his St. Louis home through foreclosure on a two-thousand-dollar mortgage, though retaining possession as a tenant. He had entered the Senate a large landowner and acquired more plantations through the family of Mrs. Benton, but over the years the Bentons' property was sold off piece by piece to maintain the family and to pay off ongoing cycles of debt.[11]

In addition to the Spanish land claimants and the fur companies, Benton also served as spokesman for mining interests in his home state, pressing for private operation of the government-owned lead mines, which were another major source of potential wealth for Missouri's economy. At the time of Benton's arrival in the Missouri Territory, there were over forty separate "diggings" in Ste. Genevieve, St. Francis, and Washington counties, including Moses Austin's *Mine à Breton* at Potosi. Despite the crudeness of early mining methods—pick and shovel work to remove minerals from pits that were seldom more than ten feet deep—the quality of the lead thus extracted promised sufficient profits to ignite violent disputes over land claims in southeastern Missouri.

The Federal government had a long-standing policy of reserving mineral lands for its own uses. The Land Ordinance of 1785 provided that "one third of all gold, silver, lead, or copper mines, [were] to be sold or otherwise disposed of as Congress shall hereafter direct." Legislation enacting a system of leasing mineral lands was not enacted until 1807. Since southeast Missouri towns such as Ste. Genevieve, Potosi, and Cape Girardeau lived largely off the products of the mines, Benton found the notion of a government monopoly over these lands abhorrent. In addition, the growing "Boonslick" region along the lower Missouri River was home to numerous "Saline" creeks and streams also under government control as a source of salt. As an attorney, Benton had fought for recognition of individual titles to land against government claims, and he argued that only "freehold titles" in the mines would assure their being exploited to their full potential.[12]

In April 1823 Benton submitted a resolution requesting information from the executive concerning the government's lead mine leases. He wanted to know who held the leases, and under what terms. Were they granted by private contract or public auction? Were the leases making money for the government? His criticisms of both the Indian factories and the lead leasing system brought him into conflict, for the first time, with Secretary of War Calhoun. The War Department was responsible for administering both programs, and Calhoun viewed Benton's efforts as part of an attack on the Monroe administration by opponents of a nationalist economic program. On January 21, 1823, Benton reported from the Committee on Public Lands a bill authorizing the President to "expose" to public sale the lead mines belonging to the United States. Several weeks later Benton spoke in support of the bill. He ridiculed "deriving a national revenue from . . . lead ore diggers," and he charged the federal government with overstepping the bounds of its authority.

He denied to the federal government the capacity to hold a "body of tenantry" within the limits of any state. "The monarchies of Europe," said Benton, "have their serfs and vassals, but the genius of the Republic disclaims the tenure and the spirit of vassalage, and calls for freemen, owners of the soil, masters of their own castles, and free from the influence of a foreign sovereign."[13]

Benton insisted, moreover, that the government had received no rents from the leasing system. This, in fact, was not the case. In 1816 Land Commissioner Josiah Meigs had reported to Treasury Secretary Crawford revenues amounting to $1,622. Benton was either unaware of this figure or chose to ignore it. "The spirit of tenantry . . . is a spirit adverse to improvement, always leaning toward the injury of the property in possession, and always holding back from the payment of rent. God placed lead . . . in Missouri for the use of the people who go there to live . . . but, by the intervention of a foreign Government, the people are denied the benefit of the use and profits of supplying their neighbors."[14]

Even though Benton believed his bill could easily have passed if brought to a vote, it was tabled "for want of time to take it through the House." After several more years of pushing for an end to the lead leasing system, Benton was finally successful in 1829—only to see his act nullified by the Supreme Court. Not until 1847 was the leasing system finally abandoned in favor of the free market, but Benton's continued championing of the cause enhanced his popularity with constituents in the mineral-rich regions of his home state.[15]

As the Seventeenth Congress came to a close, Benton had yet to distinguish himself as anyone other than a proponent of particular business interests. His efforts on behalf of the holders of Spanish grants, the fur companies, and the lead and salt mining entrepreneurs reveal him as the spokesman for a state still very much in transition from the expeditionary frontier of its colonial and territorial phases to the sedentary agrarian frontier that would characterize Missouri during the remainder of the antebellum period. Nonetheless, Benton was careful to emphasize the benefits his entire state would derive from the policies at issue: he stressed the benefits that liberal confirmation of the Spanish land claims would provide to farmers with small unconfirmed claims; the abolition of the factory system would not only benefit the fur trade but the entire state, which would profit from handling the necessary trading goods and provisions. He also displayed, in his speeches concerning the Indian trade, certain aspects of his "modern" attitude concerning Native Americans that had been absent in the national government's Indian policies during its early years. Thus far, however, Benton had not managed to synthesize his attitudes concerning race, free enterprise, and westward expansion into a message that was broadly appealing to the growing electorate of his home state. In the space of a few months, though, economic depression was to spur a movement toward greater democratization in Missouri that Benton was quick to seize upon.[16]

"Country Democracy" and the Panic of 1819

In 1821 the effects of the great financial Panic that had begun two years earlier reached Missouri. By the spring of that year the crisis was so acute that the newly elected state government faced calls for action. The change from flush times to hard times had occurred with shocking suddenness. Perhaps due to the depression in the East, perhaps the result of controversy over the slavery question and the resulting uncertainty about statehood, immigration to Missouri had dropped off during the latter part of 1820. The influx of families to the Boonslick country suddenly came to a halt, as did the growth of towns in the Missouri Valley. Land prices tumbled as settlers stopped coming and speculators were left hopelessly in debt for lands that they had bought from the government on credit. Farmers who had acquired more land than they needed in expectation of selling the extra acres to newcomers at a higher price than they had paid were left holding the land and the debt. To make matters worse, 1820 produced a bumper harvest and farmers watched their surplus rot as the markets for their crops disappeared. Some who had been part of the great migration to Missouri only a few years before, gave up and went home to Tennessee or Kentucky. Merchants had likewise gone deeply in debt for supplies to sell the expected immigrants who failed to arrive, stocking shelves with goods for which eastern creditors now demanded payment. Storeowners who had themselves extended liberal credit to customers now found collection nearly impossible. When Missouri's only financial institutions, the Bank of St. Louis and the Bank of Missouri, both failed, the disaster was complete. The state was left without currency and banking services that were now needed worse than ever.[17]

The newspapers were filled with complaints of "hard times." Farms were sold off to pay taxes and the law was still such that scores of those unable to meet their obligations were imprisoned for debt. Individuals who felt trapped by circumstances beyond their control—a growing faction among Missourians—demanded state action to provide relief and stimulate the economy. The question of how the state government should respond to the economic crisis shaped Missouri's earliest political controversies as a state. Farmers, speculators, and landholders generally condemned government inaction and demanded remedial legislation. Lawyers, merchants, and creditors denounced the stay laws and cheap currency schemes adopted by other western states as dishonest means of escaping the payment of legitimate debt.

These controversies were nothing new. Conflicts between indebted landowners and their creditors went back to the prerevolutionary period. The North Carolina Regulation of the 1760s, in which Benton's grandfather Samuel had figured so prominently, was one manifestation of this perennial struggle. During the Confederation period, when the authority of government at all levels was in question, "Liberty Men" in Maine, "Wild Yankees" in Pennsylvania, and "Green Mountain Boys" in Vermont all challenged governments they perceived as supporting local elites at their expense. When peaceful efforts to obtain redress failed, rural grievances might take on the nature of armed rebellion, as had been the case in colonial North Carolina and occurred most famously in the New England Regulation of 1786–1787, commonly known as Shays's Rebellion. By the early 1820s, with the authority of national and state governments more firmly established, resort to armed rebellion was less likely on the rural frontier. Conflicts between debtors and creditors, though, remained as fierce as ever and were heightened by the economic difficulties following the Panic. The latest round of these age-old antagonisms, most strongly felt in the new states of the West, would therefore be fought out not with black powder but at the ballot box and in the courts.[18]

In Kentucky, a pro-debtor "Relief Party" won a legislative majority in 1819 and enacted measures abolishing imprisonment for debt, greatly extending the time allowed to pay creditors, and replacing the conservative Bank of Kentucky with a new Bank of the Commonwealth, authorized to issue huge amounts of inflationary paper currency. Creditors appealed to the state courts, which promptly declared the measures unconstitutional. The makeup of the courts thus became the key issue in Kentucky's 1824 elections, which again returned a solid pro-relief majority. The new legislature then passed a bill reorganizing the state judiciary and creating an appellate court system friendly to the state's indebted farmers. Members of the established courts, however, refused to step down, and for several years Kentucky underwent a constitutional crisis as "Old Court" and "New Court" parties vied for legitimacy.[19]

In Missouri, Governor Alexander McNair convened a special session of the General Assembly to address the crisis. Meeting on June 4, 1821, the Assembly followed the example of Kentucky and several other western states, passing a stay law by which landholders, under certain conditions, might redeem land sold for debt. It exempted from execution for debt certain family possessions, including one cow, one calf, a bed and furniture, one spinning wheel, one loom, and other articles of property. The legislators abolished imprisonment for debt in certain cases and, rather than establishing a new bank, set up a system of loan offices to remedy the currency situation.[20]

The most controversial aspect of the reform legislation, the loan offices, were intended to take the place of a state bank. By providing for the issuing of $200,000 worth of paper certificates and making them receivable in payment for taxes, salaries, auditors' warrants, and certain debts, the Assembly hoped to provide badly needed currency, the absence of which a majority of members considered to be the major cause of the depression. In the unstable economic climate that followed the Panic, however, the certificates were not widely accepted. On the contrary, they were discredited almost as soon as they were issued and, if anything, only contributed to making the currency situation worse than ever.

Public opinion was divided over the question of loan offices. One faction, mostly composed of those demanding relief, insisted that still more paper money be put into the economy. The opposition demanded the legal repudiation of paper and repeal of the Loan Office Law. Political campaigns in Missouri during the remainder of 1821 and 1822 were waged primarily on the issues of the loan office and relief measures. The debate had an element of class struggle, but the lines between the contesting parties were neither clear nor permanent. Because relief legislation was in some ways an issue popular with the rural majority, many pro-reliefers were found later among the supporters of Andrew Jackson. Duff Green, later a leading editor of the Jacksonian press, was in the pro-relief faction during the early 1820s. But Jackson himself opposed similar legislation in Tennessee during the same period. In the fall elections of 1822 the anti-relief group won and pro-relief amendments to the state constitution were defeated. In addition, the Loan Office law was later declared unconstitutional, both by the State Supreme Court and by the U.S. Supreme Court. The state of Missouri was unable to collect on notes issued under the Loan Office Act, thus becoming burdened with a debt of $70,000 that took twelve years of difficult financing to pay off. Benton was already distrustful of banks as the result of his own experiences. Now coming under the influence of Macon, Randolph, and the Old Republicans, he concluded that a "hard money" policy was the only appropriate economic course for his state.[21]

The currency dispute was an aspect of larger questions concerning the nature of governance in Missouri. As politics became more democratic nationwide, there was genuine concern over the degree to which the state government was accountable to the voters. The state elections of 1820 had reflected popular dissatisfaction with a state constitution that voters perceived as undemocratic. It was these elections that had unseated William Clark as governor and produced a legislature that only narrowly chose Benton for the Senate. Demands for constitutional change continued during the governorship of Alexander McNair. The First General Assembly, in addition to passing relief legislation and establishing the loan office, also proposed amendments to the state constitution that would abolish the minimum salary for judges, empower the General Assembly rather than the governor to appoint those judges, and vacate judgeships at the end of the First General Assembly or as soon thereafter as their successors had been duly appointed and qualified. Other amendments sought to abolish the $2,000 salary for the governor and to transfer the appointive power for secretary of state, attorney general, and auditor from the governor to the legislature. Supporters of the amendments wanted to reduce the power of unelected judges and of the governor while increasing the role of legislators, who were directly accountable to the people. Opponents saw in the amendments only the designs of the pro-relief party, and viewed the judicial reform measures as weapons that would be used to threaten state judges who were inclined to invalidate recently enacted relief legislation.

The amendments were the foremost issue in the 1822 state elections. By now, however, initial public anger over the constitution of 1820 had subsided and the traditional elites had reestablished their influence. Only six of the original fifty representatives and four of the original eighteen state senators elected in the first flush of opposition to the constitution were returned to the Second General Assembly. The anti-relief group greeted the outcome as a victory "for the integrity of the constitution and the honest payment of debts." The rejection of proposals to transfer appointive powers from the governor to the legislature meant no change in the personnel of the state court system. The failure of these proposed changes, in turn, added to a current of popular discontent below the surface of the electoral outcomes that might yet be harnessed by political leaders capable of seeing its potential.[22]

Benton, still reassessing the political landscape in Missouri, refused to become involved in the debate at the state level. His Senate career to this point had essentially been that of a dignified ombudsman for the wealthy Creoles and their Anglo-American allies, whom Joseph Charless had once described as the "little junto." At the time Missouri entered the Union, Benton apparently still supported property qualifications for the electoral franchise. By 1824 a majority of voters and elected officials in states west of the Appalachians, as well as many forward-thinking politicians back east, had come to regard such voting restrictions as unfortunate anachronisms that should be abandoned in the name of democracy. Four years into his term, Benton must have looked back in wonder and thanked heaven that his name was not also associated with the unpopular 1820 constitution.

Sensing the shift toward popular government, in the Eighteenth Congress Benton introduced two proposals that marked a significant departure from his legislative record heretofore. The first was a proposal to enhance what Benton termed the principle of "*demos krateo*"—government by the people and majority rule—by offering a constitutional amendment abolishing the Electoral College and substituting a plan for direct presidential elections. His amendment would divide the states into districts equal in number to their senators and representatives and the candidate winning the most districts by popular vote would be elected. Fears of tumult resulting from popular election, said Benton in defense of his measure, were misplaced. Instead of violence, he argued, it was apathy that posed the greatest danger to our presidential elections. Benton esteemed the incorruptibility of the people and their desire to have the best man for president over any advantages to be derived from a more enlightened, but smaller—and therefore more corruptible—body. He opposed the intervention of Electors, "because the double process of electing a man to elect a man, would paralyze the spirit of the people, and destroy the life of the election itself.... It interposes a body of men between the people and the object of their choice, and gives a false direction to the gratitude of the President elected." Despite Benton's exhaustive three-day address, which reviewed the constitutional convention of 1787, the *Federalist Papers*, and the methods of choosing presidential electors in the various states, the Senate voted to postpone debate on the proposed amendment indefinitely.[23]

Seeking to enhance his popularity with the yeomen and small slaveholders who now constituted a majority of voting Missourians, Benton also offered a plan to reform national land policy. At that time the most desirable land was distributed by means of auction to the highest bidder. In the wake of the Panic, Congress had passed the Land Act of 1820, which both ended the practice of selling public lands on credit and set a minimum price of one dollar and twenty-five cents per acre. Land not disposed of by auction sometimes remained on the market for years. In April 1824 Benton introduced a bill proposing that any public lands not sold within five years were to be offered again at a reduced or "graduated" price. The price of land was subject to annual reductions of 25 cents per acre with any land unsold after it was offered at 50 cents an acre (Benton later reduced this still lower to 25 cents) subject to free donation to any bona fide settler "upon inhabiting and cultivating the same for three successive years." Benton acknowledged in his introduction that it was too late in the session to pass the measure, but that he sought to turn the minds of his colleagues to reforming the land policy. His proposal offered to farm families, increasingly threatened by the disappearance of available land in the East, an extension of the free-holding system through cheap land in the West.

Benton's graduation/donation proposal, as it came to be called, had enormous popular appeal among the people of Missouri. As the elections of 1824 approached, he was increasingly identified by Missourians—and westerners generally—as the advocate of greater democracy in the political process and greater economic opportunity for the common white man.

The Election of 1824: Benton Joins the Jackson Men

Benton's first term in the Senate coincided with the end of that brief period of one-party government associated with the misleading phrase "Era of Good Feelings." James Monroe was the last president of the so-called Virginia Dynasty. For 32 of the Republic's first 36 years, Virginians had served in the presidency. Monroe was the last chief executive to have been an adult during the War for Independence, and to the younger political generation his customary attire of knee-breeches and stockings was as quaintly out of style by the 1820s as his notions of government by the "natural aristocracy." Monroe's administration coincided with a period of both intense nationalism and the unchallenged supremacy of Jeffersonian Republicanism following the War of 1812. The president encouraged this trend toward "amalgamation" as the Federalists disappeared from the scene. He sought to create consensus behind the nationalist economic program now being promoted by Clay, Calhoun, and other Republican nationalists. Randolph, Macon, and the "Old Republicans," as well as northern "Radicals" like Martin Van Buren, found this repudiation of Jeffersonian principles abhorrent. But despite the controversies resulting from the Panic of 1819 and Missouri's entry into the Union, partisan rancor was notably absent during Monroe's two terms in office. At the end of his eight years as president, however, Monroe followed the example of his predecessors and declined to stand for a third term. With the presidential field wide open as the election of 1824 approached, the illusion of Republican unity was about to be shattered once and for all.[24]

The office of secretary of state had traditionally been a stepping-stone to the presidency. The current secretary, John Quincy Adams, having ably served for eight years in Monroe's cabinet, was confident his time had come. A more recent tradition was the selection of party nominee by congressional caucus. With the demise of the Federalist Party, this meant that congressional Republicans effectively chose the chief executive in 1816 and in 1820. Treasury Secretary William Crawford of Georgia was the favorite of the caucus, and his candidacy was strengthened when President Monroe, ignoring precedent, let it be known that he too favored Crawford. By 1824, however, there was growing dissatisfaction with the notion that a small group of political leaders, however distinguished, could choose among themselves who the next president might be. With the tenuous consensus that characterized the "Era of Good Feelings" coming to an end, the various sections of the country were producing their own favorites. A majority of New England voters supported Adams, but John C. Calhoun of South Carolina, the current secretary of war, challenged Crawford's position as champion of the South. Andrew Jackson of Tennessee and Henry Clay of Kentucky vied for the support of the West.

It was in the West and the South that reaction to the outcome of this confusing presidential race would serve as a catalyst for the beginnings of a Second Party System. Missouri's early history is best understood as a narrative of competing regional interests over the ground of a state where different sections of the country—North and South, East and West—come together. The difficulty Missourians would have in sorting out their preference among the sectional candidates during the 1824 election was reflected in the unusual degree of soul-searching among the state's political leaders as well. As early as 1822, the members of the Missouri General Assembly had pledged their support to Henry Clay. Benton initially considered supporting Crawford, as did his associates

Randolph, Macon, and Van Buren, but by the summer of 1823 settled on backing Clay's candidacy. It was a shift in Benton's political stance, away from endorsing the choice of the caucus and spokesman for the plantation interests of the Southeast, but it was a risk he felt must be taken if he was to serve more than one term as senator. By supporting Clay, Benton was attempting to break free of his long-standing identification with the St. Louis junto, which, in the eyes of many legislators, made him the hireling of the city's Creole merchant elite. Slowly reinventing himself as the tribune of Missouri's "common man," by 1823 Benton was seeking a broad new base of support among the small slaveholders and yeoman farmers in the rural areas outside of St. Louis. His proposals in the Senate to abolish the Electoral College and reform the sale of public lands were his first steps in this direction.

Many Missourians were natives of Kentucky who regarded Henry Clay as a favorite son. It was a natural step for Benton, whose editorials in the *St. Louis Enquirer* some six years earlier had called for a system of transportation improvements and protective tariffs to enhance western development strikingly similar to much of what Clay was now promoting—a program shortly to be known as the "American System" after a speech delivered by Clay in March 1824. That same month, the Missouri *Republican* reported that 66 of the 261 members of Congress had met in caucus to choose Crawford as the Republican candidate. "We consider congressional caucuses a dangerous exercise of influence," concluded editor Joseph Charless, who consequently endorsed Clay. Many westerners blamed the congressional caucus, with its power to select candidates, for the continuing dominance of the Virginia Dynasty. In 1820 Monroe had been reelected without opposition. By 1822, however, public opinion in Missouri, as in much of the country, was turning against the caucus system for selection of presidential candidates.[25]

The three members of Missouri's congressional delegation agreed that Henry Clay was the best choice for president in 1824. They agreed on little else. Barton's opposition to direct election was symptomatic of differences that had existed between Benton and himself since they had been elected to the Senate in 1820. At that time, members of the territorial elite had formed a common front to maintain their positions of power and influence. Despite the fact that Benton and Barton had both been members of the junto faction with certain common conservative political views, the two had never been close personally. In 1823 their personal rivalry for power and influence flared into open political warfare when Joshua Barton, the senator's brother, was killed in a duel with

Thomas Rector, a friend and political associate of Benton's. The time was not yet ripe for the issues involved to form the basis of party identification, but the Barton-Bates faction—eventually the core of what would become Missouri's Whig party—began to gather support just as Benton was in the midst of his own delicate change of political positions. When Barton ran for reelection in the summer of 1824 (he and Benton had drawn lots to decide who would get a four-year term and who six years), Benton returned to Missouri not only to campaign for Clay, but against his Senate colleague.[26]

In general elections that summer, there were omens of victory for the conservative status quo. John Scott was returned to the House of Representatives by a wide margin while Frederick Bates, a wealthy St. Louis attorney and former territorial secretary, won the governorship with the support of a group of influential St. Louis businessmen and land speculators. Bates's opponent was William Ashley, general of the state militia and head of the Rocky Mountain Fur Company who, despite his loss, created a base of considerable popular support, which would result in his election to Congress as a nominal Jacksonian in 1831. Barton's legislative record had little to do with the senatorial contest that took place in the General Assembly in November. As Benton's land and Electoral College proposals had not yet received enough attention to influence voters, his faction emphasized Barton's fondness for whiskey as evidence that he was unfit to hold office. The opposition underestimated Barton's popularity among Missouri legislators. The General Assembly chose Barton over William Clark's informal candidacy 50–15. Benton's opponents cheered Barton's reelection over "the most outrageous slander circulated . . . by his enemies Rector, Benton, Govn'r McNair and others." The "aspiring political *genius*," as one correspondent dubbed Benton, had failed in his attempt to manage politics within Missouri. This was not the last time that Benton would be accused of trying to play the role of "dictator" within the state.[27]

During the course of the summer campaign, Benton had traveled over eight hundred miles, stumping in nearly every part of Missouri in an attempt to rally support for Clay and seeking to counter the increasing popularity of General Jackson. The previous year a personal reconciliation between Benton and Jackson had, in fact, taken place, and the makings of a political alliance forged when Jackson had arrived in Washington as a newly elected senator from Tennessee. Upon entering the upper house, the tall, white-haired Hero found only one vacant desk and that next to Benton. There was a tense interlude. Other members anticipated a resumption of the violence left unfinished in Nashville ten years earlier until, without comment, Jackson took his seat. Shortly, Benton was assigned to the Committee on Military Affairs, of which Jackson was chairman. Thereafter the two served together in committee and "did business together just as other persons." At length they exchanged inquiries as to the health of each other's wives. When the Bentons found themselves with General Jackson at a dinner party hosted by President Monroe, the two men bowed to each other and shook hands as friends, after which Benton introduced Elizabeth to his erstwhile enemy.[28]

Some time later Rachel Jackson received a letter from Senator John Eaton of Tennessee assuring her that the General was "in very fine health," even if too busy to write, and that "all his old quarrels have been settled, including "what you never would have expected Col. Benton." Jackson added a postscript in his own hand, telling his wife, "It is a pleasing subject to me that I am now at peace with all the world." For his part, Benton simply commented, "Well, how many changes in this life."[29]

In the short term, however, Benton remained a Clay supporter as the electoral field narrowed. In May, Crawford had suffered a debilitating stroke, eliminating him from the campaign for all practical purposes. Crawford's misfortune gave Jackson unexpected strength in the South, which was enhanced when Calhoun dropped out of the contest to accept the vice presidency. When the voters of Missouri went to the polls to choose electors, Clay carried the state with 1,401 votes, Jackson received 987, Adams 311, and Crawford none. Nationwide, Jackson won a total of 152,901 votes, followed by Adams 114, 023, Crawford 46,979, and Clay 47,217. The ballots of qualified voters were not decisive, however; in 1824 half a dozen states still required that presidential electors be chosen by their state legislatures. Jackson carried 99 electoral votes, Adams 84, Crawford 41, and Clay 37. None of the candidates had a majority of the Electoral College. The Constitution therefore required that the House of Representatives choose a president from among the top three electoral vote-getters. Clay was eliminated.[30]

In Missouri, the vote distribution revealed that a deep division between St. Louis and outstate areas continued to define state politics. While Clay's strength was obvious throughout the state, Jackson proved surprisingly popular among new settlers in the central and western parts of the state. The western counties ignored Adams in favor of Jackson (though Clay still led by a two-to-one margin). The southern counties split between Clay and Jackson, with Adams getting only a few votes. In St. Louis, however, the New Englander made a strong showing, especially in the city center. The reasons for this distribution are not entirely clear. Jackson's reputation as an Indian fighter and victor of New Orleans certainly appealed to the frontier population. But social and economic factors seem to have played the crucial role. "Western farmers and traders," wrote Alan S. Wiener, "tended to resent the Creole aristocrats in the eastern part of the state." On the other hand, wealthy residents of the southeastern counties regarded Jackson, as the squire of the Hermitage, a westerner, yet possessed of some refinement and taste. Only in St. Louis was there organized opposition to Jackson. "Mercantile and banking interests distrusted the General's temper, and saw a threat in his appeal to the 'vulgar herd' that streamed St. Louis and held noisy Jackson rallies."[31]

The news that Clay had been struck from the competition and would not be one of the three candidates among whom the House would choose had the effect of dissolving popular consensus in Missouri. Crawford, who had not received a single popular vote, was no longer seriously considered. Adams received most of the votes from urban Cape Girardeau and St. Louis, but had run a distant third, statewide, behind Clay and Jackson. Jackson's supporters now claimed that their man's nationwide victory in the popular vote, in addition to his finish as close second to Clay in Missouri, entitled him to the state's vote in the House of Representatives. They demanded that the General Assembly instruct John Scott, Missouri's lone member of the House, to cast his vote for Jackson. Adams supporters argued that Missouri's representative was committed to follow whatever course the winner of the state's popular vote—Clay—chose. And Clay now supported Adams. The General Assembly debated for a month in December 1824 and January 1825 without agreeing on instructions for Scott. Increasingly pursued by the Clay-Adams faction in the capital and without guidance from the legislature, Scott began to lean towards voting for Adams.[32]

As for Benton, Clay's defeat placed him in perhaps the most awkward position of his political career. He had cut his ties to the St. Louis junto and staked his political future on Clay's popular appeal among Missourians, but Clay was now out of the running. Benton could not follow the Kentuckian in his support of Adams. That would entail having to mend his fences with the very interests from which he had so recently disassociated himself. Neither Benton nor a majority of western voters favored Adams, whom many viewed as an "aristocratic" candidate and who had come in a distant third in the Missouri polling. Benton and other Missourians also blamed Adams for his 1818 treaty with Spain, under which the United States had surrendered any claim to Texas. Benton briefly considered the idea of supporting Crawford and certain Crawford supporters in Congress momentarily counted Benton as one of their own, but Crawford had even less support than Adams in Missouri and his candidacy was associated with the despised caucus system. In either case, Benton believed that to support anyone other than Jackson involved repudiating the voice of the people—the qualified voters of the state. There was nothing for it but to come out for the General, a decision that would involve a permanent break with both Clay and supporters of his American System in Missouri. On the other hand, it was a decision consistent with the concept of *demos krateo* that had driven Benton's proposal for electoral reform. It was a practical decision and Benton knew it. "I preferred the General," he wrote later, "because he was preferred ten to one by the people of Missouri." Jackson was both a fellow westerner and a popular national hero—a fabled Indian fighter who appealed to the white egalitarianism of the region. His success in Missouri was also aided by the decision of editor Duff Green to support him after Calhoun's withdrawal from the race.[33]

Reaction to Benton's change of allegiance was mixed. To his enemies, it seemed that he was an unscrupulous opportunist who had ceased to support Clay when it became impractical to do so and who now embraced the candidate whom he had formerly opposed with the most contemptuous rhetoric. Barton, who had wholeheartedly supported Adams and whose erstwhile alliance with Benton was long over, commented, "Of all the unnatural coalitions (not to say the most insincere) is that of our Senator Pomposo, of imperial port and mien, with the General." In his opinion, anyone who stood for one candidate, then another, and another was both unreliable and self-serving.[34]

By contrast, John Scott, Missouri's lone member of the House of Representatives, had remained a friend and political ally to Benton since territorial days. That relationship, however, was also coming to an end as Scott was coming to a decision concerning his vote. On February 5, he wrote Benton that "Notwithstanding the conversation we had on Thursday evening and on Friday, from which you might justly conclude that I would not vote for Mr. Adams, I am now inclined to think differently, and unless some other change in my mind takes place, I shall vote for him."[35]

Benton was surprised and infuriated by his colleague's decision. Three days after Scott had written his letter (February 8), Benton penned his reply: "Sinister rumors and some misgivings of my own had been preparing my mind for an extraordinary development, but it was not until I had three times talked with you, face-to-face that I could believe in the reality of an intention so inconsistent with your previous conversations, so repugnant to your printed pledges, so amazing to your constituents, so fatal to yourself." Benton admonished Scott that the vote he intended to cast was not his own—"it belongs to the people." They were against Adams, and Benton, "'in their name' he solemnly protested against Scott's intention and denied his "moral power to thus bestow your vote." For nine years, since Benton's arrival in Missouri, the two had been closely connected in their political destinies; now the connection was dissolved "under circumstances which denounce our everlasting separation. . . . Tomorrow is the day for your self-immolation; if you have an enemy, he may go and feed his eyes upon the scene; your former friend will shun the afflicting spectacle."[36]

Over the past month, while the Missouri legislature had debated who should receive the state's vote, Clay began to exert pressure on Scott to support Adams. Scott was hesitant, but was growing increasingly irritated with Benton's attempts to control the voting in Missouri. By January 20, Illinois Congressman Daniel Cook, who had convinced his own state's delegation to dump Jackson in favor of his friend Adams, reported to the New Englander that Scott was "very well disposed to go with the other western delegations" and would probably cast Missouri's vote for Adams. The following day Scott and Adams met face-to-face. During their discussion, the Missourian pleaded the case of his brother, a federal judge in the territory of Arkansas, who had killed a man in a duel. Adams promised Scott that, if elected, he would dismiss a petition for the judge's removal, and Scott thereby agreed to vote for Adams. On the basis of Adams's account of their meeting, Jackson biographer Robert Remini charged that Scott's vote was "purchased in another, smaller version of a 'bargain and sale.'" More likely, the crucial factor in determining Scott's vote was his devotion to Clay. Adams mentioned nothing in their encounter about the details of forming an administration, but indicated that if he should be elected by the suffrages of the West, he should naturally look to the West for much of his support. As Scott left, Adams observed that he was "apparently satisfied.[37]

At noon on February 9, 1825, the House of Representatives convened to cast their votes, state by state, for the next president. John C. Calhoun had already received an electoral majority to become the next vice president. The House roll was called and ballot boxes distributed to each of the twenty-four state delegations. The boxes were then brought to teller's tables, where Senators Daniel Webster and John Randolph supervised the counting. Adams won thirteen states, Jackson seven, and Crawford four. Missouri's vote, cast by Scott, had gone to John Quincy Adams.

The election concluded, Adams set about naming a cabinet, which included Henry Clay as secretary of state. Jackson men, in Missouri and throughout the nation, angrily charged that a "corrupt bargain" had taken place between Adams and Clay. The General himself was among the first to reach that conclusion. In a letter written only days after the House vote, he told Major Lewis, "So you see that the Judas of the West has closed his contract and will receive the thirty pieces of silver."[38]

Historians seeking to explain the election of 1824 have tended to fall into two camps. Those like Remini, who by his own admission was a "Jackson man," have taken the rhetoric of the Jacksonians at face value. Charles G. Sellers, for instance, asserted that although the votes from the Jackson and Clay states in the House were "more than enough to sustain the manifest will of the majority," Henry Clay used his influence to "thwart the popular verdict," both to advance his own prospects of becoming next in line for the presidency and to help shape the political economy to the contours envisioned by his American System. Thus, "he was positioning himself to lead the republic to its capitalist destiny." Sellers attributes the inability of Adams and Clay to understand the disaffection of the Jacksonians to their being "insulated in the world of elite opinion." However, "by robbing the majority of its victory, Adams and Clay crippled themselves politically and made Jackson the unmistakable symbol of the demand for majority rule." Sellers is correct in his assertion that modern presidential politics originated in the majority that claimed a democratic victory for Jackson in 1824. However, by failing to examine the claims of the Jacksonians, as well as the nature of both the Jackson coalition and the National Republicans more critically, he joins a long line of historians, including Arthur Schlesinger Jr. and William N. Chambers, who incorporated the partisan spin of the rising Democratic coalition into their historical narratives.[39]

Understandably, historians of the National Republican and Whig persuasion have presented a more nuanced view of events. Daniel Walker Howe, in his examination of Whig political culture, claimed that John Quincy Adams did what any ambitious politician would do under the circumstances. He waged an aggressive fight for support among representatives in the House, "calling on every possible congressman and discussing such matters as the award of government printing contracts."

In the runoff election in the House, Adams held on to the delegations from the seven states he had carried in the general election. The bargain he struck with Clay, corrupt or otherwise—Richard Hofstadter called it "statesmanlike"—brought him the three states that Clay could deliver, including Missouri. "His own diligent calls for congressional votes," writes Howe, "won him the votes of three other states carried by Jackson. With thirteen states, Adams was elected, and his victory marked him a master of political 'old boy network.'"[40]

Merrill D. Peterson discussed Henry Clay's end of the alleged bargain at length in *The Great Triumvirate*. Adams offered Clay the post of secretary of state three days after the election in the House and Clay, at the urging of most of his friends, accepted. Peterson describes the decision as "the worst error of his political life." The bargain charge might be a lie, yet nothing could prevent people from believing it once Clay accepted Adams's appointment. "Clay," wrote Peterson, "while innocent of bargain and corruption, had done something worse for a politician; he had, as Talleyrand might have said, committed a great blunder." The conspiracy theorists around Jackson painted Clay in criminal hues based on circumstantial evidence that made an all-too-compelling narrative. Clay attempted to explain himself to his constituents; he pressed for letters and affidavits to clear his name. Were truth the issue, asserts Peterson, the lack of evidence proving the allegations would have vindicated Clay. But the issue was political power, and the more Clay protested his innocence the more guilty he seemed. "Clay was doomed to the impossible task of proving a negative, that he had not entered into a bargain. The charge was made to injure him and the Adams administration. But it was also made to promote the political fortunes of Andrew Jackson and his party." The "corrupt bargain" charge would be repeated again and again over the next four years by supporters of Jackson who felt that their man had been cheated out of the presidency by the machinations of an aristocratic faction of insiders. The Jacksonians set out, from the moment the House vote was reported, to reclaim the government in the name of "the people."[41]

Seeking to balance these partisan views of the House vote, Sean Wilentz essentially concurred with this assessment of the outcome in *The Rise of American Democracy*. Clay, he says, disregarded the cardinal political maxim that the appearance of wrongdoing can be just as damaging as the act itself. "More important, while playing by the established patrician rules of high politics, Clay did not comprehend how much and how quickly the rules were changing in the 1820s along majoritarian lines." His kinsman and former political supporter Thomas Benton well comprehended that the principle of *demos krateo* would rule from now on.[42]

Race, Ideology, and the Democratic-Republican Opposition

Much of the literature concerning Benton's behavior during the election of 1824 has portrayed him as either an opportunist who trimmed his sails to catch whatever political winds were blowing or, conversely, as a visionary western populist whose moment had finally arrived in the form of outrage over the election of John Quincy Adams. The Missourian's close friendship with John Randolph, leader of the "Old Republican" faction and, paradoxically, the die-hard enemy of democratization in electoral politics, provides certain clues to Benton's shift from spokesman for the mercantile interests of the fur companies and land speculators to the role of radical agrarian. The strict constructionist philosophy of Randolph and his fellow "Quids," in turn, cannot be fully understood without reference to their attitudes on race, slavery, and states' rights, which were entirely consistent with Benton's. The idea of republican virtue, as embodied in the heroic General Jackson, versus the alleged aristocratic corruption in the persons of Adams, Clay, and others who would shortly identify themselves as National Republicans, is essential to understanding the self-image and rhetoric of the Jacksonian movement and eventual formation of the Second American Party System. Both sides, of course, claimed to represent "the people" and both claimed to be the true heirs to the republicanism of the Founding Fathers. But the Adams and Jackson camps, as they coalesced and adapted to the new, more democratic, style of politics, redefined the republican tradition for their own purposes.

Both parties traced their roots to the Jeffersonian Republicans of the 1790s; Federalism had long since been discredited. The party of Jefferson, however, had undergone profound changes since the "Revolution of 1800" had placed its leaders in power. Under the exigencies of national power and international crisis, the Jeffersonians had adopted or endorsed many of the measures associated with the broad constitutional construction of their erstwhile opponents. These included protective tariffs, internal transportation improvements, and a national bank. As we have seen, even western Republicans like Benton were not altogether consistent in their views. In the years of the Missouri Crisis, the *St. Louis Enquirer* had called for federal transportation improvements even as it trumpeted the cause of states' rights on the slavery issue. William Chambers used the term "Roman-riding"—an ancient form of equestrian performance in which the rider controls two horses at once while standing with one foot on the back of each—to describe Benton's ideological ambivalence during his first term in the Senate. If this in fact was what he was doing, Benton was by no means alone.[43]

His shift toward a more coherent philosophy of government may be traced to his relationship with Randolph, Macon, and other conservatives from the rural Southeast—the true keepers, as they viewed themselves, of the "Old Republican" faith based on states' rights and agrarian values. Tracing their philosophical lineage through Jefferson back to the Country Whigs of eighteenth-century England, they were, by the mid-1820s, the "country party" of American government in every sense of that term: a handful of voices in the political wilderness, unyielding in their opposition to the corrupt "court" of nationalists who had betrayed their founding principles in the pursuit of greater wealth and power. The bargain between Adams and Clay, whether real or imagined, seemed the fulfillment of all the conservatives' fears and a confirmation of their warnings concerning the declension of values in the polity. It was to prove a potent symbol that would give their faction new life and new converts in the opposition.

The effects of the troubled election of 1824 were felt not only in Missouri but throughout the country, as old alignments broke up and new ones formed. Old Republicans, like Benton's friend Randolph, had initially been opposed to Jackson and had supported Crawford as the embodiment of agrarian interests and strict constitutional construction. Randolph and his supporters in the "Richmond Junto" still respected the ability and integrity of Adams, whose nationalist positions tended to be forgotten in the midst of the presidential election campaign. When Crawford was eliminated by his health, the conservatives initially saw no alternative to Adams. Always suspicious of the arbitrary exercise of power, they deplored Jackson's disregard of proper authority and the rule of law during his invasion of Spanish Florida in 1818. Nonetheless, with the appointment of Clay as secretary of state, Randolph and other conservatives began to give credence to the Jacksonians' questions as to the integrity of the administration. With support among southern and western conservatives slipping, the President's first annual message to Congress on December 6, 1825, only seemed to confirm the worst fears of strict constructionists.

President Adams recommended a national university, a comprehensive program of internal improvements, even the building of an astronomical observatory (a "lighthouse of the sky"). He interpreted the "necessary and proper" clause of Article I to empower Congress to pass "laws promoting the improvement of agriculture, commerce, and manufactures, the cultivation and encouragement of the mechanic and elegant arts, the advancement of literature, and the progress of the sciences, ornamental and profound," including scientific expeditions and a uniform system of weights and measures. Nothing in Adams's program was without precedent. The proposal for a national university dated from the Washington administration and had been taken up by every succeeding president. Jefferson had called for a national system of weights and measures and had sent Lewis and Clark's Corps of Discovery to the Pacific for purposes both diplomatic and scientific. There had even been earlier calls for a national observatory, and Adams was inspired, partly, by Jefferson's vision of an "empire of science."[44]

Nonetheless, conservative "Old Republicans" of the Randolph-Macon school were stunned by this new Hamilton-like assertion of government power. They charged that the alleged bargain with Clay was the first step in a scheme to corrupt America as a whole. Many Americans were already suspicious of the government's willingness to ally itself with banking and manufacturing interests. Adams now called for a greater expansion still of the government's economic role, further undermining, in the conservatives' view, the independence of the sturdy farmers who had been traditional guardians of republican liberty and virtue. According to Nathaniel Macon, the speech seemed "to claim all the power to the federal government, which has heretofore produced so much debate, and which the election of Mr. Jefferson was supposed to have settled."[45]

The president's program had the effect of producing an alliance between southern conservatives such as Macon and Randolph, northeasterners represented by the likes of Martin Van Buren of New York and his Albany Regency, and western agrarian interests, among whom Benton was emerging as a leader. Collectively, the opponents of economic nationalism and broad constitutional construction were dubbed "radicals" by Adams's supporters. The new "democrats," as some were now also calling themselves, considered the slur a badge of honor. Some time later, Van Buren would put forth the case for a united opposition in a much-discussed letter to Thomas Ritchie of the Richmond *Enquirer*, the leading organ of the southern conservative movement. Eschewing the antiparty rhetoric of the Era of Good Feelings, Van Buren told Ritchie, "We must always have party distinctions and the old ones are the best." In other words, since political alliances between voters of different states were unavoidable, "the most natural and beneficial to the country is that between the planters of the South and the plain Republicans of the North." This coalition, which began to form as an antithesis to the centralizing tendencies of the Adams administration, demands closer examination, for to understand the philosophy and interests that lay at the heart of it is to understand the ideology that informed Benton's public career for the next quarter-century or more.[46]

From the perspective of the opposition, the "corruption" of Adams, the New Englander, with his support for Clay's American System and his proposals for lighthouses of the sky, stood in stark contrast to the virtuous simplicity of rural life that had been touted for over a generation by Jefferson and his followers. "The mobs of great cities," he had written, "add just so much to the support of pure government, as sores do to the strength of the human body." Adams and a majority of his supporters came from the urban Northeast, where the limited potential for agriculture had—even in colonial times—led much of the population to seek a living in commerce or manufacturing. This region therefore naturally supported the Hamiltonian economic program during the Federalist period and now embraced Clay's American System as an appropriate vision of how the nation should develop. According to the opposition, such a program created artificial inequalities of wealth, based on speculation rather than honest toil, as well as a class of commercial elites—an "aristocracy"—that sought to accrue all economic and political power to itself. Borrowing imagery from prerevolutionary Whig ideology, conservatives argued that the members of this aristocratic faction now formed a "court" around the president, corrupting the nation's government from the inside out. The Republicans of earlier times and the opposition by the mid-1820s, on the other hand, comprised a "country party," made up of men who earned their bread by the sweat of their collective brows.[47]

This, at least, was the Jeffersonian myth and the ideal. Two things must be kept in mind, however, while considering the ideology of both the Jeffersonian Republicans and the Jacksonians who were to comprise the next wave of opposition to the "mercantile," "nationalist," and "corrupt" interests represented by the Federalist Party of John Adams and the National Republicans led by his son. The first point is that movements in opposition tend to be more united than movements in power. Thus, the Republicans were a close-knit group when they were presenting the Virginia and Kentucky Resolutions in response to the Alien and Sedition Acts of 1798. The Federalists, conversely, were at that time breaking apart after ten years in power, and rival camps led respectively by John Adams and Alexander Hamilton collapsed into recrimination during the campaign of 1800. From this debacle, the Federalists never recovered.

When Jefferson assumed the presidency, the same corrosive process began to work upon the unity of his own followers. Forced to pragmatism and compromise, the Jefferson administration soon adopted any number of military, financial, and constitutional policies that alienated purists within their own ranks. Though Jefferson himself escaped the wrath of conservatives who bemoaned the distance strayed from the "principles of '98," his secretary of state and protégé, James Madison (who had, after all, been among the most prominent of the early "Federalists" advocating a stronger central government), became the new *bête noir* of the strict constructionists. When Jefferson announced his decision to leave office at the end of his second term, southern conservatives led by John Randolph allied with Pennsylvania radical Republicans to form a faction that became known as the Tertium Quids (a "third sort," neither Federalist nor nationalist Republican). They supported the nomination of James Monroe for president in 1808. Randolph and the Quids went down in defeat, unable to prevent either the election of Madison in 1808 or the success of the nationalist "War Hawks" in 1812. After peace returned, Clay, Calhoun, and John Quincy Adams all appeared in the cabinet of a President Monroe now quite sympathetic to an activist role for the national government at home and abroad. By 1820 the Old Republicans seemed no more than an echo of political battles long past.[48]

A second point to be considered in regard to the realities of Jeffersonian republicanism is the phenomenon of what John Ashworth called "the absent slave." While agrarians like Macon and Randolph embraced Jefferson's assertion that "those who labor in the earth are the chosen people of God, if ever He had a chosen people," they would have been shocked if this statement (like Jefferson's other celebrated assertion that all men are created equal) were taken literally. The fact was that the majority of those with whom Jefferson, Macon, or Randolph came into contact who actually labored in the earth were African-American slaves. No group in the early republic spent a higher proportion of their time engaged in agricultural labor, yet Ashworth asserts that "slaveholders like Jefferson, and indeed white non-slaveholders too, knew that just as the slave was excluded from the egalitarianism invoked by the opening words of Jefferson's Declaration of Independence, he was not to be classified as a noble and virtuous 'cultivator of the earth.' The slave had disappeared; no one searched for him."[49]

Certainly not Thomas Hart Benton. In his new persona as champion of the common man, Benton subscribed to views on race that would characterize southern Democrats for the remainder of the antebellum period. In all of his public pronouncements he would echo the warnings of the first Jeffersonians that the greatest danger to the American republic came from an aristocracy of wealth, namely the merchants and bankers of the eastern establishment—particularly the reconstituted Bank of the United States—who accumulated fortunes by exploiting the honest farmers of the South and the West. An elitist by inclination and association, Benton nonetheless rhetorically portrayed such inequalities of wealth as inherently dangerous to American society. He was no doubt familiar with the definition of aristocracy, put forth by Virginia's John Taylor of Caroline, as the transfer of property created by one man's labor to another man by law. This definition, however, apparently did not extend to laws expropriating the slave from the fruits of his or her own labor. Indeed, among the overwhelming majority of white males, in Missouri and elsewhere, attitudes toward race and slavery were so completely internalized by the 1820s that it was not even necessary to say so. While the Old Republicans and their younger disciples spoke of the dangers inherent in a wealthy minority, it was understood that they were not referring to the slaveholding minority.[50]

The consensus on race would, at length, allow the Jacksonians, who adopted the strict constructionist views of the Tertium Quids, to elevate the political and economic equality of white males, a conclusion Randolph would not have drawn. Debate in Congress over Henry Clay's proposal for a system of internal improvements in January 1824 nonetheless revealed the extent to which agrarian strict construction was tied to the slavery issue. "If Congress has the power to do what is proposed in this bill," Randolph had warned the House of Representatives, "they may not only enact a sedition law—for that there is precedent—but they may emancipate every slave in the United States—and with stronger color of reason than they can exercise the power now contended for." Macon had stated the conclusion privately that "if Congress can make banks, roads, and canals under the Constitution, they can free any slave in the United States." Randolph's speech, however, was the first time that the connection between loose construction and emancipation had been made on the floor of Congress and it indicated a growing fear among conservatives of the ends which an activist government might ultimately pursue.[51]

The Panama Congress Debates: Catalyst for the Opposition

The first signs of a coalition developing in opposition to the new president's policies appeared in the Senate early in 1826. Martin Van Buren and Randolph—who had been elected to the upper house the previous year—were both unhappy with Adams's most recent annual message as well as his appointments to government offices. Van Buren was further alienated by the president's friendliness toward followers of his New York rival, Governor Dewitt Clinton. Randolph considered the administration to be made up of "old Sedition Law Federalists and *soi-disant* republicans who had abjured their old principles for the 'law of circumstances.'" He read the annual message in light of the appointment of former Federalists and denounced the president's policies as "the second four years of John Adams' administration." This was unfair. The younger Adams had broken with his father's party years before and was by no means alone among Republicans who had adopted certain Hamiltonian principles in developmental policy, but Randolph was never known for the moderation of his rhetoric.[52]

The opposition surfaced when Adams accepted an invitation to the Congress of American Republics at Panama. Though not required to do so, he submitted the names of his delegates to the meeting to the Senate for approval. The documents that accompanied the nominations indicated that the authors of the Pan-American Congress desired an extension of the Monroe Doctrine into a defensive alliance with the United States at its head. To some degree this was a logical next step in the diplomacy that Adams had pursued as secretary of state. He was seeking to create a hemispheric alliance, with the United States as first among equals, to further thwart any potential European designs in the region. As the debate proceeded, however, it became clear that he had seriously misread the mood of the country and of Congress. In the Senate, Van Buren and others believed the proposed alliance both unconstitutional and at odds with the country's traditionally isolationist foreign policy. They began a campaign to hamstring Adams by proposing that the chamber's usual closed-door debate on foreign policy issues now be opened to the public. Adams, failing to perceive the potential for demagoguery in such a public debate, left it to the Senate to decide for themselves this question of "an unexampled departure from its own usages, and upon the motives of which, not being himself informed, [the president] did not feel himself competent to decide."[53]

In the end, the Senate relinquished the idea of a public debate and contented itself with publication of the record after it was over. The records reveal, however, that members of the upper house lost no opportunity to utilize popular prejudices as a vehicle for attacking the administration. The question turned wholly upon the legitimacy of the mission itself, rather than the qualifications of the delegates—Richard C. Anderson and John Sergeant—to whose fitness there was no objection. In the debate that followed, the new alliance of former Quids and Northern Radicals argued that Adams had no power to accept the invitation of the Latin American states without first asking the advice and consent of the Senate. They further warned that the United States should not send delegates to a congress that quite possibly would result in a multilateral alliance. Nathaniel Macon argued that the president's assertion in his special message that he could send delegates without the Senate's advice and consent smacked of executive prerogative and was probably based on the precedent of the Monroe Doctrine, which was itself "a strong measure and of a prerogative nature." Littleton Waller Tazewell of Virginia, who had succeeded John Taylor of Caroline in 1824, likewise viewed the president's failure to seek the advice of the Senate as an attempt to circumvent the separation of powers mandated by the Constitution.[54]

Benton addressed himself to the Senate's right to decide directly on the expedience of a *new mission* such as this one. That right, he argued, was grounded in the mission's originality and when such a *new mission* was to be instituted, creating an office and not simply the filling of a vacancy, the Senate had the authority to decide upon the expediency (or constitutionality) of the office itself. Anything else was an executive usurpation of legislative powers.[55]

Benton also spoke on the subject of relations with Haiti, and his speech on this occasion is worth recounting in some detail for what it reveals of the connections between the strict adherence to the color line upon which southern society depended and the strict construction of the Constitution that the congressional opposition insisted on. Benton held that American policy towards Haiti had been fixed for over thirty years and could neither be altered nor discussed in any foreign assembly— especially the one proposed, all the other parties to which had already placed the black and white races on a basis of political equality.

"We trade with her," said Benton, "but no diplomatic relations have been established between us." The United States received no "mulatto consuls or black ambassadors" from Haiti. Why? "Because the peace of eleven states of this Union will not permit the fruits of successful insurrection to be exhibited among them." It would not permit black consuls and ambassadors to establish themselves in American cities and to "parade through our country, and give to their fellow blacks in the United States, proof in hand of the honors that await them, for a like successful effort on their part." It would not permit the fact to be seen and told "that for the murder of their masters and mistresses, they are to find *friends* among the white people of these United States. No, this is a question which has been *determined* HERE for three and thirty years; one which has never been open for discussion, at home or abroad. . . . It is one which cannot be discussed in *this* chamber on *this* day; and shall we go to Panama to discuss it?" Were Americans, asked Benton, to go there to *advise* and *consult* in counsel on issues of racial equality? Who were to advise and sit in judgment on this question, he asked rhetorically. "Five nations who have already put the black man upon an equality with the white, not only in their consultations but in real life: five nations who have at this moment (at least some of them) black generals in their armies and mulatto senators in their congresses."[56]

Only four years removed from Denmark Vessey's failed attempt at a slave revolt in his home state, South Carolina senator Robert Y. Hayne took up where Benton had left off. The federal government, he reminded the Senate, had no power to interfere with the institution of slavery and must not enter into any discussions with other nations on the subject. Haiti fell within the bounds of this argument. "We can never acknowledge her independence," argued Hayne. "Other States will do as they please—but let us take the high ground, that these questions belong to a class which the peace and safety of the Union forbids us to discuss."[57]

John M. Berrien of Georgia became even more emotional addressing the subject: "Can the people of the South permit the intercourse which would result from establishing relations of any sort with Haiti? Is the emancipated slave, his hands still reeking with the blood of his murdered master, to be admitted into their ports, to spread the doctrine of insurrection, and to strengthen and invigorate them, by exhibiting in his own person an example of successful revolt?"[58]

Despite such animated opposition, the Senate finally approved the appointment of Anderson and Sergeant, 27–17. It was a Pyrrhic victory for the administration. After all the rancorous debate, the diplomatic mission came to naught. Anderson died en route and Sergeant arrived in Panama only after the conference had adjourned. The episode, however, was an important, if largely forgotten, step in the making of the Jacksonian coalition. Up to this point, the various factions within the opposition had mostly squabbled among themselves. The Panama debates both furnished an issue around which they could coalesce and opened the administration to their attacks, which henceforth would be unceasing.

Benton's speech against the Panama Congress was a critical turning point in the creation of master race democracy. It offered, wrote Robert Pierce Forbes, the still-hazy outline of a new narrative of American destiny. Benton transformed white Americans' contempt for persons of color from a common prejudice, enshrined in custom but conceded as unjustifiable and irrational in principle, into a foundation stone of the national edifice. As elaborated in later orations, Benton put forth the doctrine that white supremacy—later paired with geographical expansion—constituted the proper and essential basis for the American republic. In so doing, he helped to crystallize the fundamental tenets of what would become the Democratic Party.

The new narrative embodied not only in the rhetoric of Benton and southern opponents of the administration, but also of northern radicals like Van Buren, "would seek to write Africans, native Americans, and even the administration of John Quincy Adams out of history." The white republic, as it would be understood in much of the country for the next hundred years and more, was taking shape in the midst of the Panama debates.[59]

In retrospect, Benton averred that no issue of the time "excited more heat and intemperate discussion, or more feeling between a President and Senate." Its chief benefit, he recalled once the heated question had long since cooled, was "a view of the firmness with which was then maintained by a minority, the old policy of the United States, to avoid entangling alliances and interference with the affairs of other nations." By the 1850s he would also be willing to concede the value of an "exposition of the Monroe Doctrine, from one so competent to give it as Mr. Adams." By the time he wrote these words, however, his perspective on the controversies between North and South had shifted yet again.[60]

Triumph of the Jacksonians

The merging of Jackson's supporters and Old Republicans at the national level was mirrored by political events in Missouri, where several newspapers portrayed the General as something of a frontier Cincinnatus—a military hero desiring only the quiet of retirement to his Hermitage, yet willing to answer the call of his countrymen to drive Adams,

Clay, and their sycophants from power. Benton, who had hurried to place himself at the head of the Jackson parade as a result of the election of 1824, now reaped the benefits of having done so, while his rivals suffered in equal measure for having supported Adams.[61]

The first indications of a change in the landscape of state politics occurred with the unexpected death of Governor Frederick Bates in August 1825. Abraham Williams, the president *pro tempore* of the state Senate, became acting governor, but with over a year-and-a-half remaining in the term, Missouri's constitution called for a special election to fill the vacancy. In the four-way contest that followed, Benton actively supported John Miller, registrar of the land office at Franklin, who ran as a "Jackson man," while Barton sponsored Judge David Todd, who was billed as an "Adams man." The *Missouri Republican* (successor to the old *Gazette*) and the new pro-Benton *Missouri Advocate* characterized the contest between Miller and Todd as a choice between the Benton-Jackson versus the Barton-Adams factions. The *Advocate* claimed that the election was an endorsement of Jackson, a vindication of Benton's shift in allegiance, and a rebuke to Barton, Scott, and the pro-administration party. Miller's victory placed the state's political patronage in the hands of a solid Jackson-Benton man who henceforth used that resource to strengthen the Jackson party in Missouri.[62]

In the elections of 1826, John Scott paid the price of voting for John Quincy Adams, losing his seat in the House to Edward Bates. Scott had failed to anticipate the extent of popular opposition to his action once the antiadministration coalition became organized. He attempted to justify his vote, arguing that such a burden should never have been placed on members of the House and that a popular referendum would have been better; that he had wanted to vote the will of the people, but had been unable to determine it (this claim had some truth, given the Assembly's inability to agree on a candidate); that he could not have affected the outcome, since Adams already had all the states he needed; and that it was in the best interest of Missouri to be on the winning side. Scott also argued that Missouri's economic future lay in establishing ties to the prosperous Northeast, which already had more capital, manufacturing, and trade than the South. Missouri farmers, seeking to emulate their cotton-growing kinsmen in the southern states, were having none of these arguments. Bates deftly announced that he belonged to "no party." He declared himself a follower of Jefferson who had supported Adams while differing from the president on certain issues. Without a candidate of their own, Jackson men voted for Bates in order to punish Scott.

In 1826 Benton was up for reelection as U.S. senator. His supporters sought to get candidates to the General Assembly to pledge themselves in advance to vote for Benton, claiming that such a litmus test was the "right of instruction"—the *demos krateo* principle in practice. Candidates willing to take such a pledge appeared in most of the state's thirty counties, an indication of Benton's broad base of popular support. In the August elections, a number of Benton-pledged candidates were elected to the Assembly.[63]

The Barton-Adams group, however, was determined to put up a fight in the legislature, supplemented by wide-ranging attacks on Benton in the press. A series of essays entitled "Torchlight" and authored by an opponent who went by the pen name CURTIUS were printed in the *Republican* during the summer. Initially CURTIUS concerned himself with Benton's opposition to Adams, which the writer viewed as a plot to undermine the president's plan for protection of domestic manufactures and the construction of internal improvements. The author concluded that Benton had become the captive of John Randolph, the "present supreme dictator of the anti-American System forces." As for Benton's shift to supporting Jackson in 1824, CURTIUS submitted that Benton had "never wavered [in his hatred of Jackson] . . . until after the electors were chosen, and the result of the presidential election, so far as it depended on them, was known—when suddenly the hostile chiefs became reconciled." The fact of Benton and Jackson's personal reconciliation over a year earlier was either not known to CURTIUS or ignored, but Barton's personal life, especially his fondness for alcohol, having been an issue two years earlier, Benton's own character was now considered fair game by his opponents.[64]

Benton's record during his first term in Congress also became the target of criticism: "Mr. Clay is the advocate of internal improvement, and Col. Benton voted against the bill for repairing the great Western avenue, the Cumberland road. . . . Mr. Clay is friendly to the protection of domestic manufactures; Mr. Benton has announced his intention of voting for a reduction of the Tariff, now but a short time in operation, and passed by the aid of his vote." Even the manner of Benton's travel to and from Washington became controversial. The allowance for travel of members, asserted CURTIUS, was for the most usual route; Benton and some other members took this to mean "crooked navigable river," charging the public for fifteen hundred, rather than eight hundred miles. The CURTIUS essays—eight in all—were later collected and reprinted in pamphlet form for distribution among the voters.[65]

Benton responded by distributing his own pamphlet reproducing his speech on public lands, an issue that even Judge Lucas had to concede "excited the liveliest interest among farmers" and "produced a considerable effect in Benton's favor." Adams himself concluded that "Benton has made himself amazingly popular by the resolution he offered for graduating and reducing the price of lands.... I have no doubt that he will be reelected."[66]

Though Benton himself warned an ally that among the legislators "every engine of intrigue will be put in motion, and every lie told that can make a *personal* or political enemy," by October he was confident of the outcome. The General Assembly met in late November 1826 at the new state capital in Jefferson City. William Carr Lane, an ally of Benton's, noted that the senator's political friends were campaigning up to the minute of voting, despite assurance over the outcome. "He will be elected—The voice of the people demands it—Who dares disobey?" On December 26, 1826, the General Assembly, meeting in joint session, nominated candidates for U.S. senator from Missouri. Only two names were presented, Thomas H. Benton and one Joseph C. Brown. Benton received 40 votes to Brown's 13. He was now the unquestioned leader of the pro-Jackson Democracy in Missouri. He enjoyed far greater support than he had in 1820, particularly in the outstate areas where his land policies seized the imagination of small farmers and slaveholders, but also in St. Louis with his promotion of far-western commerce. Opposition to Benton's reelection was centered in Ste. Genevieve, St. Francis, and Madison counties where Scott still retained influence.[67]

Both parties within the state now looked forward to the presidential election of 1828. The increased prestige of Jackson's name, as well as the development of something like a modern party organization in Missouri, led two candidates to enter the race for Congress as Jacksonians that year—William Carr Lane of St. Louis and Spencer Pettis of Cole County. The latter had the political support of central Missouri slaveholders from Howard County—a region already shaping up as a powerful force in state politics. Confronted with the possibility that a split in the Jackson vote would lead to the reelection of Edward Bates, who was now clearly identified with the Adams administration, party leaders turned to Benton.

Much was later made of Benton's "dictatorial" powers in state politics, and some historians have described Missouri as his political "fiefdom." These assertions notwithstanding, the 1828 elections were the only opportunity Benton would have to play such a role as the unchallenged leader of Jackson forces in the state. Declaring that "in obedience to the only legitimate principle of action in a republican government—that the will of the majority ought to prevail," he concluded that Spencer Pettis commanded the greater popular support. Lane withdrew from the race and later became a Whig. His supporters charged, through the *Republican*, that Benton had behaved as a dictator by choosing his party's nominee—for "what else is this caucusing umpirage of Benton but *dictation* to the Jackson party." They also charged that Benton had picked Pettis because the latter would not withdraw from the race, and that Benton's first priority was to avoid a split in the Jackson party. This was true enough, but it was consistent with Benton's *demos krateo* philosophy, which also provided the rationale for shifting his support to Jackson after the 1824 election. Further, the demand of the Boone's Lick region for national representation, and the need to relieve suspicions that Missouri politics were controlled from St. Louis, were equally important factors in awarding the nomination to Pettis. Over the course of the next twenty years and more, the slave-heavy counties bordering the Missouri River in the center of the state would become increasingly crucial to the destiny of Benton and the Democracy within Missouri.[68]

The Jacksonians worked hard to secure the election of Pettis, utilizing their now well-organized machinery at the county level to bring out the vote for their man. Bates sought unsuccessfully to distance himself from the unpopular Adams administration, but the Jackson press naturally linked him to the incumbent president in the contest against Pettis, who won over 60 percent of the votes in the August elections, which also filled the General Assembly with Benton-Jackson men. John Miller ran unopposed for reelection as governor, giving the Jacksonians an almost unchallenged supremacy in state politics that promised to be crowned by the election of their candidate as president.[69]

The 1828 presidential campaign essentially replayed the issues and alignments that had defined the state elections during the summer. The supporters of Jackson and Adams in Missouri were represented by Benton and Barton respectively. Operating as nascent political parties, both factions had grassroots organizations at the county level and both held state meetings to nominate their presidential tickets and slates of electors. Handbills, newspapers, and networks of personal relationships were utilized to drum up the vote. Mass meetings were also organized, often on county court or militia muster days when large crowds were present. Local rallies endorsed candidates for local and state offices and sent representatives to county or district assemblies. A state meeting nominated party candidates for president and vice president, chose a slate of electors, and formed a state committee to direct the campaign. In many election districts, executive committees were formed and "Committees of Correspondence" appeared in key counties. The organization was incomplete, but it reflected developments elsewhere in the nation and pointed to the elaborate party machinery that would come into being by the late nineteenth century. The Jackson forces met first, convening in Jefferson City on January 8, 1828, the anniversary of the Battle of New Orleans. In addition to choosing candidates and electors, the convention organized a state committee as well as district and county committees to plan and conduct the campaign. The Adams party followed suit in a meeting, also at Jefferson City, on March 3. Throughout the fall, both parties campaigned intensely for votes. Benton spoke on behalf of Jackson at meeting after meeting throughout Missouri. His introduction of bills on behalf of cheaper land and direct election of the president were enormously popular with rural voters, and Barton was forced to defend his opposition to both. The issue of Henry Clay's American System was more ambiguous. While the Franklin *Missouri Intellgencer* stated that Jackson was opposed to Clay's vision and that the campaign was a contest between supporters and opponents of the American System, no such clear distinctions existed. Jacksonians did not openly oppose the American System; they took their candidate's line in favor of a "judicious" tariff and avoided direct attacks on either internal improvements, which remained popular with westerners, or on the Bank of the United States, which was not. While a majority of Missourians claimed to be Jackson men after 1828, it would be some time before it became clear what party identification meant in terms of many important national issues. Jacksonian Democracy meant different things in different places. The states' rights/strict construction appeals of Jackson men in Virginia and the Carolinas, in which well-heeled latter-day Quids fought a long rearguard action against demands for greater representation on the part of poorer up-country whites, was quite different from the yawping white egalitarianism that characterized Missouri by the late 1820s.[70]

Perhaps equally important, the popular backlash against the outcome of the 1824 election had led all of the states except Delaware and South Carolina to place the choice of presidential electors directly in the hands of the voters. Despite Jackson's avoidance of particulars on the issues of the day, the coalition supporting the General scored a resounding victory on election day with the broadened electorate, winning 647,276 votes nationally to 508,064 for Adams. New England remained loyal to the incumbent president, but Jackson carried the South and the West as well as picking up ground in the Mid-Atlantic states. In Missouri 8,372 votes went to Jackson and 3,407 to Adams, adding the state's three electoral votes to Jackson's total of 178, versus 83 for Adams.

Even if the candidates and their surrogates spoke primarily in terms of personalities, the men who elected Jackson believed they understood the issues at stake. Benton would later submit that the election continued the process of party realignment along the lines of *oligarchy* versus *democracy* that had begun in 1824. Benton now undeniably counted himself among the western radicals who identified with the latter concept. In the still mostly agrarian United States of the 1820s, equality of opportunity primarily meant access to land. Land claims had been central to Benton's success as a lawyer during his early years in St. Louis and his graduation/donation plan had made him a hero to western farmers. Now Benton's agrarian vision would be joined to Jackson's record as an Indian fighter and champion of white equality. Jackson had fought the Creeks and the Seminoles to make the southern frontier safe for slaveholding whites, and now his elevation to the presidency promised to continue the process of dispossessing troublesome red men of their lands so that black men could be effectively exploited. Both a fulfillment of the republican vision of Jefferson and a reaction against its more aristocratic aspects, the master race democracy of the Jacksonians reached political maturity with the election of 1828. In the decade that followed, Benton would be foremost among congressional leaders representing the demands of country democrats who drew upon traditions dating back to the Regulators of colonial times. Stressing cheap land, hard money, and removal of the Indian tribes, Benton sought to give legislative form to the new, more egalitarian, white nation.

4 / "The Land Belongs to the People": Public Lands, States' Rights, and the "Indian Problem"

The Twenty-first Congress, the first of Andrew Jackson's presidency, assembled in December 1829. Over the next six months, two of the major issues that would define Jackson's administration—nullification and Indian removal—were heatedly debated by the U.S. Senate. Both controversies, in one way or another, touched on the relationship of the states to the federal government. Both also dealt with an area that Benton by now had made his particular legislative specialty—the availability of public lands in the West.

Perhaps no issue of the period possessed greater import than the question of administering and distributing the public lands. As a growing American population expanded westward, Congress had to deal not only with the survey and sale of acreage in the public domain but also with the competition for capital and population between the established communities of the East and the newer regions such as Missouri. At one level the debate over the price and availability of public lands was about competing visions of America's future. Would the nation develop along the lines of Jefferson's rural Arcadia with land as the true measure of wealth and the vehicle of a rough equality between white men? Or would an alternate vision—one that emphasized development of a national market economy and a more controlled distribution of the public domain—prevail? While issues of western development were complex, and the ideological lines were never as clearly drawn as they might seem in retrospect, by the late 1820s agrarian democracy based on cheap land was associated in the minds of voters with Benton and other western Jacksonians, while higher land prices and greater emphasis on commerce, manufacturing, and urban development were identified with the proponents of Henry Clay's American System. Here, indeed, were two competing concepts of American nationalism.

At another level the problem posed by the administration of public lands also meant addressing the question as to whether the Indian population had any territorial claims that whites were bound to respect. For westerners like Benton the answer was an unqualified "no." In 1812 he had enthusiastically supported a war that, in the Southwest, was largely about pacifying the hostile tribes who stood in the way of white expansion into Georgia, Alabama, and beyond. Jackson's campaign of 1813–1814 had broken the power of the Creeks and forced them to cede millions of acres to the federal government. His 1818 war against the Seminoles had brought Florida into the national domain. By 1824 Benton had put personal differences with Jackson aside to follow his old chief in a political campaign that explicitly promised to allow the southern and western states to deal with their Indian populations as they saw fit, without the interference of the federal government.

Many years after the last of the Five Civilized Tribes had been removed from their homelands and presumably after plenty of time for sober reflection, Benton would write that during the 1820s "much remained to be done to free the southern and western states from a useless and dangerous population—to give them the use and jurisdiction of all the territory within their limits." There were treaties to be were ratified and the foundation to be laid for the future removal of the Indians, followed by subsequent treaties and acts of Congress "until the southern and western states were as free as the northern from the encumbrance of an Indian population." Even at the end of his political career, when he had come to view the demands of southern "nullifiers" as singularly dangerous to the Union, Benton could not help but reflexively slip back into a bit of old-fashioned talk about states' rights when discussing the Indian problem.[1]

One might argue that Benton was simply a man of his time, sharing the racial attitudes of the majority of nineteenth-century white Americans. Such arguments have been made on behalf of Andrew Jackson. Some scholars of this unhappy aspect of our history have pointed out that, since the Indians were unwilling to submit to the laws of Georgia and other southeastern states, and since these sovereign states would not tolerate the existence of separate "dependent nations" within their borders, removal or extermination were the only alternatives and that Congress and the president chose the more humane of the two.²

In reality there was no practical reason, save the greed and hostility of southern whites, that the tribes, having gone to great lengths to adopt white culture and white methods of farming, education, and political structures, could not have remained "domestic dependent nations" within the United States. During the 1830 congressional debates over the Indian Removal Act, a number of Jackson's northeastern opponents would make just that point and only narrowly fail to carry the day. The defense of Indian rights by lawmakers such as New Jersey's Theodore Frelinghuysen was motivated, at least in part, by a sincere desire to see that justice be done to the tribes by the U.S. government. In the view of Benton and other legislators from the South and the West, however, opposition to Jacksonian Indian policy could not be separated from what they saw as the northeasterners' desire to stunt the development of their regions by limiting the availability of land to white settlers. In this light, Samuel Foot's December 1829 proposal for a moratorium on the sale of public lands and Frelinghuysen's defense of the Cherokees shortly thereafter were simply two fronts in the same war—a continuation of the sectional fight that had begun ten years earlier with the debate over Missouri statehood. The battles were to continue into the 1830s, with Henry Clay and his allies opposing the ready availability of land for "the people" whom Benton claimed to represent, and Chief Justice John Marshall joining the contest in defense of the Cherokees. In most of the later episodes of this debate, as in earlier ones, the Missourian took the side of those who argued in favor of states' rights where both land and Indian policies were concerned. On this point he was in harmony with President Jackson and the majority of his party. Like the president, however, he would stop short of condoning the right of a state—namely South Carolina—to nullify laws passed by Congress. The rights of red men and rulings by the Supreme Court were one thing. The president and the United States Congress, embodying the will of the majority, were quite another.³

Early Controversies

The question of who held legitimate claim to western lands went back to the first colonists who came into contact with America's indigenous peoples. In Benton's case, speculation in western lands and the coincidental dispossession of those lands from Native Americans were part of his birthright. The senator's father, Jesse Benton Sr., had been an original partner in the Transylvania Company founded by Richard ("Carolina Dick") Henderson and Thomas Hart. In March 1775 Daniel Boone, an employee of the Transylvania Company who had begun leading white settlers through the Cumberland Gap two years earlier, arranged a meeting between the proprietors and Cherokee leaders at Sycamore Shoals on the Watauga River. Communicating through interpreters, the chiefs signed an agreement ceding a vast area that included the entire Cumberland River valley west of the Cumberland Gap in what later became Tennessee and about two-thirds of modern-day Kentucky (some 27,000 square miles), in return for six wagonloads of merchandise described by one observer as "cheap goods, such as coarse wooden trinkets, some firearms, and spirituous liquors." The removal of the Cherokee from their Trans-Appalachian homelands, a process that the father played a role in initiating, was one that the son would play a substantial role in bringing to completion.[4]

Despite Jesse Benton's ambitious land deals, when his family moved west in 1801 his widow, Nancy, found that she could only prove only a small fraction of his original share. This experience reinforced young Thomas Benton's awareness of the transient nature of frontier land claims unfounded in written law. During his single term in the Tennessee legislature in 1809, Thomas Benton was a member of the committee on lands. At this early juncture in his political career, Benton voted in favor of preemption rights for established settlers in eastern Tennessee who lacked legal title to their own property. He also submitted a number of pleas from members of his own district seeking recognition for their claims. Perhaps mindful of the loss of a fortune in land values as the result of his father's inadequate land titles, Benton further proposed (and the state Senate passed) a bill to assure settlers the chance to hold land they had built on and improved. If someone else claimed to have stronger legal claim to the same property, the "squatters" might then acquire another, equal plot from the state. In Tennessee, at the turn of the nineteenth century, no aspiring politician could expect popular support without at least paying lip service to the Jeffersonian dream of creating an agrarian Arcadia. While the leaders of the Republican faction, like their Federalist counterparts, tended to be gentlemen of some means, usually including land and—in the South—slaves, they supported the ideal of equality of opportunity and equality before the law for white males.[5]

When he settled in the Missouri Territory following the War of 1812, Benton became involved in the tangled factional disputes surrounding the Spanish land claims. It is worth recalling that the clash of two ambitious attorneys that ended in the death of Charles Lucas was exacerbated and egged on by economic and political rivalries. One of the distinguishing features of the "junto" faction with which Benton identified himself was the relative value that Charles Gratiot, the Chouteau family, and Governor William Clark placed on peaceful relations with the Indians. This position, a legacy of Missouri's inclusive/expeditionary frontier stage, became increasingly unpopular during the postwar years. Indeed, many white Missourians viewed Clark's policies, which dated from the period when he had served as commissioner of Indian affairs, as too soft or tolerant of natives who had been attacking settlers as recently as 1815. The use of government-funded presents—a standard procedure—to negotiate a peace treaty with the Indians at Portage des Sioux in July 1815 was strongly resented by a majority of whites. "It is the Opinion of the People here," wrote a St. Louis merchant, "that we shall not have peace with the Indians until we drub them soundly into it."[6]

Clark's close association with the government's Indian policies, as well as his overt support for junto candidate John Scott in the 1817–1818 elections for territorial delegate, damaged his image in the minds of Anglo-American settlers, who poured into Missouri after the war. By 1820 the expeditionary phase of the Missouri frontier, with its lax slave code and dependence on a peaceful commerce with Indians, was coming to an end. In that year's gubernatorial election, the territory witnessed one of the first political manifestations of the new Anglo-American sedentary frontier, exclusively for white settlers and their slave-labor force, already apparent in its population patterns. Clark, the gentlemanly soldier/explorer, lost to Alexander McNair, an anti-junto leader whose administration of the land office in St. Louis from 1818 to 1820 had turned established speculators against him while gaining him the support of newly arrived settlers.[7]

After his election as U.S. senator, Benton was astute enough to take the lesson of Clark's defeat to heart. While he introduced legislation during this first term to secure recognition of the Spanish claims, as early as 1824 he was seeking to disassociate himself from his old St. Louis allies. Benton began trying to broaden his popular base of support by advocating cheap or free lands for the growing white population of his state and removal of the remaining Indians. On the new frontier of the Jacksonian era, there was no place for the Indian. The foremost question now became how to distribute the land from which the tribes had been removed.

The Public Domain to 1820

The concept of a federal public domain originated as a condition for ratifying the Articles of Confederation during the revolutionary period. Several of the newly independent states had claimed large areas west of the Appalachians under their colonial charters. States holding no land claims in the West demanded the surrender of such claims, and in 1781 an agreement was reached under which the claimant states were to cede the lands to the new national government. The creation of the public domain carried with it the seeds of an ongoing dispute between the states and the central government over how the lands should be used or distributed. This controversy over the role of public lands has, in fact, continued in various forms down to the present day. The land ceded by Virginia and the other states among the original thirteen was considered "a common fund for the use and benefit of... the United States." The parties to these agreements understood at the time that Congress would use revenue from the sale of the lands to pay off the public debt—a vital concern during the 1780s. As a consequence, in May 1785 Congress passed a Land Ordinance that provided for the survey and sale of the public domain. Public lands were to be retained by the national government until they could be sold. Within the original thirteen states, however, there was no public domain. Such lands as they possessed were disposed of by the states as they saw fit. And while the Northwest Ordinance of 1787 guaranteed that the new states entering the Union would do so on the same basis as the original thirteen, there was a significant difference in the fact that the new, western states encompassed large tracts of land not their own but still possessed and administered by the Congress. This anomaly seemed, to many, to deny the very sovereignty that the states claimed as their birthright and that they were guaranteed by the Articles of Confederation, by the Northwest Ordinance, and by the Constitution of 1787.[8]

Sales under the national land system began in 1800, and during the first decade of the nineteenth century the system put in place by Congress appeared to work well enough. Settlers buying land on credit did experience widespread difficulty making the minimum installments on their payments. Nonetheless, payments were forthcoming—if often late. The conclusion of the War of 1812 and the elimination of the Indians as a danger to white settlement, however, changed the circumstances of public land sales dramatically. Millions of acres of western lands were suddenly available for development. Glowing reports from recent arrivals like Benton and steadily rising prices for crops encouraged immigrants to move westward. Four new states—Indiana, Illinois, Alabama, and Mississippi—were able to join the Union in the four years from 1816 to 1820 as a result of dramatic population increases. While editors and boosters in the new states, such as Benton, dreamed of an empire spanning the continent and westerners began to make their growing power felt in Congress, still more settlers arrived, seeking after the choicest lands.

The Treasury Department's General Land Office was unable to keep pace with this "Great Migration." Despite the legal prohibition against trespassing on public lands, as government surveyors and land officers fell behind the pace of settlement, squatters cleared the forests and built their cabins where they pleased. Executive decrees against this practice proved unenforceable, and Congress at length authorized squatters to remain so long as they secured permission from local land offices. Few bothered to do so. Adding to the instability of the land market was the fact that, by 1819, an increasing proportion of the acreage was being purchased by men who intended to resell it for a profit rather than to settle and farm it themselves. The boom in speculation was fueled by easy credit from local banks that kept little specie on reserve. During these years nearly every prominent westerner, including Andrew Jackson, played the game of land speculation. In Missouri, Benton vented his frustrations at not having the capital to speculate on the scale his father had. "If I had brought with me twenty or thirty thousand dollars," he wrote in May of 1818, "I would have been worth today from a quarter to half a million." When he arrived in 1815, "people ... would not believe it possible that ground about St. Louis, then selling for thirty dollars an acre, should sell at this day [two years later] for two thousand." But Benton had enough experience with land values to know how quickly they could appreciate and he "daily saw splendid fortunes passing in review before me, and falling into the hands of those who look ahead."[9]

By the fall of 1820, however, land purchases had ground to a halt. The Second Bank of the United States (or B.U.S.), whose open-handed policies had done much to create the speculative bubble, began calling in loans during the summer of 1818 to shore up its dangerously overextended credit. The B.U.S. now demanded specie payments from state banks that were themselves overextended and unable to collect from their debtors. The result was the most severe economic collapse the young republic had yet seen. Property values dropped as prices plummeted. In the year before the Panic, buyers had purchased some four million acres of public land at an average price of $3.37 per acre. Purchasers who had assumed that land prices would go up indefinitely now owed the federal government a total of 22 million dollars.[10]

The effects of the depression were not immediately felt in Missouri, but in other quarters there was real concern that the enormous land debt threatened to undermine the Union itself. Since the Jefferson administration, fiscal conservatives like Treasury Secretary Albert Gallatin had advocated replacing the credit system with a system of public land sales based exclusively on cash purchases. Westerners regarded the credit system as essential to attracting new settlers, and many in the western states suspected that the push for cash sales was a scheme on the part of the eastern states to strangle population growth in the West. The Missouri *Gazette* opined, in April 1819, that abolition of land office credit was "a measure calculated to vitally stab the future growth of this country." Occurring as it did, almost simultaneously with the controversy over the admission of Missouri as a slave state (an issue that resonated not only with proslavery southerners but with westerners as a matter of self-determination), the debate concerning the credit system of land sales also reflected growing sectional rivalries.[11]

Legislation passed by Congress during 1820 and 1821 allowed settlers to keep the portion of their land that was already paid for. If settlers wished to keep all their lands, they might receive extended credit for up to ten years, with substantial discounts for immediate payment in cash. Henceforth, all land sales were to be conducted in cash with the minimum price reduced from $2.00 an acre to $1.25 and the minimum amount that could be purchased reduced from 160 acres to 80. Under these terms, the debt for public lands was halved in two years. A farm could now be bought for a hundred dollars and the social tensions inherent in the controversy over land policy were deferred for the moment.[12]

Federal Indian Policy to 1829—Benton's Views

Land tenure had never been so democratic, but neither had the hunger for new land ever been so voracious. The eyes of white settlers and speculators quite naturally turned to areas occupied by Native Americans. Here the controversy over Federal land policy would assume a different form. "From the earliest periods of colonial settlement," wrote Benton, "it had been the policy of the government, by successive purchases of this territory, to remove these tribes further and further to the west." Since the War of 1812, which had been disastrous for the tribes east of the Mississippi, this policy had accomplished much toward freeing the states of the Southwest "from this population, which so greatly hindered the expansion of their settlements and so much checked the increase of their growth and strength." Still, as the administration of James Monroe drew to a close, large portions of many of the states and territories remained in the hands of the Indian tribes. "Justice to the other states and territories required the same relief." Applications were incessantly and urgently made to the Federal government, which had jurisdiction over the purchase of Indian lands by the states. "It was evident that the encumbered states and territories would not, and certainly ought not to be satisfied, until all their soil was open to settlement and subject to their jurisdiction."[13]

Benton enthusiastically shared the views of his former commanding general, Andrew Jackson, concerning the claims of Indians to lands desired by whites. Having defeated the Creeks and forced them to cede millions of acres in the state of Georgia and the Alabama territory, Jackson spent the years following the War of 1812 pursuing the Seminoles into Florida (which was subsequently purchased from Spain) and extinguishing titles held by the Cherokees to other lands in the Southwest. Jackson had concluded that the pressure of white immigration into the region would eventually force the Indians to either become assimilated into the white population—to "become industrious citizens" and accept the authority of the states in which they resided—or, if they preferred to retain "their ancient customs and habits," to remove to a country where they might do so. By implication, this referred to the "permanent Indian frontiers" west of the Mississippi. Assimilation or removal were the only options as far as Jackson was concerned. The possibility of the Indians retaining their distinctive ethnic identity and cultural traditions within their own territorial boundaries was not a choice he was prepared to consider. Jackson told John Coffee around this time (1817) that removal of the Indians was "the only means we have in preserving them as nation, and of protecting them."[14]

In his memoirs, Benton echoed the Old Hero's views on the matter, stating that "To the Indians themselves it was equally essential to be removed." They had dwindled under contact with the white race and the pressure of white expansion was fatal to them. The natives "degenerated, become depraved, and whole tribes extinct, or reduced to a few individuals, wherever they attempted to remain in the old States; and [they] could look for no other fate in the new ones."[15]

This assertion is disingenuous for a number of reasons. While Benton rightly traces the idea of removal to Jefferson's presidency, he conveniently ignores a long history of federal policy granting the tribes status that Chief Justice Marshall would later describe as that of "domestic dependent nations," with rights to the lands they had not yet ceded to whites. This policy had existed for decades in harmony with the concept of "Indian reform." Leaders of the early republic, educated in the values of the Enlightenment, viewed Native Americans not as inherently savage, but as capable of learning to become "civilized"—that is, to convert to Christianity and to adopt a sedentary agricultural lifestyle. To this end, missionaries representing groups like the Quakers and the Moravian Brethren had gone to live and work among the various tribes since before the Revolution. The Quakers set up demonstration farms to teach the men proper methods of agriculture and husbandry, established saw mills and iron forges, and taught native women to spin and sew. During the 1790s evangelical Protestants flooded Congress with petitions calling for the establishment of more mission schools among the Indians, as well as the restriction or elimination of the whiskey trade that was so detrimental to Indian communities. The federal factory system, established by Congress during that decade and administered by the federal superintendent of Indian trade, for years carried on substantial commerce with the Indians without resort to liquor. As we have seen, Benton was instrumental in promoting the 1822 law that abolished the factory system in favor of fur company agents who had no scruples about using whiskey in their bargaining with the Indians.[16]

The presidency of Thomas Jefferson represented a crossroads in federal policy toward the Indians. Having observed the Federalist program for "civilizing" the Indians during the 1790s, he publicly held out the possibility that the Indians might eventually adopt white farming methods and become assimilated as citizens of the United States. But privately, he was more skeptical about the chances for peaceful assimilation of the Indians. Even before the Louisiana Purchase was a reality, Jefferson was contemplating removal of the eastern tribes beyond the Mississippi. As part of the constitutional amendment, he sought to pacify critics of the Purchase, Jefferson proposed closing Upper Louisiana (including the future states of Missouri and Arkansas) to further white settlement. To enforce the restriction, Congress could not have sold any of the lands in this territory to white settlers until authorized to do so by a new constitutional amendment. The object of this proposal was to ensure a peaceful and orderly process of settlement in which Indians living east of the Mississippi exchanged their lands for tracts in the part of the Louisiana Territory closed to whites. In Jefferson's thinking, relocation of the Indians to the Trans-Mississippi provided an opportunity for whites to fill up the eastern side rather than disperse into the newly acquired territory. Only after those parts of the United States already open to settlement had been occupied fully would it be necessary to allow expansion into Louisiana. Jefferson considered his plan much more practical and efficient than the uncontrolled land rush he feared would occur without its implementation. Nothing came of Jefferson's proposed constitutional amendment and under his successor, James Madison, the focus of the government's Indian policy became pacification through military means—the "drubbing" favored by settlers in Missouri and other frontier regions—rather than peaceful removal.[17]

"It was reserved for Mr. Monroe's administration," wrote Benton, "to take up the subject in its full sense." At the time of Benton's election to the U.S. Senate, Indian policy was the nominal responsibility of Secretary of War John C. Calhoun. With traditional government goals of "Indian reform" in mind, Calhoun initially pursued the goal of "civilizing" the remaining eastern tribes, looking toward the day when tribal lands would be distributed among individual Indian farmers as private property. Nonetheless, despite the progress of missionaries in constructing schools and transforming the former warrior/hunters of the Cherokee and other tribes into independent farmers, Calhoun at length concluded that such reformist measures could not succeed before the degradation resulting from contact with white civilization did its ultimate damage. With pressure increasing among whites on the southwestern frontier for the federal government to solve the Indian "problem," Calhoun reluctantly concluded that removal was the only humanitarian option. Following Jackson's lead, he became an advocate for negotiation of extensive land cessions in the area from western Georgia to the Mississippi and for transportation of those Native Americans who would not give up their "hunting" way of life west of the great river. By 1824 President Monroe's message to Congress called for the eventual removal of all Indians beyond the Mississippi.[18]

Thus, in Benton's view, "a great act of justice was rendered to the South"—the removal of all the tribes to the west side of the Mississippi, "to the wide and wild expanse of Louisiana," country thought to be so unfit for white settlement that it was labeled on maps as "the great American Desert." Calhoun and like-minded proponents of assimilation viewed removal as necessary to buy time for the processes of education and civilization to take effect among the tribes, far from the interference of white settlers. Benton was much more clear-eyed in his assessment.

As for the Indians, he would write, "their preservation and civilization, and permanency in their new possessions were to be their advantages in this removal—*delusive it might be, but still a respite from impending destruction if they remained where they were.*" Benton, even in later years, proudly claimed ownership of his role in these proceedings "of incalculable value to the southern and western states" who were thereby to be freed "from the encumbrance of an Indian population." As a member of the crucial Committee on Indian Affairs, he "was an actor in these transactions, who reported the bills and advocated the treaties which brought this great benefit to the south and the west." Incapable of regarding Indians as anything other than savages impeding the advance of white settlement, Benton had little esteem for the educational and other benevolent activities of groups sponsored by the American Board of Commissioners for Foreign Missions. He wrote, "Some societies, and some individuals, no doubt, with very humane motives, but with folly, and blindness, and injury to the objects of their care which generally attend a gratuitous interference with the affairs of others, attempted to raise an outcry, and made themselves busy to frustrate the plan but to no avail."[19]

Calhoun had managed to give a paternalist gloss to the Indian policies of the Monroe administration. By the time John Quincy Adams assumed office, however, such pretensions were breaking down in the face of a hunger for land among southern whites who defied even the authority of the Federal government. In 1802 Georgia had surrendered its claims on territories in the Southwest in return for the promise of the national government to extinguish the remaining Indian claims within the state as soon as possible. Having already been cheated or coerced into surrendering large tracts, the Creek Indians by the 1820s refused to make any further cessions. The outgoing Monroe administration was unwilling to force the issue, but the dynamics of Georgia politics shortly played a role in the matter. Governor George M. Troup, representative of the state's planter-gentry, faced formidable opposition in his bid for reelection from a candidate who embodied yeoman opposition to banks and the "monied power," and who supported debtor relief and Jackson for president in 1824. Troup was able to win the election by pressing for aggressive expropriation of remaining Indian lands. Upon returning to office he negotiated a treaty securing title to the remaining Creek lands in Georgia with a faction led by William McIntosh, a mixed-blood Creek chieftain who was, as it turned out, Troup's cousin. Although McIntosh and the collaborationist chiefs were shortly killed by order of the tribal council for this unauthorized sale, the governor proceeded to order the survey of Creek lands and submitted the questionable Treaty of Indian Springs to President Adams for submission to Congress. The Treaty was ratified in the Senate by a vote of 34 to 4.[20]

Before the end of his first year in office, Adams became aware of the circumstances under which the Creek cession had been made. He refused to authorize the survey of Creek lands; directed federal troops under General Edmund Gaines to prevent it, by force if necessary; and called for renegotiation of the treaty. The leaders of the Creeks assembled in Washington early in 1826 and concluded a new treaty with the United States by which the earlier Treaty of Indian Springs was annulled and all Creek lands in Georgia—though none in Alabama—were ceded. Adams sent this treaty to the Senate, where it was referred to Benton's Committee on Indian Affairs. The committee reported against ratification of the new treaty on grounds that it annulled and thereby implied the illegality of the Treaty of Indian Springs (apparently justifying the fate of McIntosh and his supporters); because it did not cede the whole of the Creek lands in Georgia; and because it ceded none in Alabama. Benton's committee recommended further negotiations, which were commenced under the auspices of President Adams, and on March 31, 1826, a supplemental article was concluded whereby all the Creek lands in Georgia were ceded and the Creeks within the borders of the state were required to emigrate beyond the Mississippi.[21]

Senate approval, which quickly followed, was made all the more urgent by a growing confrontation between the federal government and the state of Georgia. Although the new treaty delayed the cession until January 1, 1827, Governor Troup ordered his surveyors into the disputed area on September 1, 1826, the effective date of the McIntosh Treaty. When Secretary of War James Barbour informed Troup that the president would "employ, if necessary, all the means under his control" to enforce the terms of the Washington treaty, the governor unfurled the banner of state sovereignty. Georgia, he announced, would resist "any military attack which the Government of the United States . . . think proper to make on the territory, the People, or the sovereignty of Georgia. . . . From the first decisive act of hostility, you will be considered and treated as a public enemy . . . and, what is more, the unblushing allies of the savages, whose cause you have adopted." Troup then ordered the militia into readiness "to repel any hostile invasion of the territory of this state."[22]

Seeking to calm these troubled waters, the report from Benton's committee concluded that there was no evidence of Georgia's determination "to resist the civil authority of the United States" and rejected "any measure in anticipation of an issue which they... [did] not apprehend." Faced with such bold defiance, the administration backed down. In earlier cabinet deliberations regarding the refusal of the Creeks to negotiate cession, Secretary of War Barbour idealistically proposed that, rather than retaining tribal sovereignty which required continual treaty negotiations with the U.S. government, Native Americans should be incorporated within the states of the Union and placed under the same laws that governed white citizens. When President Adams asked whether a change so essential in the character of the government's relations with the Indians wouldn't raise questions over the constitutional powers of the national government, Barbour conceded that it would, but "it will soon be unavoidably necessary to come to such a system." Secretary of State Clay now weighed in. Far from taking Barbour's view, he submitted that the goal of civilizing the Indians was impossible, and that there was never a full-blooded Indian who took to civilization. It was not in their nature. "He believed," wrote Adams, "they were a race determined to extinction, and, although he would never use or countenance inhumanity towards them, he did not think them, as a race, worth preserving... as [they were] essentially inferior to the Anglo-Saxon race, which were rapidly taking their place on this continent." Clay asserted that the Indians "were not an improvable breed, and that their disappearance from the human family will be no great loss to the world." Barbour was shocked at these opinions, but, faced with Georgia's defiance of the federal government, the president concurred. He wrote that he feared Clay's opinions had "too much foundation."[23]

Thus, with northern support and the acquiescence of the administration, the Senate voted, in Benton's words, "to do this great act of justice to Georgia... and thus was carried into effect, after a delay of a quarter century, and after great and just complaint on the part of Georgia, the compact between that State and the United States of 1802. Georgia was paid at last for her great union of territory, and obtained the removal of an Indian community out of her limits, and the use and dominion of all of her soil for settlement and jurisdiction." Though he was careful to acknowledge northern support for a treaty that acted exclusively to the benefit of a slave state, Benton did not blush, either at the time or in the 1850s when writing his account, at this early instance of the threat of armed force to nullify a federal policy.[24]

During the presidential campaign of 1828, there was a clear distinction between the candidates on the issue of land and Indian removal. Adams, his program of internal improvements and economic nationalism in ruins, had managed to alienate southerners and westerners by his opposition to Benton and others who advocated cheap land for settlers. Benton, now firmly in the Jackson camp, advised the candidate to maintain a lofty silence on controversial issues, and avoid "particular confession" on internal improvements and the tariff. Jackson followed the script, issuing an enigmatic pronouncement that he favored a "judicious" tariff. In the West, however, Benton and other Jacksonians made it clear that it was the party of Adams that had voted against his bill to graduate downward the price of public lands. This was not entirely true; in the western states where the public land issue was hottest, Adams's supporters, with the exception of David Barton, were calling for graduation as loudly as the Jacksonians. The General let this debate go on without making positive statements on the sale of lands, but he let it be known to supporters with whom he corresponded, and it was widely understood by the voters, that he was committed to removing the Indians beyond the Mississippi, and that where Adams had vacillated, he would show decisive leadership.[25]

The Graduation/Donation Proposal and the Quest for a Sectional Alliance

While southwestern states like Georgia and Alabama began making claims on Indian lands and using lottery systems to allocate tracts among eager whites at less than market prices, other states, including Missouri, possessed millions of acres of federal land that could not be sold—even at the new minimum price. Land not disposed of by auction remained on the market at the minimum price of one dollar and twenty-five cents per acre. In the western states, the idea of a further reduction in the price of federal lands was increasingly popular as a means of restarting the migration that had been the basis of these states' earlier prosperity. Following the requests of members from several other states, Benton launched his graduation-donation campaign in the spring of 1824. Any public lands not sold within five years were to be offered again at a reduced or "graduated" price. The price of land was subject to annual reductions of 25 cents per acre, with any land unsold after it was offered at 50 cents an acre (later reduced to 25 cents) being subject to free donation to any bona-fide settler "upon inhabiting and cultivating the same for three successive years." Much later he would assert that he did not know "when I first took up the notion that sales of land by a government to its own citizens, and to the highest bidder, was false policy; and that gratuitous grants to actual settlers was the true policy, and their labor the true way of extracting national wealth and strength from the soil." It might have been in childhood, "when reading the Bible, and seeing the division of the Promised Land among the children of Israel," or later when he learned the operation of the feudal system "in giving lands to those who would defend them." The latter provides an interesting parallel. In the Dark Ages, local barons capable of providing forces to resist the incursions of Norsemen or Magyars would have been granted fiefdoms in return for their services. The senator, whose family had constructed "Benton Town"—the fortified station on the Natchez Trace—a quarter century earlier, may well have still felt cheated of recognition of his father's Tennessee land claims in light of the family's contribution to defending the frontier.[26]

Benton's critics charged that his true motives sprang from more practical considerations, namely his desire for an issue to use against David Barton in the latter's 1824 bid for reelection. Barton strongly opposed Benton's graduation plan, and the two Missouri senators clashed bitterly over the issue. Barton voiced his support for free donations of land to the industrious poor, but viewed graduation, in practice, as benefiting the big land speculators. "Not one man in ten," he declared in 1828, "of the honest and understanding part of the community of Missouri," understood the graduation proposal, which he charged with being "the first bold and direct attempt since the foundation of our Government to bribe the people with their own lands." Benton's introduction of his land proposal—too late in the 1823–1824 session for debate—lends credence to the charges of his enemies that the bill was nothing more than an "electioneering project." The outcome was, at any rate, a defeat for the pro-Benton faction in Missouri. Barton was returned to the Senate by a healthy margin.[27]

Benton had, nonetheless, fixed on an issue of enormous and growing popularity. His timing, as it turned out, could not have been better. He had already been seeking to shift his base of support from the St. Louis land and fur-trading interests whom he had represented since arriving in Missouri, to the swelling population of outstate yeoman farmers and the expectant capitalists who tied their fortunes to that class. Benton's shift to the Jackson camp in the 1824 presidential elections was decisive. The issue of generous government land policy became identified with the Jacksonian movement.

The graduation/donation proposal offered farming families, increasingly threatened by the disappearance of available land in the East, an extension of the free-holding system through cheap land in the West. As a magnet for increased settlement and trade in the western states, it promised to benefit local merchants as well. Further, the proposal offered a new life to urban workingmen in the eastern cities. While few established wage earners could easily move west to become farmers, many young men in the cities or on the shrinking older farms of the East could do so. This would have the effect of reducing the competition for jobs in the East and thus have a favorable effect on wages there. Congressmen from the eastern states interpreted the graduation policy as an attempt to undermine their section's supremacy in population and representation. So it was. Manufacturers opposed the bill because they feared it would diminish the reservoir of affordable labor on which they depended. Fiscal conservatives opposed the plan as a threat to the nation's financial soundness, since it threatened to diminish the public revenues that had historically been derived from the sale of western lands. Benton was undeterred by any of these arguments as the years went by and debate continued to rage over land policy. For himself and like-minded reformers, the issue was not revenue, but rather, greater equality of opportunity.[28]

In the Nineteenth Congress (1825–1827), Benton once more introduced his graduation/donation bill. The ground had been prepared by John Randolph and Martin Van Buren in speeches opposing the use of revenues from the sale of public lands to fund internal improvements. This proposal was an element of Clay's American System and was supported by President Adams as sound nationalist policy. Despite their personal friendship with Benton, Randolph and others among the Old Republicans were no friends of either western interests or majoritarian democracy. Concern that cheaper lands and relief for land debtors endangered the revenues upon which depended the long-sought goal of eliminating the national debt led Randolph and Nathaniel Macon to oppose those measures. At the core of their opposition, however, was the ideological fear that the control of public lands was yet another instrument by which a powerful and activist central government might interfere with the sovereignty of the states. Therefore, Randolph added a crucial qualifier. While proclaiming his hostility to the West as the theater of federally funded internal improvements, he added his opinion as "the friend of state rights" that every new state should control all the lands within its borders. Van Buren supported this view, though in more restrained language, and Virginia senator Littleton Waller Tazewell submitted a resolution calling for the Federal government to "cede and surrender" its lands within the states "upon such terms and conditions as might be consistent with the due observance of the public faith and with the general interest of the United States."[29]

For Benton, this proposal presented the opportunity to form a coalition of the West and South in favor of dissolving the federal land system in the name of states' rights. On May 16, 1826, he rose to speak formally on behalf of his graduation/donation plan for the first time. Appealing to the agrarian roots of Jeffersonian ideology, he charged that the government kept millions of idle acres locked up while the nation's landless poor suffered the lives of tenants and "wage slaves." Was it right, he asked rhetorically, that a government created to serve the people should act as a cruel landlord towards its own citizens? Echoing Jefferson, he proclaimed his belief that the future of republican government lay with its freehold farmers. "I speak to Senators who know this to be a Republic, and not a Monarchy; who know that the public lands belong to *the People* and not the Federal Government."[30]

Benton's bill would reduce the price of lands unpurchased at auction to twenty-five cents an acre within four years, and donate free lands to actual settlers. Why sell all the lands at the same "odious and arbitrary *minimum*" of $1.25 an acre? Why not sell them for what they were worth and realize an immediate return, "instead of waiting for a future, distant, and uncertain rise" in the market? Though he thought his own proposal for graduation had the best chance of success in the Senate, Benton also endorsed Tazewell's resolution to cede the public lands to the western states. The national government's retention of public lands, Benton charged, was a policy "fraught with injustice" and "destructive of the sovereignty and independence of the new states."[31]

The graduation plan was tabled, but Benton's arguments were reprinted in a pamphlet edition aimed at the growing population of land-hungry freeholders in Missouri and other western states. Beyond the argument in favor of cheap land, Benton's speech and its accompanying notes and appendices were an attack on the American System and on the Adams administration. The president had said nothing thus far about either graduation or cession—though he opposed both as antithetical to his own ideas concerning national consolidation and development. Adams ignored supporters who urged him to recommend one plan or the other. Benton bided his time, waiting for the administration to break its silence, while support for his proposal continued to grow.[32]

In fact, two competing programs for the use of public lands existed. While many western farmers favored either Benton's graduation-donation plan or Tazewell's cession proposal, Adams and Clay adhered to an alternative scheme under which the revenues from the sale of these lands were used to finance internal improvements. Since roads and canals were an essential element of developing the economies of the western states, this approach retained a good deal of support among westerners throughout the 1820s and 1830s. But the emphasis on getting the most revenue for the public lands—whether for development or for paying off the national debt—came at the expense of encouraging settlement, the goal uppermost in the minds of leaders like Benton. Many easterners and some western followers of Clay, on the other hand, viewed the lure of western lands as pulling capital and labor away from the East, where both were needed by the nation's growing industrial sector. To easterners, it seemed only fair that their region, which had contributed people and wealth to the West, but received neither land nor any other compensation, should receive a share of the benefits reaped from the public domain. In 1821 the legislature of Maryland had begun a movement to distribute a portion of the public lands to all the states for the funding of education and other purposes. Congress had already appropriated some eight million acres for the same purposes among the western states. Although Congress rejected the Maryland plan, the idea of distribution of the proceeds from public lands to the states found a champion in Clay. As the depression subsided in the 1820s, the elimination of the debt for public lands under the relief legislation presented new possibilities for policy makers. The concept of aiding internal improvements (as opposed to retiring the national debt) by distributing the proceeds of the public lands was increasingly popular among the supporters of Clay and Adams. This policy had the added benefit of keeping up protective tariffs as a source of revenue to replace money distributed from the Treasury, hence aiding the growth of American manufacturing as well.[33]

With the elections of 1828 approaching, John Quincy Adams sought to avoid making any controversial recommendations on domestic policy. Nonetheless the president was becoming alarmed by the growing din in favor of cheap land, and he addressed the issue in his December 1827 message to Congress. The present system, he asserted, "was the result of long, anxious, and persevering deliberation." Modified by the lessons of experience as the population progressed, it had "been hitherto eminently successful." More than 90 percent of the lands still remained the common property, "the appropriation and disposal of which," Adams reminded Congress, was a "sacred trust" in their hands.[34]

The president's message was not popular in the West, even though Adams implied, rather than explicitly stated, his opposition to graduation or cession. Four days later, Treasury Secretary Richard Rush asserted in his annual report that "The creation of capital is retarded rather than accelerated by the diffusion of a thin population over a great surface of soil. Anything that may serve to hold back this tendency to diffusion from running too far and too long, into an extreme, can scarcely prove otherwise than salutary." Rush was critical of what he called a "legislative incitement to emigrate" to the western states, which annually drew inhabitants from the East "into the settlement of fresh lands, lying still farther and farther off." He asserted that "the nation at large would gain" if the population of the settled eastern states "remained fixed in more instances . . . by extending the motives to manufacturing labor."[35]

Coupled with Adams's message, the Treasury report provided Benton with the proof he sought that the administration, already identified with the manufacturing and commercial interests of the Northeast, was opposed to graduation. While Van Buren worked to bring Pennsylvania and New York into the Jackson movement by renewing the Jeffersonian alliance of "planters of the South and the plain Republicans of the North," Benton sought to bring South and West together for Jackson on the issues of states' rights and strict construction as defined by the issue of public lands.[36]

Randolph and Tazewell had opened the door to such an alliance by their offer to yield on public lands in the interests of strict construction. The task of unifying the South would not be difficult: both the Southeast and the newer states of the Southwest were in agreement on the defense of slavery. Southwesterners embraced the internal improvements opposed by Randolph and his band of conservatives, but shared the Old Republicans hostility to the tariffs that made commodities more expensive. Voters in the northwestern region, however, supported both tariffs and internal improvements, while opposition to slavery in the old Northwest grew with every Yankee family that settled in the area. This impasse had seemed to preclude the possibility of cooperation between the Northwest and the Southern Atlantic states. The Rush report now promised to break the impasse. Just as the tariff was unpopular throughout the South, cheap land was almost universally popular in the West. Jacksonian leaders could now denounce the Adams-Rush stance as the product of northeastern hostility to the development of the West. Benton could thus present the tariff as appearing "under new and revolting auspices, as the antagonist to my

Graduation bill, as well as having the foundations of its success laid in a diminution of immigration to the West."[37]

In April 1828 Benton once more brought his graduation bill before the Senate and pressed it to a vote. Lengthy debate followed. William Hendricks of Indiana and John McKinley of Alabama delivered speeches in support of an amendment substituting cession for graduation. In their view, the real issue was not settlement but state sovereignty. But cession was too extreme a measure to draw support from the Southeast, and the debate went forward on the issue of graduation. Senators from East and West rehearsed well-worn arguments as to which section had derived the greater share of benefits from the public domain. Benton played to the Old South by emphasizing the tariff recommendations put forth by Secretary Rush, and the Missourian offered to accept any amendments to his bill put forth by the "friendly hands" of southern senators.[38]

On the first roll call on Benton's proposal, David Barton proposed an amendment to increase the period between reductions in land prices from one year to five. Still firmly allied with proslavery expansionists from the Old Southwest, Benton charged that Barton's plan favored the North over the South in order to shift population and political power to the former by creating a new free state before a slave state could be settled. Such a scheme would upset the delicate political balance that had been maintained since the Missouri Compromise of slave and free states entering the Union more or less in tandem. Benton's seizure of the slavery issue aimed at gaining southern support for his measure, and graduation did come close to passage in 1828 with more southern than northern support. But even after Benton had conceded to extensive changes in his proposals so as to please southerners, the Old South still failed to deliver a majority in favor of graduation. Benton's use of slavery as what today we might call a "wedge-issue" created something like the coalition of southern and western interests that he had hoped for—though still not quite the margin needed for passage of his graduation bill. It was defeated in the Senate by a vote of 25 to 21.[39]

From Public Lands to the Nature of the Union: The Webster-Hayne Debate

The culmination of Benton's attempts to forge a sectional alliance between the West and the South took place in 1830, when Senator Samuel Foot offered a resolution to inquire into "the expediency of limiting for a certain period the sales of public lands" to those that had already been offered for sale and to suspend further surveys. Benton was to play a rather secondary role in the drama that ensued as a result of this seemingly limited measure and was overshadowed by other players, as the land question was buried under weighty oratory concerning sectional differences and the nature of the Union itself. Nonetheless, the 1830 debates, primarily identified with Senator Hayne of South Carolina and Senator Webster of Massachusetts, are worth considering for what they reveal about both the issues and the personalities involved.

Foot's bill was introduced on December 29, 1829. Three weeks later, on January 18, 1830, Benton responded. The practical effects of the resolution, he argued, would be to check emigration to the new states, limit their settlement, and deliver up large portions of their surface "to the dominion of wild beasts." It was the latest in a long series of "measures of the same class, all tending to check the growth, and to injure the prosperity of the West, and all flowing from the same geographical quarter." High tariffs and Foot's resolutions were complementary parts of the same plot by eastern manufacturers to close off the West and reduce eastern workers to wage slavery. "A most complex scheme of injustice, which injures the West, to pauperize the poor of the North!" Benton appealed to the South as "the ancient defender and savior of the West," and to the "scattering reinforcements" of northeastern Republicans, to come to the aid of his section.[40]

Benton's practical goal was to achieve an alliance of South and West in favor of his graduation plan. His rhetorical obsequies appeared to be falling upon fertile ground when Senator Hayne joined the discussion. Comparing the sufferings of the West to those of the South under the 1828 "Tariff of Abominations," Hayne agreed with Benton that the new states should "be invested in due season with the control of all the lands within their respective limits," and echoed the call for alliance between West and South. At this juncture, Daniel Webster entered the debate. Taking up the charges of northeastern hostility to the growth of the West, Webster answered, "I deny that the East has, at any time, shown an illiberal policy towards the West. I deny it in the general and I deny each and all its particulars." Among the benefits conferred upon the Northwest by the East, he asserted, had been the Ordinance of 1787, which banned the introduction of slave labor into the region.[41]

Webster chose to ignore Benton and to reply to Hayne, who had not only condemned the Northeast for its role as the aggressor in the Missouri controversy but had also dredged up the secessionist Hartford convention of 1814 to tar New England with the odium of disunion. This provided Webster with the opportunity he sought. South Carolina had recently been the setting for a number of meetings at which local patriots had avowed the right of any state to judge the constitutionality of federal laws. The context of these meetings was resistance to the 1828 tariff. An election year measure passed by Jackson's congressional allies, it targeted items such as molasses, hemp, and iron for protection in order to appeal to voters in the Mid-Atlantic region. Cotton-state southerners, on the other hand, whose support for Jackson was taken for granted, would suffer both as consumers of manufactured goods and from foreign retaliation. The remedy suggested for the unpopular tariff derived from Jefferson's assertion during the crisis of 1798 that states had the right to nullify—to refuse to enforce—certain federal laws within their own borders. Webster was familiar with the doctrine of nullification, both from the Virginia and Kentucky Resolutions and, more recently, from Hayne's speeches and from the anonymously authored *South Carolina Exposition and Protest*, which he correctly suspected was the work of Vice President Calhoun. The New Englander rejected the extreme states' rights doctrine in favor of a concept of Union based on a single sovereign people who had established a *national* state. He condemned the small-minded machinations of those who spoke of the Union as a league in which the value of one's membership would be calculated, or of such delusional matters as "Liberty first and union afterwards." Rather, Webster concluded with his memorable peroration, "that other sentiment, dear to every true American heart—Liberty *and* Union, now and forever, one and inseparable."[42]

Webster's initial reply to Senator Hayne, seeking to link East and West in opposition to the South, praised the ban on slavery contained in the 1787 Northwest Ordinance and contrasted the prosperity of the states north of the Ohio River to the economic backwardness of those to the south. Both Hayne and Benton issued angry responses to Webster's linking of slavery to the economic problems of the South. Hayne insisted that slavery was a blessing, not a curse, for blacks who were wholly unqualified for freedom and who were much better off in slavery than in the "savagery" of Africa. Webster's words had obviously opened wounds hardly scarred over since the Missouri controversy ten years earlier. Vice President Calhoun, presiding over the Senate, nodded approvingly at Hayne's remarks as the senator responded that it was not slavery but the tariff that was responsible for the backwardness of the southern economy, and went on to outline the case for nullification as the last resort of the oppressed slaveholding minority.[43]

Benton answered Webster's charges with another three-day speech, beginning on February 1. He said that he regarded with admiration "the sublime morality of those who cannot bear the abstract contemplation of slavery, at the distance of five hundred or a thousand miles off." Such morality, said Benton, affected a vast superiority to that of the early Christians and even Christ himself, who had lived in the midst of slavery, yet had said nothing against the institution. Christ "preached no doctrines which led to insurrection and massacre; none which, in their application to the state of things in our country, would authorize an inferior race of blacks to exterminate that superior race of whites, in whose ranks he himself appeared upon earth."[44]

Benton went on to mingle the issues of land, slavery, and Indian removal still further. He described a vision he possessed of a banner, "floating over the head of the Senator from Massachusetts [Webster] while he was speaking," with various inscriptions on it: "Missouri Question, Colonization Society, Anti-Slavery, Georgia Indians, Western Lands, More Tariff, Internal Improvement, Anti-Sunday Mails, Anti-Masonry." Under the banner marched "a cavalcade...a motley group...the speckled progeny of many conjunctions—veteran Federalists—benevolent females—politicians who have lost their caste—National Republicans—all marching to the next Presidential election, and chanting the words on the banner, and repeating 'under these signs we conquer.'"

Benton avowed that he meant "no disrespect" to the "benevolent females" for whom he had found a place in the procession.

> Far from it. They have earned the place by the part they are acting in the public meetings for the instruction of Congress on the subject of these Georgia Indians. For the rest, I had rather take my chance, in such a cavalcade, among these benevolent females than among the unbenevolent males; had rather appear in the feminine than in the masculine gender; had rather march in bonnet, cloak, and petticoats, than in hat, coat, and pantaloons. With the aid of the corset-maker Madame Cantalo, to draw me up a little, I had rather trip it along as a Miss, in frock and pantalets, than figure as a war chief of the Georgia Cherokees, bedecked and bedizened in all the finery of paint and feathers.[45]

In his backhanded "apology" to the female activists who opposed both slavery and dispossession of the southwestern tribes, Benton managed to trivialize their efforts with his paternalistic language—not to mention the absurd vision of the formidable senator in drag—while casting aspersion upon the manhood of both northern male reformers and southwestern Indians: the courage of neither was up to the standards of the "little lulus" whom they would abandon when routed by their enemies.[46]

Slavery, the tariff, and the relationship of the states to the national government—and now even Indian removal—were becoming hopelessly entangled as the debate went on, taking in more and more ground. Webster, in his masterly summation, denied either enmity toward the South or any desire to interfere with slavery—the disposition of the institution, he said, should be left to the states. But, once the subject had been broached, southerners reflexively identified the issue of states' rights with the protection of slavery as well as opposition to the tariff. By 1830, slaves outnumbered whites in South Carolina. White masters were hypersensitive to any disturbance that threatened the racial hierarchy, a sensitivity seemingly justified in light of Denmark Vessey's abortive 1822 slave rebellion. Now, they argued, the unbearable burden of the 1828 tariff threatened to undermine the plantation system that supported both the economy of South Carolina *and* white supremacy. Hayne and his cohorts responded to Webster's assessment of slavery with such vehemence, including references to nullification and even secession, because Webster's assertion of national authority, paired with his identification of slavery as the root of southern economic backwardness, touched a nerve. If a sufficiently broad interpretation of constitutional powers allowed Congress to impose objectionable tariffs upon the states at will, asked the nullifiers, what then was to prevent a growing northern majority from legislating emancipation as well?

Missouri, States' Rights, and the Calhounites

By 1832 the South Carolina legislature authorized a state convention that overwhelmingly nullified both the Tariff of Abominations and a reform tariff passed earlier in the year that reduced rates on some items but not others. The nullification ordinance forbade the collection of duties in the state after January 1, 1833. Calhoun, whose relationship with Jackson had soured over both personal and political matters, resigned as vice president and was promptly elected to the U.S. Senate, where he now had greater freedom to speak on behalf of nullification. By early 1833 Henry Clay proposed a compromise tariff to provide South Carolina, and any states that might be inclined to follow its example, with a face-saving way of backing out of the nullification posture. The president's response was measured—at least in public. Confronted with open defiance of federal law, he requested from Congress a "Force Bill" authorizing him to use the army, if need be, to ensure compliance in South Carolina. Privately he threatened to hang Calhoun if a single drop of blood was shed in defiance of federal law. Getting wind of this, Hayne expressed his doubts that Jackson would really hang anybody. "Hayne," replied Benton, "when Jackson begins to talk about hanging, they can begin to look out for ropes!"[47]

Though Missouri was far from the center of this crisis, its citizens and political leaders followed events closely. In 1832 Daniel Dunklin, an avid states' rights Jacksonian, was elected to the governorship. A supporter of Benton's graduation plan for the public lands, he also embodied Jacksonian opposition to the Bank of the United States, federal control of internal improvements, and the protective tariff. During the nullification crisis, Dunklin moderated his states' rights philosophy with recognition of the power of the national government. When the General Assembly considered South Carolina's request for support in nullifying the Tariff of 1832, Dunklin elaborated his views on the matter. He favored the process of nullification, he wrote, where it meant disregarding a process or mandate of the federal courts in order to check the encroachment of the judiciary on the powers of the states. Thus, Dunklin agreed with Georgia's failure to comply with the Supreme Court's rulings concerning state jurisdiction over the Cherokees, since he considered it an invasion of state sovereignty. He also favored nullification if it meant protecting the reserved rights of a state against the federal government. But if nullification meant that a single state could void a law passed by Congress because of an assumed abuse of power, Dunklin was opposed. Such action, he told the General Assembly, would destroy the liberties, peace, and harmony of nation. Distinguishing between violations of a constitutionally reserved power and an abuse of delegated power, the governor rejected the latter as a legitimate reason for nullification. Missouri rejected South Carolina's call for support. Though states' rights sentiment in Missouri was widespread, the crisis of 1832 failed to create a schism among Missouri's Jacksonians. Neither did it create a state's' rights wing of the Whig Party in Missouri comparable to that which developed nationally.[48]

Benton thus found himself faced with a dilemma as Clay's compromise tariff made its way through the Senate. The bill, while retaining the principle of protection, effected a gradual reduction in duties over the next ten years. Benton took no active role in the debate on the measure. It signaled the end of the alliance of South and West that he and Hayne had sponsored. The nullifiers, seeking a way out of the trouble they had created for themselves, united in support of Clay's proposal. The shift on the part of Calhounites to supporting a tariff bill conceived by the senator most identified with protection seemed to herald a new anti-Jackson coalition. Benton, considering the measure to be both bad policy and contrary to certain key western interests, found himself voting with Daniel Webster against the bill.

Benton did not speak in the Senate on Jackson's Force Bill either, but presumably he was in the midst of reassessing his views concerning the South as represented by Calhoun and the nullifiers. He abstained from voting on the bill. At the time, his sympathies in this contest of doctrines lay with Hayne, whom he complimented on his noble effort "to vindicate himself, his State, and the South." Later, however, he was to rethink his views on the matter. By the time of his retirement from the Senate, Benton's outlook was closer to that of Webster. Long after the fact, Benton praised both Jackson and Webster, whose committee had reported the measure, for "supporting with transcendent ability the cause of the Constitution and of the country, in the person of a chief magistrate to whom he was politically opposed, bursting the bonds of party at the call of duty, and displaying a patriotism worthy of admiration and imitation."[49]

By the time he composed this tribute, Benton obviously wanted to agree with the verdict that history had rendered among those who shared his own understanding of the national government. It was, as he would point out repeatedly, a *union* and not a league or confederation, as some would have it. As the years went by, Benton, the slaveholding southern frontiersman, came more and more to see his career and his place in history as inseparable from "the people"—the united and expanding American nation in which the white yeoman farmer and the rising class of Jacksonian entrepreneurs represented the perfect (if sometimes confused) harmony of Enterprise and Arcadia. Over the years, he had his political differences with many of his contemporaries: Barton, Foot, President Adams, and for many years notably Clay and Webster (during the period when economic issues seemed transcendent). The Missourian's growing enmity for John C. Calhoun, however, was of an entirely different order. Calhoun, the former nationalist, had by the 1830s become the uncompromising sectionalist, standing on principles of nullification and—in the last instance—secession, if his region did not get everything he believed was its due. During the 1830s Benton's role as western sectionalist more and more became subsumed in the politics of class interests that largely defined the struggle between Whigs and

Democrats. When sectional loyalties once again came to the fore over the renewed slavery controversy, Jackson's coalition, as well as the Union itself, was endangered by the demands of the Calhounites. For one who identified himself as totally as Benton did with the destiny of the nation, the threat of disunion was to become a personal struggle. He had gone to war in 1812 to vindicate his nation's honor. He had resorted to pistols more than once to uphold personal reputation. In Benton's struggle with Calhoun and the forces of disunion, the personal and the political eventually became joined beyond the point of separation.

The Indian Removal Act of 1830

By the time of Jackson's inauguration, Benton's narrative informs us, "a political movement on the part of some of the southern tribes of Indians, brought up a new question between the States and those Indians, which called for the interposition of the federal government." Though they were still called Indians, "their primitive and equal government had lost its form, and had become an oligarchy, governed chiefly by a few white men, called half-breeds, because there was a tincture of Indian blood in their veins." These factions, "in some instances, set up governments within the States, and claimed sovereignty and dominion within their limits." The "oligarchy" to which Benton referred was an obstacle to removal of the Indians from the Old Southwest. Possessing some degree of white ancestry, usually on the father's side, these leaders formed a distinct social class among the southern Indians. They were often men of some means who had made their fortunes among the Indians, had married Indian women, and had raised their children to speak English. These children grew up to emulate whites in many respects. They acquired private property and established their own cotton plantations, complete with black slaves, though they still identified themselves as Indians within the matrilineal tribal community and often acted as intermediaries between their fellow tribesmen and whites.[50]

One of the most prominent members among the Native American planters' "oligarchy" was the Cherokee chief John Ross. The owner of a substantial plantation in western Georgia, Ross favored the "civilization" of Native Americans in their tribal homelands through the introduction of missionary schools and artisanal training. He was instrumental in the creation of a republican constitution for the Cherokee modeled on that of the United States. As head of the new tribal government, Ross was also leader of the major faction within the tribe that opposed the removal policy put forward by Jackson and Governor Troup. The rise of men like John Ross posed a threat to the aspirations of white southerners. It was the civilization, not the "savagery" of the Indians, that land-hungry whites feared most. The efforts of the Cherokees, Choctaws, Chickasaws, and Creeks to establish independent sovereignties within the states were intolerable to whites who coveted the very land over which these native republics claimed dominion. [51]

This being the case, President Jackson's annual message to Congress in 1829 called for either submission to state laws on the part of the Indians (under which they would have virtually no rights that whites were required to observe) or removal. Jackson acknowledged that it had long been the policy of the government to introduce among the Indians "the arts of civilization, in the hope of reclaiming them from the wandering life." This policy had been undermined, however, by the contradictory practice of purchasing the Indians' land at every opportunity, thereby pushing them further into the wilderness. "By this means they have not only been kept in a wandering state, but been led to look upon us as unjust and indifferent to their fate." Despite lavish spending on the civilization program for the tribes, the government constantly defeated its own policy, "and the Indians, in general, receding further and further to the West have retained their savage habits."[52]

Jackson then got to the crux of the matter. A portion of the southern tribes, "having mingled with the whites, and made some progress in the arts of civilized life," had lately attempted to erect an independent government within the limits of Georgia and Alabama. This was forbidden by Article IV, Section 3 of the Constitution, which declared that "no new State shall be formed or erected within the Jurisdiction of any other State" without the consent of its legislature. Refusing to sustain the southern tribes in their attempts to set up independent governments within the states of Alabama and Georgia, Jackson recommended the passage of an act enabling him to provide for the removal of the Indians to west of the Mississippi.[53]

Administration supporters, including Benton, immediately moved to enact into law the president's proposals for large-scale Indian removal. As the debate over nullification riveted the nation's attention, the Senate Committee on Indian Affairs reported out a bill on February 22, 1830, calling for an exchange of land with all eastern tribes. Debate over the proposal commenced on April 6 and continued for eighteen days. The text of the bill authorized the president to set aside an Indian territory on public lands west of the Mississippi and to exchange districts there for land now occupied by the Indians in the East. The tribes were to be granted absolute ownership of their new homes "forever." The government was to ensure that property left behind by the emigrating Indians be properly appraised and fair compensation paid, and that aid and assistance be given the emigrants on their journey and for the first year after their arrival in their new country.[54]

Benton, curiously, took no active role in the debates over the Indian removal bill. He planned to make another legislative attempt at securing passage of his graduation measure for public lands later in the session and presumably did not want to dissipate his energies when he knew the administration's position had ample support. He later wrote that the bill introduced in the Senate providing for removal "was an old policy, but party spirit now took hold of it, and strenuously resisted passage of the act."[55]

Senator Theodore Frelinghuysen of New Jersey, a former president of the American Board of Commissioners for Foreign Missions, led the opposition. He was joined by most of the senators from the northern states, who identified with the National Republican principles of John Quincy Adams. Frelinghuysen argued that the Indians had every right to refuse to leave their ancestral homes. The actual intent of the administration's proposal, he submitted, was to "rescind, modify, or explain away, our public treaties with the Indians." Such treaties, which professed to grant the tribes perpetual rights to their lands, were but "plighted covenants" to whites whose "insatiated cupidity" hungered for more Indian land "than we shall dispose of at the present rate to actual settlers in two hundred years." Frelinghuysen reminded his colleagues that the government was bound by treaty to protect the Cherokee in "the exercise and enjoyment of their civil and political rights." Yet in defiance of federal law, the state of Georgia had again proceeded with the survey of Indian land. "Do the obligations of justice change with the color of the skin?" asked the senator. "Is it one of the prerogatives of the white man, that he may disregard the dictates of moral principles when an Indian shall be concerned?"[56]

So far as many senators from the South and the West were concerned, the answer was a resounding "yes." Senator John Forsythe of Georgia made a lengthy address on April 13 in which he presented views on the Indians that arguably mirrored those of Benton. Pointedly replying to Frelinghuysen's rhetorical challenge, Forsythe submitted that the Indians were "a race not admitted to be equal with the rest of the community; not governed or completely dependent; treated somewhat like human beings, but not admitted to be freemen; not yet entitled, and probably never to be entitled, to equal civil and political rights." Forsythe charged that the "zeal and industry in the Indian cause" on the part of Frelinghuysen and others suggested an eagerness to "arrest the progress of Georgia." Forsythe did not believe that Indian removal would accelerate the civilization of the tribes. "You might as reasonably expect that wild animals, incapable of being tamed in a park, would be domesticated by turning them loose in the forest." The goal of civilization could not be obtained without destroying the tribal character and subjecting the Indians, as individuals, to "the regular action of well digested laws." Rather, Forsythe believed, the removal act was necessary in "hope of relieving the States of a population useless and burthensome" and to open new land to "survey, sale and settlement" for the white population. Nonetheless, the Georgian promised that the Indian emigrants would be "humanely provided for" in the trans-Mississippi West. The southern tribes had no alternative. They "must remove, or remain and be subjected to the State laws, whenever the States choose to exercise their power."[57]

Among those who remained skeptical of the administration's professions of paternal responsibility and promises that the Removal Bill would not lead to the forced emigration of the southern tribes was Benton's archrival David Barton, who offered amendments to guarantee that neither secret negotiations nor intimidation would be used to secure the signing of removal treaties. Barton denied any intentions either to question the motives or impugn the integrity of the Jackson administration. On the contrary, "It would be a feather in the cap of this administration to [declare] by a law, to govern all our public agents, President, and Commissioners, that neither force, nor fraud, nor direct, secret bribery, shall be resorted to in acquiring the land of those helpless people, whose guardians we affect to be."[58]

Barton's amendment, along with similar ones designed to safeguard the rights of southern Indians should the Removal Bill become law, were all defeated by the Jacksonian majority in the Senate. David Barton returned to Missouri later that summer and was at last turned out of office by an Assembly now dominated by Jackson men. In the meantime the Removal Bill passed the Senate 28–19. Benton voted with the majority, though he later asserted that "It was one of the closest and most earnestly contested questions of the session; and finally carried by an inconsiderable margin."[59]

An Alternative Proposal for Public Lands: Clay's Distribution Plan

Following on the heels of this legislative victory for the expansive white nation, Benton resubmitted his graduation bill in May 1830. Senator Hayne of South Carolina, the hero of states' rights following his confrontation with Webster earlier in the session, supported Benton in his latest effort to reduce the price of public lands. After attempts to postpone voting on the measure were defeated, the graduation bill passed the Senate by a vote of 24–22 on May 7. The West-South sectional alliance that Benton had labored so long to forge finally seemed to be bearing fruit. The limits of this strategy were immediately manifested, however, when the bill was tabled in the House.[60]

On the same day that Benton's graduation bill came up for a vote in the Senate, the vulnerabilities of the West-South alliance were further demonstrated when President Jackson vetoed an appropriation to subsidize a road from Maysville, Kentucky, to Lexington. By doing so, the president was both striking at the proponents of Clay's American System, who were already coalescing into something like a nascent opposition party, and taking a stand on principle against federally funded internal improvements within a single state.

For once Benton found himself at odds with his party's leader. While he had argued, in opposition to the Foot Resolution, that the system of internal improvements had been "a fraud upon the West" since most of the money went to projects in the North and East, his attempt to align himself with southern opinion on the issue could only go so far. Missouri, after all, was a western state as well as a southern one and in need of transportation improvements. When David Barton had earlier addressed the Senate on his differences with Benton, he pointed out, among other things, Benton's growing opposition to internal improvements. Weighing the interests of his constituency against party ideology, Benton voted in favor of the Maysville Road bill and advised Jackson to sign it. Jackson turned to Martin Van Buren, who was becoming the president's closest political confidant, for counsel. Arguing that federal spending on public works projects such as the Kentucky road would create new opportunities for congressional deal-making at the public's expense, Van Buren urged the president, in the spirit of strict construction, to veto the bill. Much later, Benton endeavored to support Jackson after the fact. He approvingly described the veto as a "killing blow" to the overall system of internal improvements, without attempting to further explain his own position on the issue.⁶¹

Jackson's veto was also a blow to the prestige of Henry Clay as a rival for the loyalties of westerners. Already contemplating the presidency in 1832 and seeking an issue by which he could counter the popularity of Benton's support for Indian removal and cheap land, Clay eventually developed an alternate scheme for the disposal of the public domain. He proposed a five-year experiment in distribution, under which the states would receive all income from the sale of western lands at current prices (about $3 million in 1831) for purposes of education, internal improvements, and the colonization of free blacks. In a single stroke Clay countered Benton's claim to leadership of western voters on the question of public lands. He simultaneously addressed the concerns of his eastern constituents who supported the American System. On the one hand, the eastern states would share in the annual dividends from public lands; on the other, they would benefit through the continuing protection of tariffs, which would be kept at a higher level by distributing the income from public lands that might otherwise go to swell the treasury surplus.⁶²

Benton was infuriated. "It is a tariff bill; it is an ultra tariff measure," he raged. The opposition was once more favoring "the principle of money-money-money" over the human value of "an increase of man— free man." Benton, in other words, appreciated the value of cheap land as a lure to settlers coming to populate the West over using land sales at higher prices as a source of revenue for whatever purpose. Beyond his objections on sectional economic principles, Benton further took issue with the proposed use of the land revenues for the colonization of free blacks, "a delicate question for Congress to touch." The slave question, Benton submitted to fellow senators, could not be "agitated by the federal legislature, without rousing and alarming the apprehensions of all the slaveholding States, and lighting up the fires of the extinguished conflagration which lately blazed in the Missouri question." Slavery was confined to the southern and middle states. If it was to be removed, it was their business and not the federal government's to remove it. The slavery issue, like the public lands and Indian policy, was a question of justice to the states. "Raise no more money from them than the exigencies of government require, and then they will have the means, if they feel the inclination, to rid themselves of a burden which is theirs to bear and theirs to remove."

By adding the colonization of free blacks to the goals of distribution, Clay hoped to appeal to moderate reformers, both North and South, who sought a solution to the growing controversy over slavery. The American Colonization Society had been founded in 1816 as a typically Jeffersonian solution to America's race problem and presumably a means to gradually end slavery as well. Clay had been a founding member of the ACS and would later serve as its president, but by the time his distribution bill was offered, the once bright hopes for colonization were fading. Younger southerners considered the idea an attack upon the institution of slavery itself, and northern abolitionists rejected the tenets of colonization because it was too slow and failed to address the moral sin of slavery. Thus as the decades passed and the followers of Calhoun and Garrison became increasingly intransigent, Benton and Clay would find their differences growing less important while their common concerns for the Union became greater.[63]

Benton moved to amend Clay's bill, replacing its distribution features with provisions lowering the minimum price of public lands from $1.25 to $1.00 an acre and adopting the principle of graduation. The amendment was defeated, with most members from the southeastern states voting against price reduction. Benton's hopes for an alliance of South and West had suffered another blow. Clay's distribution bill passed the Senate, but debate was postponed in the House as controversy over rechartering the Bank of the United States crowded out all other issues.

Clay's introduction of distribution as a means of funding internal improvements signaled a further shift from sectional to partisan divisions on the question of public land. As with other, related, issues like the tariff and the National Bank, voters and their representatives were aligning into what would shortly become a new party system. The opposition to Jackson had yet to come together firmly and, although Clay had a comprehensive platform—including distribution—in 1832, he did not yet have the kind of party apparatus that Van Buren and others had created for the Democrats. The use of the land issue in the presidential campaign of that year hastened the process of party formation. Jackson himself had yet to take a position on the issue, however. Thus far he had mentioned the public domain only as a source of revenue for his goal of retiring the national debt. In December 1832, though, Jackson publicly came out in favor of lower land prices. "It seems to me," he stated in his message to Congress, "to be our true policy that the public lands shall cease as soon as practicable to be a source of revenue, and that they be sold to settlers in limited parcels at a price barely sufficient to reimburse to the United States the expense of the present system."[64]

Benton responded with a new price-reduction bill, making a speech in which he condemned distribution as a new element of the despised American System. But, with the nullification crisis approaching its climax in early 1833, Clay now linked support for his distribution plan to his proposal for a compromise on tariffs. Clay won the round. Benton's renewed proposal to reduce land prices was defeated when a temporary coalition of Calhounites and supporters of the American System passed distribution in both houses. The president, however, refused to approve the measure. The bill was passed in the last hours of the session, but Jackson killed it with a pocket veto.[65]

In a message issued upon the convening of the next Congress nine months later, Jackson reiterated his support for cheap lands and condemned the idea of creating a surplus for distribution to the states. In the wake of the greatest controversy over the relation of the states to the central government prior to the Civil War, Jackson warned, "a more direct road to consolidation [of national power] cannot be devised." Under Clay's distribution plan, "the state governments ... would lose all their independence and dignity"; state offices would become dependent on the federal government, which provided the money for their salaries; and they would thus become "the mere stipendaries and instruments of the central power." Therefore, the president attested that "the harmony and union of the states" called for an end to the "continued agitations over public lands.... I do not doubt that it is the real interest of each and all the States in the Union, and particularly of the new States, that the price of these lands shall be reduced and graduated."[66]

The new partisan alignment had actually produced a standoff between the executive and legislative branches. With the West-South alliance that Benton had hoped for in ruins, prospects for passage of his graduation bill in a Congress whose majority was united in their opposition to the president were increasingly dim. He would continue to press for it—as Clay would continue to press for distribution with somewhat greater success—but as the 1830s wore on, Benton's attention turned to other issues and his stance on public lands shifted to the more acceptable program of favoring preemptive rights for settlers.

Indian Removal and Master Race Democracy

While Congress debated the most equitable policy for disposing of the public domain, leaders of the Cherokee nation sought to prevent the seizure of their remaining lands. Both President Jackson and the governments of Georgia and Alabama were growing increasingly anxious for the Removal Act of 1830 to be implemented. Part of the Cherokee had already emigrated west of the Mississippi. The remainder were split between one faction willing to negotiate the sale of tribal lands and another, led by John Ross, determined to hold on to such territory as the tribe still had.

"Intrusive counselors," wrote Benton, "chiefly from the Northern States, came in to influence dissension, aggravate difficulties, and impede removal." The removals would eventually be effected "but with great difficulty, chiefly on account of a foreign, or outside influence from politicians and intrusive philanthropists." In fact, Benton's accusation that "party spirit" was responsible for many of the difficulties had some merit. Following passage of the Indian Removal Act and during the approach to the election of 1832, National Republicans coupled Jackson's Indian policy with his positions on the tariff, internal improvements, and the National Bank as evidence of his cruelty and willingness to use coercion against those who stood in his way. Henry Clay, no friend of the Indians as a race, sought to exploit public opinion against the Removal Act as a campaign issue.[67]

Clay, Frelinghuysen, and other anti-Jacksonian leaders encouraged the Cherokee to appeal to the U.S. Supreme Court and to employ former attorney general William Wirt to argue their case. Wirt undertook the defense of the Indians in the summer of 1830. Although he was initially sympathetic to arguments that it was in the interest of the Cherokee themselves to remove, Wirt quickly came to the conclusion that the Cherokees had a legal right to remain in Georgia. In the case of *Cherokee Nation v. Georgia*, he brought suit for an injunction that allowed the Cherokee to remain where they were without interference by the state. The core of his argument was that the Indians constituted an independent nation and had been regarded as such by the United States in its history of making treaties with them.[68]

The Court handed down its decision on March 18, 1831. Chief Justice Marshall, writing for the majority, rejected Wirt's argument that the Cherokees were an independent nation, but he also rejected Jackson's assertion that they were subject to state law. The Indians, said Marshall, were "domestic dependent nations," subject to the United States as a ward would be to a legal guardian. Indian lands were part of the United States but were not subject to action by individual states. The Cherokee might now, with some justification, believe that they had won. Informed by John Ross that the Supreme Court had decided in their favor, they determined to stay where they were. Protestant missionaries—the pseudo-philanthropists of Benton's account, who had long been active among the Indians—supported their decision. In December 1830 the state of Georgia sought to address this "foreign interference" by passing a law prohibiting whites from entering Indian territory after March 1, 1831, without a license for the state. After the effective date, eleven missionaries were arrested for violating the law. Governor George Gilmer pardoned nine in return for promises that they would cease their illegal activities. Two others, however, Samuel A. Worcester and Dr. Elizur Butler, refused the offer of pardon and were sentenced by Judge Augustine Clayton to four years in the state penitentiary. The missionaries appealed their case and the Supreme Court reviewed it.[69]

Marshall's opinion for the majority in *Worcester v. Georgia* (March 3, 1832) went beyond his previous decision in upholding the rights of the Cherokee and the sovereignty of the national government in relation to the states. He declared the laws of Georgia relating to the Cherokees unconstitutional, null, and void. In addition, he reversed Judge Clayton's decision and ordered the two missionaries released. The Court, however, had no power to enforce its decision without the compliance of the executive branch, which was not forthcoming. "The decision of the Supreme Court," said Jackson, "has fell stillborn, and they find that it cannot coerce Georgia to yield to its mandate."[70]

In addition to his own recounting of these events twenty years later, Benton tells the story of one George Tassels, an Indian who "instigated by foreign interference, and relying upon its protection, committed a homicide in resisting the laws of Georgia." A writ of error was obtained for the case to be reviewed before the Supreme Court and, by Benton's account, William Wirt attempted to use the trial of George Tassels as a forum for revisiting the question of the right of Georgia to exercise jurisdiction over the Indians within her limits. Governor Gilmer refused to cooperate, insisting that the federal government stick to the business of fulfilling its 1802 "contract" with the state. "The day for the execution of Tassels came round," wrote Benton, "he was hanged: and the writ of the Supreme Court was no more heard of."[71]

Twenty years after the fact, we find the Missourian treating the decision and authority of the nation's highest court in much the same dismissive tone that his president and party chief used at the time. While Benton and Jackson—former attorney and judge, respectively—could hardly have been hostile to the role of the court, per se, as a forum of last resort for deciding constitutional questions, it appears to have been an essential element of Democratic philosophy to oppose the power of judicial review where policies reflecting the will of the "majority" of white male citizens were involved. Partly, such opposition reflected the natural democratic suspicion of power in the hands of unelected judges; this issue had divided Missourians during the factional disputes of the early 1820s in which the courts were the instruments for enforcing the collection of payments from indebted farmers. Partly, the hostility stemmed from an unwillingness, on the part of Jackson and his followers, to see policies reflecting the will of that same "majority" of the people *nullified*—either by the Calhounite minority in South Carolina or by the tiny judicial clique on the Court. Benton's hostility to judicial review would be more fully elaborated near the end of his life in response to the *Dred Scott* case. As far the Cherokees and Georgia, the remaining Indians made their treaty and removed west of the Mississippi. "And that was the end of the political intrusive philanthropical interference in the domestic policy of Georgia," wrote Benton, "One Indian hanged, some missionaries imprisoned, the writ of the Supreme Court disregarded, the Indians removed." The "pseudo-philanthropical intermeddlers" were left to reflect upon the great mischief they had done in assuming to become the defenders and guardians of the Indians—"a race which the humanity of our laws and people were treating with parental kindness."[72]

Benton never ceased to argue that the government had been more than just in its treatment of the southern tribes. The few Cherokees who were left in Georgia "instead of subjugation and destruction of their liberties, were to be paid a high price for their land, if they chose to join their tribe beyond the Mississippi." Benton, glossing over the fact that the removal treaty finally concluded in 1835 was made with a minority faction among the tribal leadership, reminded his readers that federal payments "for the improvements on the ceded lands to defray the expenses of removal to their new homes beyond the Mississippi—to subsist them for one year after this arrival ... with some liberal grants of money from Congress, for the sake of quieting complaints," amounted to over $12 million. The effort "being almost as much for their single extinction of Indian title in the corner of two states, as the whole province of Louisiana cost!" If the Indians chose not to remove to the West, "they were to be protected, like the white inhabitants of the countries they lived in."[73]

This was patent nonsense and Benton's comments throughout his memoirs concerning Indian policy reveal that he was no doubt aware of it. While the authorizing legislation may have paid lip service to the legal protection of those Indians who did not wish to migrate westward, such distinctions were ignored in the practice of enforcing removal. Indians no longer had a place in a southern society that was designed to admit only two classes of people: white masters and black slaves. Native Americans were an anomaly that had to be eliminated—peacefully or otherwise.

His assertions of paternal care notwithstanding, Benton's views of both Indians and blacks are more accurately revealed in his accounts of the Second Seminole War, different versions of which appear in his speeches to Congress and in *Thirty Years' View*. Hostilities in Florida, which had become an American possession as the result of Jackson's campaign against the Seminoles in 1818, renewed in December 1835. The Seminoles had agreed in the 1832–1833 Treaties of Payne's Landing to cede their lands to the government and to move west of the Mississippi within three years. The majority of the tribe did move west, but a substantial group of holdouts under the leadership of Osceola chose to resist.

The first and most infamous action of the Second Seminole War was the ambush of 112 soldiers under the command of Major Francis Dade. Despite the death of most of the officers early in the action, the desperate troops charged the concealed Seminoles to drive them from their cover. "At the end of an hour," wrote Benton, "successive charges had roused the savages from the grass, (which seemed to be alive with their naked bodies, yelling and leaping) and driven them beyond range of shot." Benton's description of the Seminoles sounds more like a passage from one of Fenimore Cooper's novels than an account of combat in Florida. Dade's soldiers had constructed a makeshift fort of pine logs to protect the growing numbers of wounded and there to make a last stand. "The savages, slowly and cautiously approaching, were a long time before they would venture within the ghastly pen, where danger still might lurk under apparent death." For the senator, the atrocities of the Seminoles were compounded by the presence of "a squad of about forty negroes—fugitives from the Southern States, more savage than the savage.... They came with knives and hatchets, cutting throats and splitting skulls whenever they saw a sign of life."[74]

The war, which would drag on until 1842 and eventually cost the U.S. government $20 million and the lives of 1,500 white soldiers, was, according to Benton, simply "one of flagrant aggression on the part of the Indians... whose very name (Seminole-wild) define them as fugitives from all tribes, and made still worse than fugitive

Indians by a mixture with fugitive negroes, some of whom became their chiefs."[75]

Seeking a strategy that combined the twin goals of free land and pacification of the hostile Seminoles, Benton, in February 1839, presented a bill providing for the armed occupation and settlement of the Florida territory. He wanted to grant 320 acres each to white men who were willing to settle and defend Florida against the Indians and runaway slaves. Clay, who objected to grants of land in principle, argued that the settlers would squander their claims by selling them to speculators and derive no benefit themselves from the awards. Senator Thomas Morris of Ohio also opposed any plan that meant federal aid to a slaveholding territory. He submitted that St. Domingo had declined and decayed under a slaveholding regime and that the present "desolate" condition of Alton, Illinois, was the result of divine wrath for the murder of abolitionist Elijah Lovejoy. Benton scoffed at Morris, who seemed to have forgotten "the horrid massacre of the white race" that had occurred on St. Domingo forty years earlier—"the true cause of the decline of the island." But what had Florida done to make her dread divine vengeance? "She has done nothing to cause the Deity to make her a place of desolation; but desolate she is—desolate in forty-one thousand square miles of her territory, made so by the ravages of the colored races upon the white."[76]

Benton recounted the massacre of white families in Florida and of Major Dade's command. "This has been the conduct of the colored races in Florida," Benton argued. Morris should see that it was "his own white race which has been the sufferer in Florida; and that the colored races have exulted in the slaughter and destruction of men, women, and children, descended, like the Senator himself, from the white branch of the human race." After three years of fruitless and costly military campaigns, the country remained under the control of "the marauding and murdering Indians which now roamed over it, savaging where they went." The government had already spent $20 million without success. Benton now proposed to give away four million dollars' worth of land that was presently useless as "the most humane method of terminating the war."[77]

More humane? Benton certainly believed so. Not least with respect to the Indians themselves, for the effect of the settlements would be "to expel them from the country by the advance of population, and almost without bloodshed." The establishment of Benton's ten thousand pioneers, occupying hundreds of fortified blockhouses or "stations," as in frontier Kentucky and Tennessee decades earlier, would soon have its desired effect on the Indians. "They will recede as the stations advance; they will retire beyond the Mississippi when they hear, from the Okefinokee Swamp to Cape Sable, the sound of the ax, the crack of the rifle, and the fierce barking of the house-dog."[78]

When Senator John Davies of Massachusetts objected to the novelty of linking Indian or defense policy to awards of land for prospective settlers, Benton climbed to new heights of eloquence in defense of his vision. "The Senator seems to have forgotten," he replied, "that every inch of territory on this continent, now occupied by white people, was taken from the Indians by armed settlers, and that *preemptions and donations of land have forever rewarded the bold settlers who rendered this service to the civilization of the world.*"[79]

Here we have the most explicit statement made during Benton's long career in the Senate linking the prize of cheap land for whites to the removal of the Indians. The lands, as Benton asserted, might belong to "the people," but Native Americans were excluded from the Jacksonian definition of that term. The old expeditionary/inclusive frontier of Benton's youth had been replaced by a sedentary/exclusionary frontier, and the process that led from one stage to the other is a large part of the story behind the rise of democracy in nineteenth-century America. "The savages," said Benton, "have given way before the armed settler from the day the New World was discovered up to the present time ... and in every instance grants of land have rewarded the courage and the enterprise of the bold pioneer."[80]

So it was. Benton's bill passed in the Senate but died in the House. The Seminole War dragged on for years without a formal peace but, as the 1830s came to a close, the "Indian problem" had been largely resolved elsewhere in the states and territories east of the Mississippi. In 1841 Henry Clay linked preemption to a renewed effort to secure the passage of his distribution plan. Western senators, including Benton, voted against it, but the bill passed. The preemption clause allowed any adult male or family head the right to settle on 160 acres of public land, which could later be purchased at the minimum government price free of competitive bids. Long one of Benton's best-loved programs, it became law as part of a Whig measure.

In the debate over Florida, Benton had dismissed the concerns of northern senators that additional slave territory would be added by conquest of the Seminoles. By the 1840s, however, he was becoming increasingly concerned over the threat posed to the Union by the expansion of slavery into the still racially inclusive Mexican borderlands. The origins of Benton's opposition to John C. Calhoun and his followers lay in the political battles and personal vendettas that had taken form during the 1830s. But during the following decade, Benton came to regard the expansionist program of southern slaveholders as a danger to both his goal of greater economic equality for white men and to the nation itself.

5 / Old Bullion and the Borderlands: Mexican Dollars

On June 12, 1844, Thomas Hart Benton stood before the Senate to address the annexation of Texas. In addition to his claim that the addition of another slave state threatened the precarious sectional truce established by the Missouri Compromise, Benton made a further argument concerning the importance of the southwestern border with Mexico that has gone unnoticed by historians. The depression years 1837 to 1840 had witnessed the closing of banks unable to redeem their paper currency in specie and the depreciation of the notes issued by those banks to a quarter, or less, of their value. This calamitous suspension of specie payments had its origins, charged Benton, in the policies of the Bank of the United States. "We are a paper money people," he said, "with a thousand paper banks, and not one mine of silver.... What would become of these banks—or rather what would become of their currency in the hands of the people—were it not for Mexican dollars?" Benton argued that the decline in the supply of Mexican silver to the Unites States that had occurred since 1836 was directly related to "the depreciation of currency and the ruin of commerce."[1]

It is one of the curiosities of Benton's career as a white nationalist that the virulent rhetoric of race he applied to both Indians and blacks was not extended to Mexicans as well. This difference becomes all the more striking when Benton's favorable descriptions of the Hispanic peoples occupying the lands to the southwest of the American republic are contrasted with the language of many of his contemporaries. Other political leaders and editors of the time routinely referred to the citizens of Mexico as a "mongrel," "indolent," or "degraded" race. Waddy Thompson of South Carolina, for example, who served as minister to Mexico in 1842, described the general population as "lazy, ignorant, and, of course, vicious and dishonest." Benton, on the other hand, acknowledged that while the United States was the first, Mexico was "the second power of the NEW WORLD. We stand at the head of the Anglo-Saxon—she at the head of the south-European race—but we all come from the same branch of the human family—the white branch—which, taking its rise in the Caucuses Mountains, and circling Europe by the north and by the south, sent their vanguards to people the two Americas."[2]

The privileged status that Benton awarded the Mexican people in his personal racial hierarchy should be viewed in several aspects. Earlier biographies have generally dealt with Benton's opposition to the annexation of Texas and the later declaration of war against Mexico as the result of his growing opposition to Calhoun and the "slave power" that, by the mid-1840s, Benton viewed as the greatest threat to the Union. This element of Benton's quest for a peaceful resolution to the crisis along the U.S.-Mexican border was genuine enough, and his inability to square his opposition to calls for annexation and war with the desires of his most vital constituency would at length lead to his fall from power.[3]

The crisis of the 1840s and the debate over the expansion of slavery to the former Mexican territories, however, only came as the latest act of political battles reaching back decades. Almost from the moment of Benton's entry into the Senate, his home state had been engaged in a lucrative trade with the Mexican provincial capital of Santa Fe. Mules, textiles, and other trade goods from Missouri—initially from Franklin in the politically important Boonslick region—were traded for furs and silver via the Santa Fe Trail. By 1836, as the Jacksonian campaign against the Second Bank of the United States and paper money reached its conclusion, $8.3 million in Mexican silver entered the United States. This windfall allowed Benton both to trumpet the superiority of a monetary policy based on specie and to utilize his hard-money stance to consolidate political support among proslavery Missourians in the Boonslick. Significantly, 1836 was also the year in which the Republic of Texas won its independence from Mexico, precipitating a long and divisive debate over American annexation (or "reannexation" as Benton had deemed it since his days at the *St. Louis Enquirer*).[4]

Historians have long erred by treating Benton's advocacy of federal protection of the Santa Fe trade, like his role as representative for the interests of the fur companies, simply as an episode in his early sponsorship of western mercantile interests. After 1825 there was little further mention of it. William Chambers, Elbert Smith, and others dealt with the New Mexican trade as a discrete policy issue, Benton's role as "Old Bullion" in the Bank War of the 1830s as another, and his opposition to the Calhounites' agenda for expanding slavery into the West during the 1840s as still another. But their approach overlooked crucial links between those issues that help explain Benton's opposition to the annexation of Texas and war with Mexico during the 1840s.

The Santa Fe trade, the hard-money policies of the Democrats, and the rancorous debate over slavery and the Mexican War cannot be understood in isolation from one another—at least as regards the career of Thomas Hart Benton. The imperatives of economic policy, state politics, and the survival of the white nation influenced and sometimes conflicted with each other as the years progressed. By the end of the 1840s, Benton would find the coalition he had forged on the basis of his advocacy for cheap land, hard money, and white supremacy was abandoning him over of his perceived hostility to the expansion of slavery into the West.

Benton's Education in Banking and Currency

As a young man coming of age on the Tennessee frontier, Thomas Benton must have noticed the lack of cash and credit available to settlers not only for land purchases, but for buying seed, labor, and other necessities. As counsel to the St. Louis junto in territorial Missouri, Benton became intimately aware of the need for sufficient capital to fund the enterprises his clients were involved in. Trade in early Missouri was frequently carried out by barter. Lead, salt, and furs, the most common articles of export, were viewed as legal tender for the payment of debts. St. Louis's origins as a fur trading post were reflected in the fact that pelts were the chief medium of trade. Different kinds of pelts were redeemable in one another, and a note was payable in peltry unless it was expressly stipulated that the payment should be in Spanish milled dollars. The first recorded payments in coin in Upper Louisiana consisted of silver sent to pay the Spanish garrison in St. Louis during the colonial period. Early American officials in the territory, however, were impressed by the almost complete absence of specie.[5]

With the growth of commerce resulting from the Louisiana Purchase, the demand for banking facilities increased. In the East, state banks had been developing during the period of sound currency that coincided with the life of the First Bank of the United States. Eighty-eight such banks had been created by the time the charter of the Bank expired in 1811. During the War of 1812, when there was no central bank to regulate currency, state institutions proliferated until, by 1816, there were 246 in operation, while their note circulation increased from $45 million dollars to $100 million. In 1816 Congress chartered a Second Bank of the United States. Economic nationalists such as Henry Clay and John C. Calhoun envisioned the Bank, a semiprivate corporation based in Philadelphia, providing credit and a sound national currency, while at the same time regulating local bank-note issues by refusing to accept unsound paper for government accounts.[6]

Three years earlier, Auguste Chouteau and other St. Louis businessmen had petitioned the General Assembly of the Territory of Missouri to charter a corporation to be known as the Bank of St. Louis. Wartime dislocations had delayed opening, but by July 1816 sufficient stock had been subscribed for the bank to begin business. On September 2 the first election of directors was held, and by the end of the year the Bank of St. Louis began making sizable real estate loans by issuing its own notes to borrowers. Though this policy was beneficial to newly arrived American speculators, in a short time the bank had overextended itself and was in serious trouble. Some of the bank's original backers, including Chouteau, had already withdrawn from the venture, and some of the more conservative of the remaining directors accused the bank's cashier, John B.N. Smith, of mismanagement for his role in the issuance of unauthorized notes. Benton had been a stockholder in the Bank of St. Louis, and as an attorney he was authorized to act as agent for the other stockholders. In this capacity, he allied himself with Joshua Pilcher, leader of a conservative minority-stockholder group, who condemned the bank's management for overlending and for failure to redeem its notes in specie. Pilcher succeeded in securing Smith's removal, but the minority block failed to win support for fundamental changes in the bank's policies. To dramatize their dissatisfaction, three of the dissenting directors resigned.[7]

On February 11, 1818, what the bank's officers called a "tumultuous assemblage"—a group led by Pilcher, Benton, and Elias Rector—gathered in front of the bank and held an informal stockholders' meeting. A resolution was adopted authorizing the leaders to demand the keys from bank officials. When the officers refused to comply, Pilcher, Benton, and Rector ordered everyone out of the bank and padlocked its doors. Having taken this step, the minority established a committee to see that the bank did not reopen until the directors ensured that their interests would be protected. Two days later the insurgents were called before a grand jury and indicted for their high-handed actions in taking possession of the bank and its assets. Pilcher, Benton, Rector, and their followers were required to post bonds to keep the peace toward the bank's president Eric Clemson and the new cashier Theophilus Smith. Dr. Bernard Farrar and Robert Wash posted one thousand dollars bond for Benton, while he provided surety for Elias Rector. On February 16 the minority stockholders' committee, which included Benton, returned the keys to the bank officers. Despite an announcement that business would resume on February 23, however, the bank's doors remained closed. At the end of February, the minority, led by Pilcher, Benton, and Rector, prepared a statement protesting the failure of the bank to pay notes in cash and its failure to reopen. The fifteen signatories declared these actions likely to "materially injure the interest of the stockholders." Thomas H. Benton signed for "self" and three others. The bank finally reopened early in 1819 but by July had to close its doors again permanently. Internal dissension and poor management had contributed to its failure. So had inability to collect its debts and the collapse of other banks whose paper constituted nearly all of the currency of the region.[8]

Benton's role in Missouri's early experiments with banking occurred simultaneously with his stint as editor of the *St. Louis Enquirer*. Throughout 1819 the *Enquirer* dealt frequently with the very issues of banking and currency that were causing problems in St. Louis and across the land. Seemingly converted by his experience with the Bank of St. Louis, Benton considered it his duty to expose institutions that issued doubtful paper currency. In April 1819 he censured the Farmers and Mechanics Bank of Cincinnati for issuing notes on "empty boxes" and for sending fifty thousand dollars' worth of these "new made notes...to Missouri and Illinois to be 'swapped' for something that would pass where they would not." In May, Benton warned that the Bank of Georgetown, Kentucky, had cleverly altered its one-dollar bills to $100 notes. The Edwardsville Bank near St. Louis in Illinois, he wrote in June, was insolvent despite the fact that it had recently shown $20,000 of specie "all arranged, like a china-workshop, to catch [the] eye."[9]

The *Enquirer* also discussed the Bank of the United States, although with greater ambivalence than it did the state banks of the West and South. In its early years the Second B.U.S., like its state-sponsored counterparts, had indulged in speculation and in an immense overissue of bank notes. Unlike the state banks, however, the B.U.S. had not failed to redeem its paper issues in specie. Though Benton pointed out particular instances of mismanagement on the part of the national bank, he did not as yet oppose its existence as an institution. His attitude at the time is indicated by an editorial in the *Enquirer* on the occasion of the Supreme Court's 1819 decision in *McCulloch v. Maryland*. In this case, the state of Maryland had passed a law imposing a fifteen thousand dollar annual tax on notes issued by the Baltimore branch of the B.U.S. The Court, in a decision rendered by Chief Justice Marshall, ruled that "the power to tax is the power to destroy" and upheld the Bank as a "necessary and proper" function of the enumerated powers of Congress. "Let the end be legitimate, let it be within the scope of the constitution," wrote Marshall, "and all means which are appropriate, which are plainly adapted to that end, which are not prohibited, but consist with the letter and spirit of the constitution, are constitutional." Benton wrote, "This decision," came "very opportunely to give confidence to the public authorities to *oppose* the resolutions to plunder [by taxing] the branch banks in Kentucky and Ohio." The Court dictum, he believed, added to the fact that "the institution may now be considered permanent and national." His editorial is remarkable in light of his later stance against the B.U.S. and the broad constitutional construction associated with the National Republican and Whig parties. It demonstrates to some degree just how radical was the change in his political philosophy that occurred over the following decade.[10]

The *Enquirer* was already giving attention to the broader problems of currency. After 1819, though Missouri was not immediately affected, a general collapse of the "paper system" occurred throughout much of the country. Viewing these events, Benton increasingly concluded that specie—"hard money"—was the only sound form of currency. He became more and more identified, as time went on, with the abolition of paper currency altogether and adherence to gold and silver. It was a stance popular with the farmers who would support him later in his career and who desired that "a dollar stands for a dollar."[11]

Benton's views may have been influenced by the difficulties of a second financial institution that he was associated with during the same period. Even before the Bank of St. Louis had embarked on its troubled career, Auguste Chouteau, Manuel Lisa, and several other original backers had dissociated themselves from it to promote a new bank guided by more fiscally conservative principles. Directors of the Bank of St. Louis did all they could to block the charter of a competitor, but by early 1817 the Bank of Missouri was serving customers from the basement of Chouteau's mansion as a fully chartered institution. In contrast with its rival, the Bank of Missouri got off to an auspicious start, proudly offering to redeem its notes in specie. In 1820 it became the depository for U.S. government funds for the land district of Missouri, and prosperity seemed ensured.[12]

Benton held only a small amount of stock in the Bank of Missouri, but he was a large depositor and an increasingly prominent member of the business community. In May 1820 the other stockholders elected him to the Bank of Missouri's Board of Directors. Enemies charged that his role in the Bank of St. Louis controversy had been motivated by a developing interest in its rival, and they cited this interest as new evidence of his function as a lackey for the "little junto." Benton, like other directors, borrowed heavily from the Bank of Missouri, and he was plunged into debt when it, too (in violation of its charter), was forced to suspend payments in August 1821. By this time Missouri was belatedly feeling the effects of the Panic of 1819, and the ill-fated experience of its two territorial banks produced a strong public reaction against banking generally. There would not be another state-chartered financial institution in Missouri until 1837.[13]

Benton spent most of his life under the burden of a Federal judgment of approximately seven thousand dollars as his share of the loss. The burden of this financial obligation no doubt spurred him to embrace the anti-bank policies of John Randolph and other strict constructionists with whom he allied himself during his first term in Washington.[14]

The Santa Fe Trade: A Solution to the Specie Shortage

Benton's challenge as he took his Senate seat in the early 1820s was to find the source of enough specie for Missouri, let alone the nation as a whole, to embark upon his hard-money experiment. As events would have it, the answer to his quandary was shortly provided by developments far to the Southwest in the former Spanish province of New Mexico.

Despite the Spanish government's ban on trade with foreigners, the lure of profit, coupled with the volatile political landscape in Mexico, had long enticed venturesome American citizens to attempt business with the New Mexican capital of Santa Fe. A number of these would-be entrepreneurs had been jailed in Santa Fe and Chihuahua and their merchandise confiscated by Spanish officials determined to enforce their government's mercantilist trade policies. They were released upon promising not to return. During his stint at the *Enquirer*, Benton had angrily denounced the American government's apparent indifference to its own citizens languishing in Spanish jails.

In 1821, the same year that Missouri finally achieved statehood, Mexico gained independence from Spain. That June, Captain William Becknell, a trader from Franklin, Missouri, advertised for men to join him in an expedition to the Southwest "for the purpose of trading horses and mules and catching wild animals of every description." Becknell and his party of thirty left Franklin with only limited trade goods for their stated purpose, and without knowledge that Mexico had declared independence. Nonetheless, along the way they met a group of Mexican soldiers who both informed them of political developments and invited them to trade in Santa Fe. Becknell's party returned to Missouri with a handsome profit from the sale of his merchandise. Local legend described Becknell and his companions triumphantly opening their saddlebags to pour gold and silver coins onto the streets before a crowd of admiring townspeople. Thus was initiated a lucrative trade that brought between $100,000 and $200,000 in silver bullion back to Missouri annually. The Santa Fe trade promised the necessary specie to fulfill Benton's vision of a hard-money economy. He thus naturally became the advocate for the federal government taking a role in the trade between Missouri and Mexico.[15]

When Congress convened in December 1824, Benton presented a petition from the citizens of Missouri noting the value of the trade with Santa Fe and pointing out that "the intervening tribes of Indians presented the only obstacle to the successful prosecution of the trade upon a large scale." To address this potential danger, Missourians asked that the national government negotiate treaties with the various tribes to secure for traders the right of safe passage along a specified route. To back up the treaties, they asked for construction of a fort where the route crossed the Arkansas River. Benton saw to it that the bill was referred to the Committee on Indian Affairs, of which he was chairman.[16]

On January 25, 1825, Benton addressed his colleagues concerning the petition. He described the profitable trade carried by caravans of men and horses across what was still viewed as the "Great American Desert." Over the past year alone, the fruit of these enterprises amounted to $190,000 in gold, silver, and precious furs. Considerable in itself and "in the commerce of an infant state" (that is, Missouri), these profits were chiefly of interest to statesmen as a promise of what might be expected from a "regulated and protected trade," not only with Santa Fe but with the mining communities of Chihuahua and Durango that lay hundreds of miles to the south.

"The principal article given in exchange" for this bounty, Benton informed his colleagues, was that which Americans had "in the greatest abundance"—cotton, "which grows in the South, is manufactured in the North, and exported from the West." The merchandise carried from Missouri to the internal provinces of Mexico was the same that had previously been brought down the Ohio from Atlantic ports and factories. "The cotton goods thus carried out ... are the same which, after paying the cotton grower for the raw material, and leaving a profit in the hands of the manufacturer, the first, second, and third sellers, and giving employment to numerous carriers, are still sold at another profit in the Internal Provinces, and yet sold so low as to drive out every competitor from the Mexican ports. . . . Allied by nature, the internal provinces are now allied by fact, with the valley of the Mississippi."[17]

This trade was of the greatest value to the people of the West, whose own interior position cut them off from foreign commerce, stated Benton. It was one of the few sources from which they could derive precious metals, and the coin brought in constituted the circulating medium of the country in western Missouri. "It is paid into the offices for public lands, and then comes into the coffers of the government, whose protection it now solicits."[18]

An unmolested passage between Mexico and the United States was "as necessary in a political, as in a commercial point of view." The two chief powers of the New World stood "at the head of that *cordon* of Republics" in the western hemisphere, which were "destined to make the last stand in defense of human liberty." The bill before the Senate would "bring together the two nations whose power and whose positions make them responsible to the world for the preservation of the Republican system."[19]

Unfortunately, these momentous developments were endangered by "a parcel of miserable barbarians, Arabs of the desert, incapable of appreciating our policy, and placing a higher value on the gun of the murdered hunter, than upon the preservation of all the republics in the world." True to form, Benton offered a solution to "the problem of Indian civilization" that was uniquely beneficial to his white constituents. History had demonstrated the failure of efforts to improve the life of the Indians through religion and education except in the South. There, roads had been built through Indian lands, causing the natives to settle near the crossings and to trade with white travelers. "This imparted the idea of exclusive property in the soil and created an attachment for a fixed residence," said Benton. If the process could occur in the South, it could be repeated in the Southwest. "This ... [was] the true secret of the happy advance which the southern tribes have made in acquiring the arts of civilization."[20]

Benton's argument demonstrates both a faith in the benefits of road construction typical of westerners at the time as well as certain assumptions about "the preservation and improvement of their race" that were likely not shared by Native Americans. His argument rings particularly hollow in light of his contempt for the rights of the same "civilized tribes" of the Old Southwest during the following decade.

Nonetheless, he pressed on, answering critics who asserted that there was no precedent for the construction of a road through foreign territory by the federal government. To demonstrate that there was indeed precedent for such an undertaking, Benton recounted his visit the previous Christmas to Monticello to pay his respects to Thomas Jefferson. Jefferson informed the Missourian that during his own administration, Congress had authorized a road from Georgia to New Orleans, then under Spanish control. Jefferson recalled that a map of the project existed in the Library of Congress, along with the authorizing statute. Upon his return to Washington, Benton had located both the authorization and the map, just as Jefferson had described them, and he now triumphantly showed his fellow senators the map of the road to New Orleans. Despite the objections of strict constructionists, including Nathaniel Macon, that this precedent had nothing to do with the legislation at hand, the bill passed 30–12 with all of the nay votes coming from eastern states. The measure was shortly passed by the House as well and signed into law by President Monroe as one of his last official acts.[21]

Benton's Early Views on Texas

Benton's 1825 speech on "the internal trade with Mexico" touched on nearly every important theme that he was to deal with as a lawmaker over the next fifteen years: not only the importance of Mexican markets to the commerce of his native Missouri and of Mexican specie to his hard-money experiment, but public lands, Indian policy, the growth of cotton as a cash crop in the South and the complementary boom in northern textile manufactures, even states' rights (they were, Benton reassured the Senate, in "no danger" from the actions he proposed). Another area he mentioned briefly concerned a part of Mexico that Benton considered to have been wrongly sacrificed by the United States in its 1819 Transcontinental Treaty with Spain. That area was Texas. Since his days as editor of the *St. Louis Enquirer*, Benton had noisily been charging that the treaty negotiated by then-secretary of state John Quincy Adams with ambassador Don Luis de Oñis surrendered land that rightfully belonged to the

United States. The treaty established the boundaries of American Louisiana at Sabine and Red Rivers, thence north along the one-hundredth meridian to the Arkansas to its source in the Rocky Mountains, and west to the Pacific along the forty-second parallel.

"If these lines are correctly given," Benton had written at the time, "the United States will have lost an immense country between the Red River and the Rio Grande del Norte." Already looking to a political and economic partnership between the United States and Mexico, Benton charged that "the policy of Spain in demanding [the boundary], and the spirit of the American government in yielding it, become equally apparent. To prevent the contagion of republican principles from reaching Mexico, in the direction of San Antonio, the settlements of the lower Mississippi are stopped on the Red River; to prevent them from reaching Santa Fe, from the people of Missouri, the settlements of the upper country are to be stopped below the three forks of the Arkansas."[22]

While conceding that Mr. Adams was "thus far . . . entitled to much approbation" as concerned other issues he had negotiated with the Spanish, Benton charged that by surrendering Texas "he departed from the character of an American statesman." The secretary of state had agreed to give up a part of the water that fell into the Mississippi—"Not, indeed the whole that Don Luis had demanded, but enough to startle the people, who would as soon submit to the dismemberment of their own bodies as to the dismemberment of that noble stream. . . . The magnificent valley of the Mississippi is theirs, with all its fountains, springs and floods; and woe to the statesman that undertakes to surrender one drop of its water, one inch of its soil, to any foreign power."[23]

It was another ten years before Benton again took up the subject of Texas. During the summer and fall of 1829 he penned a series of articles for the St. Louis *Beacon*. Seeking to pose as an ordinary contributor, rather than a prominent lawmaker, Benton used first the pen name AMERICANUS—a generic American citizen—and later LA SALLE— the French explorer who first laid claim to the Mississippi Valley. In the first of these editorials, Benton stated that "the idea . . . of endeavoring to obtain from Mexico, by friendly negotiation, and for ample equivalents, the retrocession of that part of the valley of the Mississippi which was ceded to the king of Spain by the Florida treaty of 1819, is beginning to engage, as it ought to do, the most serious attention of the Western people." Still hostile to "the author of this sacrifice"—former president Adams—Benton dismisses him as "done, and done forever with public affairs. He belongs to that class of actors who have done acting . . . and whose feelings should be respected." The senator then goes on to argue that "this narrative of the facts" proved that the boundary between the United States and Mexico established by the treaty was drawn out of hostility to Mexican independence and subservience to Spain, "interposing a vast wilderness to shut out the lights of republicanism, which might otherwise break into that benighted region." Benton further went on to argue that "the *time*, the *place*, the *negotiator*, his *associates*, their *occupation* at the time ... lead irresistibly to the conclusion that a desire to diminish the extent of the West, and in that diminution prevent the birth of four or five slaveholding states, was a subsidiary and powerful motive."[24]

In the next editorial, Benton elaborated his criticisms, claiming that a huge territory had been ceded away "for the purpose of establishing a desert between the frontiers of the United States and Mexico ... for the *avowed* purpose of obstructing Mexican independence, and for the *palpable* object of abiding the territorial extent of the West, and preventing the future existence of slave states which might have been formed upon it." Mexico, a non-slaveholding empire, now bordered upon the states of the lower Mississippi and would naturally become the refuge of fugitive slaves from that quarter. "The desertion of slaves, besides the loss in property, will endanger the peace of the frontiers, by the pursuit to which they will give rise, and the affrays which may take place."[25]

Benton continued to enumerate his objections, points one through twelve, including the charge that Texas would furnish safe harbor "to the Indians who kill and rob our citizens on their way to Mexico." Missourians had complained of their depredations, but had done so in vain while the "projector of the desert they inhabit" was president. Only upon the accession of Jackson were the complaints of white traders heard. "But military protection, while eminently desirable, is still inferior to the true remedy, the retrocession of the country upon the Arkansas and Red Rivers to its natural owners, whose mounted volunteers would quickly teach these marauders to respect the lives and property of American citizens." Somewhat contradicting his previous point, Benton later claimed that the treaty erred "in diminishing the outlet for emigration of the Indians which inhabit the states of Mississippi, Alabama, Georgia, and Tennessee." *These* Indians, he argued, should emigrate; it was due to the states they presently inhabited. The states north of the Potomac and the Ohio had sent their Indians away, and their territories had been "cleared of the encumbrance of a population which pays no taxes, counts nothing in the federal census, bears no arms except for mischief to the whites, and obstructs the settlement and cultivation of the states." Indeed, it was better for the Indians themselves that they should go, wrote Benton several months before the Senate debate over the Indian Removal Act: "Since the time that the children of Israel were in Egypt, it has been seen that two different nations could not live together without injury to the weaker, and that the road of salvation to the weaker party, was through the door of emigration. This truth is now enforced upon the Southern Indians; the land of promise for them—described by Gen. Pike, 25 years ago, as the terrestrial paradise of savages—is beyond the Mississippi."[26]

By the fall, when he had changed his byline to LA SALLE, Benton sharpened his attacks to focus on the secretary of state's motives in light of the Missouri controversy, which had occurred contemporaneously with the Adams-Oñis agreement. Adams was to be found both among the "Louisiana opposers of 1804" and the "Missouri agitators." He was "the friend, both personally and politically of both parties, which, in fact, constituted but one party at the time of the restriction." The occupation of this faction by 1819–1820 had been "to establish the latitude of 36–30, as the line, *north* of which slavery should not be admitted; and the treaty having ceded nearly the whole of Louisiana *south* of that line to the king of Spain . . . Slavery was excluded from Louisiana *north* of a certain line by *compromise*, south of it by surrender of that territory to a foreign power, the small area comprehended in Missouri, Arkansas, and the western half of Louisiana only excepted."[27]

Revisiting this controversy, Benton now averred that the free states had nothing to fear from the political superiority of the slave states, while the latter had everything to fear from the great and excessive preponderance of the former. This fact was to be demonstrated in speeches, writings, essays, newspapers, legislative acts, and judicial decisions "all issuing for a series of years from the non-slaveholding states, all thickening as time advances, and all tending to one point, *the abolition of slavery, under the clause in the Declaration of Independence, which asserts the natural equality of all men.*" Benton warned that whenever a majority might be found in Congress or on the Supreme Court to act upon these principles and to carry them out to their legitimate conclusion, "the fate of the slave societies in this Union will be as much more lamentable and terrible than that of the French inhabitants of San Domingo in '93, as the cruelties of Indian war, superadded to the atrocities of negro insurrection can exceed the horrors of negro insurrection alone."[28]

Benton ridiculed the hypocrisy of those in the free states who had sounded the alarm at the anticipated preponderance of influence among the slave states. "No, the reality of the danger is precisely the reverse of this affectation of it, and so is the reality of the fact as to the anticipated preponderance of the slave states." On which side, he asked, lay the real danger, "with us, or with the alarmists?" As far as numbers were concerned, the slave states could expect only a brief respite before the superior population of the North made itself felt politically to put an end to the institution of slavery in the southern states. "That there were *many* in the non-slaveholding states ready to have acted so during the terrible crisis of the Missouri agitation, is most certain; that there were still *more* in those same states who were unwilling so to act, is equally certain, and to us, most joyfully true. Upon *these* then ... and not upon our own numbers, we have to rely for future exemption from the combined horrors of servile and Indian war." They were men upon whom reliance could be placed:

> Christians who will never become the accomplices of fanatics in the destruction of their fellow Christians ... whose morality affects no superiority over that of Christ and the apostles; who are able to put up with the mild slavery of the black man in a part of this republic as *they* were to put up with the rigorous slavery of the white man, in the whole Roman empire, where slavery existed in its direst form ... and far from instigating insurrections, exhorted the slave to fidelity, and the master to humanity! Where St. Paul, far from being the encourager of runaways, sent back a fugitive slave to his owner, with a letter of apology and supplication.[29]

At the time of the AMERICANUS and LA SALLE articles, Benton, as he would be for years to come, was still firmly allied to the interests of Missouri's slaveholders and was still seeking to forge a sectional alliance of western and southern states based on mutual self-interest against the Northeast. John Quincy Adams and the "Federal" party of the northern states were still the villains of Benton's political morality play. His 1853 memoir *Thirty Years' View*, however, gives a very different version of events. Recounting his editorials in the *Enquirer* concerning the 1819 treaty, Benton frankly admitted that "Mr. John Quincy Adams ... was the statesman against whom my censure was directed, and I was certainly sincere in my belief of his great culpability. But the declaration which he afterwards made on the floor of the House, absolved him from censure on account of that treaty and placed the blame on the majority of Mr. Monroe's cabinet, *southern men*, by whose vote he had been governed in ceding Texas and fixing the boundary which I so condemned."³⁰

It is important here to keep in mind that by the time Benton was writing his *View*, Texas was part of the United States, Adams was dead, and the debate had moved on to the question of slavery in the Mexican Cession. Under the circumstances, perhaps Benton felt justified indulging in a bit of revisionism. The treaty, he noted, very nearly completed the extinction of slave territory within the limits of the United States, "and it was the work of southern men with the sanction of the South." At the time of the treaty and the contemporaneous Missouri Compromise which forbade slavery north of the 36°30' line,

> slave soil, except in Arkansas and Florida was extinct in the territory of the United States. The growth of slave states was stopped ... and there was not a ripple of discontent visible on the surface of the public mind at this mighty transformation of slave into free territory. No talk then about dissolving the Union, if every citizen was not allowed to go with all his "property," that is, all his slaves, to all the territory acquired by the "common blood and treasure" of all the Union.³¹

For Benton, the answer to the enigma as to why influential southerners would not only consent to, but push for the surrender of so much valuable territory, was to be found in the effect that the Missouri controversy was having on national politics. "The introduction of the slavery question into the federal elections" was "a test which no southern candidate could stand ... to prevent the slavery extension from becoming a test in the presidential election, was the true reason for giving away Texas."³²

What "southern candidate" is Benton referring to in the machinations prior to the chaotic 1824 contest? Henry Clay is exonerated both by his absence from the president's cabinet and his opposition to the treaty as Speaker of the House. Benton could be including Georgian William Crawford, Monroe's treasury secretary and the favorite of the Old Republican faction. But Crawford's career was effectively ended by the stroke he suffered in the midst of the election, and he is barely mentioned after the early chapters of *Thirty Years' View*. Both the theme of Benton's memoirs and the totality of his legislative career make it clear he can be referring to only one person—Secretary of War Calhoun, who was to become vice president in 1824 and—eventually—the embodiment of all that Benton, the nationalist, despised.

Benton, Calhoun, and Slavery "Agitation"

The antagonism between the two men first became manifest during the short 1835 session of Congress over a committee report, presented by now Senator Calhoun, alleging that the Federal budget and government payroll had doubled under Jackson and that the growing surplus in the treasury was a potential source of tyranny in the president's hands. He suggested a constitutional amendment that would permit the distribution of the Federal surplus to the states. Benton answered that it was the costs of Indian removal and Indian wars that were responsible for the increased expenditures, that routine spending had increased hardly at all, and that the senator from South Carolina had falsified the facts. This was equivalent to calling Calhoun a liar on the floor of the Senate, and the members burst into an uproar amid the presiding officer's calls to order. Calhoun responded by quoting Benton's own 1826 speech against the Adams administration on the "powers, patronage, privileges" of the executive. Benton, said Calhoun, had once agreed that too much executive power was dangerous, but he had since gone over to the spoils men. For a few days Washington buzzed with rumors of a duel over the exchange. Nothing came of it, but neither party forgot. New York Whig Philip Hone recorded in his diary that Calhoun had been insulted by "the fiercest tiger in the den" of the Democratic Party. He doubted, however, that Calhoun would challenge Benton. "I would as soon think of challenging one of the hyenas at the geological institution for snapping at me as I passed his den."[33]

By 1836 Benton and Calhoun were again at odds, this time over the slavery question. The issue before Congress was the increasing volume of abolitionist literature in the southern mails. In Charleston a mob had broken into the federal post office, seized the "incendiary publications" and burned them along with effigies of antislavery spokesmen. In his December 1835 message, President Jackson condemned "inflammatory appeals addressed to the passions of the slaves, in prints, and various sorts of publications, calculated to stimulate them to insurrection, and to produce all the horrors of servile war." Noting that the government was responsible for maintaining peace within the borders of the United States, Jackson suggested "passing such a law as will prohibit, under severe penalties, the circulation in the Southern States, through the mail, of incendiary publications intended to instigate the slaves to insurrection." The president's proposal was equivalent to federal censorship of the mails.[34]

Calhoun immediately proposed a bill to prevent postmasters from delivering the antislavery tracts in areas where state law made it illegal. He portrayed an impending danger of the abolition of slavery and the necessity for extraordinary means to prevent such dire consequences. While unwilling to call for direct federal intervention, Calhoun asked that the federal government assist the states in the enforcement of such laws as they might enact for the protection of their own citizens. Even many southern senators refused to endorse Calhoun's measure, which they believed would only serve to cause further agitation over the slavery question. Others objected on First Amendment grounds. Benton shared their view. While he was unwilling, he told fellow senators, that the "United States mail should be made a pack-horse for the abolitionists," he warned that placing the power of censorship in the hands of individual postmasters even for the "suppression of so great an evil" would "lead to things they might all regret."[35]

A second controversy involved the flood of petitions to Congress calling for the abolition of slavery in the District of Columbia. Historically, such petitions were referred to a committee upon arrival and never heard of again. Calhoun now proposed that Congress refuse to receive the offending petitions at all. Opponents charged him with deliberately fomenting the very agitation he condemned. When Calhoun read excerpts from an abolitionist newspaper on the Senate floor to bolster his point, Benton suggested that Calhoun's own action would multiply the paper's notoriety and circulation and asked that the quotation be struck from the record. The "black question," he had observed, was "like a pretentious cloud... gathering and darkening." Benton "trembled, not for the South, but for the Union." After two months of debate, which served only to strengthen extremists on both sides, the Senate voted pragmatically to accept the petitions, but to reject the proposal for abolishing slavery in the Federal District.[36]

By the mid-1830s Benton was moving away from the uncompromising proslavery stance that had characterized his position during the Missouri Controversy. Henceforth "a new point of departure was taken on the slave question" when it was debated in Congress "with avowed alternatives of dissolving the Union, and conducted in a way to show that dissolution was an object to be attained, not prevented." He later wrote, "From the beginning of the Missouri controversy up to the year 1835," he had "looked to the North on the point of danger from the slavery agitation"; but from that point forward, he looked to the South "for that danger," although he remained "equally opposed to it in either quarter."[37]

Benton's opposition to the threat he perceived from proslavery ideologues took some time to surface. He was, of course, himself a southerner and a slaveholder. As such, he possessed a sympathy and commonality of interest with white slaveholders that would continue to temper his outlook. He likewise continued to exhibit a genuine distaste for abolitionism as well as opinions of African-Americans that went rather beyond the rhetoric of white paternalism in their assessment of the "savagery" of the black race. A second factor was Benton's relationship to the powerful "Central" or "Fayette" Clique, a group of planters and merchants in the slaveholding counties of the Boonslick region along the Missouri River. It was this faction that had purged Missouri's Democratic Party of "counterfeit Jacksonians" who paid lip service to the president's leadership, but supported the monetary policies of the B.U.S. and the Whig opposition. In a state where overt Whiggery stood little chance of success, this Trojan-horse strategy was the best chance of undermining the hard-money agrarian policies favored by Benton and the radical wing of the Jacksonian coalition.

Franklin, in Howard County, was the original terminus of the Santa Fe trade. The Boonslick faction, a tightly knit group of small slaveholders and merchants, originally from the Upper South like Benton, possessed mercantile connections that allowed them to profit greatly both from the Mexican trade and the hard-money policies that Benton desired. They agreed with him as well that adherence to the Old Republican ideology of Randolph and Macon was the best formula for protecting the rights of white men generally and Missourians in particular. The Central Clique was an ideal base of power for Benton during the late 1820s and 1830s while he served as Jackson's point man in the Senate. Their campaign to weed out soft-money apostates paid off handsomely in the state and national elections of 1836, when they carried Missouri for Martin Van Buren. By 1840, with Boonslick Democrat Thomas Reynolds in the governor's mansion, Meredith M. Marmaduke as lieutenant governor, and both senators—Benton and Lewis Linn of Ste. Genevieve—ideological allies of the Central Clique, the faction's control of the state was unchallenged.

Governor Reynolds's inaugural address exemplified the strict-constructionist philosophy of Boonslick Democrats. He warned against the encroachment of the central government, "by almost imperceptible degrees, upon the reserved rights of the states." Reynolds, like other members of the Boonslick group, viewed states' rights as inseparable from the institution of slavery. He condemned the abolitionists' "headlong fury" that threatened to "trample upon the rights of the slaveholding states and expose us to all the horrors of a servile war." The peculiar institution, said the governor, was the sole prerogative of the states in which it existed, and Missourians would "be wanting in self-respect, and regardless of our undoubted rights, were we to suffer the least interference with this delicate question."[38]

It was upon the rock of "this delicate issue" that Benton's relationship with the powerful Boonslick faction would, at length, break apart. Whig observers charged that Benton ran Missouri as his personal political fiefdom, ordering his "sycophants" to form a "rotten borough system" of seventeen new counties in order to preserve Democratic dominance in the Assembly. Another described Benton as the leader of a political organization that "hunts down every man who possessed enough independence to act without consulting the great 'solitary and alone.'"[39]

The role of Benton as political "dictator" in Missouri was widely misunderstood. While, as an unquestioned champion of Jacksonian/Old Republican principles, he enjoyed enormous personal influence among members of the Assembly and great respect from the Missouri Democracy, decisions on matters of state politics were within the realm of the Central Clique alone. The faction, most of whom were personal friends of Benton, welcomed his advice, but they did not feel obligated to act on it. On the contrary, Benton was required to lobby the Boonslick leadership to receive support for his measures and to carefully court the favor of this powerful group for his national policies.[40]

Texas Annexation: "I am Against It!"

The first signal that Benton's nationalism might diverge from the interests of Missouri slaveholders came over the issue of Texas. Mexico's achievement of independence in 1821 provided new opportunities for Americans who had their eyes on settling there. Missourian Moses Austin and his son Stephen were granted privileges as *empressario* to establish a colony of Anglo-American immigrants. Compelled to look to Louisiana and Mississippi for his colonists, Austin had no practical choice but to tolerate slavery in Texas. In 1830 Mexico prohibited the importation of additional slaves into the province, but by now the Anglo-American fever for land had been ignited. Over the next five years, thousands of Americans poured into Texas, bringing their slaves with them in defiance of the law. When the antislavery government in Mexico City attempted to crack down, slaveholder fears for the security of their human property helped feed the desire of Anglo-Texans for independence. In 1836, led by former Tennessee governor Sam Houston, who had served under Benton in the War of 1812, they routed a Mexican army at San Jacinto, forced the dictator Santa Anna to recognize Texan independence, and applied for annexation to the United States.

Jackson had attempted to purchase Texas from the Mexican government and repeatedly used the American military to intimidate Mexico. He officially recognized the new republic in February 1837, only days prior to the end of his administration. He was loath, however, to raise the specter of sectional controversy by taking the final step of annexation. Jackson was also reluctant to bring on war with Mexico and international condemnation of the United States. With the inauguration of Martin Van Buren, annexation receded into the indefinite future; the Little Magician was unwilling to alienate the support of northerners who felt that too much had already been conceded to the "slave power."[41]

In 1840 Van Buren, clearly identified with the Jacksonian economic policies that many blamed for financial Panic of 1837, was further weakened among southern Democrats by his ambiguous position on issues related to slavery. Although the presidential campaign of that year is largely remembered for the partisan buffoonery of log cabins and hard cider, the Whigs, by nominating Virginia-born military hero William Henry Harrison and converted states' rights ideologue John Tyler, trounced the Democrats in the southern states for the first time. Nonetheless, with Harrison's cabinet consisting of solid supporters of the American System and Henry Clay looking prospectively to a successful agenda of Whig economic measures in Congress, the Texas issue might well have continued to sleep had not fate repeatedly taken a hand to recast the government's principal players.[42]

Within a month of his inauguration, Harrison had died of pneumonia. His vice president, whom no one had expected to play a major role in the administration, suddenly occupied the chief magistracy. The party formed in opposition to Jackson's policies once again found themselves thwarted by a president who shared few of the goals of his party colleagues. Tyler quickly dumped cold water on Henry Clay's demand for a renewed national bank. Whigs excoriated Tyler as "His Accidency" while Benton and fellow Democrats rejoiced. The Whigs' congressional caucus officially read Tyler out of the party, and his cabinet, with the exception of Daniel Webster at the State Department, resigned in protest.[43]

Denied the support and influence of his erstwhile copartisans, Tyler sought to build a new party of states' rights southerners along the ideological lines drawn by Calhoun. Freed of the requirement to consider northern antislavery opinion, the president determined to secure the annexation of Texas as the centerpiece of his administration. In January 1843 Thomas W. Gilmer, former governor of Virginia and now Calhounite congressman from that state, authored a letter calling for the immediate annexation of Texas in order to forestall British designs upon that country. These designs, Gilmer alleged, were aimed at the political and military domination of the southwestern border of the United States with a view to abolishing slavery. The letter appeared in the administration newspaper, the *Madisonian*, and a copy was sent to Andrew Jackson by Aaron V. Brown, Democratic congressman from Tennessee. Jackson replied that he had always favored the attachment of Texas to the United States. He now claimed that the failure to accomplish this objective during his own administration had been his greatest mistake. Old Hickory's letter was shown about Washington to demonstrate his support for annexation. Benton was astounded by this turn of events. Great Britain had given no indication of any disposition to wage war upon the United States or to incite insurrection among the slaves. Texas and Mexico remained at war, and to annex Texas was to adopt that war. The Gilmer letter was "a clap of thunder in a clear sky. There was nothing on the horizon to announce or portend it."[44]

Benton was convinced that the renewed agitation over Texas had the fingerprints of Calhoun on it. When Webster, who was opposed to Texas annexation, stepped down to be succeeded at the State Department by Virginia Calhounite Abel Upshur, Benton's suspicions were confirmed. The legislative session of 1843–1844 was to be consumed with debate over the Texas question. At the end of the first day of session, Benton was descending the steps of the Capitol with a group of other members when Congressman Brown accosted him. As an original enemy of the "loss" of Texas and an early advocate of reannexation, said Brown, surely Senator Benton would now take a prominent role in its recovery. Benton answered abruptly and heatedly that the movement was "on the part of some, an intrigue for the presidency and a plot to dissolve the Union—on the part of others, a Texas scrip and land speculation; and I am against it!"[45]

The detection of both an "intrigue" to control the presidency and a "plot" to break up the Union had some foundation in reality. The election of 1844 would be Calhoun's final chance at the White House. He had been laying the foundation of his campaign for years, strengthening his already wide southern following during the petition controversies and enhancing his national standing upon his return to the Democratic Party in the late 1830s. Benton, Silas Wright, and others among the "radical" wing of the party were entrenched in their opposition to the South Carolinian. Calhounites viewed the annexation of Texas and the addition of another slave state as their most effective campaign issues. Sam Houston, now president of the Republic of Texas, meanwhile played an artful game of diplomacy in response to rejection by the United States, by openly courting the friendship of Great Britain. The British had arranged a truce in the ongoing war between Texas and Mexico, and members of President Tyler's administration were concerned that the republic might become a British province on the southwestern border of the United States. Mindful of congressional opposition, President Tyler had rejected two annexation offers from Houston while Webster was secretary of state. By early 1844, however, Webster was gone, replaced by Upshur. In addition, Thomas Gilmer, whose public letter had launched the agitation for Texas, was appointed secretary of the Navy. Upshur, believing reports of British designs on Texas, reopened the stalled negotiations with Houston for a treaty of annexation.[46]

Three months after Benton's outburst to Congressman Brown on the steps of the Capitol, the Missouri senator joined both Upshur and Gilmer for an event seemingly unrelated to either Texas or slavery. On February 28, 1844, the three were among a party of guests aboard the U.S.S. *Princeton*, a new man-of-war, for an excursion down the Potomac. On the return trip most of the guests went forward to observe the firing of a big new gun dubbed the "Peacemaker." Benton followed the advice of a junior officer that he could follow the flight of the ball better if he stood several feet back from the breech. This quirk of scientific curiosity may have saved his life, for a moment later the "Peacemaker" exploded, killing a number of people, including both Upshur and Gilmer. Benton suffered from trauma and a burst eardrum but escaped the countless pieces of flying metal from the explosion.[47]

In the aftermath of this tragedy, President Tyler cast about for someone to replace Upshur as secretary of state. He shortly offered the position to Calhoun, and the South Carolinian, by now aware that his bid for the presidency had failed, accepted with alacrity. By April 12 the treaty providing for the annexation of Texas was signed by President Tyler, and American naval protection departed for the Texas coast. The treaty made no mention of boundaries. The government of Texas claimed the area between the Nueces and Rio Grande rivers. Never included within the Mexican state of Texas and still claimed by Mexico, this disputed area had formed a kind of no-man's land between the two countries over which a deadly conflict had sputtered since 1836. The treaty of annexation thus meant either taking on the continuing border war with Mexico or surrendering the claims. In the meantime, Calhoun had found among Upshur's papers a statement by Lord Aberdeen that denied any British designs to end slavery in Texas. The letter added, however, that "although we shall not desist from those open and honest efforts which we have constantly made for procuring the abolition of slavery throughout the world, we shall neither openly nor secretly resort to any measures which can tend to disturb [the southern states'] internal tranquility . . . "[48]

The secretary of state seized on this passage to dispatch an immediate reply accusing Britain of threatening slavery in Texas and the United States, rebuking the British, announcing the treaty of annexation, and concluding with a lengthy paean to slavery as a wise and humane institution. "In no other condition or in any other country in the world," wrote Calhoun, "has the negro race ever attained so high an elevation of morals, intelligence or civilization" as under the southern Christian slave system. Officially a diplomatic communiqué, the "Pakenham Letter," as it became known, was leaked to the press for domestic consumption just as the treaty of annexation went to the Senate.[49]

Both Benton and his longtime ally, publisher Francis Blair, saw in the Pakenham Letter a determination to make Texas a sectional issue. They viewed Calhoun's essay on the benefits of slavery and his demand for federal protection of the peculiar institution as a maneuver to make annexation unacceptable to Van Buren during an election year. Blair contended that Calhoun "knew that it [the Pakenham letter] would array the whole North against the treaty, and prove fatal to it. His aim, then, was to make it an exclusively southern sectional question, to make himself the champion of the southern rights involved, and take the chances for advancement held out by a project which involved in its consummation the dissolution of the confederacy."[50]

A series of public letters on the Texas question appeared in the last week of April 1844, Clay opposed annexation "at this time" as likely to lead to war with Mexico. Van Buren, likewise, questioned the wisdom of immediate annexation, expressed his fear of war with Mexico, and refused to trim his opinions "for the unworthy purpose of increasing my chances for political promotion." James K. Polk of Tennessee, however, viewed by many as the best choice for Van Buren's running mate, declared himself unequivocally for "immediate *re-annexation*."[51]

Benton's own views on the matter appeared in the Washington *Globe* at the end of the month. In answer to a letter from members of the Texas Congress, he reminded readers that he had been "the first opponent of the treaty which dismembered your territory from our Union." In time "the recovery of Texas" was inevitable, but annexation at this time would renew the hostilities between Texas and Mexico, which had abated for the moment. Benton also denounced the boundaries being claimed by Texas. "I, who consider what I am about, always speak of Texas as constituted at the time of the treaty of 1819, and not as constituted by the Republic of Texas." Benton called on readers to "not repeat the blunder [of 1819] and double the calamity, by the manner of recovering [Texas] in 1844."[52]

From Tennessee, Andrew Jackson wrote to Blair that he had "shed tears of regret" when he read the letters of Van Buren and Benton. He warned that Van Buren's tenuous claim to the Democratic nomination was in jeopardy as his letter would "lose him many western and southern votes at the Baltimore convention," and he warned that Benton's position would "enable Penn jnr. to put Col. Benton politically down in Missouri" in the upcoming senatorial election. Regarding Benton as the stronger personality, Jackson concluded that he had "led Van Buren into his unfortunate Texas position." Benton and the Old Hero found themselves in bitter disagreement for the first time in twenty years, and it was left to Blair to patch things up between the two old allies.[53]

Senate debate over Calhoun's treaty began, in secret session, in mid-May. Benton opened his attack on annexation with a long, elaborately documented review of the negotiations leading to the treaty. He pointed out that the administration was "explicit in presenting the Rio Grande del Norte, in its whole extent," as the southern and western boundary of the area to be annexed. This policy would involve "the seizure of two thousand miles of a neighbor's dominion, including the capital of New Mexico." The justification for this outrage was a nonexistent British threat to slavery. Texas, said Benton, should be annexed "for great national reasons, obvious as day, and permanent as nature," when possible "with peace and honor, or even at the price of just war against any intrusive foreign power" but not on "weak and groundless pretexts, discreditable to ourselves, offensive to others, too thin and shallow not to be seen through by every beholder and merely invented to cover unworthy purposes." In response to Calhoun's rationale, Benton cited British denials. Even if these were insincere, said Benton, British efforts to drive slavery from the "hearts, customs, and interests" of white Texans would take years. Still, Calhoun had found no time to consult with the government of Mexico before presenting it with this fait accompli.[54]

Thus, the country was faced with the question of war. The "satisfaction of the treaty would, of itself, mean war between the United States and Mexico." Such a conflict would be "unjust in itself—upon a peaceable neighbor—in violation of treaties and of pledged neutrality—unconstitutionally made." Benton further condemned the timing of the treaty— "its sudden explosion upon us, like a ripened plot and a charged bomb," on the eve of the Democratic Party's Baltimore convention. What was the purpose of raising an unnecessary sectional quarrel at this time? To give the Texas "bomb" time "to burst... blowing up candidates for the presidency... and furnishing a new Texas candidate, anointed with gunpowder."[55]

In concluding, Benton addressed the issue of slavery. He reckoned that about half of the area claimed by annexationists was unsuited to slavery; therefore the question of its further expansion was neutralized. Benton regretted that "a different aspect has been given to it." He went on to state his views on slavery in general:

> I am southern by birth, southern by my affections, interests and connections—and shall abide the fate of the South in everything in which she has right upon her side. I am a slaveholder, and shall take the fate of other slaveholders in every aggression upon that species of property... but I must see a real case of danger before I take the alarm. I am against the cry of wolf when there is no wolf. I will resist the intrusive efforts of those whom it does not concern, to abolish slavery among us; but I shall not engage in schemes for its extension into regions where it was never known—into the valley of the Rio del Norte, for example, and along a river of two thousand miles in extent, where a slave's face was never seen.[56]

Benton had spent most of his adult life fostering the transformation from expeditionary frontiers of inclusion to frontiers of exclusion fit for white agricultural settlement. He had played this role in Tennessee, in Missouri, and for the West generally since before the War of 1812. At the frontier of the Mexican borderlands, however, he ceased his drumbeat as advocate for the white republic. Both the New Mexico trade and the Union itself were now, in Benton's view, at risk. By 1843 there was too much to be sacrificed by pursuing the course of white nationalism further into the Southwest.

Strains in the Democratic Coalition: The 1844 Convention and After

At the end of May the scene of the debate shifted to the Democratic convention at Baltimore. Until the Texas issue had emerged, most members of the party assumed that the nomination would go to Van Buren. By the time the delegates met, however, controversy over the New Yorker's anti-annexation letter had made things less certain. Robert J. Walker of Mississippi and others were working to build a coalition of South and Southwest in order to nominate a candidate in favor of Texas annexation. No sooner had convention officers been selected than a southern delegate proposed the adoption of a rule requiring a two-thirds majority for the nomination. With the passage of this measure Van Buren's prospects were scuttled, and the delegates became stalemated between his supporters and those pushing for Lewis Cass. The deadlock was broken when Polk's name was put forward by Massachusetts educator and historian George Bancroft. Thus, in a deal largely brokered behind the scenes, Polk became the first "dark horse" candidate in American political history to win his party's nomination. The vice presidency was offered to New Yorker Silas Wright, but Wright, a staunch ally of both Benton and Van Buren, declined and the place on the ticket went to George Dallas of Pennsylvania.[57]

Benton was deeply disappointed with the result. Writing to Jackson during the deadlock, he compared it to 1824–1825, "when the will of the people was put down in your presence by the intrigues of the members of Congress.... Offices, 100 millions of Texas lands, ten millions of Texas stock—are making fearful havoc among our public men." Publicly, however, Benton played the role of loyal party supporter, writing to the *Missourian* that "neither Mr. Polk nor Mr. Dallas has anything to do with the intrigue which has nullified the choice of the people, and the principles of our government in the person of Mr. Van Buren; and neither of them should be injured or prejudiced by it."[58]

In the meantime, the Senate debate over the annexation treaty continued. On June 8 the treaty, far from receiving the required two-thirds for Senate approval, was defeated by a vote of 35 to 16. While all but one Whig member voted against the treaty, Democrats split with 15 in favor to 7—including Benton and Wright—opposed. Fellow Missourian David Rice Atchison, who had been appointed the previous year to replace the late Lewis Linn, significantly voted with the yeas.[59]

Two days later, Benton presented his own plan for the annexation of Texas. Under its provisions, the Rio Grande valley was left to Mexico, the area of Texas to be admitted was no larger than the largest existing state, and it was to be divided more or less equally into slave and free territories—under which "the danger of future Missouri controversies" was to be avoided. Further, the president was required to negotiate with both Texas and Mexico, securing the consent of the latter unless Congress should declare such consent unnecessary. Benton's proposal aimed at avoiding either foreign or sectional war. He particularly emphasized the damage that would result from violating and abrogating the commercial treaty between the United States and Mexico that had served Missouri so well since the 1820s, particularly as a source of hard money.

Benton recounted the trade that had commenced with Mexico the year that nation's independence had been declared, "humbly to be sure, but with a rapid and immense development." In 1835, the year before the Texas revolution, American exports to Mexico amounted to about $1.5 million. Specie imports from Mexico to the U. S. totaled $8.3 million, independent of merchandise imported from that country. "With every sympathy alive in favor of the Texians," Benton still wished to conciliate their return to the Union following their successful revolt with "the great object of preserving our peaceful relations, and with them our commercial, political, social, and moral position in regard to Mexico, the second power of the NEW WORLD after ourselves, and the first of the Spanish branch of the great American family."[60]

Six years after the Texas revolution, however, American trade with Mexico had declined precipitously, while over twenty million dollars worth of silver went annually to the British government. Benton laid the blame for this turnabout at the feet of the immediate annexationists, whose ill-conceived plans were a matter of concern to the whole of the Union, but particularly to the Great West. "The Mexican trade is emphatically a western trade! And New Orleans is its great emporium. There arrives—there did arrive—the ship loads of Mexican dollars to meet the steamboat loads of western produce! And every measure that repulses or diminishes that importation of silver, diminishes in the same degree the capacity of New Orleans to purchase western produce, and carries loss and damage to the growing crop of every western farmer."[61]

Finally, Benton added one more view from which to regard the value of the Mexican trade. "We are a paper money people, with a thousand paper banks, and not one mine of silver. . . . What would become of these banks—or rather what would become of their currency in the hands of the people—were it not for Mexican dollars?" In the depression years 1837 to 1840, the country had seen those banks shut up and their paper sink to a half, a quarter, or less of its value in the hands of the people. The "great calamity of this general and prolonged suspension of specie payments had its origin and root in the conduct and condition of the Bank of the United States, yet the loss of the customary supply of silver from Mexico favored her criminal design, and brought the local institutions more completely within subjection to her diabolical policy." Benton argued that the decline in the supply of Mexican silver to the United States during those years was enormous and was directly related to

> the depreciation of currency and the ruin of commerce ... I have before traced the working of this commerce, and shown the ignorance of the superficial observer who, looking to the direct trade alone, is ready to say Mexico takes but little from us, and that of very few articles. This is an error—a gross error: she takes—she did take—much from us—and that of everything—but at a double operation, not injurious to any interest, and beneficial to navigation, by giving it a double employment.

Economic arguments notwithstanding, his bill remained unacceptable to the advocates of immediate annexation. It was tabled by a vote of 25–20, much of the opposition coming from members opposed to any annexation at all.[62]

Three days later, George McDuffie of South Carolina rose to deliver a reply to Benton. McDuffie, who before January 1844 had been an opponent of annexation, now eagerly endorsed Calhoun's program. He accused Benton of seeking to prevent any future annexation without the consent of Mexico and revisited the record of atrocities committed by Mexican troops in the 1836 war with Texas. McDuffie's attacks became more personal. Perhaps as a result of his painful expulsion from Chapel Hill, Benton had redoubled his efforts to acquire learning during his years in Tennessee and Missouri. Gold eyeglasses hanging from his neck, a frown of concentration usually preceding his cannonades of verbiage, Benton was never known to display his erudition lightly. McDuffie derided the Missourian's tendency to play schoolmaster to the Senate, "to stand up and say, 'I am Sir Oracle, when I open my mouth let no dog bark.'" McDuffie warned that Benton would have no place at a forthcoming Democratic meeting at Nashville—"in the great division of parties ... under what flag shall we find him?" Benton would be thrown out of the Democratic positions he had so ably occupied. McDuffie concluded by comparing the Texas treaty, killed in the Senate, to the ghost of Caesar who had appeared to Brutus, warning "thou shalt see me at Philippi." The ghost of the dead treaty, said McDuffie, might well haunt Benton when he sought reelection in Missouri.[63]

As McDuffie sat down, Benton rose to respond. A large crowd had filled the gallery to observe the drama, including John Quincy Adams, who sat just behind the Missourian and thought McDuffie's speech extremely "violent and rancorous." Benton admitted his penchant to play schoolmaster, "a faint imitation of the elder Cato," but asserted in reference to McDuffie, "I never overtax my neophytes." He then turned to the treaty itself. For some, disunion was the purpose of the Texas agitation. By dividing Texas into slave states, the treaty was "an open preparation for a Missouri question and a dissolution of the Union." As for the Nashville convention, Edmund Burke had once described "a cluster of old political antagonists ... all pigging together (that is, lying like pigs, heads and tails, and as many together) in the same truckle bed." Never was there such a "medley of bedfellows" as would meet in Nashville. But let the members take care. General Jackson would be there as well. "If he should happen to find old tariff disunion, disguised as Texas disunion, lying by his side. . . . Teeth and claws he will have, and sharp use he will make of them! Not only skin and fur, but blood and bowels may fly."[64]

McDuffie had complained that Benton was arrogant, overbearing, and dictatorial to those who opposed him. So far as this was true, Benton apologized, but he had "been laboring under deep feeling." He, who hated intrigue and loved the Union, could "only speak of intriguers and disunionists with warmth and indignation." The oldest advocate for the recovery of Texas, he "must be allowed to speak in just terms of the criminal politicians who prostituted the question of its recovery to their own base purposes, and delayed its success by degrading and disgracing it." As a westerner, coming "from a state more than any other interested in the recovery of this country so unaccountably thrown away by the treaty of 1819," he "must be allowed to feel indignant at seeing Atlantic politicians seizing upon it, and making it a sectional question, for the purposes of ambition and disunion."[65]

Benton stalked toward his antagonist and struck his fist on McDuffie's desk. The Carolinian had described Benton as the Brutus who would betray his homeland. "The Senator," said Benton, "compares the rejected treaty to the slain Caesar, and gives it a ghost, which is to meet me . . . as the specter met Brutus at Philippi. . . . I can promise the ghost and his backers that if the fight goes against me at this new Philippi . . . and the enemies of the American Union triumph over me . . . I shall not fall upon my sword as Brutus did . . . but I shall save it, and save myself for another day, and for another use—for the day when the disunion of these states is to be fought—not with words, but with iron—and for the hearts of the traitors who appear in arms against their country."[66]

John Quincy Adams, attending the session, thought the attack "so merciless and personal that nothing but bodily fear could have withheld the hand of McDuffie from a challenge; but he put up with it, quiet as a lamb." Applause swept the galleries, and another extraordinary scene took place when Adams complimented Benton and offered his hand. The Missourian accepted this gesture from his longtime political enemy and reportedly told the former president, "Mr. Adams, you are passing off the stage, and I am passing away also, but while we live we will stand by THE UNION." Jackson, when informed of this incident, inquired of Blair whether it could be true and warned the editor that further support for Benton would ruin the Democratic *Globe*. To Polk, Jackson confided that the only explanation for Benton's behavior was the injury his brain had suffered as the result of the *Princeton* explosion.[67]

Congress adjourned on June 17 without action on Benton's Texas proposal. Directly afterward, he set out for St. Louis, where a stiff fight was shaping up for the 1844 Senate race. Benton's speeches in opposition to Calhoun and McDuffie were dynamite to Missouri Democrats already divided over currency issues between so-called "Hards" and "Softs." To answer the continuing need for some kind of central financial institution, the Bank of the State of Missouri had been chartered by the General Assembly in 1837 along rigidly Jacksonian lines, with strict requirements for the ratio of specie reserves on hand to the value of notes issued. Hard-money Democrats, who identified with Benton, favored these conservative banking policies and continued to seek the suppression of paper notes in order to make gold and silver the only currency in the state. Soft-money Democrats and Whigs (who remained a permanent minority in Missouri) wanted to force the state bank into accepting devalued paper as legal tender and to liberalize its credit policies in order to promote commerce. While partisan divisions were never entirely clear, the Softs generally drew political support from St. Louis business interests while the Hards came from outstate areas, with the Boonslick region as the foundation of support for Benton and his economic policies. Banking and currency controversies gained new salience in Missouri as the state experienced the effects of the nationwide depression that had begun in 1837. Calls for monetary reform grew more heated with each passing month.[68]

Into this already volatile mixture was now injected the Texas issue and the question of one or more additional slave states admitted to the Union. It was to strain Benton's alliance with the hard-money, proslavery Fayette Clique to the breaking point. Many Missourians accepted Benton's claim that the United States could still acquire Texas legally and peacefully through negotiations with Mexico. He retained some degree of political cover from the fact that Calhoun's treaty had been soundly rejected by the Senate with half-a-dozen other Democrats besides himself voting against it. Others were not so sure. White Missourians overwhelmingly supported annexation and had assumed that their senior senator would too. In the view of many, Benton, by questioning the unconditional right of slavery to expand into the West, had embraced heresy. Never mind that Benton's position on slavery itself had not essentially changed and that he still claimed to represent the interests of the white yeomanry, and wanted greater white emigration to Texas to balance the power of its small planter class prior to statehood. Missouri annexationists were in no mood for subtleties. Interpreting the defense of slavery and the interests of the West as one and the same, they now included the future of Texas as an issue that affected the destiny of Missouri as well. The *Missouri Register* warned that Benton "must not be permitted to stand in the way of the onward and upward destiny of our country to those high and holy destinies to which God and nature seem to have designed. May a dishonorable grave and a name forever infamous be the fate of him who will thus sacrifice the highest hopes and the dearest interests of his native land." Benton's political enemies accused him of being motivated "by contemptible jealousy of Calhoun" in his Texas policy and compared him to Benedict Arnold, who "in need of money, bargained for the sale of West Point. . . . Mexico, France, and England are opposed to the annexation of Texas and they have the money and to spare."[69]

The pro-Benton *Missourian* responded by publishing Benton's 1819 *Enquirer* articles on Oregon and Texas in pamphlet form and declared that the issue was "*Benton or no Benton*: MAKING UP THE ISSUE AND THROWING OFF THE MASK." Even before the Texas treaty had come to a vote in the United States Senate, the state Democratic convention met in Jefferson City, where the hard-money majority made support for both Benton and Atchison the litmus test for Assembly candidates. Upon his arrival in Missouri, Benton traveled to Boonville where he delivered a three-hour speech declaring that his position was more important than his reelection. He spoke out in support of Polk, especially approving "Young Hickory's" announcement that he would retire after a single term. Continuing to speak favorably of Van Buren, despite the choice of the national party convention, Benton called for a "Democratic candidate for 1848 taken from the North"—if not Van Buren then Silas Wright, going so far as to suggest that the South had had too many presidents. Here in the heart of slaveholding Missouri, Benton condemned "Mr. Tyler's Texas Treaty" as a ploy to portray annexation as "wholly directed to the extension, perpetuation, and predominance of slavery." Citing the resolution passed recently in Calhoun's South Carolina that called for "Texas without the Union rather than the Union without Texas," Benton presented his own bill as the only safe alternative. He appealed to voters in language that at once impugned the motives of the opposition and appealed to white solidarity against the growing influence of large planters and their slave labor force. Honorable annexation of Texas, Benton argued, could be yet be achieved, "but for none of the Negro reasons—or as it ought to be pronounced on this occasion, *nigger* reasons."[70]

In the August election for the Assembly, the Whigs sharply increased their number of seats in the legislature. The real possibility of an alliance between Whigs and soft-money Democrats to defeat Benton seemed to be shaping up. In the face of this threat Benton remained unshaken, at least publicly. At Hannibal in October, he called for the state to give Polk and Dallas a ten-thousand-vote majority. Speaking again on the Texas issue he declared, "the people of the state—both parties exclusive of the *Softs*, who are *Calhoun men*—are with me." In mid-October Benton gave a climactic speech in St. Louis. He would yield the high ground on the reannexation of Texas to no man. In his long Senate service, he had "acted a part on every public measure which can now claim public attention." Benton pointed to his protests against the surrender of Texas in 1819 as proof of his *bona fides*. The Democratic platform planks on Oregon and Texas were "my own measures! Children of twenty-five years ago! And then treated as humbugs! And their author ridiculed as a visionary projector.... Five and twenty years ago. I put these two balls in motion! Solitary and alone I did it! Millions now roll them forward!" Benton once more damned the Tyler-Calhoun "intrigue," restating and elaborating his position. Not explicitly mentioned, but embodied in Benton's campaign rhetoric, was his belief that the proper course on Texas was inextricably linked to good relations with Mexico and the Mexican silver on which his hard-money economic philosophy rested. Indeed, his charge that the Calhoun men and the Softs were one and the same had some plausibility in light of Calhoun's marriage of convenience with the Whig Party during recent years. With everything that he had championed for decades at stake, Benton privately stated that he was "ready to die politically" for his position.[71]

As it turned out, that would not be necessary. When the Thirteenth General Assembly met in late November, the Boonslick faction was once more firmly in control. In return for votes for Benton, the Central Clique came out in favor of dividing the state into single-member congressional districts. To further ensure Benton's election, the Central Clique supported a series of resolutions instructing Missouri's congressional delegation to vote for immediate annexation. However, with Speaker Claiborne Fox Jackson taking the lead, the language of the instructions was eventually softened, the word *immediate* being removed in favor of annexation "at the earliest practicable moment." Although the issue remained in doubt until the balloting took place, party discipline and Benton's long-standing popularity in the state won the day. Atchison, the immediate annexationist, was easily elected by a 34-vote margin to complete the unexpired term of Lewis Linn. For Benton the margin was much closer: 71–57 over a loose coalition of Softs, Whigs, and individual opponents. The alliance of Benton and the Boonslick Democrats had held, but the disagreements of the 1844 campaign did not bode well for the future.[72]

Annexation, the Advent of Polk, and the Death of Jackson

In the meantime the voters had gone to the polls in early November to give James K. Polk a victory over Henry Clay, who had unsuccessfully tried to straddle on the issue of Texas annexation. Though Polk's margin of electoral votes—170 to 105 for Clay—was impressive; the popular vote was much closer—1,339,494 to 1,300,004. Missouri gave Polk the ten thousand-vote majority that Benton had urged, but elsewhere, as voting from one state to another was spread over a twelve-day period, the issue was in doubt until the very end. In the critical state of New York, Polk won by a mere 5,000 out of 486,000 votes cast. Benton was convinced that Wright, who had agreed to leave the Senate and run for governor, had played a crucial role. The influence of the old radical may have had something to do with the Democratic victory, but more important still was the candidacy of James G. Birney of the antislavery Liberty party, who won sixty-two thousand votes (2.3%) nationwide and took enough votes away from Clay to ensure that Polk would win New York, and thus carry his program of expansion into the White House.[73]

In Tennessee, Old Hickory observed these developments with anxiety. In September he wrote to Blair that his affection for Benton was "not abated," but with Texas the great issue in the national election, "Col. Benton's speeches has injured the Democratic cause more than all the whiggs." In the fall of 1844, Jackson began working through Blair and through his nephew, Andrew Jackson Donelson (soon to be chargé in Texas), to persuade Benton to reestablish himself with a Texas bill based on the Louisiana Purchase. The indistinct boundary of the 1803 agreement would presumably leave sufficient latitude for negotiations between the United States and Mexico. Both Jackson and Donelson were close to Polk, and they assured Benton that the president-elect would pursue an honorable treaty. Writing from Texas, Donelson urged Benton to omit mention of either slavery or boundaries from the bill in order to get Texas back to the 1803 footing. Benton replied that he would "expect from you all a treaty which I can candidly support." On December 22, 1844, Blair wrote to Jackson that Benton would support a Polk treaty.[74]

President Tyler, in the meantime, arguing that Polk's election was a mandate for immediate annexation, asked Congress for a joint resolution to put the rejected treaty of annexation into effect. McDuffie in the Senate and Democrat Stephen A. Douglas of Illinois in the House offered bills for this purpose. Benton stubbornly reintroduced his own previous bill in response. The debate raged through December and into the new year. In a letter to Donelson, Benton commented that "the real friends to the acquisition of Texas have a hard time of it between two parties one of whom is utterly hostile to the whole measure, and the other fatally bent upon using it for selfish and sinister purposes. . . . Mr. Polk's administration is not to, 'sleep on a bed of roses.' Do not be surprised if you see two conventions in session for the dissolution of the Union before his four years are out. Massachusetts and South Carolina are each in a bad state, and each creating bad feelings around them."[75]

Interpreting his instructions from the Missouri General Assembly as backing his own position on Texas, Benton introduced a new bill on February 5, 1845, that omitted all mention of Mexico or slavery. A state "formed out of the present republic of Texas" was to be admitted as soon as the United States and Texas could agree on the terms. Benton explained that there were no conditions such as those he had insisted on in the previous session, because of the difficulty of getting agreement on them and because any action "must devolve upon the new President," Polk, in whom the Senate had full confidence. In omitting the conditions from the bill, "I do not withdraw them from the consideration of those who may direct the negotiation." As for the issues of slavery and making peaceful adjustments of the boundary line with Mexico, "I shall consider all this as remaining just as fully in the mind of the President as if submitted to him in a bill."[76]

Later in the month the House passed a resolution calling for annexation without negotiation and permitting the division of Texas into as many as five states. Those north of the Missouri Compromise line were to be free, which meant that the majority of Texas would be slave. With the end of the session approaching, the Senate appeared unable to muster the necessary votes to approve either Benton's bill or the new House measure. At length, Robert J. Walker of Mississippi arranged a compromise, combining the two proposals into a joint resolution and giving the president authority to choose between the two. The Senate approved the compromise, 27–25, on February 27 with Benton and four followers providing the deciding votes. The next day the House concurred. With only three days left in office, President Tyler now decided not to leave the matter of Texas to his successor. Pressed by Calhoun and concerned, no doubt, for his place in history, he chose the House plan over Benton's. On the evening of March 3, with only hours left in his term, Tyler sent a message to Donelson, the American Chargé d'Affaires in Texas, ordering him to proceed under the House plan.[77]

Benton and fellow radicals felt betrayed. Some, including Blair, charged that the compromise Texas bill had been passed by "fraud." Benton believed this as well. The votes of a handful of key senators, according to this account, were given on the basis of McDuffie's declaration that Tyler and Calhoun would not have the audacity to act on the measure and Polk's alleged assurance to Blair that he would proceed under Benton's negotiation plan. No doubt McDuffie, if sincere, underestimated the "audacity" of Calhoun and Tyler while Polk denied that he had made any commitments concerning Texas. Still, without the votes of Benton and his followers, no Texas bill would have passed. Polk was inaugurated on March 4, 1845. Faced with accepting or reversing Tyler's decision to annex Texas on the basis of the House resolution, the new president chose to let it stand.[78]

Three months later, as he lay on his deathbed, Andrew Jackson dictated a last message to Benton. "I thank the Colonel," he said, "for his kind recollection of me in my old age and sore afflictions; it would give me great pleasure to see him once more, but that, I fear, is impossible, as my life is drawing rapidly to a close. The Colonel is not only an able and distinguished statesman, but a warm and sincere patriot, and his country is under great obligation to him. I feel grateful for the able and efficient support he gave me during the whole of my administration, and I beg you, when next you see him, to remember me to him." In an ironic twist of fate, William B. Lewis, whom Benton had unsuccessfully tried to goad into a duel over thirty years earlier, delivered the Old Chief's last message.[79]

Jackson's passing marked the end of his era as well. The Democratic Party that had been founded on his leadership had now split over the annexation of Texas and the related question of the expansion of slavery. In the process of that division, the radical leadership of the party had been overthrown and Benton's own power in his home state had sharply declined. In Missouri, as in the nation as a whole, the Texas controversy demonstrated the vulnerabilities of the white egalitarian democracy championed by Benton and other radical Jacksonians against the demands of an uncompromising slaveholder elite. In the face of growing southern anxiety over slavery, the radicals and northern Democrats were forced to go along with one concession after another to Calhounite intransigence. Consensus on economic issues was no longer enough to unite the party. As time went on, the imperious ultimatums of the southern "slave power" (including their supporters in the Boonslick region of Missouri) undermined the ideals of the egalitarian white republic that had been championed by Benton since the late 1820s. The growing strain on Van Buren's old coalition of southern planters and "plain republicans" raised the question whether the old radicals could remain with the party at all in the new political climate.

Angered over the outcome of the Baltimore convention and still smarting at the manner in which the Texas treaty had been forced upon them, Van Buren Democrats appeared to be the natural enemies of the incoming Polk administration. Benton, in particular, was expected to use his influence in opposition to the president, who further alienated the old radicals when he replaced Francis Blair's venerable *Globe* with a new party paper edited by Thomas Ritchie, of the conservative Richmond Junto. Nonetheless, perhaps because of his unofficial role as leader of the radical-agrarian wing of the Democrats, Benton sought to establish amicable relations with Polk at the outset. With Elizabeth and their daughters, he called on the president-elect and Mrs. Polk upon their arrival in Washington, and the two families attended the same Presbyterian Church on Sundays for the next four years. In the aftermath of the election and the bitter debate over Texas, Benton had ample reason to hold grudges, but more urgent matters soon called for his attention.[80]

War for the Borderlands

Mexico responded to President Tyler's message of annexation by severing diplomatic relations with the United States and sent troops to the Rio Grande border. Upon assuming the presidency, James Polk found himself confronted with potential conflicts against both Mexico in the Southwest and Britain over the Oregon boundary. By 1846 the British government, its profits from the northwestern fur trade dwindling, indicated willingness to negotiate a boundary settlement at the forty-ninth parallel, and Benton proved instrumental in securing Senate approval for the treaty that summer. Polk thus avoided a war that no one, save a few die-hard northern expansionists, wanted to see. Mexico was a different matter. Polk was determined to have not only Texas, but California and New Mexico as well. He sent John Slidell of Louisiana to Mexico City, authorized to offer the government up to $40 million for California, New Mexico, and settlement of the Texas boundary at the Rio Grande. The Mexican government, in the midst of an internal power struggle, refused to receive Slidell. Upon receiving news of the failure of Slidell's mission, Polk ordered an American army under Zachary Taylor to advance from Corpus Christi on the Nueces River, where it had been encamped since August 1845, to the Rio Grande opposite Matamoras.[81]

The president's order was an open invitation to war with Mexico, which Benton still fervently hoped to avoid. As recently as February 1846 he had written to Pierre Chouteau Jr. that he was promoting a plan whereby private American claims against Mexico would be paid from the United States Treasury as an "equivalent" to serve the basis for negotiations "for a new boundary and for terminating all differences between us." Polk met with Benton several times during the spring of 1846. The president was aware of Benton's "decided aversion to war with Mexico if it could be avoided consistently with the honor of the country." On April 9 Polk informed Benton of Slidell's rejection. The senator commented that "our ablest men should be Ministers to the South American States; that we should cultivate their friendship and stand with them as the crowned heads of Europe stood together."[82]

Twenty-five years of peaceful trade between Missouri and Mexico had created ties that Benton was loath to break. Events, however, had now taken on a momentum of their own. Near the end of April an American patrol was attacked by Mexican troops just north of the Rio Grande. When news of the incident reached Washington, Polk asked Congress for a declaration of war. On the morning of May 11, the president consulted with congressional leaders, including Benton. The Missourian declared that he would vote for men and money "for defense of our territory," but he was not prepared to make aggressive war on Mexico. He "disapproved the marching of the army from Corpus Christi to the left bank of the [Rio Grande] Del Norte," and he "did not think the territory of the U.S. extended "beyond the Nueces." The president was unable to convince one of the leading senators from his own party that the Mexican army had "invaded our territory and shed American blood on American soil."[83]

Nonetheless, before the day was out, the House of Representatives drafted a bill substantially identical to the president's view and providing money and troops for war against Mexico. In the Senate, declaring war was a somewhat longer process. Though Calhoun insisted on a full-scale debate of the war message, Benton, as chair of the Committee on Military Affairs, prevented deliberation from interfering with the mobilization of men and supplies by moving for a division of the message between his own committee—to deal with military preparations—and the Committee on the Foreign Relations, which would address the question of relations between the United States and Mexico. Back at the White House that evening, however, Benton told the president that "in the 19th Century war should not be declared without full discussion and much more consideration than had been given to it by the House of Representatives."[84]

The following day Benton told fellow senators that "the door was still open for adjustment of our difficulties." For a time it appeared that a handful of Democrats, including both Benton and Calhoun, might join with the Whigs to defeat the declaration of war. When the vote came, however, the opposition melted. Many members "extremely averse to this war," wrote Benton, acted out of a feeling of "duress in the necessity of aiding our own troops." Only two Whigs voted against the declaration while Calhoun abstained.[85]

Much later, Benton took issue with Polk's argument that the war was a defensive measure. In the first place, "the legal state of war ... was produced by the incorporation of Texas, with which Mexico was at war." The United States government then assured that an actual, as well as legal, state of war existed, "by the immediate advance of the army to the frontier of Texas, and the Navy to the Gulf of Mexico, to take the war off the hands of the Texans." Finally, "the actual clash of arms was brought on by further advance of the American troops to the left bank of the Lower Rio-Grande." It was then, "under these circumstances that the Mexico troops crossed the river, and commenced the attack.... The laws of nations, and the law of self-defense, justify that spilling of blood; and such will be the judgment of history."[86]

Notwithstanding his view of the administration's justifications for war, Benton cooperated closely with the president as the conflict progressed, serving as both chairman of the Senate Committee on Military Affairs and as a kind of informal chief-of-staff for the commander-in-chief. Polk, who had ascended to his role as commander-in-chief largely based on his effectiveness as a partisan Democrat, now found that his top generals, both Zachary Taylor who commanded the army in Northern Mexico and Winfield Scott, the general-in-chief in Washington, had Whig affiliations. Benton possessed low opinions of both men as military leaders. He described Taylor as "unfit for command" and advised the president that Scott be "forthwith ordered to some post on the northern frontier, as a merited rebuke" for his resistance to carrying out orders. Still searching for means to effect a peaceful settlement with Mexico, Benton denounced Taylor's campaign in the north-Mexican provinces as insufficiently bold to bring about an end to the hostilities. He proposed a seaborne invasion of central Mexico by way of the coastal city of Vera Cruz, to be followed by "a rapid crushing movement" on Mexico City. As his plan developed, Benton also suggested that a high-level, bipartisan commission, with authority to make peace, should accompany the military headquarters. In addition, "there ought to be a Lieutenant General of the army who should be General-in-chief," and who would be "a man of talents and resources . . . as well as a military man." It was understood by the president and cabinet members that the plum appointment would go to Benton himself. Though he had not donned a uniform for over thirty years, the ever-confident senator argued that he deserved the appointment as he "had been a colonel in the army before either of the present generals held that rank."[87]

In June 1846 the president had requested a written summary of Benton's views on conducting the war. The result was an 11-page document which, after editing and comments by Polk, was included in a set of instructions to General Taylor. The "inhabitants" of Mexico should be treated with kindness to counteract charges that the war was one of national survival in response to American invasion and plunder. Every opportunity should be taken to assure both civilians and captured Mexican officers that "the war itself is only carried on to obtain justice, and that we had much rather procure that by negotiation than by fighting." Benton went on to explain that "in a country so divided into races, classes, and parties as Mexico," it should be easy for the United States to exploit these divisions. "Between the Spanish who monopolize the wealth and power of the country... and the mixed Indian race who bear its burthens, there must be jealousy and animosity... the lower and the higher clergy, the latter of whom have the dignities and revenues, while the former have poverty and labor... the political parties... some more liberal and friendly to us than others... rival chiefs, political and military." All such rifts in the social fabric, the existence of which must be the cause of much bitterness, must be utilized "in bringing about a just and speedy peace." Above all, Benton concluded, the war should be conducted in such a way as "to leave no lasting animosities behind, to prejudice the future friendships and commerce of the two countries; nor to permit injurious reports to go forth to excite the ill will of the other Republics of Spanish origin, against us." It was a remarkable document, showing a keen awareness of Mexican politics and society from a lawmaker who possessed long experience as an observer of American relations with Mexico both before and after her independence from Spain. It also revealed Benton, at an early date, contemplating *post bellum* relations between his beloved West and "the Mexican nation."[88]

Benton's archrival, Calhoun, had opposed the war from the first. Declaring that "Mexico is to us the forbidden fruit; the penalty of eating it is to subject our institutions to political death," the South Carolinian told friends in his home state that the war "has dropt the curtain on the future." Like Whig opponents of the administration, however, he dared go only so far. Calhoun favored a strategy of "masterly inactivity," or holding the existing line of advance until the Mexican government sued for peace. Voting with the Whigs, Calhoun and his supporters were able to either block or delay much of Polk's legislation for prosecuting the war. Benton objected to such a strategy of "sedentary occupation" as contrary to the active temperament of the American people. He advised the president, "It was a mode of warfare suited to the Spanish temper, which loved procrastination... and would certainly out-sit us in Mexico." It would also raise the question of Polk governing the conquered territory of Northern Mexico without applying to Congress, and once again raising the question of annexation by conquest, "and that beyond the Rio Grande."[89]

After considering both the Calhoun recommendation and Benton's objections, the president came down on the side of a continuing, vigorous prosecution of the war. When the Congress of 1846–1847 convened, Polk submitted a message to this effect, incorporating both Benton's proposal for an amphibious assault upon Veracruz and his idea to create the office of lieutenant general. The lieutenant general would have the authority to settle disagreements between the senior commanders in the field without the delay that the usual appeals to Washington involved, and his bipartisan council of distinguished statesmen could work for both peace and the success of the "republican" faction within the government of Mexico.[90]

It was a sensible and all-embracing program to lend direction to the haphazard prosecution of the war, but partisanship and personal jealousy doomed it to failure. The first wheel to come off involved appointments to the peace commission. On December 3, 1846, Benton submitted the names of Silas Wright, John J. Crittenden, and himself. Polk agreed, but wanted to add John Slidell. This was unacceptable to Benton, who viewed the former envoy as an irritant to Mexican sensibilities. Both the president and the senator refused to give in, and Polk abruptly dropped the whole idea of the commission. This was a major blow, not only for the purposes of peace, but because the inclusion of Crittenden, a Kentucky Whig, had been calculated to carry support from his party in favor of the lieutenant general bill.[91]

The bill to create the new position was introduced in the Senate by Benton's friend and ally John Dix of New York in January 1847. Opponents saw creation of the post and the administration's support for Benton to fill it as an intrigue on the part of the president to arrange for his successor. Despite Benton's insistence that he and Polk desired only to "show the deceived people of Mexico that just and honorable peace is all we want" and that there was no "ulterior and covert design" to elevate any successor for the presidency, the House rejected the lieutenant general bill on January 9, and the Senate followed a week later with a vote of 28 to 21. Calhoun Democrats voted with the Whigs to provide the margin of defeat. Rather remarkably, in light of his earlier argument for his own appointment, Benton would later lament a situation where "A major general, in right of seniority, would command other major generals; while everyone accustomed to military, or naval service, knows that it is rank, and not seniority, which is essential to harmonious and efficient command."[92]

Calhoun was pleased at the failure "to build up, through Benton, the old Van Buren party." Members of the cabinet, who agreed with Calhoun on little else, likewise had no desire to see the radical Benton–Van Buren wing of the Democratic Party regain national power. Secretary of State Buchanan was increasingly resentful of Benton's unofficial role as foreign policy advisor. Benton charged that Secretary of War William

Marcy, Van Buren's most bitter enemy from his home state of New York, had "covertly" lobbied to kill the measure; likewise Treasury Secretary Robert J. Walker, who had clashed with Benton over the legality of Texan claims to the Rio Grande. Walker wanted the United States to annex all of Mexico and refused to support any plan giving Benton control of the final settlement.[93]

The surviving element of Benton's proposal for a "vigorous prosecution" of the war with the aim of achieving the soonest possible peace was the request for an additional ten regiments and a special loan of first two million, then of three million dollars. With these funds, Polk hoped to induce Mexico to end the war and to cede the areas claimed by the Mexican government, including New Mexico and California, to the United States. Complications arose in the House when a "proviso," authored by antislavery Democrat David Wilmot of Pennsylvania, was attached to the loan bill. The Wilmot Proviso stipulated "that no part of the territory to be acquired should be open to the introduction of slavery." The bill as amended passed the House but was filibustered in the Senate, delaying passage of the war appropriation until early the following year. Although the Proviso ultimately failed to become law, for many northerners it served to link the war with Mexico to the expansion of slavery.

When the measure came before the Senate in February 1847, Calhoun responded by introducing his own Resolutions on the Slave Question. He condemned the Missouri Compromise and slavery restrictions generally as hostile to the "safety" and "self-preservation" of the slaveholding states. The time had come for the South to consider its position in the Union should slavery be excluded from the territories to be secured from Mexico. The South was a minority everywhere in the government; the Senate was its only remaining check on the northern majority. "Sir the day that the balance between the two sections of the country—the slaveholding states and the non-slaveholding states—is destroyed, is the day that will not be far removed from revolution, anarchy, civil war, and widespread disaster. The balance of the system is in the slaveholding states. They are the conservative portions." Although he had been willing to acquiesce in expediency of the Missouri Compromise line, its very principle was false and subversive of the Union. Calhoun therefore offered his resolutions holding that the territories were "the joint and common property" of the several states, that Congress could not "deprive the citizens of any of the states of this Union from emigrating with their property [slaves], into any part of the territories," and that in forming a constitution the people of a territory were entirely free to decide matters for themselves except for the constitutional requirement for a republican government.[94]

Benton immediately rose to protest. "We have some business to transact.... If anybody thinks that I am going to lay aside the necessary business of the session to vote on such a string of abstractions, he is greatly mistaken." He charged Calhoun with injecting the "firebrands" of disunion into the debate when he should be assisting in the practical business of ending a war he himself had started. Calhoun replied that he had expected Benton, as "the representative of a slaveholding State," to support his resolutions. "I shall be found in the right place," answered Benton. "I am on the side of my country and the Union."[95]

Four days later, with Polk's entire cabinet seated in the gallery, Benton undertook to "skin Calhoun" and lay to rest his strategy of masterly inactivity. On all Texas matters, said Benton, Calhoun had been tragically wrong. He was "wrong in 1819, in giving away Texas—wrong in 1836 in his sudden and hot haste to get her back—wrong in all his machinations for bringing on the Texas question of 1844—wrong in breaking up the armistice and peace negotiations between Mexico and Texas—wrong in secretly sending the army and navy to fight Mexico while we were at peace with her . . . wrong in writing to Mexico that he took Texas in view of all possible consequences, meaning war—wrong in offering Mexico . . . ten millions of dollars to hush up the war which he had created—wrong now in refusing Mr. Polk three million to aid in getting out of the war which he had made—wrong in throwing the blame of this war of his own making upon the shoulders of Mr. Polk—wrong in his retreat and occupation line of policy . . . and more wrong now than ever, in that string of resolutions which he has laid on the table." Benton singled out for criticism Calhoun's intervention in the peace negotiations between Mexico and Texas prior to annexation in 1844. What if two individuals were engaged in a fight, and two others should part them, and make them agree on an amicable settlement? And what if, while that settlement was going on, another man should secretly instigate one of the parties to break off the agreement and renew the struggle, and promise to take over the fight if he did? "What would morality and Christianity say to this?" asked Benton. "Surely the malediction of all good men would fall upon the man who had interfered to renew the strife. And if this would be the voice of all good men in the case of mere individuals, what would it be when the strife was between nations, and when the renewal of it was to involve a third nation in the contest, and such a war as we now have with our sister republic of Mexico?" This was the awful picture that now presented itself to the moral sense of the world as the result of Calhoun's machinations.[96]

Just prior to the end of its session the Senate approved a three million dollar loan without the Wilmot Proviso. Benton was among those voting against the antislavery measure, which was rejected 31 to 21. Where the Proviso was concerned, he was in agreement with Polk, who thought the Proviso "a mischievous and foolish amendment," as well as with other slave state senators, including Calhoun. For once he found himself out of step with radical Democrats like Dix and his old friend Silas Wright. The latter thought the restriction of slavery in the territories "clearly right . . . expedient . . . necessary." In the North the Proviso sparked a popular reaction, lending to public meetings and legislative resolutions in support of slavery restriction. Even Francis Blair, an old friend and political ally, thought Wilmot's measure the correct policy. Benton would justify his vote, after the fact, by arguing that the Proviso and the Calhoun resolutions were twin evils—"two halves of a pair of shears, neither of which could cut until joined together"; but which, once joined, endangered the map of the Union. Benton further argued that the slavery-restriction Proviso was "nugatory and could answer no purpose," because the territory it was intended to cover was already free soil under Mexican law. The whole slavery agitation, whether originating from North or South, was, Benton believed, the portent of a violent new "sectional struggle" that threatened to tear the Republic apart.[97]

Relations between Benton and the president had become somewhat strained since the defeat of the lieutenant general proposal, though the two men continued to be on friendly terms for the moment. Polk—harassed, overworked, mistrusting of his top generals, and feeling himself surrounded by political enemies—was increasingly concerned over the divisions within his own party. Benton's latest salvo against Calhoun was only one manifestation of the Democrats' disarray. The "Democratic Party in Congress were in a most distracted and feeble condition," wrote the president. Calhoun was "perfectly desperate in his aspirations for the Presidency," and had seized upon the slavery issue "as the only means of sustaining himself." Polk worried that northern Radicals, supporting Silas Wright for the nomination in 1848, "would be rejoiced at the opportunity to take issue with Mr. Calhoun on such a question." He despaired that there was "no patriotism on either side." Calhounites, on the other hand, fretted over Benton's continuing influence as a kind of one-man Kitchen Cabinet within the administration. One wrote that, in the event he replaced the ailing Robert Walker as secretary of the treasury, "Benton might become Dictator of the Administration." Another warned Calhoun that "something must be done to head Mr. Benton" in his effort to develop alliance with the North. The Missourian was now clearly the foremost obstacle to Calhoun's efforts to forge a new coalition that would allow *him* to dictate the terms on which peace was concluded with Mexico and the status of slavery in the newly won territories was decided.[98]

Benton, Frémont, and Polk

The break between Benton and Polk, when it finally occurred, took place not over policy at all, but over the career of the senator's son-in-law. John Charles Frémont had been introduced to the Bentons a half-dozen years earlier when he was a young lieutenant in the Army's Corps of Topographical Engineers. Ever promoting westward exploration and settlement, Benton often hosted the men involved in such projects at his home. Frémont, then twenty-eight, was immediately smitten with Benton's seventeen-year-old daughter, Jessie. In defiance of her father's wishes, Jessie secretly married the dashing young officer in October 1841. When confronted with this fact, Benton quickly overcame his objections and Frémont moved into the Benton home, where he commenced to work together with his ambitious wife and father-in-law on a series of projects for the development of the far West. In 1842 Frémont had set out in command of the first of several mapping expeditions that would lead him into the Rocky Mountains and beyond. Upon his return to the East, his report—embellished by Jessie's literary skill—shortly made him famous as the "Pathfinder of the West."[99]

In the summer of 1845, Benton and Navy Secretary George Bancroft had sent Frémont on the third of his expeditions to the far West. Accompanied by 60 well-armed and experienced men, Frémont left St. Louis in June to explore certain river sources in the Oregon Country, even as debate raged in Washington over the boundary dispute with Great Britain. By December of 1845, Frémont and his men were in central California. Ordered out of the region by the Mexican governor, the force retired northward to Oregon. In early May 1846, a Lieutenant Gillespie of the U.S. Marine Corps managed to find the party on the shores of Oregon's Klamath Lake. Gillespie carried letters from Benton and others, as well as dispatches from the administration, concerning the diplomatic crisis between the United States and Mexico. Interpreting this intelligence as justification for returning south to finish what he had started, Frémont arrived back in California just as the Anglo-American population rose in revolt and declared themselves an independent republic under the Bear Flag. Frémont, commanding the most potent military force in the region, declared himself "protector" of Anglo-American interests, resigned his commission in the U.S. Army, and declared his intention to conquer all of California. This pronouncement was all the more remarkable because it was made at a time when Frémont had no definite knowledge as to whether or not Mexico and the United States were actually at war.[100]

Shaky legal grounds notwithstanding, Frémont and his "California Battalion" set about wresting the territory from Mexican control with the assistance of an American naval squadron under Commodore Robert Stockton. The fighting shortly became subsumed into the general war with Mexico and resulted in California's "incorporation with the American Republic," in which Benton could take justifiable pride. When General Jose Maria Castro, Frémont's former adversary in northern California, alleged to the Mexican government that the Americans had pillaged the homes of Californios, Benton promptly set out to chronicle and to justify his son-in-law's actions in a public letter to Polk. The movement for independence, he argued, was the salvation of California, and had snatched it out of the hands of the British just as they were ready to take it. "The fate of California," he later wrote, "would have been the same whether the United States squadrons had arrived or not; and whether the Mexican War had happened or not. California was already in a revolutionary state, already divided from Mexico politically as it had always been geographically."[101]

The senior American officer on the spot, Commodore Stockton, had appointed the Pathfinder as civil governor of California. In December 1846, however, this arrangement was upset by the arrival of Brigadier General Stephen Watts Kearny, in command of a force that had marched overland from Fort Leavenworth to Santa Fe and thence to San Diego. Kearny insisted that Frémont, as an army officer whose resignation had not yet been formally accepted, came under *his* command. Caught in the middle of this early case of interservice rivalry, Frémont chose badly, siding with Stockton for his own purposes. Kearny, thereupon, charged the insubordinate officer with fomenting a mutiny, dismissed his troops, and sent Frémont east to face a court-martial.

The powerful Senator Benton charged to the rescue of his heroic son-in-law, the victim—as he saw it—of jealous regulars who resented his achievements and fame. During the late summer and early fall of 1847, Benton plead Frémont's case with Polk, as did both Jessie and the Pathfinder's stalwart guide Kit Carson. The president refused to commit himself on the matter but noted that Benton's "deepest concern in life was to see justice done to Col. Frémont." In November, Benton resigned as chair of the Committee on Military Affairs over Secretary of War Marcy's alleged "persecution" of Frémont. The court-martial began on November 2 and continued into January 1848. In the end, the tribunal found Frémont guilty of all charges and sentenced him to dismissal from the service. Nonetheless, noting the unusual circumstances, six of the thirteen officers on the court recommended executive clemency. The matter now rested with Polk and his cabinet. With the exception of Marcy, the majority agreed that the sentence was unwarranted and overly harsh. The secretary of war, however, felt that the honor of the army was at stake. He finally suggested that Polk approve the verdict but remove the sentence. Polk ruled Frémont guilty of insubordination rather than mutiny and ordered him to "resume his sword" at the rank of lieutenant colonel. This may have been more than generous from the president's perspective, but Frémont, feeling his honor had been sullied by the implications of guilt, angrily resigned his commission. Benton's strained relations with the president now broke off completely. Henceforth, although the two continued to attend the same church every Sunday, Polk lamented that Benton "never speaks to me as he was in the habit of doing."[102]

The Peace Settlement

In February of 1848, the nation mourned the death of John Quincy Adams. He had collapsed on the floor of the House and died shortly after. Benton, as senior member of the U.S. Senate, was selected to give the eulogy there. "Punctual to every duty," said Benton, "death found him at the post of duty; and where else could it have found him, at any stage of his career, for the fifty years of his illustrious public life?" Thus had the Missourian's bitterness over the events of 1825 faded into memory.[103]

In the midst of the nation's mourning, news arrived in Washington that peace had at last been concluded with Mexico. An unusual set of maneuvers by Nicholas Trist, a State Department official whose authority had been withdrawn in the midst of negotiations, produced the Treaty of Guadalupe Hidalgo. Despite reservations, Polk sent the treaty to the Senate for approval. There, the Committee on Foreign Affairs, led by Benton and Webster, recommended rejection and the appointment of a commission to be composed of three or five persons belonging to both political parties, to proceed to Mexico to negotiate a new treaty. Benton and Polk were now so estranged that the president wrote, "What Mr. Benton's reason for opposing [the peace treaty] may be no one can tell." He speculated, however, that Benton had "heretofore maintained that the true boundary of Texas was the Nueces instead of the Rio Grande, and he is apt to think that nothing is done properly that he is not previously consulted about."[104]

Before debate in the Senate had concluded, amendments were offered to the treaty, on the one hand for annexing either further territories in Mexico or the whole country, and on the other for annexing no land whatsoever. The first provision, offered by Jefferson Davis of Mississippi and supported by several leading Democrats was, on its face, unacceptable to Mexico. In addition, there were concerns about the ability of the United States to absorb the "mongrel" peoples who populated Mexico south of the Rio Grande. Benton's friend Senator John Clayton of Delaware later explained that to take all of Mexico meant including "Aztecs, Creoles, Half-breeds, Quadroons, Samboes, and I know not what else" within the boundaries of the United States. The latter amendment, which gained the support of numerous Whig members, North and South, was unacceptable to a majority of Americans at the conclusion of a costly and controversial war. Support by a majority for either amendment would have had the practical effect of voting to continue a war that had by now become highly unpopular in many parts of the country. A majority of senators therefore voted on March 10 to approve a peace agreement by which the United States gained an immense territory from Mexico. Absorbed as he had been with Frémont's court-martial, Benton took no part in the debate over the treaty. When the roll was called, however, he was among 14 senators voting in opposition to it.[105]

Despite counsel from Benton urging "total abstinence from the agitation of the question," citizens of the territory of New Mexico, meeting in convention at Santa Fe, had drawn up petitions that were sent to both Benton and Dix, requesting a territorial government and proclaiming that "we do not desire to have domestic slavery within our borders." In his final message to Congress, James Polk quoted "the great republican maxim . . . that the will of the majority, constitutionally expressed, shall prevail [as] our safeguard against force and violence." The president called on Congress to establish territorial governments for New Mexico and California, avoiding "geographical divisions, and heated contests for political power." Congress was now so divided by party and section that unified action was impossible. Benton asked that the petitions be assigned to Stephen A. Douglas's Committee on Territories, but Calhoun immediately attacked the move as showing "disrespect to one-half of the people of the Union." Benton responded that the signers had the right to have their petition printed regardless of opinions for or against it. The petition was referred to committee, but no action resulted for the remainder of the session.[106]

In the New Year, the presidency of James K. Polk drew to a close. Having worked closely together early in the administration, Polk and Benton were now bitterly estranged as the result of Frémont's court-martial. Polk recorded that Benton "would never have quarreled with me" had it not been for his anger over the outcome. Worn out by the pursuit—almost completely successful—of the goals he had established for his presidency, the workaholic Polk returned to Tennessee, where he died only a few months later. In his own memoirs, Benton managed a more forgiving assessment of the president he had served with. "He was an exemplary man in private life... and patriotic in his public life, aiming at the good of his country always. It was his misfortune to have been brought into the presidency by an intrigue, not of his own, but of others." The "intriguers" who composed his cabinet "required the exclusion of all independent and disinterested men from his counsels and confidence." Polk's "own will was not strong enough for his position, yet he became firm and absolute where his judgment was convinced and patriotism required decision." The war with Mexico, "under the impulse of speculators... was the great blot upon his administration; and that wholly the work of the intriguing part of his cabinet." Polk had proven his friendship to the Union by opposing the absorption of the whole of Mexico when many around him advocated such a policy. "The acquisition of New Mexico and California," wrote Benton, "were the distinguishing events of his administration." Nonetheless, the Missourian believed to the end of his life that the Mexican borderlands could have been acquired by peaceful means had the men in power but listened to his counsel.[107]

6 / The Destiny of the Races: The Free Soil Schism

In the aftermath of the war with Mexico, new forces sought to carry Benton's vision of the white republic to its logical conclusion, even as the party of Jackson was increasingly becoming the political arm of what some northerners referred to as the "slave power." During the presidential election of 1848, the acquisition of the Mexican Cession once more brought the question of the expansion of slavery into the territories front and center. Benton wanted to see the Democrats nominate a northerner to check the influence of the southern slave power. By his account, the Calhounites were attempting to plant slavery in areas where the population did not want it and were tearing apart the national party organizations with their fanaticism. At first the Benton-Blair-Van Buren wing of the Democracy were united behind Silas Wright. The New Yorker seemed a sure winner, but his sudden death in August 1847 left the radicals without a challenger. When the Democrats gathered for their convention at Baltimore near the end of May 1848, they were greeted by the spectacle of *two* delegations from New York, conservative "Hunkers" under the leadership of William F. Marcy, and the old Loco-Foco radicals who remained loyal to Van Buren. A heated debate ensued over which group possessed the proper credentials to be seated. Striving for harmony, the convention leaders adopted a rule allowing both factions to participate, with each delegate getting half a vote. Already aroused over the Wilmot Proviso and the threat of slavery expanding into the Mexican Cession, Van Buren and his "Barnburners" were in no mood to make concessions. When a rule was added requiring all candidates to support any candidate chosen, Van Buren and the Barnburners angrily withdrew and prepared to hold a separate convention at Utica, New York. Democratic unity was further called into question by the absence of a delegation from South Carolina. With the leading spokesmen of the sectional controversy refusing to attend, the controversies and power struggles were muted.[1]

The leadership of the Barnburners included some of Benton's closest political allies. Aside from the former president, there was his son John Van Buren, New York senator John Dix, and Churchill C. Cambreleng. Like Benton a native of North Carolina, Cambreling had settled in New York and had represented hard-money New Yorkers since the bank wars of 1830s. From St. Louis, Frank Blair Jr. warned that the dissenters were not simply New York Loco-Focos, but rather "a large portion of the Democrats in every free state" who were now in favor of slavery restriction." As the radicals saw it, the issue was neither abolition in the interest of blacks, nor simply one of the sectional balance of power; rather, the question was whether the economy of the new territories would be dominated by free labor or by slave labor. The Van Burenites saw themselves as the true heirs of the Jacksonian legacy—the ideal of broader opportunity for yeoman farmers and urban workingmen. From this perspective, opposition to the spread of the slave-labor system was keeping faith with the original interests and doctrines that had created the Jacksonian movement. Would the newly acquired territories and the opportunities they represented be dominated by freeholding farmers and free labor in the towns of the west—*"the grand body of white workingmen,"* as Brooklyn radical Walt Whitman submitted—or by a "few thousand rich, 'political,' and aristocratic owners of slaves"?[2]

Members of the Free Soil Party, as they styled themselves after the Utica convention, advanced the argument that free labor was more efficient than slave labor because the wage incentive and the desire for social mobility were superior motivations to violent coercion; that slavery undermined the dignity of manual work by associating it with servility; and that slavery resulted in ignorance and social backwardness wherever it existed, for poor whites as well as slaves. These socioeconomic arguments were powerful enough on one level. But as free soil ideology evolved in the late 1840s and through the 1850s it also made another, frankly racist argument to white northern voters. David Wilmot himself had insisted that his Proviso of 1846 was a "White Man's Proviso," intended to preserve the territories of the Mexican Cession for free white laborers. Wilmot was unconcerned for the slaves themselves—his proposal did not arise from any "squeamish sensitiveness... nor morbid sympathy for the slave.... The negro race already occupy enough of this fair continent... I would preserve for free white labor a fair country... when the sons of toil, of my own race, and my own color, can live without the disgrace which association with negro slavery brings upon free labor." An abolitionist observer noted that Wilmot's speeches often contrasted "black labor" and "free labor," "as though it were the negro and not slavery which degraded labor." By the summer of 1848 another editor pointed out that New York Barnburners tended to place their opposition to slavery extension "on the ground of an abhorrence of 'black slaves,'" rather than of slavery itself.[3]

The Democratic convention at Baltimore had meanwhile nominated Lewis Cass of Michigan, a stolid old party regular, to bear the standard. Cass neatly avoided the twin hazards of slavery extension versus Wilmot Proviso restriction by announcing that the question should be left to the inhabitants of the territories themselves. This "dogma of squatter sovereignty" as Benton referred to it, while not entirely new, was given its first full exposition by Cass; it was well suited to the purposes of the political brokers in the Democratic Party who sought to position themselves between the extentionists and the restrictionists.[4]

Benton once more found himself on the horns of a dilemma. His own desire to see white freeholders rather than slave labor dominate the territories, as well as his personal and political ties to the leadership of the free soil movement, exercised a strong pull on his sympathies. Nonetheless, his stronger concern was the danger posed to the Union by all forms of slavery agitation, whether originating from the South or North. A united Democratic Party was, he believed, the country's best hope for sectional peace. Benton also had to take the opinions of voters back in his home state into consideration. He agreed "in principle with the Utica convention, and was for keeping free territory clear of negroes," but, he reminded Blair, "his was a location which required that he should have the advantage of favorable circumstance to act successfully in support of what he wished."[5]

Benton kept his reservations over the party's choice to himself, campaigning with Cass in a show of unity tour that took him to Philadelphia and thence to New York City. There, evoking the late Silas Wright, Benton made an eloquent appeal for party unity. Convinced that "harmony, union and concession among the Democrats" were "the only sure guaranty of success," he argued that Cass would be a president "honorable to the country" and "satisfactory to the whole Democratic Party." Having performed his duty to the party, Benton returned to Washington while Cass continued on to his Michigan home.[6]

Party regulars suspected that Benton's support for Cass was less than wholehearted. In any case, northern Democrats were unconvinced by the show of unity, and the free soil movement continued to gather momentum through the summer. Democrats, former Liberty Party supporters, and "conscience" Whigs, unhappy with their party's nomination of General Taylor, all fell in with the Barnburners to form a new party based on the principle of slavery restriction. On August 9 they formed the Free-Soil Party and nominated Van Buren for president. Charles Francis Adams, grasping the antislavery standard from his late father John Quincy, was nominated for vice president. Francis Blair, Benton's longtime Jacksonian ally, provided editorials in support of Free-Soilism, and in Missouri, Frank Blair Jr. and his brother Montgomery attempted—without success—to establish a Free Soil ticket. Among other national heroes, they invoked the name of Thomas Hart Benton. But Benton remained noncommittal. Lacking enthusiasm for Cass, yet unwilling to bolt the Democratic Party, he found reason to be delayed by "business" matters in Virginia and Kentucky. After his appearances for Cass in June, the most prominent Democratic senator sat out the remainder of the campaign.[7]

On election day, predictably, the Free Soil defection resulted in victory for the Whig candidate Zachary Taylor, the hero of Buena Vista. New York was again crucial. Although the combined votes of Democrats and Free-Soilers were well above the Whig total, the Barnburner-Hunker schism gave the state—and the presidency—to Taylor. While Democrats were demoralized by the results, Van Buren and his supporters had reason to be optimistic. The Free-Soilers had moved far beyond the performance of the old Liberty Party, sending 13 new representatives to the House and electing Salmon Chase of Ohio to the Senate, as well as taking 10 percent of the popular vote nationwide. Van Buren thought the party had achieved "much more than there was good reason to expect" and looked forward to victory in 1852, with Benton as the candidate for a northern-oriented, free soil, radical Democracy.[8]

High Wall and Deep Ditch

By 1849, however, Benton's own position on slavery in the territories was becoming increasingly untenable back in Missouri. By now his principles had changed dramatically from his unconditional support for slavery in the Missouri controversy thirty years earlier. In the face of Calhounite statements to the contrary, Benton argued that Congress *did* have the power to legislate on the slavery issue in the territories. While he thought the Wilmot Proviso unnecessary, and likely to aggravate sectional discord, he believed it no different in essence from the antislavery clause that Congress had included in the Northwest Ordinance of 1787. Benton went still further to declare that he was now against the institution of slavery itself. "If there were no slavery in Missouri today," he declared to voters in Jefferson City, "I should oppose its coming in; if there was none in the United States, I should oppose its coming into the United States; as there is none in New Mexico or California, I am against sending it to those territories."[9]

During the summer of 1849, Benton undertook a grueling speaking tour of Missouri appealing to the voters to reject Calhounite extremism and to support him for a sixth term in the U.S. Senate. While he had managed to mend his fences with Missouri Democrats following the Texas controversy of 1844, neither his ego nor his understanding of national interests would long constrain him. His early stance on the war with Mexico, insisting that the conflict was inconsistent "with the honor of the country," led Howard County Democrats to "condemn those, who would oppose the action of the government in the efficient and energetic prosecution of the war." Once hostilities commenced, Benton's well publicized role as chair of the Senate committee on Military Affairs and his influence with the Polk administration offset this criticism to some degree, as did his continuing control of Federal patronage in Missouri. Nonetheless, a growing faction of political opponents and newspaper editors awaited an issue that would provide the opportunity to unseat the great senator.[10]

That issue was the extension of slavery to the territories of the Mexican Cession. Late in December 1848, Calhoun orchestrated a meeting of southern members of Congress with the goal of uniting on a sectional platform. The *Address of the Southern Delegates in Congress to their Constituents* was published the following January. The members denounced the "aggression and encroachment" of the North against the South on "this most vital subject"—slavery. The "Southern Address" asserted that "the Federal Government has no right to extend or restrict slavery, no more than to establish or abolish it," and demanded that southerners "shall not be prohibited from migrating with our property into the Territories of the United States, because we are slaveholders." The address concluded by raising the specter of emancipation and its consequences—the white race prostrated, blacks and their white sympathizers in control of the national government, the country becoming "the permanent abode of disorder, anarchy, misery, and wretchedness." Southerners must unite in an effort to deter the North from the course of abolitionism. If the effort failed, "nothing would remain for you but to stand up immovably in defense of rights involving your all—your property, prosperity, equality, liberty, and safety. As the assailed, you would stand justified by all laws, human and divine, in repelling a blow so dangerous, without looking to consequences, and to resort to all means necessary for that purpose."[11]

At nearly the same moment, anti-Benton Democrats in the Missouri General Assembly, led by Claiborne Fox Jackson, introduced a set of resolutions designed to put the state squarely in Calhoun's camp. The Jackson Resolutions, as they came to be known, sought to force Benton's hand on the slavery issue by imposing legislative instructions on him that its authors knew he would never follow. The Resolutions declared that Congress had no right to legislate against slavery in the territories. They further upheld the principle of popular sovereignty in the territories themselves in relation to the extension or exclusion of slavery and argued that the "aggressions" of the North, motivated by "antislavery fanaticism," released the slaveholding states "from all further adherence" to the Missouri Compromise of 1820. Nonetheless, "for the sake of harmony, and for the preservation of our Federal Union," Missourians would agree to the application of the old 36°30' line of demarcation between slave and free territory, "if by such concessions future aggressions upon the legal rights of the states may be arrested and the spirit of anti-slavery fanaticism be extinguished." The legislators then declared that if Congress were to pass any act contrary to these Resolutions, "Missouri will be found in hearty cooperation with the slave-holding states." Finally, they instructed "our Senators in Congress ... to act in conformity to the foregoing resolutions." Both the state House and Senate quickly passed these measures by large majorities and by March, Governor Austin A. King had signed them into law.[12]

Upon learning of the Jackson Resolutions, Benton declared them the "offspring of the Calhoun address" and thus "fundamentally wrong." In May 1849 he returned to his home state, launching his great "appeal" to "the People of Missouri" with a public letter on May 9 in which he denounced the resolutions and set forth his case. The power of legislatures to instruct the senators they had chosen was a long-standing feature of Democratic ideology, but Benton now sought to extend the principle by insisting on his right of appeal from the Assembly to the people who had chosen the legislators.[13]

Speaking in the House chamber in Jefferson City on May 26, Benton denounced Calhoun as the "prime mover and head contriver" of the southern "nullifiers" and "ultras" whose goal was "the subversion of the Union." Rejecting the assertion of the Southern Address and the Jackson Resolutions that Congress had no authority over slavery in the territories, Benton declared war against the followers of Calhounite principles in Missouri. "Now I have them," he cried, "and between them and me, henceforth and forever, a high wall and a deep ditch! And no communication, no compromise, no caucus with them."

Benton conceded that "he was born to the inheritance of slaves" and had always had them. He had "bought some, but only on their own entreaty, and to save them from execution sales." He had "sold some but only for misconduct." He had lost two slaves to the abolitionists, "and never enquired after them and liberated a third who would not go with them." Benton had slaves in Washington, and was "not the least afraid that Congress will pass law to affect this property either here or there." Knowing that slavery was perfectly safe wherever it presently existed, Benton would not alarm slaveholders as his enemies did by creating a nonexistent threat.[14]

Benton traveled the state all summer, first stumping in the central Missouri river counties with larger slave populations, then moving north and west into the frontier counties. At Lexington, Benton brought roars of laughter by describing the genealogy of the Jackson Resolutions. "CALHOUN, the father; NAPTON, the Granny; CLAIB JACKSON, the nurse and clout washer." At New Franklin several members of the Fayette group, including Jackson himself, appeared unannounced. Some observers feared violence, but at the end of his two-hour speech, "Col. Benton took his hat and marched off without deigning to cast a look even of scorn upon the pigmy defender of the disunion resolutions—so called by Col. Benton." On another occasion, Benton effectively silenced Jackson and two front-row companions by pointing them out with the description, "as demure as three prostitutes at a christening."[15]

Pushing on to David Atchison's home ground to the northwest, Benton spoke at Platte City (Atchison's home). The editor of the *Argus* related that after speaking to the hostile crowd, Benton was heard to say, "GOD DAMN PLATTE CITY, - GOD DAMN IT, I wouldn't make another speech there to save it from the fate of Sodom and Gomorrah . . ." The reporter added, "Such were his denunciations of a whole community, whose only offense was that they did not agree with him in his opinions. We want no such tyranny as this."[16]

On the first day of September, Benton arrived in Fayette, the seat of Howard County and the center of the hard-money, slaveholding political clique that had dominated Missouri politics and supported Benton for fifteen years. News that he intended to speak there without invitation brought threats against Benton's life. "Pistols and bowie knives were largely in demand," and Benton received threats that he would be tarred and feathered, and if he did not answer questions he would have to walk over dead bodies to leave the Central College chapel where he was speaking. An admirer later recalled that when Benton arrived, "he entered, walked majestically to the stand, and as he did so a tumult of discordant sounds from his opponents broke forth—braying, whistling, yelling, and groaning, which lasted for several moments." Benton impassively removed his hat and gloves and "facing the crowd, looked round upon it with unblanched face and haughty defiance." He then launched into a typically Bentonian philippic, in which he began by denying the charge of Calhoun and his followers that northerners sought the abolition of slavery in the states. The question of abolition, said Benton, was no more than agitation—a "barefaced attempt to pick a quarrel" for the purpose of uniting the South against the North in an effort to break up the Union. Reviewing the origins of the Southern Address and the Jackson Resolutions, Benton characterized them as a new form of "nullification ... [an] odious and treasonable doctrine ... the assertion of the right of the minority to govern the majority—to do so by military violence—to resist acts of Congress by force." Such doctrines were mirrored by the "killing sentiments" among the audience Benton was addressing: "knives are carried for my benefit, and revolvers prepared to give me six out of the half dozen bullets they contain ... my life is wanted [because] I am an obstacle to nullification."

Benton went on to offer his analysis of the Jackson Resolutions, declaring them and their instructions to him to have been passed "for alarm and agitation at home. To fire the people. To stir them up. To hold them to the attack upon Benton and the North." The purpose of Jackson, Napton, and their fellows was transparent: "Knowing that I would not obey [the instructions]," they had provided the basis for a new campaign to unseat Benton, complete with stump speakers, editorialists, and letter writers "all repeating the fundamental falsehood of 'abolition of slavery in the states,' and all shouting the wolf howl, 'obey or resign.'" It was against this "conspiracy" that Benton had launched his "appeal." The Jackson Resolutions, he declared, "should be repudiated as a disgrace to the state." At the end of the three-and-a-half-hour speech, according to a friendly observer, "the insulters were cowed."[17]

Benton's campaign began to have an effect far beyond the borders of Missouri. Mississippi's Henry S. Foote, in a public letter to former congressman Henry A. Wise of Virginia, charged Benton with "treachery to the South" and the unforgivable crime of attacking Calhoun. Foote insisted that the "traitor" Benton could never become the presidential candidate of the Democratic Party because he was for the Wilmot Proviso and a Free Soiler. For these reasons, Benton could not even be returned to the Senate from Missouri. Calhoun himself authored an elaborate *Address... to the People of the Southern States* in which he sought to unify the planter class around opposition to Benton. In a private letter to anti-Benton editor Samuel Treat, Calhoun declared that Benton had been "false to the South for ten years, and can do us much less injury in the camp of the abolitionists than he could in our own camp."[18]

The question of Benton's "treason" against southern, slaveholding interests bears further examination. Old Bullion's alienation not only from the planters of the deep South, whom he once courted as the natural allies of the developing West, but from his own base of support among Boon's Lick slaveholders had taken a long time to become final. In part, the rupture indeed had occurred over the issue of nullification and disunion, a question on which, for Benton, there could never be "compromise" or "caucus" with the hated Calhoun and his minions. Beyond the political and constitutional questions involved in Benton's ideological shift from states' rights agrarian to Free Soil Democrat were economic developments that did not go unnoticed by the senator, who had represented the interests of Missouri in a growing, industrializing nation for nearly thirty years.

In his speech at Fayette, Benton had asserted that it was now the North that was the true friend of westerners. The "men of the North are working men, and they feel for working men in other places," including "the man who waters the soil with his sweat, and makes an improvement in the wilderness." Improvement was the key element in this view. Like many southern-born men, particularly those of the Upper South, Benton saw the plantation economy creating a distinct and economically backward region out of step with the industrial development the rest of the nation was experiencing. When seen against this background, Benton's campaign for cheap land, for transportation improvements, and for peace with the Mexican provinces that poured silver into Missouri coffers, all appear as pieces of a master plan as intricate as Clay's American System.

Missouri and particularly the city of St. Louis were filling with white immigrants. For a visionary westerner such as Benton, slavery itself was not so much an evil (though he was coming to believe, like Jefferson, that it *was* an evil and should quickly be phased out) as it was an irrelevancy.[19]

The growth of the commercial metropolis at St. Louis was driven home in October when Benton attended a national railroad convention being held there. Earlier in the year Benton had introduced a bill in the Senate for a "central national road" from St. Louis to San Francisco. The road, with a branch to the Oregon territory, was to consist of "iron railways where practicable and advantageous," and of "macadamized or otherwise constructed" roads where railroads were impractical. Having advocated such a route as a freshman senator in the 1820s, Benton argued that in the wake of the California gold rush, inland communication between the two sides of the continent had become a national necessity. The majority of aspiring promoters competed for government land grants and subsidies for privately owned railroad companies. Benton wanted no part of proposals to "make a great national work of this kind a matter of stock jobbing" to profit "individuals or companies." The work must be undertaken by the national government and the government, ultimately, would own it. Benton proposed to finance his railroad with 75 percent of the revenues generated by California land sales and 50 percent of the sales of all other public lands (thus late in the day was the prophet of graduation-donation converted to the use of land revenues for internal improvements). The right-of-way was to be a mile wide to accommodate additional tracks in the future—"a national, central road, a highway, not merely for ourselves, but for posting for all time to come." Of course nothing came of Benton's proposal. By now it was one railroad scheme among a host of others and, like nearly everything else, was becoming a matter of sectional controversy.[20]

The convention in St. Louis was an opportunity for Benton not only to advocate the central route for the proposed transcontinental railroad, but to confront the presidential ambitions of fellow Democrat Stephen Douglas, whose popularity in his home state of Illinois hinged upon his own support for the northern route. Benton assured St. Louis Whig John Darby that he would attend the railroad convention. "I shall be there, sir. . . . Douglas never can be president, sir. No, sir; Douglas never can be president, sir. His legs are too short, sir. His coat, like a cow's tail, hangs too near the ground, sir." The meeting, with over eight hundred delegates present, convened in the rotunda of the federal courthouse on October 15, 1849. The address presented by Benton on the convention's second day was a tour de force of both his visions for national economic development and for Anglo-Saxon dominance.[21]

Benton called enthusiastically for a road built along his central route between the 38th and 39th parallels of North latitude, a road "national in its location by being central—national in its construction, being made by the nation—national in its title, by belonging to the nation." The road would be a "Western route to Asia." Having "the effect abroad, of carrying and diffusing the lights of American civilization to regions remote and hitherto involved in the darkness of pagan idolatry and imperial despotism; the effect at home, of producing a more perfect fusion of the different elements comparing our own National Union."[22]

> Along the proposed route would travel ... the furs of the North, the drugs and spices of the South, the teas, silks and crapes of China, the cashmeres of Tibet, the diamonds of India and Borneo, the various products of the Japan Islands, Manchuria, Australia, and Polynesia, the results of the whole fishery, the gold, silver, quicksilver, jewels and precious stones of California, and the innumerable and unimaginable elements of commerce which could be brought into life from the depths of the sea, and from new and unexplored regions by the enterprise and ingenuity of our countrymen ... Our surplus ... products would find a new ... market in return, while the Bible, the Printing Press, the Ballot Box, and the Steam Engine, would receive a welcome passage into vast and unregenerated fields, where their magic powers and blessed influences are greatly needed.[23]

Describing the enterprising nature of the American character, Benton stated that it must have employment; if no war or great object were available, it would take up speculation, "and the whole country go a planting bushes, and counting fortunes at the rate of thousands of dollars for each opening bud." The same "restless spirit of enterprise" was "panting for employment." A hundred thousand men could finish the railroad in seven years, creating "a band of iron, hooping and binding the states together, east and west. "People of the North and the South" would meet in the great line which would go east from the Mississippi, and feel again as their fathers did in the time of the revolution—feel that they were brothers, children of the same mother country, with a heart to love and a hand to support each other...."[24]

"Three and a half centuries ago," said Benton, "the great Columbus ... departed from Europe to arrive in the East by going to the West."

A king and a queen started him on his enterprise; it now lay in the hands of a republic to complete it:

> Let us rise to the grandeur of the occasion. Let us complete the grand design of Columbus by putting Europe and Asia into communication . . . through the heart of our country. Let us give to his ships, converted into cars, a continued course . . . Let us now rise above everything sectional, local, personal. Let us beseech the National Legislature to build the great road upon which the great national line which unites Europe and Asia—San Francisco at one end, St. Louis in the middle, New York at the other; and which shall be adorned with its crowning honor—the colossal statue of the great Columbus—whose design it accomplishes, hewn from a granite mass of a peak of the Rocky Mountains, overlooking the road—the mountain itself a pedestal and the statue part of the mountain—pointing with outstretched arm to the western horizon, and saying to the flying passengers, "There is the East; there is India."[25]

Benton's conclusion was greeted with thunderous applause. The speech was an enormous success. The convention itself, however, was inconclusive. The delegates adjourned having passed only an ambiguous resolution calling on Congress to provide a Pacific railroad with branches to St. Louis, Memphis, and Chicago. The question of the road's eastern terminus remained open, and over the next few years would become tied up in other national issues over which Benton and Douglas were contending.[26]

Benton spent several more weeks carrying his message to Missouri's eastern counties along the Mississippi. The majority of these counties, like those along the Missouri River, had large slave populations. By now his political odyssey had become an event of national importance. Southern partisans, the honor of their section at stake, were at a loss to understand the defection of a fellow slaveholder. "The Platte, the Osage, the Jackson, and the St. Genevieve [sic] have all been trampoosed by the great champion of free soil," wrote one Virginia editor, "and the thunder of his declaration made to reverberate from the confluences of the Missouri and Mississippi to the base of the Rocky Mountains. There is a slight touch of the moral sublime in the majestic stride of the old Bison, as he winds his way over the stamping grounds it was his wont years since to claim as his own undisputed possessions." Like the Scottish Lord Selkirk, Benton could once exclaim, "I am monarch of all I survey"; now, however, he had thrown away his birthright in the fruitless effort to attain the object of his unhallowed ambition—the presidential nomination. "Benton," the editorial concuded, "will be consigned to the obscurity which is justly due to such moral degeneracy."[27]

Northerners, on the other hand, were beginning to see Benton as one of their own in the debate over slavery expansion. An antislavery publication mused that "Col. Benton has some faults besides his wrong politics, and conspicuous among them is his excellent opinion of his own opinions. But he is a laborious, pains-taking Senator who seldom speaks without knowing whereof he is talking, and it would be rather hard to find another Loco-Foco in Missouri to fill his place, though there are many ready enough to *take* it. That you see is quite another thing."[28]

Benton's "appeal" thus ended without changing the perceptions of southerners who viewed him as a turncoat, while northern Free-Soilers, on the other hand, increasingly viewed him as one of their own. It was an extremely awkward position for a politician seeking reelection in a region where voters were identifying their interests more and more with the slaveholding South. Benton must henceforth sever himself from his longtime base of support among outstate Missouri voters and look to antislavery elements, both in Missouri and in Congress, for allies in his war against "nullification." Having made his appeal and now determined to let the political chips fall where they might, in early November 1849 Benton left again for Washington.

The 1850 Debates

Benton returned to Washington confident of the success of his efforts in Missouri. His enemies were equally confident that Old Bullion's days as the leading Democratic voice from Missouri were numbered. Benton had been in tight political spots before and had successfully chosen which way to tack with the prevailing winds. Far from having constructed his high wall and deep ditch, Benton was just as adept at "Roman-riding" in 1850 as he had been thirty years earlier. Now, though, he seemed not to realize that the horses beneath his feet were about to go off in opposite directions.

The most urgent issue before the new Congress was the request of California for admission to the Union as a free state. President Taylor supported the admission without concessions to slave states as part of any grand bargain. While Calhounites were unpleasantly surprised at the nationalist tones of the message from a southern, slaveholding president, Benton was pleased. He thought that Taylor "comprehended the difficulties of his position, and was determined to grapple with them," through "frankly and firmly presented remedies."[29]

Further debate arose over the perennial question of the extent of the state of Texas, which continued to claim the Rio Grande as its *western*, as well as its southern, boundary. Benton objected to the further expansion of slaveholding Texas into federal territory and proposed that the Texas–New Mexico boundary should be drawn "four degrees east of Santa Fe." Texas, in return, was to be compensated with 15 million dollars from the Federal government to pay the public debt of the former Lone Star Republic. Antislavery northerners still desired an end to slavery in the District of Columbia or—failing that—an end of the slave trade in the capital. Southerners wanted the free states to demonstrate their good faith by supporting passage of a strict new fugitive slave law.

Stepping forward once more in an attempt to unravel the snarl of controversies before the Senate was Henry Clay. Now 73, the "Great Compromiser" offered a package that he hoped would settle all outstanding sectional differences for good. California was to be admitted as a state without congressional action on either the exclusion or introduction of slavery. The remainder of the Mexican Cession was to be organized into two territorial governments (New Mexico and Utah), also without congressional action concerning slavery; Texas would surrender its land claims to New Mexico in return for federal assumption of the Texas debt; the slave trade, but not slavery itself, was to be abolished in the District of Columbia; a more effective fugitive slave law was to be enacted; and Congress was forbidden to interfere with the domestic slave trade in the states. All of these measures taken together were to constitute a quid pro quo—substantial concessions to the South in return for the admission of California as a free state. Benton was opposed to Clay's "omnibus" bill from the outset, considering it "a *capitulation* to those who threatened secession."[30]

Through February, March, and into April, debate raged over Clay's proposals. A high point was Calhoun's address on the March 4. Suffering from tuberculosis and too ill to speak, Calhoun looked on as James M. Mason of Virginia read his speech. Calhoun's speech did not directly address Clay's plan, but, in its ominous predictions of disunion, most likely contributed more powerfully to the goal of compromise than any number of more measured speeches. Before the month was out Calhoun was dead. It was Benton's responsibility as senior senator to arrange for the observation of the great man's passing in Congress, but while Clay, Webster, and Cass all offered eulogies, Benton remained silent.

Webster urged him to be magnanimous and speak, but Benton reportedly answered, "He is not dead, sir—he is not dead. There may be no vitality in his body, but there is in his doctrines . . . . My people cannot distinguish between a man and his principles—between a traitor and treason. They cannot eulogize the one and denounce the other." Some vestige of the unforgiving hatred that caused Benton to hound Charles Lucas into a second duel in 1817 followed Calhoun even in death.[31]

In February, Benton had attempted to dissuade northern senators from pushing for an application of the Wilmot Proviso doctrine. Such legislation, he argued, was unnecessary, as slavery had been abolished in the republic of Mexico in the 1830s. The actions of the Mexican government, Benton asserted, proved "that there is not the least ground for fearing, or hoping that it [slavery] can ever exist in California or New Mexico." Benton's effort to convince his northern colleagues, with whom he agreed on the substance of the slavery extension issue, from drafting explicit free soil legislation was linked to the imperatives of party politics back in Missouri. In this, Benton had to skillfully ride the twin horses of being both nationalist and southerner. His opposition to the Clay's omnibus bill was not simply a question of whether the necessary sectional compromises could be passed as a "lump" or a piece of "logrolling," but was closely tied to the objectives of his great appeal to Missouri voters the previous summer and his campaign to win reelection.[32]

Benton's major effort on behalf of the separate admission of California was launched on April 8. Addressing himself to this issue on the basis of "a separate consideration, and an independent decision, upon its own merits," Benton desired not to "mix up" the admission of California "with all the questions which the slavery agitation has produced." He objected to the proposed omnibus bill as a surrender to the threats of a minority in Congress, whom he described as agitated without cause. Benton's speech suggests the importance of his partisan political interest in devising a republican issue salient to Missouri voters. If state political concerns were indeed behind Benton's position on the compromise package, he was choosing a curious strategy. His opposition to Clay placed him on the side of President Taylor and a majority of northern Whigs who favored a piecemeal settlement of the outstanding issues. Most of Benton's fellow Democrats, on the other hand, led by Lewis Cass and Stephen A. Douglas, supported Clay.[33]

Three days later, Benton moved that the Senate take up a separate bill to admit California. His motion was tabled, leaving the admission of California to a Select Committee of Thirteen, chaired by Clay. Although the Kentuckian and his allies had won the first round in the Senate, supporters of the omnibus found themselves at an increasing disadvantage as debate moved into the national arena. Among other issues, southern ideologues and Texans would settle for nothing less than the entire area disputed with New Mexico. President Taylor, on the other hand, was determined to grant New Mexico immediate statehood and let the Supreme Court settle the boundary dispute.[34]

Benton watched the debate over the omnibus rage on for a month. On June 10 he entered a motion to postpone consideration of the California–Texas–New Mexico–Utah legislation until March 1851—or until the life of the Thirty-first Congress had expired. He then embarked upon a lengthy speech attacking the omnibus bill and setting forth his views on slavery. The omnibus, argued Benton, was a "monster" in which the admission of California was made "the scapegoat of all the sins of slavery." With everything from the territorial question to the Texas–New Mexico border dispute "packed upon her back," California's plea for admission was likely to be "sacrificed under the heavy load." Benton traced his opposition to slavery extension to the principles of Jefferson and John Randolph:

> The men of that day were not enthusiasts or fanatics: they were statesmen and philosophers. They knew that . . . emancipation . . . was not a . . . question of property merely—but a question . . . between races; and what was to be the consequence to each race. The incurability of the evil is that greatest objection to the extension of slavery. It is wrong . . . to inflict an evil which can be cured: how much more to inflict one that is incurable, and against the will of the people who are to endure it forever! . . . It is a question of races, involving consequences which go to the destruction of one or the other. . . . It seems to be above human wisdom but there is a wisdom above human wisdom! And to that we must look. In the meantime, do not extend the evil.[35]

The speech was popular in the northern states where opposition to slavery extension prevailed. Benton was the only senator from a slave state to explicitly announce his opposition to slavery as an institution and the extension on slavery through the vehicle of Clay's omnibus compromise. He was vilified as a traitor throughout the South for having done so. Clay's bill, in the meantime, remained stalled in the Senate. In the midst of this impasse, Zachary Taylor suddenly died on the July 9. Benton declared Taylor's passing to be a "public calamity"—"no man could have been more devoted to the Union, or more opposed to the slavery agitation." In point of fact, the removal of the combative old warrior from the scene and the ascension of the conciliatory Millard Fillmore brought new support for Clay's plan and an "armistice" between North and South for another decade. Still, despite the support of the president, it was impossible to pass all of the measures as an omnibus. Clay was exhausted and frustrated. In August he left for a holiday in an attempt to recover his fading health. Leadership of pro-compromise forces in the Senate thereupon fell to Douglas of Illinois, who broke up the omnibus into its constituent measures and successfully built coalitions in support of each.[36]

One by one the various provisions of the compromise were stripped from the omnibus bill until only the Utah provision was left. The Texas–New Mexico boundary remained a crucial issue. Texas apparently came out ahead, gaining its southwestern panhandle and ten million dollars from the federal government. Feeling the settlement rewarded Texas too generously, Benton joined the minority voting against the bill, which passed 30–20. California was admitted (34–18) and New Mexico granted territorial status without explicit provisions concerning slavery. By mid-September the new fugitive slave bill came before the Senate. Benton abstained from voting on the measure, later explaining that he believed the bill so freighted "with such multiplied and complex provisions" as to make it "inexecutable," except at great trouble and cost. Benton also thought the act was "attended with an array and machinery which would excite disturbance, and scenes of force and violence, and render the law odious." As it turned out, implementation of the Fugitive Slave Act in the northern states, "verified all the objections taken to it." The bill to end the slave trade in the District of Columbia passed at the same time (33–19), with Benton voting in favor of the measure.[37]

As the session drew to a close, Benton perhaps sensed that his time in the Senate was also ending. On September 16 he rose to put his observations concerning the omnibus measures on record. Although he had been severely criticized for his opposition to the Clay's approach, the voting on the various measures recently passed had proved him right. An examination of the roll calls on the California, New Mexico, Utah, and boundary dispute questions revealed that only seventeen members of the Senate had voted for all four measures. Thus, he insisted, he had been right to call for voting on the measures separately from the outset: "Right to resist a measure, come from whom it may"—referring to Clay. Four months, argued Benton, had been wasted and the admission of California endangered "about a matter which was unparliamentary and which has failed, and the moment that it failed everything which was proposed was accomplished; at that moment the cats and dogs that had been tied together by their tails for four months, scratching and biting, being loose again, every one of them ran off to his own hole and was quiet."[38]

If Benton intended this final serving of wit to vindicate himself before the voters of Missouri, he was too late. On August 5 the state's voters had cast their ballots for members of the General Assembly. Benton Democrats, who had been doing their best to present their man as staunchly opposed to the Wilmot Proviso or any other measures smacking of Free-Soilism, won 55 seats to only 37 for the militantly proslavery anti-Benton faction of the party. With the majority Democrats thus divided, the Whigs held a plurality with 64 seats in both houses. On January 9, 1851, the Missouri legislature met to nominate candidates for U.S. senator. Whig leaders who opposed the extension of slavery favored Abiel Leonard of Howard County. Leonard, however, let it be known that he agreed with Benton on the power of Congress to legislate the slavery question in the territories. This made him unacceptable to pro-southern Whigs. Another opposition member from the Boonslick region, John B. Clark, was free of any association with Benton's views on slavery in the territories, but was unacceptable to St. Louis Whigs and moderates, who believed his candidacy would disrupt both the party and the Union. Whig members from St. Louis then put forth the name of Henry S. Geyer, a lawyer from the city who had previously stated that Congress had no power over slavery in the territories. This was good enough for anti-Benton Democrats.

The General Assembly began voting for U.S. senator on January 10. On the first ballot Geyer received 64 votes, Benton 55, and anti-Benton Democrat James Green 37. With factional lines thus drawn, the voting continued through 40 ballots. Benton's support came primarily from areas of the state where small farmers predominated. Here was the last echo of the Jacksonian movement that had been Benton's base of power since 1825. As the balloting continued, anti-Benton Democrats gradually shifted their support to Geyer. Sixteen of them finally voted with the Whig members to give Geyer a majority of 80 votes on January 22. Benton's thirty-year career in the Senate was over.[39]

"The Huge Wild Buffalo of the Missouri Prairies"

Returning to the Senate for his final session in early 1851, Benton once more took up the issue of land claims—this time concerning California.

He argued in favor of safeguards for the original population, proposing amendments to the bill settling land claims that contained "all the equitable and favorable provisions heretofore allowed to land claimants in Upper and Lower Louisiana and in Florida." Benton's efforts to help the older natives of California came to nothing; his amendments were all voted down.[40]

At 69, defeated in his bid for reelection to the Senate and recovering from a recent illness, Benton refused to go quietly into retirement. Determined to return to Congress, he set his sights on the city of St. Louis. He began by participating in municipal elections during April 1851, speaking at the courthouse and at smaller venues in support of pro-Benton Democrats. The Missouri *Republican* charged that the senator's popularity among the city's Irish and German immigrants linked him to "Socialism, Red Republicanism, Infidelity, Communism, Free-Soilism, Anti-Catholicism, and every other ism!" Anti-Benton congressman James Bowlin estimated that half of the city's eighty thousand inhabitants were Irish- or German-born and complained that Benton had come to St. Louis to stump "for the Free Soil candidate" by "pandering to the foreign prejudice against slavery."[41]

These charges had some truth. In fact, Benton had determined to run for Congress in 1852 as the representative from St. Louis. The frontier village that he had first come to in 1815 had changed beyond recognition. At that time a settlement of some three thousand souls, St. Louis had grown to a city of over sixteen thousand by 1840 and 77,860 by 1850. Nearly 43 percent of the population was composed of German or Irish natives. When the children of foreign-born parents and second-generation Germans from Pennsylvania are added, more than half the population of St. Louis were Germans or Irish. St. Louis Whigs, who had controlled the city government until 1842, were divided. Most of the old Creole elite, with whom Benton had long ago burned his bridges, identified with the party of Clay and Webster even as they retained their French Catholic cultural and religious affiliations. Other St. Louis Whigs, including Joseph Charless Jr., the son of Benton's old publishing rival from *Enquirer* days, represented the growing anti-immigrant, anti-Catholic "Native American" wing of the Whig party that would grow into the Know-Nothing movement during the following decade. Benton was typical of his own party in his tolerance of both immigrants and Catholicism. Indeed he went well beyond most Democrats in his long-standing support of Catholic causes, had counted Bishop Louis DuBourg and Father Pierre-Jean De Smet among his intimates, and as far back as

1818 had contributed to the construction of a new brick church for St. Louis Catholics to replace the dilapidated log structure that had served since the 1760s. Just before his death at age 22, Benton's son Randolph had converted to Catholicism under the tutelage of Father De Smet. Benton penned a note to the famous missionary telling him, "You are giving me peace in giving it to him."[42]

Benton's celebration of white Anglo-Saxon nationhood stopped short of religious chauvinism. For this reason he remained popular among the St. Louis Irish who were also drawn to the anti-bank, hard-money, and cheap land policies that Benton had advocated during the 1820s and 1830s. As the immigrants saw it, Benton remained the champion of the "little man" and enemy of the elitists whom they believed the Whigs represented both in St. Louis and in Washington. Germans in St. Louis admired Benton for many of the same reasons, but also agreed with him that the expansion of slavery should be checked. The Germans overwhelmingly endorsed the ideology of free white labor, commercial progress, and political equality of white men that had long been advocated by Benton, the Blairs, and others among the old radical wing of the Democratic Party. While they did not yet support abolitionism in significant numbers, they did want to ensure that Missouri and the West remained a "white man's country," free from the domination of the slave power. Benton's former allies—the hard-money advocates from the central countries and the most militant proponents of the unrestricted spread of slavery—now styled themselves the "National" Democrats.[43]

At the center of Benton's campaign for the House was his call for the repeal or "expunging" of the Jackson Resolutions, and the defeat of "nullifiers" such as Jackson and Atchison. He promised to continue his push for a "homestead" act and once again spoke in favor of his road and rail system "on a direct line from St. Louis to San Francisco." He was happy, he said, to be running for that branch of Congress directly elected by "my real friends—the people," and to join the battle against the tendency of "slipping away the power from the immediate and responsible representatives of the people to those whom they neither elect nor control—from the many to the few—converting the government into an oligarchy instead of a democracy." The anti-Benton press, including the Missouri *Republican*, denounced Benton as "an old fogy" whose influence had dissipated—"his hand uplifted against every prominent man in public life." Benton received strong support from Henry Boernstein's German daily *Anzeiger des Westens*, from speakers like Frank Blair, and from Alexander Kayser, who often gave his speeches in German for the benefit of immigrant voters. A new paper, the *Missouri Democrat*, was also established at this time by B. Gratz Brown, a twenty-six-year-old Kentuckian and a cousin of the Blairs.[44]

The election took place on August 2, 1852. Benton, admitted the *Republican*, had "made a Duke of Wellington affair of it—a perfect Waterloo defeat to us—and that too, we believe, solely by the aid of Blucher and the Prussian forces." The pro-Free-Soil Germans and other white workingmen had apparently been decisive in Benton's election. "The huge wild buffalo of the Missouri prairies" as a southern newspaper described him, "this strange, powerful, hateful, spiteful, remorseless man," would return to Congress as a representative from Missouri's First District.[45]

While he waited for the Thirty-third Congress to meet—it would not convene for over a year after the day of his election—Benton set to work on a project he had been contemplating for some time. Writing to his former Senate colleague John Dix for advice on finding a publisher, Benton described his intended literary endeavor. His speeches to the Senate had covered "all subjects, civil and military, legislative and diplomatic, for thirty years; and never ... for rhetorical or clap-traps effect; but always to the business in hand." His speeches were "enough to make them constitute ... the framework and scaffolding—the outline, and the salient points—of all our history during the eventful period from 1820 to 1850—they only want some filling up between, and some connecting by notes and illustrations, to become a complete history of the working of our government during that time ..."[46]

The resulting work, a two-volume legislative "memoir" entitled *Thirty Years' View*, was Benton's account of the political history of the United States during his six terms as U.S. senator. Printed in double columns of small type, the weighty tomes contain extracts of speeches by Benton, Clay, Calhoun, and others, as well as the author's post hoc commentary on the issues he describes. Filled with pedantry and self-justification, the work is pure Benton, and anyone who would understand the statesman should examine at least selections of his *Thirty Years' View*. Like the man, the book is something of a monument that no one interested in the period can ignore. For the first hundred years after the author's passing, his biographers, without exception, echoed Benton's own high opinion of the role he had played in the great issues of the day. Nonetheless, Benton attempted as best he could to evade narrow partisanship and to be generous to former adversaries like Henry Clay. The twin villains of the narrative, of course, were the nullifiers and the abolitionists—"the two halves of a pair of shears, neither of which could cut until joined together. Then the map of the Union was in danger."... Benton had "seen the capacity of the people for self-government tried at many points, and always found equal to the occasion." Two crucial questions remained, however: whether presidential elections should be "governed by the virtue and intelligence of the people, or... become the spoil of intrigue and corruption," and whether nationalism should "remain co-extensive with the union, leading to harmony and fraternity; or, divide into sectionalism, ending in hate, alienation, separation, and civil war."[47]

Benton's final term in Congress coincided with the administration of Democrat Franklin Pierce. Initially, the Missourian's allies hoped that Pierce would support him for the speakership of the House or offer him an important diplomatic post. They were soon disappointed. The new cabinet was dominated by pro-states-rights, proslavery men, including William Marcy at the State Department and Jefferson Davis as secretary of war. Federal patronage appointments were lavished upon anti-Benton Democrats from Missouri. Other Democratic House members from the state, John S. Phelps and James Lamb, originally elected as Benton Democrats, quickly sensed the prevailing direction of political winds and shifted to the camp of Atchison and the "antis-." Benton, unwilling to openly criticize Pierce, could only assure his allies that shifting allegiances would "have no effect on my *political* course... a point at which a vulgar heard of hack politicians cannot understand me."[48]

From his position at the War Department, Secretary Davis had begun to promote a southern route for the Pacific railroad. Stephen A. Douglas, meanwhile, continued to lobby for a northern route with Chicago as the eastern terminus. Benton tried to persuade Jefferson Davis to send an army expedition to explore the central route. Davis, who had his own plans, politely rejected Benton's suggestion and sent an expedition to survey an extreme southern route instead. Having been frustrated in his attempt to gain official sanction, Benton returned to Missouri to see off Edward Beale, a tough frontiersman who had served with Frémont and who had recently been named superintendent of Indian affairs for California. En route to his post, Beale and his companions, traveling by mule, would cross the Great Plains west of Missouri and pass through the Utah territory along a route mapped out by Frémont, to estimate the practicability of a railroad. While at the frontier towns of Kansas, Westport, and Independence, Benton spoke to assembled crowds of "that *'American road to India'*... a cherished vision of mine for thirty-eight years... you stand on the brink of a mighty enterprise, and everyone should thank God that he lives in an age, and in a country, and under a form of government which enables him to act a part in the great undertaking, which is to unite two oceans and three continents, consolidate our Union, and make America the thoroughfare of Europe and Asia." The unorganized status of the Kansas-Nebraska region remained an obstacle to the central route, but Benton promised to work for immediate territorial government and the extinction of Indian titles, despite the efforts of others to secure an alternative route for the railroad. Meanwhile, Benton declared that the lands previously granted to those Indian nations removed from the East in the 1830s, but never actually occupied, were already open for white settlement by right of preemption. The listeners were delighted with his invitation to defy existing law by occupying Indian lands.[49]

Returning to Washington, Benton pressed forward with his railroad promotion. By fall he could report that Beale had found "the Central Route" to be "good for roads and settlements, and inviting the hand of the farmer to improve it." Benton also sent a map of the Nebraska territory to the commissioner of Indian affairs, asking him to mark the assigned and unassigned lands. When this request was met, Benton had the map published, and boldly claimed that it was an official designation of lands already open for settlement. The commissioner denied that this was the case, but the damage was done. Benton's ploy contributed to growing public pressure for territorial organization.[50]

In the Congress that was called to session in December 1852, Benton devoted much of his time to the sort of constituency service expected from members of the House. Long the advocate of outstate farmers and planters, Benton now found himself representing the interests of the St. Louis mercantile community for the first time in nearly thirty years. Shortly, however, such routine matters were pushed to the background as the controversy over the Pacific railroad revived the toxic issue of slavery in the territories. Douglas, seeking both to win the western railroad for Chicago and unite the Democrats behind his own presidential ambitions, introduced a proposal that called for the organization of the area west of Missouri hitherto known as "Nebraska" into *two* new territories. In January 1854 Douglas reported his "Kansas-Nebraska Bill" to the Senate. Ordinarily this should have been no particular cause for controversy. The entire area to be organized was north of the 36°30' line, which meant it was closed to slavery under the 1820 Missouri Compromise. Certain southerners, however, led by David Atchison, threatened a renewed sectional crisis if the territory was organized on the basis of the

1820 agreement. Atchison had already vowed that "I had rather see the whole territory sunk into hell, than see it organized as free territory." He was anxious to undermine Benton prior to Missouri's election of a new U.S. senator in 1855.[51]

Douglas was gambling on the apparently self-evident truth that Kansas was unfit for slavery and that northerners would have no objection to a bill allowing the concept of popular sovereignty—of the settlers deciding the slavery question for themselves—to be put to the test. The formula was designed to mollify the South while achieving Douglas's railroad and political objectives in one blow. Still not satisfied, Atchison pointed out the inconsistency between the "popular sovereignty" measure and the legal restrictions of the Missouri Compromise. Douglas at length added a clause to the bill explicitly repealing the provisions of the 1820 Compromise.

Benton, the Blairs, and other members of the old radical Democracy were outraged, to say nothing of those like Van Buren and Wilmot who openly embraced free soil ideology. The proposal was greeted with protest meetings throughout the North, and Douglas commented that he could travel to Chicago by the light of his own burning effigy. To Benton the shattering of the fragile truce of 1850 was inexcusable. Ignoring his own substantial role in reopening the quarrel, in conversation with New York's William H. Seward, he urged all antislavery men to "save ourselves from Douglas's bill" by remonstrations throughout the North "in public meetings and in legislative resolutions."[52]

On April 25 Benton formally addressed the House on the Kansas-Nebraska controversy. He began speaking in defense of the Missouri Compromise. He "had stood upon it above thirty years, and intended to stand upon it to the end—solitary and alone, if need be; but preferring company." He condemned "intermeddlers" who sought to require Democratic members of Congress, under the instant penalty of political damnation, to support "every bill which they call administration." To make his point, Benton recounted the fable of an ass that donned the skin of a lion to scare his master. The master recognized his braying, and rather than running in fear picked up a cudgel and beat the animal nearly to death. The moral of the story: "A caution to all asses how they undertake to scare their masters." The Compromise, said Benton, had brought peace in 1820 when the Union had been divided like "enemies on the field of battle," yet now it was to be "abrogated" not by the inhabitants—not by any one human being living, or expecting to live on the territory ... but upon a motion in Congress...." If, as the

Kansas-Nebraska bill stated, the Compromise of 1850 had nullified that of 1820, then why, asked Benton, do it again in 1854? If the bill intended neither to legislate slavery into nor out of the territories, then why legislate at all? Why all the disturbance if no effect was intended? All of this "untrue, contradictory, suicidal and preposterous" reasoning was an effort to blame others for the effect of the bill—destroying... all confidence between the North and South, and arraying one-half the union against the other in deadly hostility."[53]

When Benton's allotted hour had elapsed, John Wentworth of Chicago rose to offer the Missourian as much of his own hour as was needed to finish. This declaration was met by angry objections from southern members. Wentworth stood his ground. "I want the whole country," he said, "to understand that the oldest man living in Congress, the man who was here when the Missouri Compromise was adopted, and the only man in the whole Congress, is now refused a courtesy which has been refused to no other living man."[54]

At length, Benton was allowed to continue. He cited one precedent after another of congressional control of the territories. Yet what was the excuse for "all this turmoil and mischief? To keep slavery out of Congress! Great God! It was out of Congress completely, entirely and forever out of Congress, unless Congress dragged it in by breaking down the sacred laws which settled it." The slaveholders would gain "nothing but an unequal and vexations contest" they could not win. Indeed, Benton concluded, the movement had begun "without a memorial, without a petition, without a request, from a human being. There had not yet been a "word in its favor from the smallest public meeting or private assemblage of any slave state." This was "the response of the south to this boom tendered to it by northerner members under a northerner President... the response of silence—more emphatic than words..."[55]

Antislavery members congratulated Benton on his speech. The St. Louis *Democrat* opined that Benton had stripped "the Douglas fraud... naked in its many deformities," and celebrated Benton as the only congressman from slaveholding Missouri to oppose the Kansas-Nebraska bill. The *Union*, on the other hand, attacked the "former idol of his party" for "aiding the abolitionists in their war upon a bill entrusting the domestic affairs of the people to their own care and oversight!"[56]

Several weeks later, on May 19, as the debate in the House neared its conclusion prior to voting, Benton spoke once more on the Kansas-Nebraska proposal. Noting that a Georgia congressman had hinted at possible future applications of the Kansas-Nebraska "principle," Benton demanded to know the "ulterior operations" of the bill "containing a principle to be asserted in the future?" The answer, he believed, lay in the aggressive diplomacy of the Pierce administration. James Gadsden of South Carolina—a protégé of Jefferson Davis—had been dispatched to Mexico with the authority to spend up to fifty million dollars to secure a large section of Mexican territory. Gadsden returned with "a small slice only of the desired territory," but asserted that on a second attempt he might acquire new territory and convert it from "free soil" to "slave soil." Further evidence of southern-driven "grand movements" to expand the empire of slavery lay in the machinations of Pierre Soulé, American ambassador to Madrid. Soulé was attempting to purchase Cuba from Spain, "and a rumpus kicked up if the island is not got." These, claimed Benton, were "indexes" to what the Georgia member might have had in mind when he spoke of the future.[57]

Benton had spoken his piece. Whether there was any direct connection between the Kansas-Nebraska bill and the negotiations with Spain and Mexico remains open to debate. At the end of May the Kansas-Nebraska bill was approved by the House 113–110 and signed into law by President Pierce. Now alienated from both the administration and the leadership of his party, Benton was condemned in the Washington *Union* as a "Whig adjunct and abolition ally." This, of course, was nonsense, but Benton did find himself working more with Free-Soil Democrats like Salmon Chase and Charles Sumner.[58]

Even before the president's signature was on Douglas's volatile bill, Benton had announced as a candidate for reelection to the House—subject to a "primary" election—*and* as a candidate for the Senate. Pro-Benton candidates for the Missouri General Assembly were already promising to return him to the upper house. The novel primary election to choose party candidates was held on June 24 with some 4,500 self-identified party members participating. No one filed against Benton for Congress, but the Democratic nomination for General Assembly was hotly contested. In a pamphlet addressed to his constituents, Benton declared that he was glad to see both a Whig (St. Louis mayor Luther Kennett) and a "Nullifier" (anti-Bentonite Trusten Polk) in the field against him. He condemned the Kansas-Nebraska Act's repeal of the Missouri Compromise, characterizing the provision as the work of a "night caucus of eight nullifiers" in Congress, designed "to govern the next presidential election, and to 'kill off Benton.'"[59]

The results of the 1854 congressional elections in Missouri were remarkable for a number of reasons. Never an independent force in state politics, the Whig Party had succeeded in winning a number of House seats as well as Geyer's election to the Senate in 1850 by exploiting divisions between Benton and anti-Benton Democrats. In 1854 with the Nebraska issue front and center, both national parties were badly divided. Kennett, who was running against Benton in St. Louis, was known to be an anti-Nebraska candidate. He was also one of the first politicians west of the Mississippi to benefit from growing nativist resentment of the German and Irish immigrant populations. Elected mayor as a "Whig-American" in 1850 and twice thereafter, Kennett and his supporters in the city government were viewed by the Germans, in particular, as unfriendly to immigrants. In 1854 Kennett perceived the growing power of the immigrant voting block and chose to make an appeal to the Irish by downplaying his nativist credentials and emphasizing his own Irish Protestant ancestry. The Whig papers also appealed to both Irish and nativists by attacking the Germans, claiming that Henry Boernstein, publisher of the *Anzeiger des Westerns* was attempting to "Germanize" St. Louis. By the summer of 1854 a new element, the American or "Know Nothing" Party, had organized itself in St. Louis and promised to upset all previous calculations. Kennett and the Whigs apparently reached an agreement with the popular Know Nothings by election day. In return for dumping several foreign-born candidates from the ticket and pledging that Kennett would join the movement after the election, Whigs won Know Nothing support for him.[60]

The election on August 7 witnessed the worst riot in St. Louis up to that time. It was fueled by charges in the *Missouri Democrat* of purposeful delay by the judge in charge of issuing naturalization papers in order to minimize the potential Democratic vote, countercharges in the *Republican* that Democrats planned to herd illegal immigrants to the polls, and predictions of violence in both papers that ultimately became self-fulfilling. When voting was delayed in the heavily Irish Fifth Ward by an election judge who minutely examined naturalization papers, a shoving match in the lengthening queue led to a stabbing. The initial bloodshed, in turn, brought a nativist mob, which stormed through the Irish neighborhoods along the riverfront, trading blows and gunfire with the immigrants. Order was eventually restored when Mayor John How called out the militia, but the riot left ten dead, thirty-three wounded, and nearly a hundred buildings damaged. Included in the damage was the congressional career of Thomas Hart Benton. Despite careful attention to the German vote by surrogates Frank Blair and B. Gratz Brown, Benton was made to appear both anti-immigrant and anti-Catholic by the Whig press. He lost by a margin of not quite a thousand votes to Kennett, who joined the Know Nothings shortly thereafter. Trusten Polk, the anti-Benton Democrat, garnered only 378.[61]

The elections included not only seats in the U.S. House but the General Assembly as well. Sixty Whigs had been chosen, fifty-seven anti-Benton Democrats, and forty-three Benton Democrats. The Know Nothings were not yet adequately organized to field a slate of candidates, but both Whig contender James S. Rollins and, more surprisingly, David Atchison courted the nativist vote. Badly divided, the Whigs finally settled on Mexican War hero Alexander Doniphan. Through 41 ballots the voting remained stalemated, and the Assembly adopted a concurrent resolution to postpone the election of a United States senator until the following November. When the 1854–1855 session of the General Assembly ended, the Missouri Whig Party quickly fell into dissolution, its victories the previous August notwithstanding; most Whigs drifted into the American Party. Likewise, with the impotence of Benton Democrats to affect the outcome of the voting for senator, Jacksonian Democracy as it had existed for thirty years was a spent political force in the state.[62]

Nonetheless, Benton was determined to fight for the cause of the Union during his remaining years. As the elections of 1856 approached, "Bleeding Kansas" became a battleground between slaveholders and free soil settlers, and a new national political party emerged. Many northern Democrats who ten years earlier had supported Van Buren and his Barnburners now joined forces with former "Conscience" Whigs, abolitionists, Free Soilers, Know Nothings, and other assorted factions in common opposition to the extension of slavery. The new coalition, whose platform adopted such remnants of Jacksonian Democracy as a homestead bill, was called the Republican Party (harkening back to Jeffersonian ideals). Francis Preston Blair, who played an important role in the formation of the new party, tried unsuccessfully to coax his old friend Benton into running. As usual, Old Bullion demurred, but a member of the family was chosen to be the standard-bearer in any case. John Charles Frémont—the "Pathfinder of the West"—was chosen to be the Republicans' first presidential candidate.

The ticket was a strictly sectional one. Frémont would not even be on the ballot in southern states. Slaveholders immediately labeled the party a "Black Republican" conspiracy to abolish slavery in the states and threatened disunion if Frémont won the election. Anticipating such a reaction from southerners, Benton regarded the new party as a source of potential division of the Union. He had tried, to no avail, to dissuade his son-in-law from accepting the Republican nomination. Relations between Benton and his family were strained and became more so when he traveled to the Democratic convention in Cincinnati to endorse James Buchanan. Benton even accepted the nomination of his party for governor of Missouri. He had no chance of success, but used his candidacy as an opportunity to travel the state speaking on behalf of Buchanan. Winding up his campaign at Washington Square in St. Louis, Benton told the assembled crowd that Frémont was as dear to him as one of his own children. "There was nothing which a father could do for a son which I have not done to carry him through his undertakings, and to uphold him in the severe trials to which he has been subjected." But, fearful of the dangers posed to the Union by a sectional party, Benton warned his son-in-law not to expect his support as the Republican presidential candidate. "I told him at once that I not only could not support him, but that I would oppose him."[63]

Nationally, as well as in Missouri, Buchanan was victorious, though Frémont and the Republicans made an impressive showing the first time upon the national stage. The Know Nothings, running former President Millard Fillmore, would soon disintegrate, with most of their northerner members moving on to become Republicans.

Benton's Legacy: The Culmination of Master Race Democracy

Eighteen fifty-six was Benton's last campaign. Still devoted to the white nation, during the last year-and-a-half of his life he watched Buchanan allow it to slip toward disunion and civil war. Benton had published the second volume of his legislative memoir, *Thirty Years' View*, in 1855 and continued working tirelessly on an *Abridgement of the Debates of Congress* as his health deteriorated from colon cancer. In the midst of his illness, Benton found the strength to pen a two hundred-page response to the Supreme Court's decision in *Dred Scott v. Sanford*, arguing that Congress, in fact, did have the power to legislate on the question of slavery in the territories.[64]

Benton died in Washington, D.C. on April 10, 1858. Even in death, the question of his last words concerning the Buchanan administration became a subject of controversy. Within days, Horace Greeley's New York *Tribune* was reporting the whispered confidence of the "dying patriot" to "an old intimate Missouri friend" that "among the greatest consolations in dying" was the knowledge that Congress had thwarted the pro-slavery Lecompton constitution for Kansas despite President Buchanan's support for the measure. The friend in question was Republican Francis P. Blair, though his son, Frank Jr., actually supplied the story and thus became the "Missouri friend." Benton's son-in-law, William Carey Jones, angrily denied the story, insisting that Benton remained loyal to Buchanan and the Democratic Party to the end. Jones was an administration appointee who regarded Frémont, his kin by marriage, and the Blairs as traitors to the old faith. Although Jones published his denial as a pamphlet, it seems that Blair had somewhat the better of the contest. He had privately reported the final conversation to Van Buren, and his version was consistent with Benton's views on slavery expansion at least since the Texas controversy of the early 1840s. William Chambers argued that Benton "could no more have supported the Lecompton constitution than he could the Dred Scott decision" and attributes this to "his attachment to both freedom and Union."[65]

Union and freedom were causes for which Benton had fought throughout his long career. But Benton's most meticulous biographer, in the last pages of his opus, was unwilling or unable to elaborate on the meaning of these words to the great proponent of western expansion and white man's democracy. In the absence of guidance from Chambers, we must turn to the "Missouri friend" at the center of the controversy. Throughout this book Benton's own words have been used to understand his life and career. In the end, the words of Frank Blair Jr., family friend and protégé of Thomas Hart Benton, are useful to shed light on his legacy.

Frank Blair was the son of Francis Preston Blair of Kentucky, editor of the flagship Democratic Party newspaper, the Washington *Globe*, and a member of Andrew Jackson's "Kitchen Cabinet" during the 1830s. Like Benton and Van Buren, Blair was a radical Democrat who became increasingly unhappy with the influence of the slave power in his party as the 1840s wore on. Unlike Benton, Blair left the party in 1848 to support the Free-Soil candidacy of Van Buren and was one of the founding members of the Republican coalition. His sons Montgomery and Frank Jr. both moved to St. Louis in the early 1840s, where they practiced law and became involved in politics as Benton Democrats before supporting the Free-Soil-Republican movement themselves. Young Frank was elected to Congress in 1852. Montgomery Blair served as one of the attorneys for the plaintiffs in the Dred Scott Case.[66]

Following the election of 1856, the Blairs had come to the conclusion that the nation could be saved from civil war only by the gradual emancipation of the slave population, accompanied by the colonization of freed African-Americans to Central America. Colonization was not a new idea. The American Colonization Society had been established in 1817 and included many of the foremost political figures of the day. Benton had opposed calls for the federal government to fund colonization schemes during the 1830s, but this was before he came to perceive the slavery issue as the greatest threat to the Union. However he may have attempted to parse the question in the interests of his own political survival, there can be little question that during the last decade of his life, Benton would have supported any practical measure that removed the troublesome issue of slavery and left the American West to be developed by free white labor. This was exactly the goal that Frank Blair addressed in a speech before Boston's Mercantile Association on January 26, 1859—less than a year after the death of his mentor.

Blair presented the merchants of Boston with two great challenges: one was to reach the commerce of India and the Far East "by means of a great national highway between the oceans, spreading the people of our own race across the great temperate zone"; the other "to create a new empire for their commerce within the tropics of America, requiring for its maintenance the peculiar organization of the colored races." The first objective was to be attained by the westward march of white settlers across the Great Plains and the Rocky Mountains to the Pacific. The process was already well under way. "Here, then, we are rapidly realizing Benton's prediction, that the line of great States which now stretch halfway across our continent in the same latitudes as Pennsylvania, Ohio, Indiana, Illinois, and Missouri may be matched by an equal number of States, equally great, between Missouri and California." Blair lingered to enumerate the developing tier of free states, including Kansas (which had "thrown off her slave fetters" and was ready to take her place as a free state in the Union), West Kansas (the gold-rich area around Pike's Peak), the "Mountain State," a fourth state encompassing the valley of the Colorado and, finally, Utah, in the Great Basin. This rapidly growing belt of states would have a decisive effect on the destiny of the Republic.[67]

The immediate result of this emerging line of free states upon the races of the continent would be "to repress far to the north and south the wild beasts and the wild tribes who pursue them." Blair predicted that white agricultural settlements would "soon fill the empty spaces now marked on the map as the hunting grounds of the Cheyennes, Arapahoes, Utalis, and Sioux, *and the reservations of the Delawares, Shawnees, and Cherokees, will become the abode of civilized communities.*" Hence the old canard that the tribes from east of the Mississippi rejected sedentary agriculture and "civilization" was once more brought into play. Benton had asserted that, during the 1830s, the survival and preservation of the Indians' culture as well as "permanency in their new possessions" were the advantages of removal for the southwestern tribes—"*delusive it might be, but still a respite from impending destruction if they remained where they were.*" Now the delusion was stripped away and the respite was ended. According to Blair, the hunting tribes "will pursue the buffalo into the sections, north and south, least adapted to cultivation, and, as the game gradually diminishes, the tribes supported by it will destroy each other for the remnants." There was reason to hope that some remnants of the "savage hunting tribes" might become herdsmen on the Western plains, "as in the Spanish settlements to the South." As for the rest, their disappearance from the continent would be the result of natural processes; they had no legitimate place in the white nation Blair envisioned.[68]

In any case, the racial amalgamation allowed in the Spanish colonies was to be avoided as "hybrid races carry degradation alike into government as into communities." The Moors and the Spanish shared the same territory for eight centuries without propagating a common stock. The "celebrated African explorer, Dr. Livingston," reported "that in the old settlement of Angola, where the Portuguese had amalgamated universally with the natives, the hybrid race does not survive but a few generations in its own line." The same rule held fast in this country where "the French who have intermarried freely with the Indians leave a posterity called half-breeds, because they do not survive an intermixture of their caste beyond two or three generations." Other observers had assured Blair "that the same fact is true of the mulatto caste."[69]

Finally, Blair turned to the dangerous problem of slavery. The decline and fall of the Roman Empire had resulted from the corruption that the spread of slavery had entailed and the emergence of modern Europe had begun only when slavery, in the form of serfdom, was effectively ended. Even backward, autocratic Russia was now taking to heart the lesson of the superiority of free labor. In America, slavery had taken its worst form. "The contrast between the races destroys the sympathies of kindred which would soften servitude." Indeed, the Supreme Court had sanctioned the idea "that the Negro is a being so alien to our nature as to have no rights which we are bound to respect as appertaining to man; that he is not included in the great declaration of the rights of humanity; and the inference is that he has no soul." This "monstrous doctrine," Blair asserted, was a last resort to render slavery compatible with the principles of a free government, but would "not such degradation attach in time to all who are constrained to labor in the service of another, no matter what class or how compelled?" This was a key argument of Free-Soilers and Republicans—that the proximity of slave labor, and the degradation that attached to slaves, eventually devalued and degraded free labor.[70]

The remedy was one "deriving its force from the nature of our Constitution.... It is Freedom. It is the deliverance of two incongruous races from an unnatural connection." Blair waxed eloquent in his condescension for "that sable race, bred in the pestilence of Africa, [which was] a blot on the fair prospect of our country." He therefore sought deliverance "from a people who cannot assimilate with our people, the subjects of an institution utterly abhorrent to our free institutions." Through the joint actions of the state and federal governments, a place in Spanish America was to be provided where emancipated African-Americans, provided with free land and civil liberties, would thrive in the torrid climates from which their race had emerged. Their colonization would create a black republic in Central America and the Caribbean, as well as new markets and resources for the expanding economy of the United States. This new nation, in fact, would become "our India, but under happier auspices; for instead of being governed by a great company, to drive the people to despair and insurrection by its exactions, it would have its own Government, which would owe fealty to ours, as Canada does to England."[71]

From his days with the *St. Louis Enquirer*, Benton had advocated an "American road to India," both to foster commerce and to spread republican institutions to the despotic empires of Asia. His goal, in those early years, had been an inclusive one, bringing both trade and freedom to the peoples of the East. As the years progressed and the notion of racial inequality as a necessity for the equality of white men became more entrenched, this optimism faded. America did develop greater ties of trade with China and Japan by 1860, but few voices were advocating the spread of representative government to these realms; the Asian races were considered incapable of it. By the time of Benton's death, the rhetoric of Frank Blair and like-minded leaders reveals plans for the creation of an American commonwealth explicitly based on separation of the races. The vision of a nation of white yeoman farmers, businessmen, and workers, long advocated by Benton, continued to find sympathetic audiences, at least in the North, in the last years before the Civil War made the colonization obsolete as an answer to slavery.[72]

Benton's career spanned the decades of America's growth from an infant republic to a continental power and from an agrarian economy to a country of rails and factories. He had contributed to its expansion and development as much as any man of his generation, but the "white republic" that he had espoused ultimately failed to materialize. Nonetheless, in the platform of the new Republican Party, the policies for which he had fought during his career as a legislator—free land for white farmers, the exclusion of slavery from the territories, and federal promotion of Western economic development—came to pass. The goal of making the West into a frontier of exclusion—a white man's country—continued into the postwar period, but the realities of race in the United States would continue to complicate that goal. At the end of his life Benton remained both a white supremacist *and* a patriotic champion of democracy and Union in varying degrees. For the nation he had served, however, the time was fast approaching when those values could no longer be reconciled.

Notes

Introduction

1. See Merrill D. Peterson, *The Great Triumvirate: Webster, Clay, and Calhoun* (New York: Oxford University Press, 1987); also Maurice G. Baxter, *One and Inseparable: Daniel Webster and the Union* (Cambridge, Mass.: Harvard University Press, 1984); John Niven, *John C. Calhoun and the Price of Union* (Baton Rouge: Louisiana State University Press, 1988); Robert V. Remini, *Henry Clay: Statesman for the Union* (New York: W.W. Norton, 1991). On Benton, see William N. Chambers, *Old Bullion Benton: Senator from the New West* (Boston: Little, Brown, 1956), 389.

2. John F. Darby, *Personal Recollections of Many Prominent People Whom I have Known and of Events* (St. Louis: G.I. Jones, 1880), 184. Chambers disputes the accuracy of this quote, but concedes that "These words catch some of Benton's expanding rhetorical spirit and his increasing tendency [by 1849], to identify himself with 'the people.'" Chambers, *Old Bullion Benton*, 354.

3. Peter Novick, *That Noble Dream: The "Objectivity Question" and the American Historical Profession* (Cambridge, U.K.: Cambridge University Press, 1988), 68–80; Richard Hofstadter, *The Progressive Historians: Turner, Beard, Parrington*, (New York: Knopf, 1968), 26–27; David W. Blight, *Race and Reunion: The Civil War in American Memory* (Cambridge, Mass.: Belknap Press of Harvard University Press, 2004).

4. Theodore Roosevelt. *Thomas H. Benton* (Boston: Houghton-Mifflin, 1888). The project was perhaps suggested to Roosevelt by Henry Cabot Lodge, who wrote the volume on Washington for the series. Edmund Morris, *The Rise of Theodore Roosevelt* (New York: Coward, McCann & Geoghegan, 1979), 320.

5. Roosevelt, *Thomas H. Benton*, 62–63. It is worth noting here that John F. Kennedy portrayed Benton in a similar light in the chapter devoted to the Missourian in *Profiles in Courage* (New York: Harper, 1956).

6. Roosevelt, 24, 27–28, & 13; review of *Thomas H. Benton*, by Theodore Roosevelt, *The Nation*, March 29, 1888.

7. William M. Meigs, *Life of Thomas Hart Benton* (Philadelphia: J.B. Lippincott Co., 1904), 3, 13, 53–54, 452. "Just as this book was passing through the press, the biography of Benton by William M. Meigs appeared and acknowledgement is made for the use of a few personal incidents." Joseph M. Rogers, *Thomas H. Benton* (Philadelphia: G.W. Jacobs & Co., 1905), 351.

8. Originally McClure's M.A. thesis at the University of Missouri, Columbia, it was also published as "Early Opposition to Thomas Hart Benton," *Missouri Historical Review* X (April 1916): 151–96.

9. McCandless never published his dissertation as a book-length monograph; however, large sections of it were republished in the *Missouri Historical Review*. See "The Rise of Thomas H. Benton in Missouri Politics," *Missouri Historical Review* 50 (October 1955): 16–29; "The Political Philosophy and Political Personality of Thomas H. Benton," *Missouri Historical Review* 50 (January 1956): 145–58 (quote page 151); "The Significance of County Making in the Election of Thomas H. Benton," *Missouri Historical Review* LIII (October 1958): 34–38. McCandless is also the author of *A History of Missouri: Volume II, 1820–1860* (Columbia: University of Missouri Press, 1972), in which Benton, if any single individual, is the central figure.

10. Chambers, *Old Bullion Benton*, 10, 15–17.

11. Review of *Old Bullion Benton: Senator from the New West* by William N. Chambers, *Saturday Review*, Sept. 29, 1956; Chambers, *Old Bullion Benton*, xi–xii. Emphasis mine.

12. Ibid., xii–xiii.

13. The following year the institution changed its name to Iowa State University. Smith was the author of numerous works on the antebellum period, including *The Death of Slavery: The United States, 1837–1865* (Chicago: University of Chicago Press, 1967); *The Presidency of James Buchanan* (Lawrence: University Press of Kansas, 1975); *Francis Preston Blair* (New York: Free Press, 1980); and *The Presidencies of Zachary Taylor and Millard Fillmore* (Lawrence: University Press of Kansas, 1988), in addition to his biography of Benton. Long active in politics, Smith ran for the U.S. Senate in 1962 and 1966.

14. See Robert Shalhope, "Thomas Hart Benton and Missouri State Politics: A Reexamination," *Bulletin of the Missouri Historical Society* 25, no. 3 (April 1969): 171–91; "Jacksonian Politics in Missouri: A Comment on the McCormick Thesis," *Civil War History* 15, no. 3 (September 1969): 210–25; John D. Morton, "'This Magnificent New World': Thomas Hart Benton's Westward Vision Reconsidered," *Missouri Historical Review* 90 (April 1996), 284–308; "'A High Wall and a Deep Ditch': Thomas Hart Benton and the Compromise of 1850," *Missouri Historical Review* 94 (October 1999), 1–24.

15. Horsman, *Race and Manifest Destiny*, 90–92.

16. See Michael A. Morrison and James Brewer Stewart, eds., *Race and the Early Republic: Racial Consciousness and Nation Building in the Early Republic* (Lanham, Md.: Rowman & Littlefield, 2002), 80–81, 113–14, 136–39. "This new Jacksonian racial modernity denied the viability of a biracial republic, doubted the efficacy of efforts to promote responsibility and uplift among people of color, and conceded only a measure of white responsibility for the well-being of an allegedly 'inferior' race" (Stewart, 136); Horsman, *Race and Manifest Destiny*, 252–53.

17. Since the 1960s the term "*Herrenvolk* democracy" has been used to describe the concept of equal rights applying to a white master race alone. Not only the racial

hierarchy of the United States, both before and after the Civil War, but the apartheid regime in South Africa prior to the 1990s have been submitted as examples of this idea. See Pierre L. van den Berghe, *Race and Racism: A Comparative Perspective* (New York: Wiley, 1967), and George Fredrickson, *The Black Image in the White Mind: The Debate on Afro-American Character and Destiny, 1817-1914* (New York: Harper & Row, 1971). Sean Wilentz uses the more Anglo-American "Master Race Democracy" to describe the same phenomenon in *The Rise of American Democracy: From Jefferson to Lincoln* (New York: Norton, 2005), 431, 517ff.

18. Saxton, *The Rise and Fall of the White Republic* (London and New York: Verso, 1990), 138, 144-45.

19. Ibid., 153-54.

20. Wilentz, *The Rise of American Democracy*, 287.

21. Another excellent synthesis, which offers a very different interpretation of the Jacksonians and their "master-race democracy," is Daniel Walker Howe, *What Hath God Wrought: The Transformation of America, 1815-1848* (New York: Oxford University Press, 2007).

1 / Honor and Country

1. The location known thereafter as "Bloody Island" was the sight of numerous duels during the early 1800s. The island lay to the east of the river's channel of navigation and was separated by a chute from the Illinois shore. It was assumed appropriate for conducting affairs of honor, as it was outside the jurisdiction of either Illinois or Missouri. In the 1850s the city of St. Louis completed a project to widen and deepen the channel, eliminating the eastern chute. The once notorious Bloody Island now lies under the railroad yards of East St. Louis, Illinois. James Neil Primm, *Lion of the Valley: St. Louis, Missouri, 1764-1980* (Boulder, Colo.: Pruett Publishing Co., 1981), 114, 149-51.

2. Frederick Jackson Turner, *The Frontier in American History* (New York: H. Holt and Company, 1920), 67-68, 107.

3. William N. Chambers, "As the Twig is Bent: The Family and North Carolina Years of Thomas Hart Benton, 1752-1801," *North Carolina Historical Review* 26, no. 4 (October 1949), 386; James Truslow Adams, ed., *Atlas of American History* (New York: C. Scribner's Sons, 1943), plate 55.

4. Chambers, "As the Twig is Bent," 387, 390. See Hugh T. Leffler and William S. Powell, *Colonial North Carolina: A History* (New York: Scribner, 1973), 217-39, esp. 231, on source of the name "Regulators."

5. Lefler and Powell, 218-19, 239.

6. Marjolein Kars, *Breaking Loose Together: The Regulator Rebellion in Pre-Revolutionary North Carolina* (Chapel Hill: University of North Carolina Press, 2002), 68-73; Lefler and Powell, 219-22.

7. Kars, *Breaking Loose Together*, 57-58

8. George Sims, "An Address to the People of Granville County," June 6, 1765, in William K. Boyd, ed., *Some Eighteenth Century Tracts Concerning North Carolina* (Raleigh, N.C.: Edwards & Broughton, 1927), 187-89; Kars, 58, 71-72.

9. William L. Saunders, ed., *The Colonial Records of North Carolina*, VII, 842; Reverend George Micklejohn S.T.D.,"On the Important Duty of Subjection to the Civil Powers," *Early American Imprints*, First Series, 10977; Paul David Nelson, *William Tryon and the Course of Empire: A Life in British Imperial Service* (Chapel Hill:

University of North Carolina Press, 1990), 71–76; Lefler and Powell, 231–34; Chambers, "As the Twig is Bent," 390.

10. Chambers, "As the Twig is Bent," 391.

11. A commonly asserted argument in the recent historiography of the American Revolution holds that the small farmers who supported the Regulation were opposed to the efforts of colonial elites, such as the Bentons, to lead them in the movement to break with Great Britain. In this thesis, much of the violence between Whig and Tory factions in revolutionary North Carolina was simply a continuation of prewar tensions. Other historians have disagreed, arguing that colonial Americans lacked a sufficient degree of class consciousness to provide the basis for a large-scale military resistance movement and that local issues and personalities defined the conflict in the Piedmont against the backdrop of the larger war against British rule. Marjolein Kars asserts that, in the years before the Revolutionary War, "it was increasingly clear to North Carolina elites that many Piedmont inhabitants had little sympathy for the Whig cause." She concludes that while the war brought bitter conflict between Whigs and Tories to the region, "when it was over, much the same men and the same social system remained in place" (Kars, 212, 214). See Wayne E. Lee, *Crowds and Soldiers in Revolutionary North Carolina: The Culture of Violence in Riot and War* (Gainesville: University Press of Florida, 2001), 209–11, for discussion of historiography on the Regulators.

12. Smith, *Magnificent Missourian*, 15–16; Chambers, "As the Twig is Bent," 391–95; Benton, "Auto-biographical Sketch," I; Jessie B. Frémont, "Biographical Sketch of Senator Benton in Connection with Western Expansion," in John C. Frémont, *Memoirs of My Life. Including in the narrative five journeys of western exploration, during the years 1842, 1843–4, 1845–6–7, 1848–9, 1853–4* (Chicago and New York: Belford, Clarke & Company, 1887), 2–3.

13. Chambers, "As the Twig is Bent," 393; Thomas H. Benton to Clay, June 22, 1813, in *The Papers of Henry Clay*, ed. James F. Hopkins (Lexington, Ky.: University of Kentucky Press, 11vols., 1992), I, 805–6. "I have been of *that soil* [i.e. the Federalist Party], but not of the New England school."

14. Indenture of the Wautauga Purchase, March 19, 1775, Office of the Register of Washington County Tennessee; A List of Jesse Benton's Taxable Property, 1788, in Orange County Records, 1788–1793, State Department of Archives and History, Raleigh, N.C.; both cited in Chambers, "As the Twig is Bent," 392, 401.

15. Chambers, "As the Twig is Bent," 396.

16. Benton, "Autobiographical Sketch," in *Thirty Years' View*, I, I; Fremont, "Biographical Sketch," 3; Will of Jesse Benton, in Benton Papers, MHS.

17. Jesse Benton to Thomas Hart, Hartford, June 29, 1788, Thomas J. Clay Papers, LOC; Walter Clark, ed., The State Records of North Carolina, XXII, 39, 49. Both cited in Chambers, "As the Twig is Bent," 402.

18. Jesse Benton to Thomas Hart, August 23, 1783, in Thomas J. Clay Papers, LOC.

19. Last Will of Jesse Benton Sr., October 21, 1790, Benton Papers, Missouri Historical Society; Benton, "Autobiographical Sketch," I; Frémont, "Biographical Sketch," 3–4.

20. Benton, "Autobiographical Sketch," i–ii; Frémont, "Biographical Sketch," 3–4.

21. Bond of Nancy Benton to Thomas Hart, October 26, 1791, Thomas J. Clay Papers, LOC (Chambers, "As the Twig is Bent," 405–6); Benton, "Autobiographical Sketch," i–ii; Fremont, "Biographical Sketch," 4.

22. Kemp P. Battle, *History of the University of North Carolina* (Raleigh, N.C.: Edwards & Broughton Printing Company, 1907-12), I, 72-74, 168-69, 194-95; Chambers, "As the Twig is Bent," 409-10.

23. Statements at an Investigation of the Faculty of the University, Faculty Records, 1799-1814, University of North Carolina; Statement of Thomas H. Benton in Faculty Records, 1799-1814, University of North Carolina, *Documenting the American South*, <http://docsouth.unc.edu>.

24. Statement of Fleming Saunders, Marmaduke Baker, Thomas King, and William Cherry, March 19, 1799, in Faculty Minutes, University of North Carolina. Cited in Biography of Thomas Hart Benton, in *Documenting the American South*, <http://docsouth.unc.edu>. These facts remained clouded in obscurity until investigated by William N. Chambers in the 1940s.

25. George Ehrhardt, "Expelled from North Carolina University on Theft Charge, Boy Becomes U.S. Senator," *Raleigh News and Observer*, February 5, 1928. Cited in Chambers, "As the Twig is Bent," 416.

26. Bertram Wyatt-Brown, *Southern Honor: Ethics and Behavior in the Old South* (New York: Oxford University Press, 1982), 350-51.

27. Benton, "Auto-biographical Sketch," ii.

28. *Nashville Impartial Review*, January 3, 1807. This issue also reports the hanging and burning of Aaron Burr in effigy by citizens of Nashville; Chambers, *Old Bullion Benton*, 24.

29. *Congressional Globe*: 30/1, 1076.

30. Thomas P. Abernathy, *From Frontier to Plantation in Tennessee: A Study in Frontier Democracy* (Chapel Hill: University of North Carolina Press, 1932), 91-102; John Buchanan, *Jackson's Way: Andrew Jackson and the People of the Western Waters* (New York: J. Wiley, 2001), 114-17; see also Arthur Preston Whitaker, *The Spanish Frontier, 1783-1795: The Westward Movement and the Spanish Retreat from the Mississippi Valley* (New York: Houghton Mifflin Company, 1927); David Weber, *The Spanish Frontier in North America* (New Haven: Yale University Press, 1992); John F. Bannon, *The Spanish Borderlands Frontier, 1513-1821* (New York: Holt, Rinehart and Winston, 1970).

31. John Umstead to Thomas Hart, August 7, 1800, in Thomas J. Clay Papers, LOC; Chambers, *Old Bullion Benton*, 18-19; Abernathy, 24-32.

32. Benton, "Auto-Biographical Sketch," ii.

33. Chambers, *Old Bullion Benton*, 19-20; Smith, *Magnificent Missourian*, 24. The following year an equally splendid cotton crop was destroyed at the point of harvest by an early frost. Benton resolved to abandon the plow and pursue a career where his own exertions rather than the whims of nature would determine the results. Frémont, "Biographical Sketch," 5.

34. Benton, "Auto-Biographical Sketch," ii. Jackson read law under North Carolina attorneys Spruce McCay and John Stoke from 1784 to 1787. See Robert Remini, *Andrew Jackson and the Course of American Empire, 1767-1821* (New York: Harper & Row, 1977), 31.

35. Thomas H. Benton to John Hardeman and Nicholas Perkins Hardeman, December 10, 1804, Benton Papers, Missouri Historical Society.

36. Thomas H. Benton to Thomas Hardeman, November 22, 1829, Hardeman Papers, MHS.

37. See Nicholas Perkins Hardeman, *Wilderness Calling: The Hardeman Family in the American Westward Movement, 1750–1900* (Knoxville: University of Tennessee Press, 1977).

38. Chambers, *Old Bullion Benton*, 22–23; Smith, *Magnificent Missourian*, 25.

39. Benton, *Thirty Years' View*, I, 736.

40. Benton, *Thirty Years' View*, I, 736. While Chambers dates this meeting sometime in the spring of 1807 (*Old Bullion Benton*, 25), Jackson's biographers make no mention of the first time the two men met. Remini, for instance, describes Benton simply as a "clever young lawyer whom Jackson had met on the circuit and recognized as a man of talent and industry." *Life of Andrew Jackson* (New York: Perennial Classics, 2001, 64). James Parton, in one of the earliest biographies of Jackson (1860), simply quotes Benton's account verbatim. *Life of Andrew Jackson* (New York: Mason Brothers, 1860), I, 345–49.

41. Parton, *Life of Andrew Jackson*, I, 29; see also Andrew Burstein, *The Passions of Andrew Jackson* (New York: Alfred A. Knopf, 2003), 60.

42. Benton, *Thirty Years' View*, I, 681.

43. Milton Lomask, *Aaron Burr: The Years from Princeton to Vice President, 1756–1805* (New York: Farrar, Straus & Giroux, 1979), 336–44; Thomas Fleming, *Duel: Alexander Hamilton, Aaron Burr, and the Future of America* (New York: Basic Books, 1999), 196–203.

44. Joseph Ellis, *Founding Brothers: The Revolutionary Generation* (New York: Alfred A. Knopf, 2000), 45; see also Joanne B. Freeman, *Affairs of Honor: National Politics in the New Republic* (New Haven: Yale University Press, 2001), 168.

45. Benton, *Thirty Years' View*, I, 682.

46. Ibid., 681–82.

47. Jackson to Brigadier General James Winchester, October 4, 1806; Order to Brigadier Generals of the 2nd Division, October 4, 1806. Both in *Papers of Andrew Jackson*, ed. Harold D. Moser et al., II, (Knoxville: University of Tennessee Press, 1980–), 110–11.

48. Jackson to Daniel Smith, November 12, 1806, Jackson to William C.C. Claiborne, November 12, 1806, in *Papers of Andrew Jackson*, II, 116–19.

49. *Congressional Globe*: 30/1, 1076; Benton, *Thirty Years' View*, I, 682. Nancy Isenberg's *Fallen Founder: The Life of Aaron Burr* (New York: Viking Penguin, 2007) offers an alternative view that presents Burr in a much more favorable light, often at odds with the preponderance of scholarly literature. Isenberg attributes alleged connections between Burr's 1804 campaign for governor of New York and Federalist secession plots to Hamiltonian "scandalmongering" (253). Charges that Burr's filibustering activities in the Southwest might also have been separatist in nature she blames on General James Wilkinson, an admittedly unattractive character who, with the aid of Republican newspapers, portrayed Burr as the "archconspirator" to salvage his own fortunes (311–15). While the debate concerning Aaron Burr's place in the early history of the United States continues, for our purposes, the point is how Burr and the threat he seemed to pose to national unity were *perceived* by Benton, whose understanding of events remained essentially unchanged for more than fifty years.

50. Benton, *Thirty Years' View*, I, 736; Chambers, *Old Bullion Benton*, 35–37; Parton, *Andrew Jackson*, I, 343–45; Joseph Howard Parks, *Felix Grundy*:

Champion of Democracy (Baton Rouge: Louisiana State University Press, 1940), 92-93.

51. See Michael Paul Rogin, *Fathers and Children: Andrew Jackson and the Subjugation of the American Indian* (New York: Knopf, 1975), 136, 142-43, 149-151.

52. On the causes of the War of 1812, see Donald Hickey, *The War of 1812: A Forgotten Conflict* (Urbana: University of Illinois Press, 1989); J.C.A. Stagg, *Mr. Madison's War: Politics, Diplomacy and Warfare in the Early Republic, 1783-1830* (Princeton, N.J.: Princeton University Press, 1983); and Robert A. Rutland, *Madison's Alternatives: The Jeffersonian Republicans and the Coming of War* (Philadelphia: Lippincott, 1975). For interpretations that emphasize the issue of national honor, see Reginald Horsman, *The Causes of the War of 1812* (New York: A.S. Barnes, 1962); Bradford Perkins, *Prologue to War: England and the United States, 1805-1812* (Berkeley: University of California Press, 1961); and Robert Wiebe, *The Opening of American Society* (New York: Knopf, 1984), especially 168-93.

53. See Wiebe, *The Opening of American Society*, 184-85.

54. Ibid., 186.

55. See Rogin, *Fathers and Children*, 140-45.

56. "The coming of war then he hailed the occasion to end his life in action rather than in the slow progress of a fatal illness." Frémont, "Biographical Sketch," 5-6; Benton to Jackson, January 30, 1812, in *Papers of Andrew Jackson*, II, 280-81.

57. Jackson to William Preston Anderson, June 16, 1807, *Papers of Andrew Jackson*, II, 167.

58. May 30, 1807, Monroe Papers, LOC.

59. George W. Hay to Thomas Jefferson, June 14, 1807, Thomas Jefferson Papers, LOC, <http://memory.loc.gov/ammem/collections/jefferson_papers/>.

60. Parton, *Life of Jackson*, I, 333-34; Remini, *Jackson*, 49; Buchanan, *Jackson's Way*, 173; Risjord, *The Old Republicans* (New York: Columbia University Press, 1965), 86-95.

61. Chambers, *Old Bullion Benton*, 30-31; Smith, *Magnificent Missourian*, 29.

62. Benton, *Addresses on the Presentation of the Sword of General Andrew Jackson to Congress* (Washington, D.C., 1855), 32-33; Benton, "Auto-Biographical Sketch," iii.

63. Jackson to Tennessee Volunteers, March 12, 1812, in *Correspondence of Andrew Jackson*, ed. John Spencer Bassett, I, 221-22.

64. Nashville *Democratic Clarion*, July 8, 1812.

65. Benton to Clay, October 3, 1812: "I count upon being in the city of Washington soon after the opening of the session. Possibly additional troops will be raised to serve in the war: I should like extremely to have an appointment among them. We are waiting here with impatience, to hear that the Ken. And O. volunteers have effaced the stain of Gen. H[ull]s conduct." *The Papers of Henry Clay*, ed. James F. Hopkins. (Lexington: University of Kentucky Press, 1992).

66. Jackson to the Tennessee Volunteers, November 14, 1812, in *Papers of Andrew Jackson*, II, 341.

67. See *Papers of Andrew Jackson*, II, 345.

68. Jackson to Willie Blount, November 11, 1812, in *Papers of Andrew Jackson*, II, 337.

69. "Quid times?" ("What is to fear?") Words of Caesar to the frightened ship's pilot as they were attempting to cross the Adriatic to Italy during the war with Pompey.

Benton, "Journal of a Voyage from Nashville, Ten. To New Orleans in the winter of the year 1813," in Nashville *Democratic Clarion*, February 9 and 16, also March 9, 1813.

70. Benton, "Journal of a Voyage from Nashville, Ten. To New Orleans."

71. Ibid.

72. Sec. of War John Armstrong to Jackson, February 6, 1813, in *Papers of Andrew Jackson*, II, 361. Accounts of Jackson's conduct during this episode, to which can be traced the nickname "Old Hickory," are found in numerous sources, including Remini, *Life of Andrew Jackson*, 65–67, and Burstein, *Passions of Andrew Jackson*, 92–93.

73. *Clarion*, April 27, 1813. Curiously, in the course of the expedition, the symptoms of his illness had disappeared. "Open air, night and day, vigorous exercise, bathing and drying in the sunshine, simple food taken regularly, and forgetting himself in pursuit of larger endeavors—all of these factors seemed to have restored him to health." Frémont, "Biographical Sketch," 6. Benton perhaps passed on to his daughter his romanticized view of the life of a soldier in the field.

74. *Clarion*, February 23, April 22, 23, 26, 27, 1813. Exchange of letters between Benton and Lewis recounted in Duel Correspondence Circular, April 1813, in Benton Papers, MHS.

75. Freeman, *Affairs of Honor*, 121.

76. Duel Correspondence Circular, April 1813, in Benton Papers, MHS.

77. Chambers, *Old Bullion Benton*, 293–94.

78. Jackson to John Armstrong, May 10, 1813, in *Papers of Andrew Jackson*, II, 405.

79. Benton to Clay, June 22, 1813, in *The Papers of Henry Clay*, ed. James F. Hopkins (Lexington: University of Kentucky Press), 11 vols., I (1992), 805–6.

80. Benton to Jackson, June 15, 1813, in *Papers of Andrew Jackson*, II, 406–7; Chambers, *Old Bullion Benton*, 48–49. One of the junior officers of the newly raised 39th Infantry was Ensign Sam Houston.

81. See Rogin, *Fathers and Children*, 136; Jackson to Benton, August 4, 1813, Affidavit of Felix Robertson, August 5, 1813, Jackson to John M. Armstrong with Armstrong's Responses, in *Papers of Andrew Jackson*, 418–21; Chambers, *Old Bullion Benton*, 49–50; Smith, *Magnificent Missourian*, 43–45.

82. Jackson to Benton, July 19, 1813, in *Papers of Andrew Jackson*, II, 413.

83. Benton to Jackson, July 25, 1813, in *Papers of Andrew Jackson*, II, 413–15.

84. Account of the Nashville fight based on circular, "Thomas H. Benton's Account of His Duel with General Jackson," September 10, 1813, in *Papers of Andrew Jackson*, II, 425–27, and Certificate of James W. Sitler, September 5, 1813, in *Correspondence of Andrew Jackson*, I, 317.

85. By that time the bullet had migrated in Jackson's upper arm and was causing discomfort. A physician was summoned to the White House and cut an incision without anesthesia to remove the slug from the president's arm. Jackson supposedly offered the bullet to Benton, with whom he had now long been reconciled. Benton declined, insisting the president should keep it "in consideration of the extra care he had taken of it" for so many years. Chambers, *Old Bullion Benton*, 194–95.

86. A number of accounts, including Burstein's, allege that Benton "fled" Tennessee after nearly killing Jackson in 1813 (*Passions of Andrew Jackson*, 152). As Chambers long ago pointed out, this is hardly an accurate characterization of what occurred. Benton continued to serve under Jackson's command, sometimes in close personal proximity, for another year after the Nashville fight. When Benton did move on, after the war's

conclusion, he most likely did so because he viewed his political future in Tennessee as blighted since he was no longer part of Jackson's inner circle (*Old Bullion Benton*, 53).

87. Rogin, *Fathers and Children*, 145–48; Remini, *Andrew Jackson and His Indian Wars*, 1–6; Prucha, *The Sword of the Republic* (Bloomington: Indiana University Press, 1977), 114–15. See also Gregory Evans Dowd, *A Spirited Resistance: The North American Indian Struggle for Unity, 1745–1814* (Baltimore, Md.: Johns Hopkins University Press, 1992), and R. David Edmunds, *Tecumseh and the Quest for Indian Leadership* (Boston: Little, Brown, 1984), both of which interpret the Red Stick campaign as an episode within a longer civil war among the Creeks.

88. Jackson to Tennessee Volunteers, September 24, 1813, in *Papers of Andrew Jackson*, II, 428–29; letter from Benton quoted in Parton, *Life of Andrew Jackson*, I, 395–96; Benton to Carroll and Carroll to Benton, September 16, 1813, in *Papers of Andrew Jackson*.

89. Chambers, *Old Bullion Benton*, 53–55; Smith, *Magnificent Missourian*, 48–50.

90. Benton and Others to the Adjutant General, October 25, 1814, Jackson Papers, LOC; Jackson to Benton, n.d., October 1814, in *Correspondence of Andrew Jackson*, II, 65–66

2 / The Transformation of Frontier Missouri

1. Jerome Steffen, ed., *The American West: New Perspectives, New Dimensions* (Norman: Oklahoma University Press, 1979), 94–123, on cosmopolitan versus insular frontiers. Elsewhere Steffen used the terms *expeditionary* and *sedentary frontiers* to describe the same stages of development (*William Clark: Jeffersonian Man on the Frontier* (Norman: University of Oklahoma Press, 1967). Stephen Aron has described this process in the North American heartland as one of racial and cultural as well as geographical "confluence" (*American Confluence: The Missouri Frontier from Borderland to Border State* (Bloomington and Indianapolis: Indiana University Press, 2006). For discussion of the transition to "racial modernity" during the Jacksonian period, see Michael A. Morrison and James Brewer Stewart, eds., *Race and the Early Republic: Racial Consciousness and Nation Building in the Early Republic*, 136–39.

2. Frémont, "Biographical Sketch"; Chambers, *Old Bullion Benton*, 57–58; Smith, *Magnificent Missourian*, 51–52.

3. Benton to Governor James Preston, November 14, 1819, in Benton Papers, MHS. In the same letter, Benton is enthusiastic about the potential of his territory: "Our country still presents the finest theater in America," he tells Preston. Benton cites the ready availability of cheap lands, the flourishing towns of the region, and the commerce plying "our noble rivers," and notes that "the tide of emigration flows in upon us with a force and steadiness which should announce to the old states that the power of this continent is gravitating to the borders of the Mississippi." Benton rhetorically asks what Preston thinks Missouri will be by 1830 and, perhaps with an eye to his political future, predicts, "From that day the West will give law to the Republic."

4. Thomas H. Benton to Governor James Preston, November 14, 1819, Benton Papers, MHS; Timothy Flint, *Recollections of the Last Forty Years* (Boston: Cummings, Hilliard, and Company, 1826), 81–82. Benton's actual route is unknown. It is reasonable to conjecture that leaving western Virginia he traveled down the Ohio, perhaps stopping in Tennessee to visit his family before continuing to Missouri, which would explain his recounting that he "crossed" the Mississippi. However, as I will explain

below, there is intriguing, if circumstantial, evidence that Benton may have traveled to St. Louis by way of New Orleans. William Chambers pointed out that not only Benton's route, but the date of his arrival in St. Louis, have been open to debate among various authors. He asserts that the matter can be definitely established based on the list of attorneys in St. Louis that Benton signed in October 1815 (Roll of Attorneys, Circuit Court for the City of St. Louis) and a letter to James McDowell, dated November 1815, stating that he was settled in St. Louis (*Old Bullion Benton*, 62–63).

5. Benton to William C. Preston, April 27, 1817, Benton Papers, MHS; "Earliest Picture of St. Louis," Missouri Historical Society, *Glimpses of the Past*, VIII (St. Louis, 1941), 7–9; William Foley and C. David Rice, *The First Chouteaus* (Urbana: University of Illinois Press, 1983), 38, 42; Clarence Alvord, *The Illinois Country, 1673–1818* (Springfield: Illinois Centennial Commission, 1920), 347, 349.

6. Steward, *Duels and the Roots of Violence in Missouri* (Columbia: University of Missouri Press, 2000), 60; Chambers, *Old Bullion Benton*, 63.

7. Flint, *Recollections*, 134; Benton, *Thirty Years' View*, I, iii–iv.

8. "Statement of facts and rules of the duel between J. Barton and T. Hempstead," St. Louis, August 10, 1816," in Benton Papers, MHS. Joshua Barton went on to serve in the Missouri legislature, as secretary of state for Missouri, and as U.S. attorney. He was killed in a duel with Thomas C. Rector on Bloody Island, June 1823.

9. Dick Steward, *Duels and the Roots of Violence in Missouri*, 43, 46–47, 65–66.

10. Lemont K. Richardson, "Private Land Claims in Missouri," *Missouri Historical Review* 50 (January 1956): 135–37.

11. Foley, *Genesis of Missouri* (Columbia: University of Missouri Press, 1989), 158.

12. Smith had a reputation as a lethal duelist who reportedly killed over a dozen men. Like Benton, he hailed from Tennessee and added the "T"—for his native state—to his last name so that he would not be confused with the other John Smiths of the world. See Dick Steward, *Frontier Swashbuckler: The Life and Legend of John Smith T.* (Columbia: University of Missouri Press, 2000).

13. Foley, *Genesis of Missouri*, 165–66.

14. Carter, *Territorial Papers*, XIII, 112–14; Richardson, "Private Land Claims," 272; Steward, *Duels*, 64.

15. Carter, *Territorial Papers*, XIV, 97–98; Foley, *Genesis of Missouri*, 172–74.

16. Foley, *Genesis of Missouri*, 183–84.

17. Ibid., 248–50; Richardson, "Private Land Claims," 281, 392–94.

18. Based on the *Registers d'Arpentage*, Chambers asserts that there were about 140 concessions of more than 800 arpents surveyed, compared with more than 325 individual farm plots of about 300 arpents and more than 535 family plots of 800 arpents or less surveyed. The surveys covered only about half the area granted by Spanish authorities, and there were hundreds or thousands of un-surveyed family claims. *Old Bullion Benton*, 65; see also Perry McCandless, "The Rise of Thomas H. Benton in Missouri Politics," *MHR* 50 (October 1955): 16–29.

19. Foley, *Genesis of Missouri*, 238.

20. "Proceedings for the first meeting of the Board of Trustees for superintending schools in St. Louis," April 4, 1817, Schools Envelope, MHS. Significantly, the issue that dominates the records of the Board during Benton's tenure is the sale of public land to pay for local schools.

21. Steffen, Jerome, "William Clark: A New Perspective on Missouri Territorial Politics, 1813–1820," *MHR* 67 (January 1973): 182–83.

22. William Russell to Rufus Easton, nd, 1817; Russell to Easton, nd, 1817; both in Easton Papers, MHS.

23. *Missouri Gazette*, August 9, 1817.

24. Foley, *Genesis of Missouri*, 291.

25. Charles Lucas to Benton, November 15, 1816; Charles Lucas, "Statement of the causes of difference between T.H. Benton and me," August 11, 1817; both in Lucas Papers, MHS.

26. Ibid.

27. Ibid.

28. Primm, *Lion of the Valley*, 113. Benton's "first friend" in St. Louis, Charles Gratiot, had died earlier in 1817 of a paralytic stroke. Benton to William C. Preston, April 27, 1817; Benton to Lucas, August 11, 1817, Duels Envelope, MHS.

29. "Articles regulating the terms of a personal interview between Thomas H. Benton and Charles Lucas Esquires," August 11, 1817, Benton Papers, MHS. Lawless was part of a circle of up-and-coming young lawyers and businessmen with whom Benton associated. In addition to the Hempsteads, that circle included Robert Wash, also a lawyer and avid hunter; Major Joshua Pilcher, who had come to St. Louis during the War of 1812 and had gone into merchandising; and Dr. Bernard Farrar, a physician who attended Benton in his duels with Lucas (Chambers, *Old Bullion Benton*, 67–68). Wash, Pilcher, and Farrar were all Virginians by birth and members of the gentry who were accustomed to assuming political leadership. Benton's relationship with the Prestons and the McDowells, as well as with Governor Clark, reinforced his inclination to identify with this group.

30. Statement by Charles Lucas, August 29, 1817; Luke E. Lawless to Charles Lucas, August 29, 1817; both in Lucas Papers, MHS.

31. Rogin, *Fathers and Children*, 58.

32. Ibid., 49–50; Wyatt-Brown, *Southern Honor*, 43–44.

33. Benton to Lucas, September 23, 1817, *Missouri Gazette*, October 4, 1817; Chambers, *Old Bullion Benton*, 68, for the date of Nancy Benton's arrival in St. Louis.

34. Lawless to Lucas, September 26, 1817, Duels Envelope, MHS; Lucas to Benton, September 26, 1817, Lucas Papers, MHS.

35. "Articles regulating the terms of a personal interview between Thomas H. Benton demanding and Charles Lucas answering," September 26, 1817, Benton Papers, MHS; Certificate of Conduct of Lucas-Benton Duel, September 27, 1817, Lucas Papers, MHS;

36. *Missouri Gazette*, September 27, 1817.

37. Amadee Soulard, "The Bloody Island Cross Mark," *St. Louis Globe Democrat*, June 25, 1899, copy in Duels Envelope, MHS; Chambers, *Old Bullion Benton*, 75–76.

38. Thomas Hart Benton, "Autobiographical Sketch," in *Thirty Years' View or, A History of the Working of the American Government for Thirty Years, From 1820 to 1850* (New York: D. Appleton and Co., 2 vols., 1854–56), I, i–vi. In fact, much of the correspondence relating to the affair was saved by other parties and is now in the archives of the Missouri Historical Society in St. Louis.

39. See Marvin Mikesell, "Comparative Studies in Frontier History," *Annals of the Association of American Geographers*, L (March 1960): 62–74; Jerome Steffen, ed., *The*

American West: New Perspectives, New Dimensions. See David Weber, *The Mexican Frontier, 1821–1846: The American Southwest Under Mexico* (Albuquerque: University of New Mexico Press, 1982) on frontiers of inclusion/exclusion. My account of slaveholding under the Creole regime is based on Carl J. Ekberg, *French Roots in the Illinois Country* (Urbana: University of Illinois Press, 1998), 145–57, and Foley, *The Genesis of Missouri*.

40. "Éditconcernant les Nègres à la Louisiane," *Publications of the Louisiana Historical Society* 4 (1908): 76 (summarized in Ekberg, *French Roots in the Illinois Country*, 147–48).

41. "Réglementsur la police pour la province de la Louisiane," Archives Nationales, Coloniales, Paris, C13A, 35: 40–51 (in Ekberg, *Illinois Country*, 148–49).

42. Ordinance regarding Slavery, 12 August 1781, in Louis Houck, ed., *The Spanish Regime in Missouri: a collection of papers and documents relating to upper Louisiana principally within the present limits of Missouri during the dominion of Spain, from the Archives of the Indies at Seville, etc., translated from the original Spanish into English, and including also some papers concerning the supposed grant to Col. George Morgan at the mouth of the Ohio, found in the Congressional library; ed. and with an introduction and notes, biographical and explanatory* (Chicago: R.R. Donnelley & Sons Company, 2 vols., 1909), I, 44.

43. Flagg, Edmund, "The Far West, 1836–1837," in Reuben Thwaites, ed., *Early Western Travels, 1748–1846, a series of annotated reprints of some of the best and rarest contemporary volumes of travel: descriptive of the aborigines and social and economic conditions in the middle and far west, during the period of early American settlement* (Cleveland, Ohio: A.H. Clark Co., 25 vols., 1904–1907), 27: 56; Ekberg, *Illinois Country*, 151; see also Ekberg, *Colonial Ste. Genevieve*, 196–238, in which the author's conclusions are based on the comments of Pierre Charles Delassus de Luzières, commandant of the town of New Bourbon. Ekberg adds, "This study.... is not the appropriate place to take up the lively debate concerning the relative merits and demerits of the respective varieties of slavery practiced in the New World. At this point, however, it seems evident that the brand of human bondage practiced in colonial Ste. Genevieve was less repressive and more humane than that practiced in the Anglo-American colonies" (236 n. 11).

44. Arvarh E. Strickland, "Aspects of Slavery in Missouri, 1821," *Missouri Historical Review* 65 (July 1971): 506.

45. Strickland, "Aspects of Slavery in Missouri, 1821," 506–7; Floyd C. Shoemaker, *Missouri's Struggle for Statehood* (New York: Russell & Russell, 1943), 17–20.

46. Trexler, Harrison, *Slavery in Missouri, 1804–1864* (Baltimore: Johns Hopkins University Press, 1914), 58; Foley, *Genesis of Missouri*, 154; Strickland, "Aspects of Slavery in Missouri, 1821," 508.

47. Rufus Babcock, ed., *Forty Years of Pioneer Life: The Memoir of John Mason Peck, D.D.* (Carbondale: Southern Illinois University Press, 1965), 146.

48. John Mason Peck, quoted in Houck, *History of Missouri* (Chicago: R.R. Donnelley & Sns, 2 vols., 1908), 3: 249.

49. *St. Louis Enquirer*, April 21, 1819.

50. Selections of Editorial Articles from the St. Louis Enquirer, on the Subject of Oregon and Texas, as Originally Published in that Paper, in the Years 1818–1819, MHS, 5, 7, & 9.

51. *St. Louis Enquirer*, June 19, 1819.

52. *Missouri Gazette*, June 9, October 20, 1819, January 26, 1820; *Niles' Weekly Register*, 42, 288 (December 25, 1819); Flint, *Recollections*, 201. Transportation improvements were one of the foundations of economic development in the West, and western Democrats, throughout the Jacksonian era, were considerably more ambivalent over the question of internal improvements than the party leadership's adherence to "strict construction" might imply.

53. "Memorial and Resolutions of Missouri Territorial Legislature, 1818 Petitioning Congress for Statehood," in Floyd Shoemaker, *Missouri's Struggle for Statehood* (New York: Russell & Russell, 1943), 325–26. Shoemaker's classic continues to be cited in scholarly works dealing with the controversy surrounding Missouri's admission to the Union from a regional perspective. Robert P. Forbes, *The Missouri Compromise and Its Aftermath: Slavery & the Meaning of America* (Chapel Hill: University of North Carolina Press, 2007) is a contemporary and comprehensive study of politics surrounding the Missouri controversy and the subsequent sectional truce over slavery through 1854. Still useful is Glover Moore's *The Missouri Controversy, 1819–1821* (Lexington: University of Kentucky Press, 1953), which also deals with national politics during the immediate period.

54. Annals of Congress 15/2: 1166, 1170; see also David D. March, "The Admission of Missouri," *MHR*, 65, no. 4 (July 1971): 428; Shoemaker, 55–56; Moore, 33–35.

55. Annals of Congress 15/2: 1214–17; March, 428–29; Shoemaker, 56–57; Moore, 32–53.

56. *St. Louis Enquirer*, May 19, 1819.

57. Ibid.; March, "Admission of Missouri," 430–32.

58. Ibid., May 19, 1819. In his argument supporting this resolution, Benton stated that the proposed slavery restriction tended to confine the slaves to the Deep South where conditions were harsher than in the Upper South or border states.

59. *St. Louis Enquirer*, May 19, 1819; Shoemaker, 84–87; Moore, 262; March, 432.

60. *St. Louis Enquirer*, July 14, 1819; Shoemaker, 92–96; March, 433.

61. *St. Louis Enquirer*, April 19, 1819; *Missouri Gazette*, May 17, 1820; Shoemaker, 127.

62. *Missouri Gazette*, April 19, 1820, May 17, 31, 1820.

63. Chambers, *Old Bullion Benton*, 56–57. Chambers attributes this story to Marquis James's *Life of Andrew Jackson* (Indianapolis & New York: The Bobbs-Merrill Co., 1938), 306. James, in turn, seems to have drawn the story from James D. Davis's *History of the City of Memphis*, Admission of Missouri... *Also, The Old Times Papers* (Memphis: Hite, Crumpton & Kelly, 1873), 70–77.

64. Wyatt-Brown, *Southern Honor*, 318–19. Marcus Brutus Winchester (1796–1856) served in the War of 1812 as an aide to his father, General James Winchester, and was captured by the British at the Raisin River in 1813. James Winchester, with John Overton and Andrew Jackson, founded the town of Memphis, and Marcus Winchester served as its first mayor from 1827 to 1829. About 1823, Winchester married Amarante Loiselle of New Orleans, known as "Mary," whom most historians agree was a woman of color. They had six daughters and two sons. "Possibly because of his marriage and the hardening of racial lines, Winchester's career declined. He moved with his family to his farm three miles outside of Memphis and was involved in a variety of lawsuits and financial difficulties." *Tennessee Encyclopedia of History and Culture*, Admission

of Missouri, <http://tennesseeencylclopedia.net>. None of the sources on Winchester mention Thomas Hart Benton. Wyatt Brown also cites Davis, *History of the City of Memphis*, as well as John De Witt, "General James Winchester," *Tennessee Historical Magazine* 1 (September 1915): 201; Samuel D. Williams, *Beginnings of West Tennessee in the Land of the Chickasaws, 1541–1841* (Johnson City, Tenn.: Watauga Press, 1930), 130; and Gerald M. Capers Jr., *The Biography of a River Town: Memphis in Its Heroic Age* (Chapel Hill: University of North Carolina Press, 1939), 52–53.

65. Wyatt-Brown, *Southern Honor*, 307–8. Consider also the career of Kentuckian Richard Mentor Johnson, ninth vice president of the United States. A hero of the War of 1812 and later a Jacksonian member of Congress, Johnson had a long-term and open relationship with Julia Chinn, a mulatto slave who bore him two daughters. This flouting of convention so offended southern standards that the 23 presidential electors from Virginia refused to vote for Johnson when he sought the vice presidency as Van Buren's running mate in 1836. Because of his scandalous behavior he became the only vice president in American history chosen by the U.S. Senate rather than by the Electoral College (ibid., 311–12).

66. Moore, 11–12. See Garry Wills, *"Negro President": Jefferson and the Slave Power* (Boston: Houghton Mifflin, 2003). See also H-Net, December 29, 2003, for a critique of Wills's thesis by Jack Rakove of Stanford and Larry Kramer of New York University School of Law.

67. Leonard L. Richards, *The Slave Power: The Free North and Southern Domination, 1780–1860* (Baton Rouge: Louisiana State University Press, 2000), 9, quoted in Wills, *"Negro President,"* 7.

68. Moore, *Missouri Controversy*, 88–89, 100–111; March, 438–39.

69. Moore, *Missouri Controversy*, 249–50, 264.

70. *Missouri Gazette*, April 5, 1820.

71. Shoemaker, 132–34; March, 440–41.

72. Lehmann, F.W., "The Constitution of 1820," *MHR* 16 (January 1922): 239–46.

73. *Missouri Gazette*, June 28, 1820.

74. *St. Louis Enquirer*, August 2, 1820.

75. Steffen, "William Clark," 193–97.

76. Perry McCandless, *A History of Missouri*, II, 1820–1860, 15.

77. Benton to John Scott, August 30, 1820, Benton Papers, MHS.

78. Darby, *Personal Recollections*, 32–33.

79. McCandless, *History of Missouri*, II, 16–18; Shoemaker, *Missouri's Struggle for Statehood*, 273.

80. Nathaniel Watkins to Henry Clay, October 6, 1820, in Thomas J. Clay Papers, LOC.

81. Thomas Benton to Nancy Benton, December 13, 1820; Benton to Robert Wash, March 14, 1821; both in Benton Papers, MHS; Frémont, "Biographical Sketch," 7.

82. Charles Francis Adams, ed., *Memoirs of John Quincy Adams, Comprising Parts of His Diary from 1795 to 1848* (Philadelphia: J.B. Lippincott & Co., 12 vols., 1874–1877), V, 128; *Congressional Directory* (1820), 41; *Missouri Gazette*, December 21, 1821; Nathan Sargent, *Public Men and Events from the commencement of Mr. Monroe's administration, in 1817, to the close of Mr. Filmore's administration, in 1853* (Philadelphia: J.B. Lippincott & Co., 1875), I, 52–55.

83. Moore, *The Missouri Controversy*, 148-49.
84. *St. Louis Enquirer*, December 30, 1820.
85. *St. Louis Enquirer*, quoted in *Niles Weekly Register*, XIX, February 3, 1821.
86. March, "The Admission of Missouri," 443-47. See George Dangerfield, *The Era of Good Feelings* (New York: Harcourt, Brace, 1952), 133-45 on the "Second Missouri Debate."
87. Shoemaker, *Struggle for Statehood*, appendix IV, 360-62.
88. March, 449.

3 / The Triumph of Master Race Democracy

1. Nathaniel Macon to Bolling Hill, June 20, 1823, quoted in Wyatt-Brown, *Southern Honor*, 178; descriptions from Schlesinger, *Age of Jackson*, 26-29 (Boston: Little, Brown, 1945), and Charles G. Sellers, *The Market Revolution: Jacksonian America, 1815-1846* (New York: Oxford University Press, 1991), 118.
2. Quoted in Sellers, *Market Revolution*, 119.
3. According to William Chambers, Benton lifted the name of Sir John Oldcastle from his reading of English history. The original was a leader of the fourteenth-century Lollard movement who was convicted of heresy and hanged in 1417 for his unorthodox opinions. "Though Sir John was the prototype of Shakespeare's Falstaff, 'my old lad of the castle,' the stage character was little like the actual person." *Old Bullion Benton*, 28. See also Christopher Allmand, *Henry V* (Berkeley: University of California Press, 1992), 288, 294-99, 302-4.
4. Benton, *Thirty Years' View*, I, 473-74; Chambers, *Old Bullion Benton*, 30, 109; Schlesinger, *Age of Jackson*, 20-21; Sellers, *Market Revolution*, 118.
5. *Annals of Congress* 17/1: 179, 297-307; 17/2: 146-47; 18/1: 787; Chambers, *Old Bullion Benton*, 110; Smith, *Magnificent Missourian*, 79-80.
6. *Annals of Congress*, 17/1: 317-31.
7. Crooks to Benton, April 1, 1822, *American Fur Company Letter Books*, 2: 241.
8. Smith, *Magnificent Missourian*, 81; Francis Paul Prucha, *The Great Father: The United States Government and the American Indians* (Lincoln: University of Nebraska Press, 2 vols., 1984), I, 134.
9. Stuart to Crooks, November 22, 1822; Crooks to Benton, December 31, 1822; both in Kenneth Wiggins Porter, *John Jacob Astor: Business Man* (Cambridge, Mass.: Harvard University Press, 2 vols., 1931), II, 713-14.
10. Porter, II, 705, 817.
11. Nancy Benton to Samuel Benton, January 12, 1823, Benton Papers, MHS; Smith, *Magnificent Missourian*, 82-83.
12. Abramoske, Donald J., "The Federal Lead Leasing System in Missouri," *Missouri Historical Review* 54 (October 1959): 28.
13. *Annals of Congress*, 17th Congress, 2nd Session, 240.
14. Carter, *Territorial Papers*, XV, 219-20; *Annals of Congress*, 17/2, 240.
15. *U.S. v. Gear*, 44 US 120 (1845).
16. See pages 75-76 and 103-10 above. The city of St. Louis remained an exception, or perhaps a qualification, to the expeditionary/sedentary dichotomy that serves so well to characterize outstate Missouri. Its growing importance as a national center of commerce and population would influence later shifts in Benton's political views during the 1840s and 1850s.

17. Dorothy B. Dorsey, "The Panic of 1819 in Missouri," *Missouri Historical Review* 29 (January 1935): 79-91.

18. See Sean Wilentz, *The Rise of American Democracy*, 15-20, for an outline of these uprisings, which he associates with the genesis of "Country Democracy."

19. Ibid., 288-90. Kentucky's "Court Wars" also provided a political apprenticeship for Amos Kendall and Francis Preston Blair, both of whom supported the "New Court" faction and who both went on to become important political lieutenants of President Andrew Jackson. See Donald B. Cole, *A Jackson Man: Amos Kendall and the Rise of American Democracy* (Baton Rouge: Louisiana State University Press, 2004), 9-94, and Elbert B. Smith, *Francis Preston Blair* (New York: Free Press, 1980), 1-25. See also Lowell H. Harrison and James C. Clotter, *A New History of Kentucky* (Lexington: University Press of Kentucky, 1997), 109-12; Murray N. Rothbard, *The Panic of 1819: Reactions and Policies* (New York: Columbia University Press, 1962), 52-55; Sellers, *Market Revolution*, 169-70.

20. Dorsey, "Panic of 1819," 87; Rothbard, *Panic of 1819*, 42-45.

21. McCandless, *History of Missouri*, II, 27; Wilentz, *Rise of American Democracy*, 287; Rothbard, *Panic of 1819*, 86; Dorsey, "Panic of 1819," 88-90.

22. McCandless, *History of Missouri*, II, 67-68. As with the eighteenth-century Regulators, for country democrats of the 1820s, the Courts became the focus of resistance to the perceived "aristocratic" tendencies of a new "monied power." Richard Ellis pointed out in *The Jeffersonian Crisis: Courts and Politics in the Young Republic* (New York: Oxford University Press, 1971) that attitudes toward the legitimacy of appointed judges was the distinguishing factor between radical and moderate Republicans during Jefferson's administration. The radicals, led by John Randolph and Nathaniel Macon, were the precursors of the Jacksonian movement several decades later. Wilentz makes a similar case in *The Rise of American Democracy*, 32, 118, 121.

23. *Register of Debates*, 18/1, 167-203. Versions of the amendment to reform the method of choosing the president and vice president were proposed by Robert Y. Hayne of South Carolina and Martin Van Buren of New York at the same time. Among other constitutional amendments offered during this session was a proposal by Senator Mahlon Dickerson of New Jersey to limit the chief executive to two terms in office—the measure that eventually became the Twenty-second Amendment in 1951.

24. The presidential election of 1824, being one of the crucial political events in the eventual rise of Jacksonian democracy, has been covered by scores of works on the period. Some of the major accounts include Andrew Burstein, *The Passions of Andrew Jackson* (New York: Alfred A. Knopf, 2003), 146-58; Merrill D. Peterson, *The Great Triumvirate: Webster, Clay, and Calhoun*, 116-31; Robert Remini, *The Life of Andrew Jackson*, 145-56, and *Henry Clay: Statesman for the Union*, 234-72; Charles G. Sellers, *The Market Revolution*, 124-25, 172-74, 178-81, 185-201; Harry L. Watson, *Liberty and Power: The Politics of Jacksonian America* (New York: Hill and Wang, 1990), 74-83; Sean Wilentz, *The Rise of American Democracy: Jefferson to Lincoln*, 240-57. For Benton's role in the political maneuvering and his eventual support for Jackson, see Chambers, *Old Bullion Benton*, 116-31; and Smith, *Magnificent Missourian*, 92-95; see also Alan S. Wiener, "John Scott, Thomas Hart Benton, David Barton and the Election of 1824: A Case Study in Pressure Politics," *Missouri Historical Review* 60 (July 1966): 460-94.

25. Missouri *Republican*, March 8, 1824; Wiener, "Scott, Benton, Barton and the

Election of 1824," 468–69; see chapter two for Benton's proposals to aid western development during 1818–1819.

26. Wiener, 469–70.

27. John K. Walker and John O'Fallon, November 15, 18, 1824, quoted in Chambers, *Old Bullion Benton*, 126; Wiener, 471–72; McCandless, *History of Missouri*, II, 72, 89.

28. Chambers, *Old Bullion Benton*, 118; Smith, *Magnificent Missourian*, 93–99; Remini, *Life of Andrew Jackson*, 71, 148.

29. *Correspondence of Andrew Jackson*, III, 217.

30. Wiener, 475. The federal census of 1820 listed 16,067 free white males over age 16 in a state population of 68,176. Only about 21 percent of the state's population could vote and considerably less did. The modest vote totals seem to indicate that, despite universal white male suffrage in the state, the idea of deferring to the propertied classes died hard even in the West, and widespread participation among qualified voters had yet to take root.

31. Wiener, 475–76. In 1824 the Hermitage was still a plain brick farmhouse, two stories high, situated on 640 acres outside of Nashville. According to the 1820 census, Jackson owned 44 slaves. The number would rise to 95 by the time he became president in 1829 and to 150 a few years later. Remini, *Life of Andrew Jackson*, 51, 61.

32. *Journal of the Senate of the State of Missouri* (Jefferson City, MO: s.n., 1821–1877), *3rd General Assembly, 1st Session*, 229–31; Wiener, 476; see also Hattie Anderson, "Jackson Men in Missouri in 1828," *MHR* 34 (April 1940): 303–4.

33. Fayette *Missouri Intelligencer*, August 2, 1826. Elbert Smith offers perhaps the most succinct assessment of Benton's decision: "It was the only possible decision consistent with the sentiments he had been shouting from the housetops throughout the preceding year. The people had spoken and Benton would obey.... Benton had already placed himself at the head of Western democracy and Western democracy had spoken for Jackson. The Senator was not going to be run over by the very forces he had helped generate." *Magnificent Missourian*, 94. See also McCandless, *History of Missouri*, II, 73.

34. Barton to Silas Bent, February 2, 1825, in Bay, *Reminiscences of the Bench and Bar*, 604–5.

35. Scott to Benton, February 5, 1825. Wiener cites Parton, *Life of Andrew Jackson*, III, 62, in which the brief note is quoted in its entirety.

36. Benton to Scott, in Parton, *Life of Andrew Jackson*, III, 62–63.

37. Remini, *Andrew Jackson and the Course of American Freedom*, 94; Adams, *Memoirs*, VI, 473–74.

38. Remini, *Henry Clay*, xvi, 271; Jackson to William B. Lewis, February 14, 1825, in *Correspondence of Andrew Jackson*, III, 276.

39. *Market Revolution*, 198–200; Sellers relies on Marquis James's 1938 biography of Jackson, as well as Remini's *Election of Andrew Jackson* (Philadelphia: Lippincott, 1963).

40. Daniel Walker Howe, *What Hath God Wrought: The Transformation of America, 1815–1848* (New York: Oxford University Press, 2007), 208–11, and *The Political Culture of the American Whigs* (Chicago: University of Chicago Press, 1979), 46–47; Richard Hofstadter, *The Idea of a Party System: The Rise of Legitimate Opposition in the United States, 1780–1840* (Berkeley: University of California Press, 1969), 232. No doubt Adams would have been shocked by this characterization of his behavior. His

inability to admit—even to himself—to playing politics is evidenced by the fact that his voluminous diary, in which he recorded nearly everything he did, contains a blank space on the day of his crucial conference with Clay prior to the House vote (*Memoirs of John Quincy Adams*, January 9, 1825). The significance of this omission is discussed in Samuel Flagg Bemis, *John Quincy Adams and the Union* (New York: Knopf, 1956), 40ff.

41. Peterson, *Great Triumvirate*, 129-30.

42. Wilentz, *Rise of American Democracy*, 255-56.

43. "A man must ride alternately on the horses of his private and his public nature, as equestrians in the circus throw themselves nimbly from horse to horse, or plant one foot on the back of one, and the other foot on the back of the other." Ralph Waldo Emerson, "Fate," from *The Conduct of Life* (Boston: Ticknor and Fields, 1860).

44. James D. Richardson, ed., *Messages and Papers of the Presidents* (New York: Bureau of National Literature and Art, Volumes 1-10, 1897), II, 299-317; see Peterson, *Great Triumvirate*, 133-34, on precedents from earlier administrations.

45. Macon to Bartlett Yancey, December 8, 1825, quoted in Risjord, *Old Republicans*.

46. Van Buren to Ritchie, January 13, 1827. Historians have argued for years that Van Buren was presenting the blueprint for a proslavery or pro-southern party in opposition to Adams and his northeastern base. See Richard H. Brown, "The Missouri Crisis, Slavery, and the Politics of Jacksonianism," *South Atlantic Quarterly* 65 (1966): 55-70. Sean Wilentz takes issue with this view, stating that Van Buren, in calling for a return to the parties of Jefferson's day, which had been based on political principles, neither shared the proslavery views of his southern copartisans, nor hoped to build a new party on them. "While deprecating the antislavery agitation in the North, Van Buren was asking potential allies in both sections—in the South, most delicately, Thomas Ritchie—to honor national compromise. The South, as well as the North, would have to eschew the politics of slavery" (*Rise of American Democracy*, 296).

47. Thomas Jefferson, *Notes on the State of Virginia*, ed. Thomas Perkins Abernethy (New York: Harper & Row, 1964), 157-58.

48. This was the faction that Benton had dismissed in his OLDCASTLE editorial written in Tennessee at the same time.

49. John Ashworth, *Slavery, Capitalism and Politics in the Antebellum Republic* (Cambridge, U.K., and New York: Cambridge University Press, 1995), 21.

50. Ashworth, 21-27.

51. *Annals of Congress*, 18/1: 1307; Macon to Bartlett Yancey, December 26, 1824, quoted in Risjord, *Old Republicans*, 242.

52. Randolph to Littleton Waller Tazewell, February 21, 1826, as quoted in Risjord, 260.

53. On the Panama Congress debates, see Benton, *Thirty Years' View*, I, 65-69; Risjord, *Old Republicans*, 260-61; Don E. Fehrenbacher, *The Slaveholding Republic: An Account of the United States Government's Relations to Slavery*, ed. Ward M. McAfee (Oxford, U.K., and New York: Oxford University Press, 2001), 115-16.

54. *Register of Debates (RD)*, 19/1: Part I, 150, Part II, 2514.

55. Ibid., 304ff. With characteristic pedantry, Benton goes on for over 20 pages, emphasizing the distinction between *Ministers* and *Deputies* in foreign affairs and explaining the advisory role of the Senate in the creation of such offices.

56. *RD* 19/1:330; Benton, *Thirty Years' View*, I, 69.

57. *RD* 19/1:166; Fehrenbacher, *The Slaveholding Republic*, 115–16. Despite calls for closer ties from both antislavery circles and commercial interests, the United States did not accord diplomatic recognition to the Republic of Haiti until 1862, once slaveholders were no longer a major force in national politics.

58. *RD*, 1/19: 290–91; Fehrenbacher, *The Slaveholding Republic*, 116.

59. Forbes, *The Missouri Compromise and Its Aftermath*, 207–9.

60. Benton, *Thirty Years' View*, I. 69; Peterson, *Great Triumvirate*, 139–40.

61. There were, of course, also a number of papers that supported the administration and were consistent in their opposition to Benton, namely, St. Louis's *Missouri Republican*.

62. *Missouri Republican*, September 12, 19, 1825; October 17, 24; *Missouri Advocate*, August 13, September 17, November 26, December 3, 10, 24, 1825; McCandless, *History of Missouri*, II, 76–77; Chambers, *Old Bullion Benton*, 133.

63. McCandless, *History of Missouri*, II, 77–79; Chambers, *Old Bullion Benton*, 141–42.

64. CURTIUS, "Torchlight—An Examination of the Origin, Policy and Principles of the Opposition to the Administration and an Exposition of the Official Conduct of THOMAS H. BENTON, One of the Senators from Missouri," *Missouri Republican* Office, 1826. McCandless, *History of Missouri*, II, 72, 78–79; Chambers, *Old Bullion Benton*, 126, 142.

65. CURTIUS, "Torchlight."

66. Lucas to Adams, September 1826, in *Letters of Hon. John B.C. Lucas from 1815 to 1836* (compiled and published by his grandson, John B.C. Lucas, St. Louis, Mo., 1905), 78; Adams, *Memoirs*, VII, 187–88.

67. Benton to Finis Ewing, September 4, 1826, Benton Papers, MHS; William Carr Lane in MHS, *Glimpses of the Past*, VII, 91, 94; Chambers, *Old Bullion Benton*, 144–45.

68. Robert E. Shalhope, "Thomas Hart Benton and Missouri State Politics: A Re-Examination," *Bulletin of the Missouri Historical Society* 25, no. 3 (April 1969): 172–73; Chambers, *Old Bullion Benton*, 148–49; McCandless, *History of Missouri*, II, 80–81.

69. McCandless, *History of Missouri*, II, 81.

70. Chambers, *Old Bullion Benton*, 147–48; McCandless, *History of Missouri*, II, 81–82.

4 / "The Land Belongs To the People"

1. Benton. *Thirty Years' View*, I, 27, 29.

2. On this subject, see in particular the work of Robert Remini, *Andrew Jackson and the Course of American Freedom* (New York: Harper & Row, 1981), and *Andrew Jackson and His Indian Wars* (New York: Viking, 2001); and Francis P. Prucha, *Great Father: The United States Government and the American Indians* (Lincoln: University of Nebraska Press, 2 vols., 1984). Benton's views on the issue of Indian removal and his active role throughout the process as a member of the Senate Committee on Indian Affairs are almost entirely absent from both earlier, book-length biographies and from the article literature dealing with his career that has appeared since the 1960s. This is a curious omission given the prominence of the Indian question during both the Adams and Jackson administrations. Chambers mentions his subject's views on race and settlement of the Southwest in passing (*Old Bullion Benton*, 159), but, on the whole, avoids anything that would detract from the adulatory tone of his work. This

oversight, intended or not, becomes all the more glaring when one examines Benton's own legislative memoir, *Thirty Years' View*, in which the former senator devoted no less than six long chapters to the subject of Indian removal and in which he made his assessment of Native Americans as a race unmistakably clear.

3. *Cherokee Nation v. Georgia*: 30 U.S. 1 (1831).

4. See pages 12-13 above as well as John Mack Faragher, *Daniel Boone* (New York: Holt, 1992), 110-12; Chambers, "As the Twig is Bent," 391-93; and William G. McLoughlin. *Cherokee Renascence in the New Republic* (Princeton, N.J.: Princeton University Press, 1986), 18-19.

5. Benton, *Thirty Years' View*, I, 105-6; Chambers, *Old Bullion Benton*, 32-33; Smith, *Magnificent Missourian*, 30-31.

6. Christian Wilt to Joseph Hertzog, March 13, 1815, Christian Wilt Letterbook, MHS.

7. See pages 59-60 above on frontiers of inclusion/exclusion. See also McCandless, *History of Missouri*, II, 14-15, and William Foley, *Wilderness Journey: The Life of William Clark* (Columbia: University of Missouri Press, 2004); and Aron, *American Confluence*, 209-11, on Missouri's transition from an inclusive borderland to a sedentary frontier of exclusion.

8. Donaldson, ed., *The Public Domain: its history, with statistics, with references to the national domain, colonization, acquirement of territory, the survey, administration and several methods of sale and disposition of the public domain of the United States, with sketch of legislative history of the land states and territories, and references to the land system of the colonies, and also that of several foreign governments* (Washington: G.P.O., 1884), 68-69; Daniel Feller, *The Public Lands in Jacksonian Politics* (Madison: University of Wisconsin Press, 1984), 3-7.

9. Benton to Governor Preston, May 20, 1818, Benton Papers, MHS; see Feller, *Public Lands in Jacksonian Politics*, 18-30, on speculation.

10. Feller, *Public Lands in Jacksonian Politics*, 22; Malcolm J. Rohrbough, *The Land Office Business: The Settlement and Administration of American Public Lands, 1789-1837* (New York: Oxford University Press, 1968), 137-40; Paul W. Gates, *History of Public Land Law Development*. (Washington: U.S. Government Printing Office, 1968), 139.

11. Missouri *Gazette*, April 28, 1819.

12. Feller, *Public Lands in Jacksonian Politics*, 27-37; Rohrbough, *Land Office Business*, 141-44; Gates, *History of Public Land Law Development*, 140-41.

13. Benton, *Thirty Years' View*, I, 27. Benton's assertion about colonial Indian policy is far from literally true. The British government's Proclamation of 1763 and the Quebec Act of 1774 were both designed to keep the peace in the Trans-Appalachian West by forbidding further white settlement on Indian lands. The activities of Jessie Benton, Richard Henderson, and the Transylvania Company were, coincidentally, in violation of both measures.

14. Jackson to John Coffee, July 10, 1817, quoted in Remini, *Life of Jackson*, 114.

15. Benton, *Thirty Years' View*, I, 27.

16. See pp. 119-122 above. *Cherokee Nation v. Georgia*, 30 U.S. 1 (1831); Anthony F.C. Wallace, *The Long, Bitter Trail: Andrew Jackson and the Indians* (New York: Hill and Wang, 1993), 35-36; Ronald N. Satz, *American Indian Policy in the Jacksonian Era* (Lincoln: University of Nebraska Press, 1975), 1-6; Francis Paul Prucha, *The Great*

Father: The United States Government and the American Indians, I, 115–54; William G. McLoughlin, *Cherokees and Missionaries, 1789–1839* (New Haven: Yale University Press, 1984), and *Cherokee Renascence in the New Republic* (Princeton, N.J.: Princeton University Press, 1986), 46–47, 72–77, 350–65.

17. Foley, *A History of Missoury: Volume I, 1673–1820* (Columbia: University of Missouri Press, 1971), 66–67; Anthony F.C. Wallace, *Jefferson and the Indians: The Tragic Fate of the First Americans* (Cambridge, Mass.: Belknap Press of Harvard University Press, 1999), 251–60.

18. Benton, *Thirty Years' View*, I, 28; John C. Calhoun, "Regulations Concerning the Civilization of the Indians," September 3, 1819, in *The Papers of John C. Calhoun (PJCC)*, ed. Robert L. Meriwether (Columbia: Published by the University of South Carolina Press for the South Caroliniana Society, 28 vols., 1959–2003), IV, 295–96; Calhoun to Henry Clay, January 15, 1820, in *PJCC*, IV, 575–76; Andrew Jackson to Calhoun, August 25, 1820, *PJCC*, V, 336–37; Jackson to Calhoun, September 2, 1820, *PJCC*, V, 243–345; Calhoun to James Monroe, February 8, 1822, *PJCC*, VI, 679–83; James Monroe to the Senate and House of Representatives, March 3, 1824, in James D. Richardson, ed., *Messages and Papers of the Presidents*, II, 234–37; James Monroe, "Eighth Annual Message," December 7, 1824, in Richardson, II, 256–57 and 261; Monroe to the Senate and House of Representatives, January 27, 1825, in Richardson, II, 280–83; Sellers, *Market Revolution*, 90–93; Peterson, *Great Triumvirate*, 90–92.

19. Benton, *Thirty Years' View*, I, 27 and 28; emphasis mine.

20. *American State Papers, Indian Affairs*, II, 563; *Thirty Years' View*, 58–59; *Memoirs of John Quincy Adams*, VII, 12; Charles J. Kappler, *Indian Affairs. Laws and Treaties* (Washington: G.P.O., 7 vols., 1903–), II, 214–17; Samuel Flagg Bemis, *John Quincy Adams and the Union*, 79–80; Sellers, *Market Revolution*, 278–79; Mary W.M. Hargreaves, *Presidency of John Quincy Adams* (Lawrence: University Press of Kansas, 1985), 202. See also Ulrich B. Philips, *Georgia and State Rights: A Study of the Political History of Georgia from the Revolution to the Civil War* (Washington: Government Printing Office, 1902), on this controversy.

21. *American State Papers, Indian Affairs*, II, 571–82; Benton, *Thirty Years' View*, I, 59; Bemis, *John Quincy Adams*, 80–81.

22. *American State Papers, Indian Affairs*, II, 727ff.

23. Adams, *Memoirs*, 7: 89–90; Bemis, *John Quincy Adams*, 82–83.

24. "To remove the Indians" would "make room for the spread of slaves." Benton, *Thirty Years' View*, I, 28, 59.

25. On removal: Jackson to Colonel John D. Terrill, July 29, 1826, in *Correspondence of Andrew Jackson*; on land issue, see Feller, 101–6; Chambers, *Old Bullion Benton*, 151; William W. Freehling, *Road to Disunion: Volume I, Secessionists at Bay, 1776–1854* (New York: Oxford University Press, 1990), 261–62, 267, 269.

26. Benton, *Thirty Years' View*, I, 102. See pp. 63–65 above on Benton Town.

27. McCandless, "Benton v. Barton: The Formation of the Second Party System in Missouri," *MHR* 79 (July 1985): 431–32, and *History of Missouri*, II, 71–72; Feller, *Public Lands*, 69; Chambers, *Old Bullion Benton*, 126.

28. Benton, *Thirty Years' View*, 102–3; Chambers, 114–15; McCandless, "Benton v. Barton," 430.

29. *RD*, 19/1: 358–59, 762, 782. See also Feller, 74.

30. Emphasis mine; *RD* 19/1: 727; Benton's full speech is on pp. 720–49.

31. *RD* 19/1: 736-37; see Feller 75-76.

32. St. Louis *Missouri Republican*, September 28 and November 26, 1826; *Memoirs of John Quincy Adams*, 7: 89, 173, 194; Buel Leopard and Floyd C. Shoemaker, eds., *Messages and Proclamations of the Governors of the State of Missouri* (Columbia: The State Historical Society of Missouri, 20 vols., 1922), I, 118-19.

33. Peterson, *Great Triumvirate*, 83-84.

34. James D. Richardson, *Messages and Papers of the Presidents*, 2, 391.

35. "Annual Treasury Report," *RD*, 20/1: 2831-33.

36. See Remini, *Martin Van Buren and the Making of the Democratic Party* (New York: Columbia University Press, 1959), 131.

37. *Mr. Benton's Speeches on Public Lands* (Washington: Green and Jarvis, 1828); Feller, 93-94, on sectional interests.

38. *RD* 20/1: 502, 518, 620-22.

39. Ibid., 483-97, 653-60, 665-67, 674-78; see also Hargreaves, *Presidency of John Quincy Adams*, 197-99.

40. Ibid., 22-26.

41. Ibid., 31-41, 43-58.

42. Ibid., 58-80.

43. Ibid., 82-93.

44. Ibid., 94-110, especially 105-7.

45. Ibid., 107-9.

46. Ibid., 109.

47. Daniel Walker Howe. *What Hath God Wrought*, 400-6.

48. McCandless, *History of Missouri*, II, 97-98; see also Leopard and Shoemaker, *Messages and Proclamations*, and James R. Sharp, "Gov. Daniel Dunklin's Jacksonian Democracy," *Missouri Historical Review* 56, no. 3 (April 1962).

49. *RD* 21/1: 4, 31-41, 42ff., 58ff., 102-19; Benton, *Thirty Years' View*, 130-43, 333.

50. Benton, *Thirty Years' View*, I, 163; McLoughlin, *Cherokee Renascence in the New Republic*, 31-32, 67-71, 75-76, 173; Satz, *American Indian Policy in the Jacksonian Era*, 2, 11, 98-99; Prucha, *Great Father*, I, 185; Wallace, *Long, Bitter Trail*, 8-9.

51. Wallace, *Long, Bitter Trail*, 9-11; McLoughlin, *Cherokee Renascence in the New Republic*, 430-57; Prucha, *Great Father*, I, 179-91, 236-42; Satz, *American Indian Policy in the Jacksonian Era*, 99-100.

52. James D. Richardson, *Messages and Papers of the Presidents*, II, 457-59.

53. Ibid.; Satz, *American Indian Policy in the Jacksonian Era*, 19-20; Prucha, *Great Father*, I, 194-95; Remini, *Life of Andrew Jackson*, 212-13; Wallace, *Long, Bitter Trail*, 121-24.

54. *United States Statutes at Large* (Washington: Little, Brown and Company, 1845-1874), 21/1: 411-412, *Senate Records*; Satz, *American Indian Policy in the Jacksonian Era*, 20-22; Prucha, *Great Father*, I, 195, 200-6.

55. Benton, *Thirty Years' View*, I, 164; Benton's renewed efforts on behalf of graduation can be found in *RD* 21/1: 413-20, 423-27.

56. *RD* 21/1: 309-20.

57. Ibid., 325-28, 332.

58. Ibid., 380-83.

59. Benton, *Thirty Years' View*, I, 164.

60. *RD* 21/1: 405-27; St Louis *Beacon*, February 20, May 1, 27, June 3, 10, September 23, 1830; see also Chambers, *Old Bullion Benton*, 166; Feller, *Public Lands*, 131-36.

61. *RD* 21/1: 115–16; 820; James D. Richardson, *Messages and Papers*, III, 1050–52; Benton, *Thirty Years' View*, I, 26, 167. Sean Wilentz analyzes the divisions among Jackson's supporters in *The Rise of American Democracy*, 328. He asserts that Jackson viewed the veto as a necessary concession to the strict constructionist Old Republicans, some of whom were "leaning dangerously toward Calhoun's more extreme state-rights views," at the time of the nullification controversy.

62. *American State Papers: Public Lands* (Washington, D.C.: Library of Congress, 1789-1838), 6:441–51.

63. *RD* 22/1: 625–38, 786, 907, 931, 1101–2, 1111, 1145–46, 1152, 1164, 1219; 22/2: 308–9, 462–73, 713–15, all on tariff and distribution debates.

64. James D. Richardson, *Messages and Papers*, 2: 600–601.

65. *RD* 22/1: 61, 208–29; Benton, *Speech in the Senate of the United States, January 24, 1833. [On Distributing the Proceeds of the Public lands]* (n.p., n.d.), passim; Benton, *Thirty Years' View*, I, 262–69.

66. James D. Richardson, *Messages and Papers*, 3: 56–59.

67. Benton, *Thirty Years' View*, I, 624; Satz, *American Indian Policy in the Jacksonian Era*, 39–40.

68. See Remini, *Jackson and His Indian Wars*, 254–55.

69. *Cherokee Nation v. Georgia*, 30 U.S. 1 (1831).

70. *Worcester v. Georgia*, 31 U.S. 515 (1832); Jackson to John Coffee, in Bassett, *Correspondence*, IV, 430. An apocryphal, though widely quoted, story has Jackson crowing, "Well, John Marshall has made his decision; now let him enforce it." In reality, there was little need for the chief executive to ignore the Court's decision, as the president had no legal grounds to act without Georgia's refusal to comply with a federal habeas corpus order where the two missionaries were concerned. Prucha, *Great Father*, I, 212.

71. Benton, *Thirty Years' View*, I, 166.

72. Benton, *Historical and Legal Examination of . . . the Dred Scott Case* (New York: D. Appleton and Co., 1858), 7–8. Though Benton denied the authority of the Supreme Court to nullify the Missouri Compromise, the core of his argument is that it had already denied Scott's right to bring suit on the basis that blacks were not citizens of the United States. Having denied Scott's standing, the Court went on to decide the merits of his case in its *obiter dicta*—essentially a lengthy appendix to the formal ruling; *Thirty Years' View*, I, 166.

73. Ibid., 624.

74. Benton, *Thirty Years' View*, II, 70–72.

75. Ibid., 72.

76. *RD* 23/3, appendix, 162.

77. Ibid. Benton's account of the Dade massacre in his 1839 speech, particularly the "savage cruelty" of the "band of forty negroes [who] came down upon the helpless survivors, sought out for each one that was alive, and gave the knife and the hatchet to every helpless being in whom breath or motion could be found," is almost identical to the account in *Thirty Years' View*.

78. *RD* 23/3, appendix, 164.

79. Ibid., 163; emphasis mine. The quote sheds light on Benton's reference to the feudal system "giving lands to those who would defend them" as an inspiration for his graduation/donation proposals (see 187 above).

80. Ibid.

5 / Old Bullion and the Borderlands

1. *Congressional Globe (CG)* 28/1: Appendix, 573.

2. Thompson, quoted in Horsman, *Race and Manifest Destiny*, 212; Benton in *Congressional Globe* 28/1: appendix, 576.

3. On Benton's opposition to Texas annexation and war with Mexico, see Chambers, *Old Bullion Benton*, 271–343; Smith, *Magnificent Missourian*, 187–231; Freehling, *Road to Disunion*, I, 432, 446–47, 441–544.

4. *CG* 28/1: Appendix, 572; *Selections of Editorial Articles from the St. Louis Enquirer, on the Subject of Oregon and Texas, as Originally Published in that Paper, in the Years 1818–1819*, MHS, 5, 7, & 9; Christopher Phillips, *Missouri's Confederate: Claiborne Fox Jackson and the Creation of Southern Identity in the Border West* (Columbia: University of Missouri Press, 2000), 62–64; Chambers, *Old Bullion Benton*, 127–28; Smith, *Magnificent Missourian*, 85–87; McCandless, *History of Missouri*, II, 128–30.

5. Harry S. Gleik, "Banking in Early Missouri, Part I," *MHR* 61, no. 4 (July 1967): 428.

6. Gleik, "Banking in Early Missouri," 429; Sellers, *Market Revolution*, 45–46, 68–69, 71–72; Wilentz, *Rise of American Democracy*, 203–5.

7. *Laws of the State of Missouri relating to banks, trust companies, savings and safe deposit institutions, speculative merchandising companies, mortgage loan companies, and credit unions* (Jefferson City, Mo.: Mid-State Printing Co., 1949), I, 175–83; *Missouri Gazette*, December 31, 1814, October 15, 1816; Walter B. Stevens, *St. Louis, The Fourth City* (St. Louis: S.J. Clarke Pub. Co., 3 vols., 1909), I, 221; J. Thomas Scharf, *History of St. Louis City and County: from the earliest periods to the present day: including biographical sketches of representative men* (Philadelphia: L.H. Everts, 2 vols., 1882), II, 1384, 1387; Foley, *Genesis of Missouri*, 257–58; Chambers, *Old Bullion Benton*, 78.

8. *Missouri Gazette*, February 20, March 6, 13, April 24, and September 4, 11, 18, 1818, and July 21, 1819; Gleik, "Banking in Early Missouri," 433; Foley, *Genesis of Missouri*, 258; Chambers, *Old Bullion Benton*, 78–79.

9. *St. Louis Enquirer*, April 28, May 26, June 9, 16, 1819.

10. *McCulloch v. Maryland*, 17 U.S. 316; *Enquirer*, April 21, 1819.

11. *Enquirer*, August 11, 1819; January 24, 1820.

12. *American State Papers, Finance*, III, 747; List of Stockholders of Bank of Missouri, Benton Papers, MHS; Gleik, "Banking in Early Missouri," 433–34; Foley, *Genesis of Missouri*, 258–59; Chambers, *Old Bullion Benton*, 90.

13. *American State Papers, Finance*, III, 720, and IV, 758; Gleik, "Banking in Early Missouri," 434–35; Dorsey, "Panic of 1819 in Missouri," 83–85; Foley, *Genesis of Missouri*, 259; Chambers, *Old Bullion* Benton, 106.

14. Smith, *Magnificent Missourian*, 65.

15. Seymour V. Connor and Jimmy M. Skaggs, *Broadcloth and Britches: The Santa Fe Trade* (College Station: Texas A&M University Press, 1977), 15–17; Stephen Sayles, "Thomas Hart Benton and the Santa Fe Trail," *MHR* 69 (October 1974): 1–22; McCandless, *History of Missouri*, II, 128–30.

16. *RD* 18/2: 6–7.

17. Ibid., 18/2, 342–43.

18. Ibid., 344.

19. *RD*, 18/2, 345.
20. Ibid., 445-346.
21. Ibid., 18/2: 347-48; Benton, *Thirty Years' View*, I, 43; Sayles, "Thomas Hart Benton and the Santa Fe Trail," 14-19; Chambers, *Old Bullion Benton*, 127-28; Smith, *Magnificent Missourian*, 85-87.
22. Benton, *Selections of Editorial Articles from the St. Louis Enquirer, on the Subject of Oregon and Texas, as Originally Published in that Paper, in the Years 1818-1819* (St. Louis, 1844), 10.
23. Ibid., 6-7.
24. St. Louis *Beacon*, August 1, 1829.
25. Ibid., August 8, 1829.
26. Ibid, August 1, 8, 1829.
27. Ibid., October 7, 1829.
28. Ibid., October 17, 1829.
29. Ibid.
30. Benton, *Thirty Years' View*, I, 15, emphasis mine.
31. Ibid.
32. Ibid., 16-18.
33. *RD* 23/2: 367-92, 417-27, 428-39; Allen Nevins, ed., *The Diary of Philip Hone, 1828-1851* (New York: Dodd, Mead, 2 vols., 1927), I, 150.
34. James D. Richardson, *Messages and Papers*, II, 1394-95; Wilentz, *Rise of American Democracy*, 410-11.
35. RD 24/1: 1136-53, 1155-71, 1675, 1721-37; Benton, *Thirty Years' View*, I, 574-75, 580-88; Peterson, *Great Triumvirate*, 257-59.
36. *RD* 24/1: 72-99, 185-211, 300-303, 471-97; Benton, *Thirty Years' View*, I, 576-80. The newspaper in question was the Concord, New Hampshire *Herald of Freedom*, a publication that assailed the remarks of a local congressman that there was little abolitionist sentiment in his state. In the face of Calhoun's attacks from the *proslavery* standpoint, on the representative's sincerity, Benton supported the antiabolitionist credentials of fellow-Democrat Franklin Pierce.
37. Benton, *Thirty Years' View*, I, 623.
38. *Journal of the House of Representatives of the State of Missouri at the first Session of the Eleventh General Assembly*, 28-33; see also Shalhope, "Thomas Hart Benton and Missouri State Politics," 179-80.
39. William M. Campbell to Abiel Leonard, December 20, 1840, Abiel Leonard Collection; George Caleb Bingham to James S. Rollins, February 21, 1841, Rollins Collection, Western Historical Manuscripts.
40. Shalhope, "Benton and Missouri State Politics," 180.
41. Freehling, *Road to Disunion*, I, 364-68; Major L. Wilson, *The Presidency of Martin Van Buren* (Lawrence: University Press of Kansas, 1984), 14, 18, 148-52.
42. Freehling, *Road to Disunion*, I, 355-63; Wilentz, *Rise of American Democracy*, 493-507; Michael Holt, *Rise and Fall of the American Whig Party: Jacksonian Politics and the Onset of the Civil War* (New York: Oxford University Press, 1999), 91-92, 94.
43. Wilentz, *Rise of American Democracy*, 521-25, is the most recent account of these events; see also Holt, *Rise and Fall of the American Whig Party*, 122-37; Peterson, *Great Triumvirate*, 297-313; Norma Louis Peterson, *The Presidencies of William Henry Harrison and John Tyler* (Lawrence: University Press of Kansas, 1989), 31-93.

44. Tyler to Webster, October 11, 1841, in Lyon G. Tyler, ed., *Letters and Times of the Tylers* (Richmond, Va.: Whittet & Shepperson, 3 vols., 1884–1886), II, 254; Jackson to Aaron V. Brown, February 9, 1843, *Correspondence of Andrew Jackson*, VI, 201–2; Washington *Globe*, March 20, 1844; Benton, *Thirty Years' View*, II, 581; Remini, *Andrew Jackson and the Course of American Democracy*, 362–68.

45. Benton, *Thirty Years' View*, II, 582–83; Chambers, *Old Bullion Benton*, 271–72; Smith, *Magnificent Missourian*, 190–92.

46. Peterson, *Great Triumvirate*, 340–42; Freehling, *Road to Disunion*, I, 378–82.

47. Columbia *Missourian*, March 13, 1844; Benton, *Thirty Years' View*, II, 567–69.

48. Lord Aberdeen to Richard Packenham, December 26, 1843, *British and Foreign State Papers, 1844–1845*, 33:232; Norma L. Peterson, *Presidencies of Harrison and Tyler*, 203–16; Freehling, *Road to Disunion*, I, 407–10; Peterson, *Great Triumvirate*, 344–47; Wilentz, *Rise of American Democracy*, 566–67.

49. *Works of John C. Calhoun*, ed. Richard K. Crallé (New York: D. Appleton, 6 vols., 1855), V, 333–47.

50. Washington *Globe*, May 6, 1844.

51. *Niles Register*, LXVI (May 4, 25, and June 8, 1844), 153–57, 160, 197, 228; *Annexation of Texas, Opinions of Mssrs. Clay, Polk, Benton, and Van Buren* (n.p., n.d.), 3, 4, 12–14, 16.

52. Washington *Globe*, April 29, 1844.

53. Jackson to Blair, May 7 and 11, and June 5 and 29; and to Benton, May 14, 1844, in *Correspondence of Andrew Jackson*, VI, 284, 286, 292–294, 298, 299.

54. *CG* 28/1, Appendix, 474–83.

55. Ibid., 483.

56. Ibid., 485.

57. "That convention is . . . to be looked back upon as the starting point in the course of usurpation which has taken the choice of President out of the hands of the people . . . " *Thirty Years' View*, II, 595.

58. *Correspondence of Andrew Jackson*, VI, 296; *Missourian*, June 15, 1844; quoted in *Thirty Years' View*, II, 595.

59. *CG* 28/1: 652.

60. Ibid., Appendix, 572.

61. Ibid., 573.

62. Ibid.

63. Ibid., 589–90.

64. Ibid., 607–9.

65. Ibid., 610.

66. Ibid.

67. *Memoirs of John Quincy Adams*, XII, 56; Blair to Jackson, July 7, and Jackson to Blair, June 25, 1844, in *Correspondence of Andrew Jackson*, VI, 298–302.

68. Christopher Phillips, *Missouri's Confederate*, 138–44; McCandless, *History of Missouri*, II, 120, 228–32.

69. Quoted in Smith, *Magnificent Missourian*, 200; Clarence H. McClure, *Opposition in Missouri to Thomas Hart Benton*, 68–71, 79–89; see Smith, *Magnificent Missourian*, 188–89, and Chambers, *Old Bullion Benton*, 273–74, for analysis of Benton's stance on slavery; see also Freehling, *Road to Disunion*, 432; William E. Parrish, *David Rice Atchison of Missouri* (Columbia: University of Missouri Press, 1961), 45.

70. *Missourian*, March 16, April 8, October 5, 1844; Washington *Globe*, August 29, 1844; McClure, *Opposition in Missouri to Thomas Hart Benton*, 85–96.

71. *Missourian*, October 5, 1844; Benton, *Substance of... Speech Delivered at St. Louis, Saturday, October 19, 1844*; Benton to A.R. Corbin, October 5, 28, 1844, MHS. On Calhoun and bank policy, see Wilentz, *Rise of American Democracy*, 204–5, 443, 524.

72. Mandated by Congress in 1841, this measure had been anathema to the state-rightist Boonslick faction who claimed that their opposition had been to federal intervention rather than the measure itself. Boonslick politicians could now claim to be yielding to pressure from within the state. *Journal of the House of Representatives of the State of Missouri*, 13th General Assembly, 1844–1845, 121–22; see Phillips, *Missouri's Confederate*, 153–54; Shalhope, "Thomas Hart Benton and Missouri State Politics," 181–82, 186.

73. Chambers, *Old Bullion Benton*, 286–87; Smith, *Magnificent Missourian*, 202; Holt, *Rise and Fall of the American Whig Party*, 194–96. 1844 was the last presidential election to be held on different days in different states. Beginning in 1848, the nation's voters all went to the polls on the same day in November.

74. *Correspondence of Andrew Jackson*, VI, 325, 331–32, 338, 342, 345–51, 354–55, 366.

75. *CG* 28/2: 16–17, 192–94; Calhoun to William R. King, December 13, to Thomas Clemson, December 27, and to R.M.T. Hunter, December 29, 1844, all in *Correspondence of John C. Calhoun*, 633, 635, 636; *Missouri Republican*, January 28, 1845; Benton to Donelson, January 10, 1845, in "Selected Letters from the Donelson Papers," *Tennessee Historical Magazine* 111, June 1917, 148–49.

76. *CG* 28/2: 244–45.

77. Ibid, 341–45, 358–63; Benton, *Thirty Years' View*, II, 632–36; Chambers, *Old Bullion Benton*, 289–90; Smith, *Magnificent Missourian*, 203–4.

78. Benton, *Thirty Years' View*, II, 637–38. "Thus was Texas incorporated into the Union—by deception and by deluding five senators out of their votes. It was not a barren fraud, but one prolific of evil, and pregnant with bloody fruit. It established, so for as the United States was concerned, a state of war with Mexico."

79. Lewis to Benton, March 4, 1846, in *CG* 29/2, 563, and in *Correspondence of Andrew Jackson*, VI, 414–15, note 2. Jackson's messages to Benton, Blair, and Sam Houston on his deathbed were transmitted verbally to Lewis. He committed the Benton message to writing nine months later, trying to recall the precise words. Chambers, *Old Bullion Benton*, 293–94; Remini, *Life of Andrew Jackson*, 357–58.

80. Benton to Mrs. James K. Polk, February 14, 1845, quoted in Chambers, *Old Bullion Benton*, 290; Smith, *Magnificent Missourian*, 206.

81. John S.D. Eisenhower, *So Far From God: The U.S. War with Mexico, 1846–1848* (New York: Random House, 1989), 40–48; Wilentz, *Rise of American Democracy*, 580–81; Chambers, *Old Bullion Benton*, 294–300, 305–6; Smith, *Magnificent Missourian*, 206–10.

82. Benton to Pierre Chouteau, February 11, 1846, Chouteau-Walsh Papers, MHS; *Diary of James K. Polk during His Presidency, 1845–1849*, ed. Milo M. Quaife (Chicago: A.C. McClurg, 4 vols., 1910), I, 71, 305–8, 325–26, 375–76, 390, 391–92; Benton, *Thirty Years' View*, II, 693–94.

83. *Diary of James K. Polk*, I, 375, 390.

84. Ibid.

288 / NOTES

85. *CG*, 29/1: 783–85, 795–804; Benton, *Thirty Years' View*, II, 679–80.

86. Benton, *Thirty Years' View*, II, 678.

87. *Diary of James K. Polk*, I, 219–28, 231–33, 239–43, 258–65; Benton, *Thirty Years' View*, II, 678.

88. *Diary of James K. Polk*, II, 5, 16, 268–70; draft of letter in Benton's handwriting [July 14, 1846], in Polk Papers, LOC; see Chambers, *Old Bullion Benton*, 309; Smith, *Magnificent Missourian*, 214–15.

89. Benton, *Thirty Years' View*, II, 693–94.

90. *Diary of James K. Polk*, II, 224–30; *Thirty Years' View*, II, 678–79; *CG* 29/2: 246–47. Allan Nevins found Polk's willingness to appoint Benton to the lieutenant general position extraordinary. "Benton was in no way qualified, as Scott distinctly was, for so important a military station. Both his headstrong and domineering qualities, and his comparative ignorance of troops and warfare, made him an unsuitable choice. But Polk liked and respected Benton, and was willing to take a chance with him." *Polk: The Diary of a President, 1845-1849*, Allan Nevins, ed. (New York: Longmans, Green and Company, 1952), 164. John S.D. Eisenhower, in his history of the Mexican War, wrote that Polk undermined congressional support for his war measures "by pursuing his quixotic request to establish the new rank of lieutenant general in the army, still intending to bestow it on Senator Benton. Not only did this measure stand no chance, but it provided a rallying point on which Whigs and Calhoun Democrats (as well as those concerned with military competence) could agree." *So Far From God*, 289.

91. *Diary of James K. Polk*, II, 262, 268–69; Blair to Van Buren, December 26, 1846, in Martin Van Buren papers, LOC.

92. *CG* 29/2: 175–77, 185–87, 246–47; Benton, *Thirty Years' View*, II, 679.

93. *Correspondence of John C. Calhoun*. In Annual Report of the American Historical Association, 1899 (Washington, D.C., 1900), 714, 717.

94. *CG* 29/2: appendix, 244–47, 346; Crallé, *Works of John C. Calhoun*, IV, 339–49; Benton, *Thirty Years' View*, II, 696–97.

95. *CG* 29/2: 356–59, 453–55.

96. Ibid., 494–501.

97. *Diary of James K. Polk*, II, 334; *Thirty Years' View*, II, 694–700; John A. Garraty, *Silas Wright* (New York: Columbia University Press, 1949), 394–98; William E. Smith, *The Francis Preston Blair Family in Politics* (New York: The Macmillan Company, 2 vols., 1933), I, 205–6.

98. *Diary of James K. Polk*, II, 334, 346, 358–59, and III, 74; Elwood Fisher to Calhoun, May 25, 1847, and J.W.A. Pettit to Calhoun, June 18, 1847, in Boucher, Chauncy S., and Robert P. Brooks. *Correspondence Addressed to John C. Calhoun, 1837-1849*, in Annual Report, American Historical Association, 1929 (Washington, D.C., 1930).

99. Tom Chaffin, *Pathfinder: John Charles Frémont and the Course of American Empire* (New York: Hill and Wang, 2002), 75–145. See also Allan Nevins, *Frémont: Pathmarker of the West* (New York & London: D. Appleton-Century Co., 1939); Chambers, *Old Bullion Benton*, 251–63; Smith, *Magnificent Missourian*, 181–82.

100. Eisenhower, *So Far From God*, 213–14; Chaffin, *Pathfinder*, 257–335.

101. Benton, "Operations of Captain Fremont in Upper California," *Niles National Register*, LXXI, November 14, 21, 1846; Benton, *Thirty Years' View*, II, 691–92.

102. *Diary of James K. Polk*, III, 52–54, 61–62, 120–23, 129–130, 197–98, 201–6, 324,

336-39, 442, and IV, 227; Benton, *Thirty Years' View*, II, 715-19; Blair to Van Buren, January 23, 1848, in Van Buren Papers, LOC.

103. William H. Seward. *Life and Public Services of John Quincy Adams, Sixth President of the United States* (Auburn, N.Y.: Derby, Miller and Company, 1849), 345.

104. *Diary of James K. Polk*, III, 363-68.

105. Clayton speech, *CG* 32/3, Appendix, 270, quoted in Horsman, *Race and Manifest Destiny*, 246; David M. Potter, *Impending Crisis, 1848-1861* (New York: Harper & Row, 1976), 5-6; see also Thomas R. Hietala, "Continentalism and the Color Line," in *Race and U.S. Foreign Policy from Colonial Times Through the Age of Jackson*, ed. Michael L. Krenn (New York: Garland Publishing, 1998), 304-44, especially 324-38.

106. James D. Richardson, *Messages and Papers*, VI, 2479, 2489-92; *CG* 30/2: 33-37; "Benton to People of California and New Mexico," August 27, 1848, *Niles Register*, LXXIV (1848), 244-45.

107. *Diary of James K. Polk*, IV, 329-30; Benton, *Thirty Years' View*, II, 737-38.

6 / The Destiny of the Races

1. *Niles Register* LXXIII (1848), 402-6; *Missouri Republican*, May 1, 4, 22, 26, 1848. The nickname of the New York Radicals came from the Dutch tale of a farmer who chose to burn down his entire barn in order to destroy the rats. Wilentz, *Rise of American Democracy*, 531, 608-17; Schlesinger, *Age of Jackson*, 450-68.

2. *Brooklyn Eagle*, September 1, 1847; Whitman, *Gathering of the Forces*, I, 208 (quoted in Schlesinger, *Age of Jackson*, 452).

3. *CG* 29/2: Appendix 314-17; *Pennsylvania Freeman*, December 7, 1848, and *National Era*, June 15, 1848, both quoted in Eric Foner, *Free Soil, Free Labor, Free Men: The Ideology of the Republican Party Before the Civil War* (New York: Oxford University Press, 1970), 267; see also Foner, "Racial Attitudes of the New York Free Soilers," *New York History* XLVI (October 1965): 311-29; Chaplain W. Morrison, *Democratic Politics and Sectionalism: The Wilmot Proviso Controversy* (Chapel Hill: University of North Carolina Press, 1967), 73; Charles B. Going, *David Wilmot, Free-Soiler: A Biography of the Great Advocate of the Wilmot Proviso* (New York and London: D. Appleton and Company, 1924), 174; Eugene H. Berwanger, *The Frontier Against Slavery: Western Anti-Negro Prejudice and the Slavery Extension Controversy* (Urbana: University of Illinois Press, 1967), 133-34.

4. Benton, *Thirty Years' View*, II, 722-23; *Niles Register* LXXIII (January 8, 1848), 293; Frank B. Woodford, *Lewis Cass: The Last Jeffersonian* (New Brunswick, N.J.: Rutgers University Press, 1950), 250-54; Schlesinger, *Age of Jackson*, 450ff.

5. Flagg to Van Buren, June 19, 1848, Benton to Van Buren, May 29, 1848, and Blair to Van Buren, June 26, 1848, all in Van Buren Papers, LOC.

6. St. Louis *Union*, June 16, 17, and 19, 1848.

7. St. Louis *Union*, July 13, August 26, September 12 and 25, October 25 and 26, 1848; *Missouri Republican*, October 10, 19, 20, 1848; "Prospectus of the Free Soil Democrat," August 30, 1848, in Political Papers, MHS; J.N. Bailey to Abiel Leonard (n.d.), in Abiel Leonard Collection, Western Historical Manuscripts; *Memoirs of John A. Dix*, I, 240; see also David M. Potter, *The Impending Crisis*, 77-80; E. Smith, *Francis Preston Blair*, 197-200.

8. Van Buren to Blair, December 11, 1848, cited in W.E. Smith, *Francis Preston Blair Family in Politics*, I, 243; Benton, *Thirty Years' View*, II, 723.

9. Benton, *Colonel Benton's Great Speech! to the People of Missouri: Delivered at the Capitol of the State* (n.p., 1849); Chambers, *Old Bullion Benton*, 345.

10. *Missouri Democrat*, April 18, 1847.

11. *Works of John C. Calhoun*, VI, 290–313.

12. *Laws of the State of Missouri*, Fifteenth General Assembly, 1848–1849.

13. St. Louis *Union*, May 8 and 9, 1849.

14. Benton, *Colonel Benton's Great Speech!*

15. *Liberty Weekly Tribune*, June 29, July 6, August 17, September 14, 1849; *St. Louis Daily New Era*, July 19, 1849; *Missouri Statesman*, June 22, 1849; Smith, *Magnificent Missourian*, 252–53.

16. Ibid.

17. David M. Grisson, "Personal Recollections of Distinguished Missourians," *MHR* (January 1924); Benton, *Speech . . . Delivered at Fayette, Howard County, Missouri on Saturday the First of September 1849*, 3–32; St. Louis *Union*, October 9, 10, 11, 1849.

18. Henry S. Foote, *Letter from the Hon. H.S. Foote of Mississippi to Hon. Henry A. Wise* (n.p., 1849), 1, 2, 7; Calhoun to Andrew Pickens Calhoun, July 24, 1849, in *Correspondence of John C. Calhoun*, 769; Calhoun to Samuel Treat, July 9, 1849, in Treat Papers, MHS; Calhoun, *Address . . . to the People of the Southern States* (St. Louis *Union*, 1849), 1, 19–20.

19. Benton, *Speech . . . Delivered at Fayette, Howard County, Missouri on Saturday the First of September 1849*, 3–32.

20. *Congressional Globe*, 30/2: 470–74; Robert S. Cotterill, "The National Railroad Convention," *MHR* 12 (July 1918): 203–7; Liberty [Missouri] *Weekly Tribune*, May 18, 1849.

21. Darby, *Personal Recollections*, 182–83.

22. St. Louis *Union*, October 18–19, 1849; Missouri *Republican*, October 18, 1849; Cotterill, "The National Railroad Convention," 207–15.

23. Ibid.

24. Ibid.

25. Ibid.

26. Ibid.

27. *Fredericksburg News*, October 12, 1849, quoted in Smith, *Magnificent Missourian*, 257–58.

28. *Liberty Weekly Tribune*, June 1, 1849.

29. James D. Richardson, *Messages and Papers*, V, 9–24; Benton, *Thirty Years' View*, II, 740–42.———.

30. For the controversies confronting the 31st Congress and Clay's omnibus proposals, see Benton, *Thirty Years' View*, II, 742; Peterson, *Great Triumvirate*, 449–60; Freehling, *Road to Disunion*, I, 487–509; Potter, *Impending Crisis*, 90–100.

31. *Works of John C. Calhoun*, IV, 542–73; Benton, *Thirty Years' View*, II, 744–47; John Wentworth, *Congressional Reminiscences: Adams, Benton, Calhoun, Clay, and Webster* (Chicago: Fergus Printing Co., 1882), 23–24; Chambers, *Old Bullion Benton*, 358; Smith, *Magnificent Missourian*, 267–69; Peterson, *Great Triumvirate*, 467.

32. *CG* 31/1: 430–32; John D. Morton, "'A High Wall and a Deep Ditch': Thomas Hart Benton and the Compromise of 1850," *MHR* 94 (October 1999): 1–24.

33. *CG* 31/1: 656–62, Appendix 446–50; Morton, "'A High Wall and a Deep Ditch,'" 19–21.
34. *CG* 31/1: 704–14, 751–64, 769–75, 780–82.
35. *CG* 31/1: 1173, Appendix 676–684.
36. Chambers, *Old Bullion Benton*, 364–67; Smith, *Magnificent Missourian*, 274–79; Potter, *Impending Crisis*, 104–20.
37. Benton, *Thirty Years' View*, II, 779–80.
38. *CG* 31/1: 1829.
39. *Journal of the House of Representatives of the State of Missouri*, 16th Assembly, 1st Session, 88–104, 107–15, 123–36; Morton, "'A High Wall and a Deep Ditch,'" 23–24; Chambers, *Old Bullion Benton*, 368–77; Smith, *Magnificent Missourian*, 279–83.
40. *CG* 31/1: 158–60, 349–51, 360–64, 373–78, 387–91, 407–8.
41. Missouri *Republican*, March 3, 12, 24, 26, and April 6–9, 1851; Bowlin to A.J. Donelson, May 5, 1851, in "Selected Letters from the Donelson Papers," *Tennessee Historical Magazine* III, December 1917, 271–74.
42. Benton to Father De Smet, April 1, 1852, Benton Papers, MHS.
43. Primm, *Lion of the Valley*, 164–66, 169; Steven Rowan and James Neal Primm, *Germans for a Free Missouri* (Columbia: University of Missouri Press, 1983), 6–10.
44. Missouri *Republican*, November 1851–August 1852, quoted in Chambers, 384–85.
45. *New Orleans Crescent*, August 13, 1852, quoted in Smith, *Magnificent Missourian*, 289; Missouri *Republican*, August 5, 1852.
46. Benton to Dix, May 15, 1851, Van Buren Papers, LOC.
47. Benton, *Thirty Years' View*, II, 787.
48. Benton to Montgomery Blair, in Blair Papers, LOC.
49. *Jefferson Enquirer*, May 28, 1853; Benton, *Letter to the People of Missouri, Central National Highway to the Pacific* (Washington, 1853).
50. Smith, *Magnificent Missourian*, 293.
51. Atchison to Samuel Treat, May 29, 1853, Reynolds Papers, MHS.
52. Letter from Seward, January 8, 1854, in Seward, Frederick W., *Seward at Washington . . . With Selections from His Letters, 1846–1861* (New York: Derby and Miller, 1891).
53. *CG*, 33/1: 986–99; Appendix, 557–61, 698–99, 743–44.
54. Ibid.
55. Ibid.
56. Missouri *Democrat*, April 29, May 1, 2, and 8, 1854; Washington *Union*, April 26, 28, 30, 1854.
57. *CG* 33/1: 1031–36; see also Chambers, *Old Bullion Benton*, 403.
58. Washington *Union*, April 25 and July 9, 1854; Chambers, *Old Bullion Benton*, 404–5.
59. Missouri *Democrat*, May 8, June, 21, 24, 30, July 1, 1854; Missouri *Republican*, April 16, 20, May 3, 5, 1854; Benton, *To the Democratic Voters of the St. Louis Congressional District* (Washington, D.C., 1854).
60. Holt, *Rise and Fall of the American Whig Party*, 850–51; Primm, *Lion of the Valley*, 167–70.
61. John C. Schneider, "Riot and Reaction . . . ," *MHR* (January 1974): 171–85; Chambers, *Old Bullion Benton*, 408; Holt, 851–52.

62. McCandless, *History of Missouri*, II, 467–68.

63. St. Louis *Leader*, November 4, 1856; Jefferson *Enquirer*, November 8, 1856; Missouri *Democrat*, November 4, 1856.

64. *Dred Scott v. Sandford*, 60 U.S. 393 (1857); Chambers, *Old Bullion Benton*, 424–40; Smith, *Magnificent Missourian*, 316–24.

65. New York *Tribune*, April 14 and May 25, 1858; William C. Jones, Colonel Benton and His Contemporaries, May 17, 1858, pamphlet in Van Buren Papers, LOC; Chambers, *Old Bullion Benton*, 441–42; Smith, *Francis Preston Blair*, 248–49.

66. Smith, *Francis Preston Blair*, 188–91, 234–37; William E. Parrish, *Frank Blair: Lincoln's Conservative* (Columbia: University of Missouri Press, 1998), 1–48.

67. Francis P. Blair Jr., *The Destiny of the Races of this Continent. An address delivered before the Mercantile library association of Boston, Massachusetts on the 26th of January, 1859* (Washington, D.C.: Buell & Blanchard, 1859), 1–15.

68. Blair, *The Destiny of the Races*, 16; Benton, *Thirty Years' View*, I, 28. See chapter four above.

69. Blair, *The Destiny of the Races*, 17.

70. Ibid., 18–19.

71. Ibid., 21–23.

72. *Selections of Editorial Articles from the St. Louis Enquirer, on the Subject of Oregon and Texas, as Originally Published in that Paper, in the Years 1818–1819*, MHS, 23.

Bibliography

MANUSCRIPT COLLECTIONS

Benton Papers, Missouri Historical Society
Blair Papers, Library of Congress
Duels Envelope, Missouri Historical Society
Easton Papers, Missouri Historical Society
Hardeman Papers, Missouri Historical Society
Abiel Leonard Collection, Western Historical Manuscripts
Lucas Papers, Missouri Historical Society
Polk Papers, Library of Congress
Reynolds Papers, Missouri Historical Society
Schools Envelope, Missouri Historical Society
Treat Papers, Missouri Historical Society
Christian Wilt Letterbook, Missouri Historical Society

GOVERNMENT DOCUMENTS

American State Papers, 1789–1838. Washington, D.C.: Library of Congress. Also available online at <http://memory.loc.gov/ammem/amlaw/lwsp.html#top≥>.
Annals of Congress.
British and Foreign State Papers. London: H.M.S.O., 170 volumes, 1814–1977.
Carter, Clarence Edwin, ed. *The Territorial Papers of the United States.* Vol. 13–15, *The Territory of Louisiana-Missouri, 1803–1821.* Washington, D.C.: U.S. G.P.O., 1948–1951.
Cherokee Nation v. Georgia, 30 U.S. 1, 1831.
Congressional Directory.
Congressional Globe.

Dred Scott v. Sandford, 60 U.S. 393, 1857.

Faculty Records, 1799–1814, University of North Carolina, *Documenting the American South*. <http://docsouth.unc.edu/unc/unc06-17/unc06-17.html>.

Journal of the House of Representatives of the State of Missouri. Jefferson City, Mo.: s.n., 1821–1877.

Journal of the Senate of the State of Missouri. Jefferson City, Mo.: s.n., 1821–1877.

Kappler, Charles J., ed. *Indian affairs. Laws and Treaties*. Washington: G.P.O.7 volumes, 1903–.

Laws of the State of Missouri relating to banks, trust companies, savings and safe deposit institutions, speculative merchandising companies, mortgage loan companies, and credit unions. Jefferson City, Mo.: Mid-State Printing Co., 1949.

Leopard, Buel, and Floyd C. Shoemaker, eds. *Messages and Proclamations of the Governors of the State of Missouri*. Columbia, Mo.: The State Historical Society of Missouri, 20 volumes, 1922.

McCulloch v. Maryland, 17 U.S. 316, 1819.

Register of Debates in Congress.

Richardson, James D., ed. *Messages and Papers of the Presidents*. New York: Bureau of National Literature and Art, Volumes 1–10, 1897.

United States Statutes at Large. Washington: Little, Brown and Company, 1845-1874.

U.S. v. Gear, 44 US 120, (1845).

Worcester v. Georgia, 31 U.S. 515, 1832.

NEWSPAPERS AND CONTEMPORARY PERIODICALS

Columbia *Missourian*
Missouri Advocate, St. Louis
Missouri Gazette, St. Louis
Missouri Intelligencer, Fayette
Missouri *Republican*, St. Louis
Nashville *Democratic Clarion*
Nashville *Impartial Review*
New York *Tribune*
Niles National Register, Washington, D.C.
Niles Weekly Register, Baltimore
St. Louis *Beacon*
St. Louis *Globe Democrat*
St. Louis *Union*
Washington *Globe*

PUBLISHED CORRESPONDENCE, DIARIES, MEMOIRS, AND PUBLIC PAPERS

Adams, John Quincy. *Memoirs of John Quincy Adams, Comprising Parts of His*

Diary from 1795 to 1848, ed. Charles Francis Adams. Philadelphia: J.B. Lippincott & Co., 12 volumes, 1874–1877.

American Fur Company Letter Books. 71 volumes, 1802–1871.

Annexation of Texas, Opinions of Mssrs. Clay, Polk, Benton, and Van Buren, n.p., n.d.

Bay, W.V.N. *Reminiscences of the Bench and Bar of Missouri*. St. Louis: F.H. Thomas and Co., 1878.

Benton, Thomas Hart. *Addresses on the Presentation of the Sword of General Andrew Jackson to Congress*. Washington, D.C. 1855.

———. *Colonel Benton's Great Speech! to the People of Missouri: Delivered at the Capitol of the State*, n.p., 1849.

———. *Historical and Legal EXAMINATION of that Part of the Decision of the Supreme Court of the United States in the DRED SCOTT CASE, Which Declares the Unconstitutionality of the Missouri Compromise Act, and the Self-Extension of the Constitution to the Territories, Carrying Slavery Along With It*. New York: D. Appleton and Co., 1858.

———. *Letter to the People of Missouri, Central National Highway to the Pacific*, Washington, 1853.

———. *Mr. Benton's Speeches on Public Lands*. Washington: Green and Jarvis, 1828.

———. *Selections of Editorial Articles from the St. Louis Enquirer, on the Subject of Oregon and Texas, as Originally Published in that Paper, in the Years 1818–1819*. St. Louis, 1844.

———. *Speech ... Delivered at Fayette, Howard County, Missouri on Saturday the First of September 1849*.

———. *Speech in the Senate of the United States, January 24, 1833 [On Distributing the Proceeds of the Public lands]*, n.p., n.d.

———. *Substance of... Speech Delivered at St. Louis, Saturday, October 19, 1844*. St. Louis, 1844.

———. *Thirty Years' View, or, A History of the Working of the American Government for Thirty Years, From 1820 to 1850*. New York: D. Appleton and Co., 2 Volumes, 1854–1856.

———. *To the Democratic Voters of the St. Louis Congressional District*. Washington, D.C., 1854.

Blair, Francis P. Jr. *The Destiny of the Races of this Continent. An address delivered before the Mercantile library association of Boston, Massachusetts on the 26th of January, 1859*. Washington, D.C.: Buell & Blanchard, 1859.

Boucher, Chauncy S., and Robert P. Brooks. *Correspondence Addressed to John C. Calhoun, 1837–1849*, in Annual Report, American Historical Association, 1929. Washington, D.C., 1930.

Calhoun, John C. *Correspondence of John C. Calhoun*, ed. J. Franklin Jameson. In *Annual Report of the American Historical Association, 1899*, II, 1900.

———. *The Papers of John C. Calhoun*, ed. Robert L. Meriwether. Columbia:

Published by the University of South Carolina Press for the South Caroliniana Society, 28 Volumes, 1959–2003.
———. *Works of John C. Calhoun*, ed. Richard K. Crallé. New York: D. Appleton, 6 volumes, 1855.
Clay, Henry. *The Papers of Henry Clay*, ed. James F. Hopkins. Lexington: University of Kentucky Press, 11 volumes, 1992.
CURTIUS. "Torchlight—An Examination of the Origin, Policy and Principles of the Opposition to the Administration and an Exposition of the Official Conduct of THOMAS H. BENTON, One of the Senators from Missouri," Missouri *Republican* Office, 1826.
Darby, John F. *Personal Recollections of Many Prominent People Whom I have Known and of Events*. St. Louis, Mo.: G.I. Jones, 1880.
Dix, John Adams. *Memoirs of John Adams Dix*, ed. Morgan Dix. New York: Harper & Brothers, 1883.
Emerson, Ralph Waldo. "Fate." In *The Conduct of Life*. Boston: Ticknor and Fields, 1860.
Flint, Timothy. *Recollections of the Last Forty Years, Passed in Occasional Residences and Journeyings in the Valley of the Mississippi . . . in a Series of Letters to the Reverend James Flint*. Boston: Cummings, Hilliard, and Company, 1826.
Foote, Henry S. *Letter from the Hon. H.S. Foote of Mississippi to Hon. Henry A. Wise*. n.p., 1849.
Frémont, Jessie B. "Biographical Sketch of Senator Benton in Connection with Western Expansion." In John C. Frémont, *Memoirs of My Life. Including in the narrative five journeys of western exploration, during the years 1842, 1843–4, 1845–6–7, 1848–9, 1853–4*. Chicago and New York: Belford, Clarke & Company, 1887.
Hone, Philip. *The Diary of Philip Hone, 1828–1851*, Allen Nevins, ed. New York: Dodd, Mead, 2 vols., 1927.
Houck, Louis, ed. *The Spanish Regime in Missouri: a collection of papers and documents relating to upper Louisiana principally within the present limits of Missouri during the dominion of Spain, from the Archives of the Indies at Seville, etc., translated from the original Spanish into English, and including also some papers concerning the supposed grant to Col. George Morgan at the mouth of the Ohio, found in the Congressional library; ed. and with an introduction and notes, biographical and explanatory*. Chicago: R.R. Donnelley & Sons Company, 2 volumes, 1909.
Jackson, Andrew. *Correspondence of Andrew Jackson.*, ed. John Spencer Bassett. Washington, D.C.: Carnegie Institution of Washington, 6 volumes, 1926–1935.
———. *Papers of Andrew Jackson*, ed. Harold D. Moser et al., Knoxville: University of Tennessee Press, 8 volumes, 1980.
Jefferson, Thomas. *Notes on the State of Virginia [introduction to the Torchbook edition by Thomas Perkins Abernethy]*. New York: Harper & Row, 1964.
———. Thomas Jefferson Papers. Washington: Library of Congress, microform, 1974.

Lucas, John B.C. *Letters of Hon. John B.C. Lucas from 1815 to 1836*, compiled and published by his grandson, John B.C. Lucas, St. Louis, Mo., 1905.

Micklejohn, Reverend George S.T.D. "On the Important Duty of Subjection to the Civil Powers," *Early American Imprints*, First Series 10977, 1768 (microform, 1981).

Monroe, James. James Monroe Papers. Washington: Library of Congress, microform, 1960.

Peck, John Mason. *Forty Years of Pioneer Life: The Memoir of John Mason Peck, D.D.*, ed. Rufus Babcock. Carbondale: Southern Illinois University Press, 1965.

Polk, James K. *The Diary of James K. Polk during His Presidency, 1845–1849*, ed. Milo M. Quaife. Chicago: A.C. McClurg, 4 volumes, 1910.

———. *Polk: The Diary of a President, 1845-1849*, Allan Nevins, ed. New York: Longmans, Green and Company, 1952.

Saunders, William L., ed. *The Colonial Records of North Carolina*. Raleigh: P.M. Hale, State Printer, 10 volumes, 1886–1907.

"Selected Letters from the Donelson Papers," *Tennessee Historical Magazine* 111, June 1917.

Seward, Frederick W. *Seward at Washington . . . With Selections from His Letters, 1846–1861.* New York: Derby and Miller, 1891.

Seward, William H. *Life and Public Services of John Quincy Adams, Sixth President of the United States.* Auburn, N.Y.: Derby, Miller and Company, 1849.

Sims, George. "An Address to the People of Granville County," June 6, 1765. In Boyd, William K., ed., *Some Eighteenth Century Tracts Concerning North Carolina*. Raleigh, N.C.: Edwards & Broughton, 1927.

Thwaites, Reuben Gold, ed. *Early Western Travels, 1748–1846: a series of annotated reprints of some of the best and rarest contemporary volumes of travel: descriptive of the aborigines and social and economic conditions in the middle and far west, during the period of early American settlement.* Cleveland: A.H. Clark Co., 25 volumes, 1904–1907.

Tyler, Lyon G., ed. *Letters and Times of the Tylers*. Richmond, Va.: Whittet & Shepperson, 3 volumes, 1884–1886.

Van Buren, Martin. Martin Van Buren Papers. Washington: Library of Congress, microform, 1960.

Wentworth, John. *Congressional Reminiscences: Adams, Benton, Calhoun, Clay, and Webster*. Chicago: Fergus Printing Co., 1882.

BOOKS AND ARTICLES

Abernethy, Thomas P. *From Frontier to Plantation in Tennessee: A Study in Frontier Democracy.* Chapel Hill: University of North Carolina Press, 1932.

Abramoske, Donald J. "The Federal Lead Leasing System in Missouri." *Missouri Historical Review* 54 (October 1959).

Adams, James Truslow, ed. *Atlas of American History.* New York: C. Scribner's Sons, 1943.

Allmand, Christopher. *Henry V.* Berkeley: University of California Press, 1992.

Alvord, Clarence. *The Illinois Country, 1673–1818.* Springfield: Published by the Illinois Centennial Commission, 1920.

Anderson, Hattie. "Jackson Men in Missouri in 1828." *Missouri Historical Review* 34 (April 1940).

Aron, Stephen. *American Confluence: The Missouri Frontier from Borderland to Border State.* Bloomington and Indianapolis: Indiana University Press, 2006.

Ashworth, John. *Slavery, Capitalism and Politics in the Antebellum Republic.* Cambridge, U.K., and New York: Cambridge University Press, 1995.

Bannon, John Francis, S.J. *The Spanish Borderlands Frontier, 1513–1821.* New York: Holt, Rinehart and Winston, 1970.

Baxter, Maurice G. *One and Inseparable: Daniel Webster and the Union.* Cambridge, Mass.: Harvard University Press, 1984.

Bemis, Samuel Flagg. *John Quincy Adams and the Union.* New York: Knopf, 1956.

Berwanger, Eugene H. *The Frontier Against Slavery: Western Anti-Negro Prejudice and the Slavery Extension Controversy.* Urbana: University of Illinois Press, 1967.

Blight, David W. *Race and Reunion: The Civil War in American Memory.* Cambridge, Mass.: Belknap Press of Harvard University Press, 2001.

Brown, Richard H. "The Missouri Crisis, Slavery, and the Politics of Jacksonianism." *South Atlantic Quarterly* 65 (1966).

Buchanan, John. *Jackson's Way: Andrew Jackson and the People of the Western Waters.* New York: J. Wiley, 2001.

Burstein, Andrew. *The Passions of Andrew Jackson.* New York: Alfred A. Knopf, 2003.

Capers, Gerald M. Jr. *The Biography of a River Town: Memphis in Its Heroic Age.* Chapel Hill: University of North Carolina Press, 1939.

Chaffin, Tom. *Pathfinder: John Charles Frémont and the Course of American Empire.* New York: Hill and Wang, 2002.

Chambers, William N. "As the Twig is Bent: The Family and North Carolina Years of Thomas Hart Benton, 1752–1801." *North Carolina Historical Review* 2, no. 4 (October 1949).

——. *Old Bullion Benton: Senator from the New West.* Boston: Little, Brown, 1956.

Cole, Donald B. *A Jackson Man: Amos Kendall and the Rise of American Democracy.* Baton Rouge: Louisiana State University Press, 2004.

Connor, Seymour V., and Jimmy M. Skaggs. *Broadcloth and Britches: The Santa Fe Trade.* College Station: Texas A&M University Press, 1977.

Dangerfield, George. *The Era of Good Feelings.* New York: Harcourt, Brace, 1952.

Davis, James D. *The History of The City of Memphis . . . Also, The "Old Times Papers."* Memphis: Hite, Crumpton & Kelly, 1873.

De Witt, John. "General James Winchester," *Tennessee Historical Magazine* 1, September 1915.
Donaldson, Thomas. *The Public Domain: its history, with statistics, with references to the national domain, colonization, acquirement of territory, the survey, administration and several methods of sale and disposition of the public domain of the United States, with sketch of legislative history of the land states and territories, and references to the land system of the colonies, and also that of several foreign governments*. Washington: G.P.O., 1881.
Dorsey, Dorothy B. "The Panic of 1819 in Missouri." *Missouri Historical Review* 29 (January 1935).
Dowd, Gregory Evans. *A Spirited Resistance: The North American Indian Struggle for Unity, 1745–1815*. Baltimore: Johns Hopkins University Press, 1992.
Edmunds, R. David. *Tecumseh and the Quest for Indian Leadership*. Boston: Little, Brown, 1984.
Eisenhower, John S.D. *So Far From God: The U.S. War with Mexico, 1846–1848*. New York: Random House, 1989.
Ekberg, Carl J. *Colonial Ste. Genevieve: An Adventure on the Mississippi Frontier*. Gerald, Mo.: Patrice Press, 1985.
———. *French Roots in the Illinois Country: The Mississippi Frontier in Colonial Times*. Urbana: University of Illinois Press, 1998.
Ellis, Joseph. *Founding Brothers: The Revolutionary Generation*. New York: Alfred A. Knopf, 2000.
Ellis, Richard. *The Jeffersonian Crisis: Courts and Politics in the Young Republic*. New York: Oxford University Press, 1971.
Faragher, John Mack. *Daniel Boone: The Life and Legend of an American Pioneer*. New York: Holt, 1992.
Fehrenbacher, Don E. *The Slaveholding Republic: An Account of the United States Government's Relations to Slavery*, ed. Ward M. McAfee. Oxford, U.K., and New York: Oxford University Press, 2001.
Feller, Daniel. *The Public Lands in Jacksonian Politics*. Madison: University of Wisconsin Press, 1984.
Fleming, Thomas. *Duel: Alexander Hamilton, Aaron Burr, and the Future of America*. New York: Basic Books, 1999.
Foley, William E. *The Genesis of Missouri: From Wilderness Outpost to Statehood*. Columbia: University of Missouri Press, 1989.
———. *A History of Missoury: Volume I, 1673–1820* [William E. Parrish, general editor]. Columbia: University of Missouri Press, 1971.
———. *Wilderness Journey: The Life of William Clark*. Columbia: University of Missouri Press, 2004.
Foley, William E., and C. David Rice. *The First Chouteaus: River Barons of Early St. Louis*. Urbana: University of Illinois Press, 1983.
Foner, Eric. *Free Soil, Free Labor, Free Men: The Ideology of the Republican Party Before the Civil War*. New York: Oxford University Press, 1970.

———. "Racial Attitudes of the New York Free Soilers." *New York History* XLVI (October 1965).
Forbes, Robert Pierce. *The Missouri Compromise and Its Aftermath: Slavery & the Meaning of America*. Chapel Hill: University of North Carolina Press, 2007.
Fredrickson, George M. *The Black Image in the White Mind: The Debate on Afro-American Character and Destiny, 1817–1914*. New York: Harper & Row, 1971.
Freehling, William W. *The Road to Disunion: Volume I, Secessionists at Bay, 1776–1854*. New York: Oxford University Press, 1990.
Freeman, Joanne B. *Affairs of Honor: National Politics in the New Republic*. New Haven: Yale University Press, 2001.
Garraty, John A. *Silas Wright*. New York: Columbia University Press, 1949.
Gates, Paul W. *History of Public Land Law Development. Written for the Public Land Law Review Commission, by Paul W. Gates; with a chapter by Robert W. Swenson*. Washington: U.S. Government Printing Office, 1968.
Gerteis, Louis. *Civil War St. Louis*. Lawrence: University Press of Kansas, 2001.
Gleik, Harry S. "Banking in Early Missouri, Part I." *Missouri Historical Review* 61, no. 4 (July 1967).
Going, Charles B. *David Wilmot, Free-Soiler: A Biography of the Great Advocate of the Wilmot Proviso*. New York and London: D. Appleton and Company, 1924.
Hardeman, Nicholas Perkins. *Wilderness Calling: The Hardeman Family in the American Westward Movement, 1750–1900*. Knoxville: University of Tennessee Press, 1977.
Hargreaves, Mary W.M. *The Presidency of John Quincy Adams*. Lawrence: University Press of Kansas, 1985.
Harrison, Lowell H., and James C. Klotter. *A New History of Kentucky*. Lexington: University Press of Kentucky, 1997.
Hickey, Donald. *The War of 1812: A Forgotten Conflict*. Urbana: University of Illinois Press, 1989.
Hietala, Thomas R. "Continentalism and the Color Line." In *Race and U.S. Foreign Policy from Colonial Times through the Age of Jackson*, ed. Michael L. Krenn. New York: Garland Publishing, 1998.
Hofstadter, Richard. *The Idea of a Party System: The Rise of Legitimate Opposition in the United States, 1780–1840*. Berkeley: University of California Press, 1969.
———. *The Progressive Historians: Turner, Beard, Parrington*. New York: Knopf, 1968.
Holt, Michael F. *Rise and Fall of the American Whig Party: Jacksonian Politics and the Onset of the Civil War*. New York: Oxford University Press, 1999.
Horsman, Reginald. *The Causes of the War of 1812*. New York: A.S. Barnes, 1962.

———. *Race and Manifest Destiny: The Origins of American Racial Anglo-Saxonism.* Cambridge, Mass.: Harvard University Press, 1981.

Houck, Louis. *A History of Missouri from the earliest explorations and settlements until the admission of the state into the union.* Chicago: R.R. Donnelley & Sons, 2 volumes, 1908.

Howe, Daniel Walker. *The Political Culture of the American Whigs.* Chicago: University of Chicago Press, 1979.

———. *What Hath God Wrought: The Transformation of America, 1815–1848.* New York: Oxford University Press, 2007.

Isenberg, Nancy. *Fallen Founder: The Life of Aaron Burr.* New York: Viking Penguin, 2007.

James, Marquis. *Life of Andrew Jackson, Complete in One Volume.* Indianapolis and New York: The Bobbs-Merrill Co., 1938.

Kars, Marjoleine. *Breaking Loose Together: The Regulator Rebellion in Pre-Revolutionary North Carolina.* Chapel Hill: University of North Carolina Press, 2002.

Kemp P. Battle. *History of the University of North Carolina* (Raleigh, N.C.: Edwards & Broughton Printing Company, 1907.

Kennedy, John F. *Profiles in Courage.* New York: Harper, 1956.

Lee, Wayne E. *Crowds and Soldiers in Revolutionary North Carolina: The Culture of Violence in Riot and War.* Gainesville: University Press of Florida, 2001.

Lefler, Hugh T., and William S. Powell. *Colonial North Carolina: A History.* New York: Scribner, 1973.

Lehmann, F.W., "The Constitution of 1820." *Missouri Historical Review* 16 (January 1922).

Lomask, Milton. *Aaron Burr: The Conspiracy and the Years of Exile, 1805–1836.* New York: Farrar, Straus & Giroux, 1982.

———. *Aaron Burr: The Years from Princeton to Vice President, 1756–1805.* New York: Farrar, Straus & Giroux, 1979.

March, David D. "The Admission of Missouri." *Missouri Historical Review* 65 (July 1971).

McCandless, Perry G. "Benton v. Barton: The Formation of the Second Party System in Missouri." *Missouri Historical Review* 79 (July 1985).

———. *A History of Missouri: Volume II, 1820–1860* [William E. Parrish, general editor]. Columbia: University of Missouri Press, 1972.

———. "The Political Philosophy and Political Personality of Thomas H. Benton." *Missouri Historical Review* 50 (January 1956).

———. "The Rise of Thomas H. Benton in Missouri Politics." *Missouri Historical Review* 50 (October 1955).

———. "The Significance of County Making in the Election of Thomas H. Benton." *Missouri Historical Review* 53 (October 1958).

McClure, Clarence H. "Early Opposition to Thomas Hart Benton." *Missouri Historical Review* X (April 1916).
———. *Opposition in Missouri to Thomas Hart Benton.* Warrensburg: Central Missouri State College, 1926.
McLoughlin, William G. *Cherokee Renascence in the New Republic.* Princeton, N.J.: Princeton University Press, 1986.
———, *Cherokees and Missionaries, 1789–1839.* New Haven: Yale University Press, 1984.
Meigs, William M. *Life of Thomas Hart Benton.* Philadelphia: J.B. Lippincott Co., 1904.
Mikesell, Marvin. "Comparative Studies in Frontier History." *Annals of the Association of American Geographers* 50 (March 1960).
Missouri Historical Society. "Earliest Picture of St. Louis." In *Glimpses of the Past,* VIII, St. Louis, 1941.
Moore, Glover. *The Missouri Controversy, 1819–1821.* Lexington: University of Kentucky Press, 1953.
Morris, Edmund. *The Rise of Theodore Roosevelt.* New York: Coward, McCann & Geoghegan, 1979.
Morrison, Chaplain W. *Democratic Politics and Sectionalism: The Wilmot Proviso Controversy.* Chapel Hill: University of North Carolina Press, 1967.
Morrison, Michael A., and James Brewer Stewart, eds. *Race and the Early Republic: Racial Consciousness and Nation Building in the Early Republic.* Lanham, Md.: Rowman & Littlefield, 2002.
Morton, John D. "'This Magnificent New World': Thomas Hart Benton's Westward Vision Reconsidered." *Missouri Historical Review* 90, no. 3 (April 1996).
———. "'A High Wall and a Deep Ditch': Thomas Hart Benton and the Compromise of 1850." *Missouri Historical Review* 94, no. 1 (October 1999).
The Nation. Unsigned review of *Thomas H. Benton,* by Theodore Roosevelt. March 29, 1888.
Nelson, Paul David. *William Tryon and the Course of Empire: A Life in British Imperial Service.* Chapel Hill: University of North Carolina Press, 1990.
Nevins, Allan. *Frémont: Pathmarker of the West.* New York & London: D. Appleton-Century Co., 1939.
Niven, John. *John C. Calhoun and the Price of Union.* Baton Rouge: Louisiana State University Press, 1988.
Novick, Peter. *That Noble Dream: The "Objectivity Question" and the American Historical Profession.* Cambridge, U.K.: Cambridge University Press, 1988.
Parks, Joseph Howard. *Felix Grundy: Champion of Democracy.* Baton Rouge: Louisiana State University Press, 1940.
Parrish, William E. *David Rice Atchison of Missouri: Border Politician.* Columbia: University of Missouri Press, 1961.
———. *Frank Blair: Lincoln's Conservative.* Columbia: University of Missouri Press, 1998.

Parton, James. *Life of Andrew Jackson*. New York: Mason Brothers, 3 volumes, 1860.
Perkins, Bradford. *Prologue to War: England and the United States, 1805–1812*. Berkeley: University of California Press, 1961.
Peterson, Merrill D. *The Great Triumvirate: Webster, Clay, and Calhoun*. New York: Oxford University Press, 1987.
Peterson, Norma Lois. *The Presidencies of William Henry Harrison and John Tyler*. Lawrence: University Press of Kansas, 1989.
Phillips, Christopher. *Missouri's Confederate: Claiborne Fox Jackson and the Creation of Southern Identity in the Border West*. Columbia: University of Missouri Press, 2000.
Phillips, Ulrich B. *Georgia and State Rights: A Study of the Political History of Georgia from the Revolution to the Civil War*. Washington: Government Printing Office, 1902.
Porter, Kenneth Wiggins. *John Jacob Astor: Business Man*. Cambridge, Mass.: Harvard University Press, 2 volumes, 1931.
Potter, David M. *The Impending Crisis, 1848–1861*. New York: Harper & Row, 1976.
Primm, James Neal. *Lion of the Valley: St. Louis, Missouri, 1764–1980*. Boulder, Colo.: Pruett Publishing Co., 1981.
Prucha, Francis Paul. *The Great Father: The United States Government and the American Indians*. Lincoln: University of Nebraska Press, 2 volumes, 1984.
———. *The Sword of the Republic: The United States Army on the Frontier, 1783–1846*. Bloomington: Indiana University Press, 1977.
Remini, Robert V. *Andrew Jackson and His Indian Wars*. New York: Viking, 2001.
———. *Andrew Jackson and the Course of American Democracy, 1833–1845*. New York: Harper & Row, 1984.
———. *Andrew Jackson and the Course of American Empire, 1767–1821*. New York: Harper & Row, 1977.
———. *Andrew Jackson and the Course of American Freedom, 1822–1832*. New York: Harper & Row, 1981.
———. *The Election of Andrew Jackson*. Philadelphia: Lippincott, 1963.
———. *Henry Clay: Statesman for the Union*. New York: W.W. Norton, 1991.
———. *The Life of Andrew Jackson*. New York: Perennial Classics, 2001.
———. *Martin Van Buren and the Making of the Democratic Party*. New York: Columbia University Press, 1959.
Richards, Leonard L. "The Jacksonians and Slavery." In *Antislavery Reconsidered: New Perspectives on the Abolitionists*, ed. Lewis Perry and Michael Fellman. Baton Rouge: Louisiana State University Press, 1979.
———. *The Slave Power: The Free North and Southern Domination, 1780–1860*. Baton Rouge: Louisiana State University Press, 2000.
Richardson, Lemont K. "Private Land Claims in Missouri." *Missouri Historical Review* 50 (January 1956).

Risjord, Norman. *The Old Republicans: Southern Conservatism in the Age of Jefferson.* New York: Columbia University Press, 1965.
Rogers, Joseph M. *Thomas H. Benton.* Philadelphia: G.W. Jacobs & Co., 1905.
Rogin, Michael Paul. *Fathers and Children: Andrew Jackson and the Subjugation of the American Indian.* New York: Knopf, 1975.
Rohrbough, Malcolm J. *The Land Office Business: The Settlement and Administration of American Public Lands, 1789-1837.* New York: Oxford University Press, 1968.
Roosevelt, Theodore. *Thomas H. Benton.* Boston: Houghton-Mifflin, 1888.
Rothbard, Murray N. *The Panic of 1819: Reactions and Policies.* New York: Columbia University Press, 1962.
Rowan, Steven, and James Neal Primm. *Germans for a Free Missouri.* Columbia: University of Missouri Press, 1983.
Rutland, Robert A. *Madison's Alternatives: The Jeffersonian Republicans and the Coming of War.* Philadelphia: Lippincott, 1975.
Sargent, Nathan. *Public Men and Events from the commencement of Mr. Monroe's administration, in 1817, to the close of Mr. Filmore's administration, in 1853.* Philadelphia: J.B. Lippincott & Co., 1875.
Saturday Review. Unsigned review of *Old Bullion Benton: Senator from the New West*, by William N. Chambers. September 29, 1956.
Satz, Ronald N. *American Indian Policy in the Jacksonian Era.* Lincoln: University of Nebraska Press, 1975.
Saxton, Alexander. *The Rise and Fall of the White Republic.* London & New York: Verso, 1990.
Sayles, Stephen. "Thomas Hart Benton and the Santa Fe Trail." *Missouri Historical Review* 69 (October 1974).
Scharf, J. Thomas. *History of St. Louis City and County: from the earliest periods to the present day: including biographical sketches of representative men.* Philadelphia: L. H. Everts, 2 volumes, 1882.
Schlesinger, Arthur M. Jr. *The Age of Jackson.* Boston: Little, Brown and Company, 1945.
Sellers, Charles G. *The Market Revolution: Jacksonian America, 1815-1846.* New York: Oxford University Press, 1991.
Shalhope, Robert E. "Jacksonian Politics in Missouri: A Comment on the McCormick Thesis." *Civil War History* 15, no. 3 (September 1969).
———. *Sterling Price: Portrait of a Southerner.* Columbia: University of Missouri Press, 1971.
———. "Thomas Hart Benton and Missouri State Politics: A Re-examination." *Bulletin of the Missouri Historical Society* 25 (April 1969).
Sharp, James R. "Gov. Daniel Dunklin's Jacksonian Democracy in Missouri, 1832-1836." *Missouri Historical Review* 56 (April 1962).
Shoemaker, Floyd C. *Missouri's Struggle for Statehood, 1804-1821.* New York: Russell & Russell, 1943.

Smith, Elbert B. *The Death of Slavery: The United States, 1837–1865*. Chicago: University of Chicago Press, 1967.
———. *Francis Preston Blair*. New York: Free Press, 1980.
———. *Magnificent Missourian: The Life of Thomas Hart Benton*. Philadelphia: Lippincott, 1957.
———. *The Presidencies of Zachary Taylor and Millard Fillmore*. Lawrence: University Press of Kansas, 1988.
———. *The Presidency of James Buchanan*. Lawrence: University Press of Kansas, 1975.
Smith, William E. *The Francis Preston Blair Family in Politics*. New York: The Macmillan Company, 2 volumes, 1933.
Soulard, Amadee. "The Bloody Island Cross Mark," *St. Louis Globe Democrat*, June 25, 1899.
Stagg, J.C.A. *Mr. Madison's War: Politics, Diplomacy and Warfare in the Early Republic, 1783–1830*. Princeton, N.J.: Princeton University Press, 1983.
Steffen, Jerome. "William Clark: A New Perspective on Missouri Territorial Politics, 1813–1820," *Missouri Historical Review* 67 (January 1973).
———. *William Clark: Jeffersonian Man on the Frontier*. Norman: University of Oklahoma Press, 1967.
———, ed. *The American West: New Perspectives, New Dimensions*. Norman: University of Oklahoma Press, 1979.
Stevens, Walter B. *St. Louis, The Fourth City*. St. Louis: S.J. Clarke Pub. Co., 3 volumes, 1909.
Steward, Dick. *Duels and the Roots of Violence in Missouri*. Columbia: University of Missouri Press, 2000.
———. *Frontier Swashbuckler: The Life and Legend of John Smith T*. Columbia: University of Missouri Press, 2000.
Strickland, Arvarh E. "Aspects of Slavery in Missouri, 1821." *Missouri Historical Review* 65 (July 1971).
Takaki, Ronald. *Iron Cages: Race and Culture in 19th Century America*. New York: Knopf, 1979.
Tennessee Encyclopedia of History and Culture. <http://tennesseeencyclopedia.net>.
Trexler, Harrison. *Slavery in Missouri, 1804–1865*. Baltimore: Johns Hopkins University Press, 1914.
Turner, Frederick Jackson. *The Frontier in American History*. New York: H. Holt and Company, 1920.
Van den Berghe, Pierre L. *Race and Racism: A Comparative Perspective*. New York: Wiley, 1967.
Wallace, Anthony F.C. *Jefferson and the Indians: The Tragic Fate of the First Americans*. Cambridge, Mass.: Belknap Press of Harvard University Press, 1999.
———. *The Long, Bitter Trail: Andrew Jackson and the Indians*. New York: Hill and Wang, 1993.

Watson, Harry L. *Liberty and Power: The Politics of Jacksonian America.* New York: Hill and Wang, 1990.
Weber, David. *The Mexican Frontier, 1821–1846: The American Southwest under Mexico.* Albuquerque: University of New Mexico Press, 1982.
———, *The Spanish Frontier in North America.* New Haven: Yale University Press, 1992.
Whitaker, Arthur Preston. *The Spanish-American Frontier, 1783–1795: The Westward Movement and the Spanish Retreat in the Mississippi Valley.* New York: Houghton Mifflin Company, 1927.
Wiebe, Robert. *The Opening of American Society: From the Adoption of the Constitution to the Eve of Disunion.* New York: Knopf, 1984.
Wiener, Alan S. "John Scott, Thomas Hart Benton, David Barton and the Election of 1824: A Case Study in Pressure Politics." *Missouri Historical Review* 60 (July 1966).
Wilentz, Sean. *The Rise of American Democracy: Jefferson to Lincoln.* New York: Norton, 2005.
Williams, Samuel C. *Beginnings of West Tennessee in the Land of the Chickasaws, 1541–1841.* Johnson City, Tenn.: Watauga Press, 1930.
Wills, Garry. *"Negro President": Jefferson and the Slave Power.* Boston: Houghton Mifflin, 2003.
Wilson, Major L. *The Presidency of Martin Van Buren.* Lawrence: University Press of Kansas, 1984.
Woodford, Frank B. *Lewis Cass: The Last Jeffersonian.* New Brunswick, N.J.: Rutgers University Press, 1950.
Wyatt-Brown, Bertram. *Southern Honor: Ethics and Behavior in the Old South.* New York: Oxford University Press, 1982.

DISSERTATIONS

Perry G. McCandless. *Thomas H. Benton, His Source of Political Strength in Missouri from 1815 to 1858.* University of Missouri, 1953.

Index

Aberdeen, Lord, 199
Adams, Charles Francis, 229
Adams, John, 122–23
Adams, John Quincy: on Benton's land rights reform proposals, 131; Benton's opposition to, 95; on Benton's speech on Texas annexation, 206; death of, 223; and election of 1824, 110, 114, 117; and federal Indian policy, 146, 148–49, 164; in Monroe's cabinet, 123; and Panama Congress debates, 125–28; and public domain land sales, 153; public works projects proposed by, 120–21; and slavery in territories, 190–91; and Transcontinental Treaty (1819), 186–87
Adams-Oñis agreement (1819), 186–87, 189, 208
Age of Jackson (Schlesinger), 12
Alabama: and federal Indian policy, 170; immigration to, 141; Native Americans in, 163
Albany Regency, 121
Alien and Sedition Act of 1798, 122

American Board of Commissioners for Foreign Missions, 146, 164
American Colonization Society, 168, 256
American Fur Company, 99, 101
American Revolution, 20–21, 264*n*11
American System (Clay), 12, 111, 122–24, 133, 136, 151–52, 166, 196
AMERICANUS (pen name), 187
Anderson, Patton, 37
Anderson, Richard C., 126
Andrews, Henry, 99
Armstrong, John, 48
Army Corps of Topographical Engineers, 221
Aron, Stephen, 269*n*1
Articles of Confederation, 140
Artisanal training, 162
Ashley, William H., 89, 99, 112
Ashworth, John, 123
Astor, John Jacob, 99
Atchison, David Rice, 202, 209, 231, 248–49, 253
Austin, Moses, 62, 102, 195
Austin, Stephen, 195

Bancroft, George, 202, 221
Banking policy, 177–225; Benton's education in, 179–83; Macon's views on, 97; and Mexican silver, 177, 178, 183–86, 203–4; in Missouri, 179–80; and Panic of 1819, 104–5; and Santa Fe trade, 183–86; and Texas annexation, 186–91
Bank of Georgetown (Kentucky), 181
Bank of Kentucky, 105
Bank of Missouri, 101, 104, 182–83
Bank of St. Louis, 104, 180, 182
Bank of the Commonwealth (Kentucky), 105
Bank of the State of Missouri, 206
Bank of the United States (First), 180
Bank of the United States (Second): debate over chartering of, 168; opposition to, 7, 124, 160, 178, 181–82; and Panic of 1819, 141
Bank War of 1830s, 179
Baptists, 76
Barbour, James, 147, 148
Barnburners, 226–27, 228
Barter trade, 179
Barton, David: and Benton's graduation/donation proposal, 150; and election of 1820, 90, 91, 92; and election of 1824, 111, 112; and election of 1828, 133; and Indian Removal Act, 165; and land rights, 149; and Missouri constitution, 87; and Missouri politics, 63–64, 88; and Missouri statehood petition, 92–93; and public domain land sales, 155, 166
Barton, Joshua, 58, 67, 70, 111–12, 270n8
Bates, Edward, 58, 87, 129
Bates, Frederick, 61, 62, 112, 129
Beacon on Texas annexation, 187–88
Beale, Edward, 247, 248

Becknell, William, 184
Benton, Ann Gooch "Nancy" (mother), 21–26, 69, 70, 138
Benton, Augustine (uncle), 19
Benton, Elizabeth McDowell (wife), 55, 83, 91–92, 113
Benton, Frances (grandmother), 19
Benton, Jesse (brother), 48–50, 69
Benton, Jesse (father), 6, 19–23, 29, 32, 96, 138
Benton, Jessie (daughter). *See* Frémont, Jessie Benton
Benton, Randolph (son), 245
Benton, Samuel (grandfather), 17, 18–19, 96
Benton, Samuel, Jr. (uncle), 19, 22
Benton, Thomas Hart: birth of, 17; Calhoun's conflicts with, 192–95; childhood of, 15–16, 21–22; and currency debate, 177–225; death of, 254–55; and Democratic Convention of 1844, 202–9; duels with Lucas, 14–15, 63–72; education of, 23–25, 30–31, 179–83; election campaigns of, 89–91, 130–31, 244–46; *Enquirer* owned and operated by, 77–78; family background, 15–26; and federal Indian policy, 142–49, 162–65, 169–76; and Free Soil Party, 244–59; and Frémont's career, 221–23; and frontier Missouri, 54–94; and graduation/donation proposal, 134, 149–55; Jackson's conflict with, 48–50, 268nn84–86; in Jackson's inner circle, 38; and Jackson's presidential campaign, 109–19; Jackson's reconciliation with, 112–13; and land rights, 135–76; legacy of, 254–59; marriage of, 83, 91–92; and Mexican War (1846–1848), 213–25; military career of, 50–53;

and Missouri Compromise, 91–94; and nationalism in Old Southwest, 26–37; and Panama Congress debates, 125–28; and Panic of 1819, 104–9; and Polk's treatment of Frémont, 221–23; and racialization of American politics, 95–134; and slavery, 72–91, 229–43; and Spanish land grants, 55–63; and special interest groups, 98–104; and Texas annexation, 186–91, 195–201, 209–11, 213–21; at University of North Carolina, 7, 24–25; and War of 1812, 42–53
Benton (Roosevelt), 3–4
Benton Town, 29–30, 150
Berrien, John M., 127
Birney, James G., 209
Black Code (*Code Noir*), 73–74
Blair, Francis, 199, 212, 220, 229, 253, 255, 276*n*19
Blair, Frank, Jr., 227, 229, 245, 252, 255–58
Blair, Montgomery, 229, 255
Bloody Island, 58, 67, 263*n*1
Blount, William, 29, 43
Board of Trustees for Schools in St. Louis, 64
Boernstein, Henry, 245, 252
Boone, Daniel, 21, 138
Boonslick Democrats, 194, 209
Bowlin, James, 244
Britain: and Oregon boundary conflict, 213; Proclamation of 1763, 29, 280*n*13; Quebec Act of 1774, 280*n*13; and Texas annexation, 198, 199; and War of 1812, 38–39, 52
Brown, Aaron V., 197
Brown, B. Gratz, 246, 252
Brown, Joseph C., 131
Buchanan, James, 217, 254, 255

Bulletin of the Missouri Historical Society on Benton's career, 9
Burke, Edmund, 205
Burr, Aaron, 26–27, 33–37, 40, 60, 266*n*49
Butler, Elizur, 171
Butler, Thomas, 41

Cabanne, Jean P., 56
Calhoun, John C.: and Bank of the United States, 180; Benton's conflicts with, 161, 191, 192–95, 234; and California annexation, 224–25; constituency of, 8; death of, 239–40; and election of 1824, 110, 113, 116; and election of 1844, 197–98; and factory system, 100; and federal Indian policy, 145, 146; Jackson's conflict with, 2, 96; and Mexican War, 216; and mining rights, 102; in Monroe's cabinet, 123; and nationalist economic program, 109–10; and New Mexico annexation, 224–25; and nullification crisis, 157, 159; as secretary of state for Tyler, 198–99; and slavery in territories, 192–95, 199, 218–19, 226, 230–32; and Texas annexation, 197, 198, 199; and War Hawks, 40
California: admitted to Union, 242; annexation of, 224–25; Frémont in, 221–22; and Mexican War, 218; petition for statehood, 238–39, 240; Polk's goal to annex, 213, 224
Cambreleng, Churchill C., 227
Carr, William C., 60
Carroll, William, 38, 48, 51, 69
Carson, Kit, 222
Cass, Lewis, 202, 228, 239, 240
Castro, Jose Maria, 222
Catholics, 244–45
Censorship of mail, 192–93

Central America, colonization of free blacks in, 255–56, 258
Central Clique, 6, 194, 195, 209
"Central national road" proposal, 235, 236, 247–48
Chambers, William, 6–8, 27, 57, 82, 117, 119–20, 179, 255, 261*n*2, 270*n*18, 275*n*3
Charless, Joseph: Benton's feud with, 81–83, 87; and election of 1824, 111; gradualist approach to slavery of, 86; on "little junto," 62, 63, 82, 88, 108; and *Missouri Gazette*, 57, 77; and Missouri's statehood petition, 81; on Scott's election as territorial delegate, 66
Charless, Joseph, Jr., 244
Chase, Salmon, 229, 251
Cherokee Nation v. Georgia (1831), 170
Cherokees (tribe): and Indian Removal Act, 169–70; land claims by, 163; and land grants, 29; and Treaty of Sycamore Shoals, 29, 138
Chickasaws (tribe), 163
Chinn, Julia, 274*n*65
Choctaws (tribe), 163
Chouteau, Auguste, 56, 60, 62, 139, 180, 182
Chouteau, Pierre, 56
Chouteau, Pierre, Jr., 213
Chouteau, Victoire, 56
Clamorgen, Jacques, 60
Clark, George Rogers, 56
Clark, John B., 243
Clark, William: and Indian relations, 139; and state government, 88, 89, 107; and territorial delegate election, 64–65; as territorial governor, 56, 63
Classical education, 24
Clay, Henry: and American Colonization Society, 168; American System program of, 12, 111, 122–24, 133, 136, 151–52, 166, 196; and Bank of the United States, 180; Benton's support for, 113; as Burr's defense attorney, 36; Calhoun eulogized by, 239; and California's petition for statehood, 239, 242; constituency of, 8; and election of 1824, 110, 114, 116, 118; and election of 1844, 209; and federal Indian policy, 148, 170; Jackson policies opposed by, 2; and Missouri's statehood petition, 79, 81, 85; in Monroe's cabinet, 123; and nationalist economic program, 109–10; and nullification crisis, 159, 161; and public domain land sales, 137, 153, 166–69, 175; as secretary of state for Adams, 117, 120; and Texas annexation, 199, 239, 242; and War Hawks, 39–40
Clayton, Augustine, 171
Clayton, John, 224
Clemson, Eli, 14–15, 70, 71
Clemson, Eric, 181
Clinton, Dewitt, 81, 125
Code duello, 25–26. *See also* Duels
Code Noir (Black Code), 73–74
Coffee, John, 38, 49, 51, 69, 143
Colonization of free blacks, 167–68, 255–56, 258
Committee on Foreign Relations, 214, 223
Committee on Indian Affairs, 146, 147, 163, 184, 279*n*2
Committee on Military Affairs, 113, 214, 223, 230
Committee on Public Lands, 102
Committee on Territories, 224
Congress of American Republics at Panama, 125–28
Cook, Daniel, 116
Cook, John B., 88

Cook, Nathaniel, 89, 90
Cotton, 185, 186, 265*n*33
"Country Democracy," 104–9, 276*n*22
Crawford, William, 110, 111, 113–14, 117, 191
Creeks (tribe): in Georgia, 146, 147, 148; Jackson's campaign against, 136, 143; land claims by, 163; Spanish alliance with, 28; and Treaty of Indian Springs, 147; and War of 1812, 50–51, 52
Crittenden, John J., 217
Crockett, David, 11
Crooks, Ramsay, 99, 100, 101
Cruzat, Francisco, 74
Cuba, attempts to purchase from Spain, 251
Cumberland Gap, 21, 138
Currency, 177–225; Benton's education in, 179–83; Macon's views on, 97; and Mexican silver, 177, 178, 183–86, 203–4; and Panic of 1819, 104; and Santa Fe trade, 183–86; and Texas annexation, 186–91. *See also* Banking policy
CURTIUS (pen name), 130

Dade, Francis, 173, 283*n*77
Dallas, George, 202
Darby, John, 235
Davies, John, 175
Davis, James D., 82
Davis, Jefferson, 224, 247, 251
Dawson's Number Two, 96
Democratic Convention of 1844, 201, 202–9
Democratic Convention of 1848, 228
Democratic Party: Convention of 1844, 202–9; and election of 1848, 228–29; factions in, 6; and Jackson, 2; and master race democracy, 11, 128; Texas annexation as dividing issue for, 212

Democratic-Republicans, 119–24
Democrat on Kansas-Nebraska Bill, 250
Demos krateo principle, 108, 115, 130, 132
De Smet, Pierre-Jean, 244–45
Dialectical Society, 24
Dickerson, Mahlon, 276*n*23
Dickinson, Charles, 72
District of Columbia, petitions to end slavery in, 193, 239, 242
Dix, John, 217, 227, 246
"Domestic dependent nations," 170
Donaldson, James, 60, 61
Donelson, Alexander, 49
Donelson, Andrew Jackson, 210
Doniphan, Alexander, 253
Douglas, Stephen A., 210, 224, 235, 240, 247, 248, 249
Dred Scott v. Sanford (1857), 254, 283*n*72
DuBourg, Louis, 244
DuBourg, William, 57
Duels: Barton-Hempstead, 58; Barton-Rector, 111–12, 270*n*8; Benton (Jesse)-Carroll, 48, 69; Benton (Thomas)-Jackson, 48–50, 268*nn*84–85; Benton (Thomas)-Lucas, 14–15, 63–72; Burr-Hamilton, 33, 34–35; code of honor for, 68; Jackson-Dickinson, 33; "posting" of correspondence for unmet challenges, 46; ritualized violence of, 25–26
Dunklin, Daniel, 160

Easton, Rufus, 59, 60, 63, 64, 66
Eaton, John, 113
Edwards, Ninian, 79
Edwardsville Bank, 181
Eisenhower, John S.D., 288*n*90
Ekberg, Carl, 74, 272*n*43
Election of 1810, 39

Election of 1816, 64–65
Election of 1822, 107
Election of 1824, 109–19, 276n24
Election of 1826, 129, 130–31
Election of 1828, 131, 132–34, 148–49
Election of 1836, 194
Election of 1840, 196
Election of 1844, 197–98, 206, 209
Election of 1848, 226
Election of 1850, 243
Election of 1852, 246
Election of 1854, 251–53
Election of 1856, 253, 254
Electoral College, 84, 108, 111, 113
Elements of History (Millot), 24
Elliot, Henry, 90
Ellis, Richard, 276n22
Enquirer. See *St. Louis Enquirer*
Episcopal Church, 21
Era of Good Feelings, 63, 109, 110
Essex Junto, 34
Evangelical Protestants, 144

Factory system, 99–101, 144
Fallen Founder: The Life of Aaron Burr (Isenberg), 266n49
Fanning, Edmund, 19
Farmers and Mechanics Bank of Cincinnati, 181
Farnham, Russell, 99
Farrar, Bernard, 14, 70, 181, 271n29
Fayette Clique, 207
Federal Indian policy: Indian Removal Act of 1830, 162–65, 169–76; and land rights, 142–49
Federalist Party, 1, 21, 34, 38, 123, 144
Fillmore, Millard, 242, 254
Flagg, Edmund, 74
Florida: Native Americans in, 136; and Second Seminole War, 173–75
Floyd, John, 55, 92, 99
Foot, Samuel, 137, 155–56
Foote, Henry S., 234

Forbes, Robert Pierce, 128
Force Bill, 161
Forsythe, John, 164–65
Fort, John, 36
Fort Mims, 50–51
Free blacks, colonization of, 167–68, 255–56, 258
Freeman, Joanne, 34
Free Soil Party, 10–11, 227–29, 244–59
Frelinghuysen, Theodore, 137, 164, 165, 170
Frémont, Jessie Benton, 221, 222
Frémont, John Charles, 221–23, 253–54
Fugitive Slave Act, 239, 242
Fur trade, 99–101

Gadsden, James, 251
Gaines, Edmund, 147
Gallatin, Albert, 61, 142
Gardoqui, Don Diego, 28
General Land Office (U.S.), 62, 141
Georgia: and federal Indian policy, 146, 170, 171; Native Americans in, 136–37, 146–47, 163, 164
Geyer, Henry S., 243, 252
Gillespie, Lieutenant, 221
Gilmer, George, 171, 197, 198
Globe on Benton's views of Texas annexation, 200
Gooch, James, 21
Gooch, William, 21
Graduation/donation proposal, 109, 134, 149–55
Gratiot, Charles, 56–57, 60, 61, 62, 75, 139
"Great Migration," 76, 141
The Great Triumvirate (Peterson), 118
Greeley, Horace, 254
Green, Duff, 106, 115
Green, James, 243
Grundy, Felix, 37, 39–40

INDEX / 313

Guadalupe Hidalgo Treaty (1848), 223–25

Haiti, U.S. relations with, 126–27
Hall, Sergeant, 77
Hamilton, Alexander, 33, 34, 38, 123
Hammond, Charles, 49
Hammond, Samuel, 63
Hard-currency proponents, 206, 207
Hardeman, John, 30
Hardeman, Nicholas Perkins, 30
Hardeman, Thomas, 30, 31
Hard-money stance, 178
Harper, William, 88
Harrison, William Henry, 196
Hart, Lucretia, 36
Hart, Nathaniel, 55
Hart, Thomas, 20, 21, 22, 138
Hay, George, 40
Hayne, Robert Y., 127, 155–59, 160, 166, 276n23
Hays, Stockley Donelson, 37, 49
Hempstead, Edward, 57–58, 60, 61–62, 63, 67
Hempstead, Thomas, 58, 85
Henderson, Richard, 20, 21, 138
Hendricks, William, 155
Henry, Isaac N., 77, 82
Herrenvolk democracy, 262n17
Hofstadter, Richard, 118
Hone, Philip, 192
Horsman, Reginald, 9, 10
Houston, Sam, 196, 198
Howe, Daniel Walker, 117
How, John, 252
Hudson's Bay Company, 99

Illinois, immigration to, 141
Immigration: to Missouri, 54, 62–63, 76–77, 104, 244; and slavery, 75; to western territories, 141
Indiana, immigration to, 141

Indian Removal Act of 1830, 9, 135, 137, 162–65, 169–76, 189
Indians. *See* Native Americans
Indian Springs Treaty (1824), 147
Interest groups, 54, 98–104
Isenberg, Nancy, 266n49
Isolationist foreign policy, 125–28

Jackson, Andrew: and agrarian republicanism, 16; Benton's conflict with, 48–50, 268nn84–86; Benton's reconciliation with, 112–13; on Benton's stance on Texas annexation, 209–10; Burr's connections to, 26–27, 35–36, 40–41; Calhoun's conflict with, 96; death of, 211–12; duel with Benton, 268nn84–85; duel with Dickinson, 33; and election of 1824, 109–19; and election of 1828, 132–34; and federal Indian policy, 143, 149, 169–70; and founding of Memphis, 273n64; and master race democracy, 10; opposition to policies of, 2; and Panic of 1819 relief programs, 106; Pensacola assault by, 52; Polk's ties to, 210; and public domain land sales, 166, 167, 168, 169; as slaveowner, 277n31; as Superior Court judge in Tennessee, 32–33; and Tennessee's constitution, 30; and Texas annexation, 196, 197, 200; and War of 1812, 38, 42, 52–53
Jackson, Claiborne Fox, 209, 231
Jackson, Elizabeth, 69
Jackson, Rachel, 113
Jackson Resolutions, 231, 233, 245
Jay, John, 28
J.B. Lippincott Company, 8
Jefferson, Thomas: Burr as vice-president for, 33; Burr's arrest warrant issued by, 36; and

development of territories, 1; and federal Indian policy, 144; and Federalist Party, 123; Jackson's break with, 41; and road construction in territories, 186; and slavery in territories, 241
Jeffersonian Republicans, 38, 109, 119
Johnson, Richard Mentor, 274*n*65
Johnston, Lyttleton, 45, 48
Jones, John Rice, 59, 88, 90
Jones, William Carey, 255
Junto, 6, 58, 64, 88, 179

Kansas: constitution of, 255; as free state, 256
Kansas-Nebraska Bill of 1854, 248–51
Kars, Marjolein, 264*n*11
Kayser, Alexander, 246
Kearny, Stephen Watts, 222
Kendall, Amos, 276*n*19
Kennett, Luther, 251, 252, 253
Kentucky, Panic of 1819 relief programs in, 105
King, Austin A., 231
King, Rufus, 81, 100
Know-Nothing movement, 244, 253, 254

Labadie, Sylvestre, 56
Lamb, James, 247
Land Act of 1820, 109
Land Ordinance of 1785, 102, 140
Land rights, 135–76; Benton's proposals to reform, 108–9, 111; in California, 243–54; and Clay's distribution plan, 166–69; early controversies, 137–39; and federal Indian policy, 142–49, 162–65; and graduation/donation proposal, 149–55; and interest groups, 54, 98–99; and public domain, 140–42; and Spanish land grants, 29, 139; and states' rights, 159–62; and Webster-Hayne debate, 155–59. *See also* Public domain lands
Land speculation: by Benton family, 20, 21; and immigration, 104; and Indian removal, 137–38; in Louisiana, 59; in Missouri, 63; and public domain lands, 141. *See also* Public domain lands
Lane, William Carr, 131, 132
LA SALLE (pen name), 187, 189
Lawless, Luke, 14, 67, 68, 70, 71, 271*n*29
Law practice by Benton, 30–33, 57, 58–59, 101
Lead mining, 102–4
Leduc, Marie Philippe, 61, 90
Leonard, Abiel, 243
Lewis, Merriwether, 61
Lewis, William B., 38, 45–46, 212
Liberty Party, 209, 229
Life of Thomas Hart Benton (Meigs), 4–5
Linn, Lewis, 194, 202, 209
Lisa, Manuel, 99, 182
"Litte junto," 62, 63, 82
Loan offices, 106
Loco-Foco faction, 226, 227
Loiselle, Amarante, 273*n*64
Louisiana, Spanish land grants in, 59. *See also* New Orleans
Lovejoy, Elijah, 174
Lucas, Charles, 14–15, 63–72, 139
Lucas, John B.C., 60–61, 63, 71, 81, 86, 90
Luzières, Pierre Charles Delassus de, 272*n*43
Lytle, Archibald, 24, 25
Lytle, John, 24

Macon, Nathaniel: and banking policy, 107; on Clay's American System, 124; on economic role of government, 121; and nationalist

economic program, 110; in North Carolina State Assembly, 20, 96; as Old Republican, 96, 120; and Panama Congress debates, 126; and road construction in territories, 186
Madison, James, 39, 41, 47–48, 123, 145
Magness, David, 37
Magnificent Missourian (Smith), 8
Mail censorship, 192–93
Maine, statehood petition of, 84
Manifest Destiny, 4
Marcy, William, 217–18, 223, 226, 247
Marmaduke, Meredith M., 194
Marshall, John, 137, 144, 171, 182
Mason, James S., 239
Master race democracy, 9–10, 95–134; and "Country Democracy," 104–9; culmination of, 254–59; and Democratic-Republicans, 119–24; and election of 1824, 109–19; and Indian Removal Act of 1830, 169–76; and Jacksonians, 128–34; and Old Republicans, 96–98; and Panama Congress debates, 125–28; and Panic of 1819, 104–9; and special interest groups, 98–104
McCandless, Perry, 5–6
McClure, Clarence H., 5
McCulloch v. Maryland (1819), 182
McDowell, Elizabeth. *See* Benton, Elizabeth McDowell
McDowell, James, 55
McDowell, Sarah, 55
McDuffie, George, 204–5, 210, 211
McGillivray, Alexander, 28, 50
McIntosh, William, 146
McKenney, Thomas, 99–100
McKinley, John, 155
McNair, Alexander, 63–64, 87–89, 106–7, 139
Meigs, Josiah, 103

Meigs, William M., 4–5
Methodists, 76
Mexican War (1846–48), 201, 213–24
Mexico: attempts to purchase territories in, 251; border disputes with, 188; independence from Spain, 184, 195; peace treaty with, 223–25; silver imports from, 203–4; and Texas annexation, 213–21; trade with, 178, 203
Micklejohn, George, 19, 22
Miller, John, 129, 132
Mining interests, 102–4
Miscegenation, 83, 273–74nn64–65
Missionary schools, 162, 171
Mississippi, immigration to, 141
Mississippi River, 27
Missouri: constitution of, 87–88, 107; currency debate in, 206; and election of 1824, 110–11, 114; and election of 1828, 134; and election of 1844, 209; immigration to, 54, 62–63, 76–77, 104, 235, 244; local politics in, 107–8, 243, 244–45; multiracial communities in, 72–73; and Panic of 1819, 104–9; politics in, 63–64; Santa Fe trade with, 178, 203; slavery in, 72–91, 237; Spanish land grants in, 55–63; statehood petition of, 2, 78–81; territorial government in, 78–79; and Texas annexation, 207, 212; as third-class territory, 63; transformation of, 54–94
Missouri Advocate on special election for governor in Missouri, 129
Missourian on Texas annexation, 207
Missouri Compromise, 85–86, 91–94, 191, 218, 231, 250
Missouri Enabling Act of 1820, 85
Missouri Gazette: on Clark's candidacy for governor, 89;

Enquirer as rival to, 77; on land office credit, 142
Missouri Historical Review on Benton's career, 9
Missouri Intelligencer on Jackson's opposition to Clay's American System, 133
Missouri Register on Texas annexation, 207
Missouri Republican: on Benton's election campaign, 245; on Benton's popularity among immigrants, 244; on special election for governor in Missouri, 129
Missouri's Struggle for Statehood (Floyd), 273n53
Monroe, James, 109–10; and federal Indian policy, 143; Jackson's support for nomination of, 41; and Missouri's statehood petition, 93; Old Republicans' support for, 123
Monroe Doctrine, 125, 126, 128
Moore, Glover, 85
Moral Philosophy (Paley), 24
Moravian Brethren, 144
Morris, Thomas, 174

Natchez Trace, 29
Nationalism, 2–3, 26–37, 136, 195–96
National Republicans, 119, 122, 164, 170
National university proposal, 120–21
Native Americans: as "domestic dependent nations," 170; and factory system, 99–101, 144; and Indian Removal Act of 1830, 95, 162–65, 169–76; and land rights, 142–49; reform programs for, 144, 162, 165; Spanish recruitment of, 28; and War of 1812, 50–51, 52, 142–43. *See also* Federal Indian policy; *specific tribes*

Nevins, Allan, 288n90
New Mexico: annexation of, 224–25; boundary with Texas, 239, 242; and Mexican War, 218; Polk's goal to annex, 213, 224
New Orleans: and Burr's separatist plots, 36; Spanish closing of port in, 27, 30; and War of 1812, 43
North Carolina: Benton family in, 16–26; entry into union by, 22; local government in, 16–18; and Regulator movement, 11, 17, 19, 105
Northwest Ordinance of 1787, 75, 80, 140, 157, 230
Nullification crisis, 135, 137, 157, 246–47

O'Fallon, John, 66
"Old Bullion." *See* Benton, Thomas Hart
Old Bullion Benton (Chambers), 6–8, 82
Old Republicans, 96–98, 107, 110, 120–23, 194
Oñis, Don Luis de, 186–87
Opposition in Missouri to Thomas Hart Benton (McClure), 5
Oregon, boundary conflict with Britain, 2, 213
Overton, John, 273n64

Packenham, Edward, 52
"Pakenham Letter," 199
Panama Congress debates, 125–28
Panic of 1819, 12, 104–9, 183
Panic of 1837, 196
Paris Treaty (1783), 27
Parton, James, 33, 41
Payne's Landing Treaty (1832), 173
Peck, John Mason, 76
Penrose, Clement B., 60, 61
Personal honor, Benton's hypersensitivity to, 2, 16, 46

Peterson, Merrill D., 118
Pettis, Spencer, 131, 132
Phelps, John S., 247
Philanthropic Society, 24, 25
Pierce, Franklin, 247, 251
Pilcher, Joshua, 180, 181, 271n29
Polk, James K.: Benton's relationship with, 212, 220, 221–23, 225; and election of 1844, 202, 209; Jackson's ties to, 210; and Mexican War, 213, 214–15, 224, 288n90; and Texas annexation, 199
Polk, Trusten, 251, 253
Portage des Sioux Treaty (1815), 139
Pratte, Bernard, 60, 99
Preston, Francis, 55
Preston, James, 55
Preston, Laetitia, 55
Preston, Thomas L., 55
Proclamation of 1763 (Britain), 29, 280n13
Prucha, Francis Paul, 100
Public domain lands: Clay's distribution plan for, 166–69; graduation/donation proposal, 109, 134, 149–55; sales of, 109, 140–42, 155–59, 235

Quakers, 144
Quarles, Dr., 70
Quebec Act of 1774 (Britain), 280n13

Race and Manifest Destiny (Horsman), 9
Railroad construction, 235–36, 248
Ralls, Daniel, 90
Randolph, John: and banking policy, 107, 183; Benton's friendship with, 12, 97–98, 119, 120, 130; and Burr's trial, 40; and election of 1824, 117; and nationalist economic program, 110; and Old Republicans, 96, 123; and public domain land sales, 151, 154; and slavery in territories, 241
Rector, Elias, 180–81
Rector, Thomas, 112, 270n8
Red Sticks, 50–51, 52
Regulator movement, 11, 17, 19, 105
Religion, 76, 144, 244–45
Remini, Robert, 116, 117
Renault, Philippe, 73
Republican Party: Benton's legacy in platform of, 259; and election of 1856, 253; and master race democracy, 10; and popular government, 11; and slavery, 258
Reynolds, Thomas, 194
Richmond Junto, 120, 212
Rise and Fall of the White Republic (Saxton), 10
The Rise of American Democracy (Wilentz), 11–12, 118
Ritchie, Thomas, 55, 85, 121, 212
Road construction, 185–86, 235, 273n52
Robertson, James, 30
Rogers, Joseph M., 5
Rogin, Michael Paul, 68, 69
Rollins, James S., 253
"Roman-riding," 120, 238–39, 240
Roosevelt, Theodore, 3–4
Ross, John, 162, 163, 170
Rush, Richard, 154, 155
Russell, William, 63, 65

St. Louis Enquirer: on banking policy, 181–82; Benton as owner and editor of, 77–78; on Missouri's statehood petition, 80, 85, 93; on Texas annexation, 207; on trade, 9–10
Sanford, Richard, 24
Santa Anna, 196
Santa Fe, trade with, 178, 183–86, 194, 203

Saunders, Fleming, 25
Saxton, Alexander, 10, 11
Schlesinger, Arthur, Jr., 7–8, 12, 117
Scott, John: Clark's support for, 139; and election of 1824, 114, 115–17; and election of 1826, 129; and Missouri's statehood petition, 79, 81; as state representative, 89, 92, 112; as territorial delegate candidate, 63, 64, 65
Scott, Winfield, 215
Second Party System, 110, 119
Second Seminole War, 173
Sellers, Charles G., 117
Seminoles (tribe), 136, 143, 173–74
Sergeant, John, 126
Sevier, John, 29
Seward, William H., 249
Shays's Rebellion, 105
Shoemaker, Floyd, 91, 273*n*53
Silver, 203–4
Simpson, Robert, 66
Sims, George, 18
Slavery: Benton family's participation in, 16; free labor devalued by, 258; gradualist approach to, 86; and Indian Removal Act of 1830, 95; legal status of slave in territories, 73–74; and master race democracy, 9; in Missouri, 72–91, 237; and Missouri Compromise, 85–86, 91–94; and nullification crisis, 157; and Texas annexation, 189–90, 201, 210–11, 226, 230–31; in western territories, 229–43
Slidell, John, 213, 217
Smith, Elbert, 8, 100, 101, 179, 277*n*33
Smith, John B.N., 180
Smith, Theophilus, 181
Smith T., John, 60, 270*n*12
Soulé, Pierre, 251
South Carolina Exposition and Protest (anonymous), 157

South Carolina, nullification crisis in, 137, 157, 159–60
"Southern Address" (Calhoun), 230–31, 233
Spain: land grants from, 58–63, 75; Mexico's independence from, 184, 195; New Orleans port closed by, 27, 30; racial amalgamation in colonies of, 257; trade with, 28, 183–84; and Transcontinental Treaty (1819), 186–87; and Treaty of Paris (1783), 27
Spanish land grants, 29, 98–99, 139
Special interest groups, 54, 98–104
States' rights: and Indian removal, 136; and land rights, 159–62; and Missouri Compromise, 85
Steward, Dick, 57
Stockton, Robert, 222
Strict constructionists, 119, 124, 183, 186, 194
Stuart, Robert, 101
Sumner, Charles, 251
Sumner, James, 50
Supreme Court (U.S.): on Indian Removal Act, 170–71; on loan offices, 106; on mineral rights leasing system, 103; on states' power to tax, 182. *See also specific cases*
Sycamore Shoals Treaty (1775), 29, 138

Tallmadge, James, 79
Tariffs, 153, 154–55, 156–57, 159–60
Tassels, George, 171
Taylor, John, 124, 126
Taylor, Zachary, 213, 215, 229, 238, 241–42
Tazewell, Littleton Waller, 126, 151, 152, 154
Tecumseh, 50, 52

Tennessee: Benton family in, 26–37; constitution of, 30
"Tertium Quid" faction, 41, 96, 119, 123, 124
Texas: annexation of, 2, 177, 195–201, 209–21; Benton's early views on, 186–91; border disputes of, 187, 239, 242; and master race democracy, 9; and slavery question, 189–90, 201, 210–11
Textile manufacturing, 186
Thirty Years' View (Benton), 33–34, 72, 190–91, 246, 254
"Thomas Hart Benton, His Sources of Political Strength in Missouri from 1815 to 1838" (McCandless), 5–6
Thomas, Jesse B., 79, 85
Thompson, Waddy, 178
Three-fifths clause, 84
Todd, David, 129
"Torchlight" essays (CURTIUS), 130
Trade: with Mexico, 178; in Missouri, 179; with Spain, 183–84
Transcontinental railroad proposals, 235–36
Transcontinental Treaty (1819), 186–87, 208
Transylvania Company, 21, 138
Treat, Samuel, 234
Treaty of Guadalupe Hidalgo (1848), 223–25
Treaty of Indian Springs (1824), 147
Treaty of Paris (1783), 27
Treaty of Payne's Landing (1832), 173
Treaty of Portage des Sioux (1815), 139
Treaty of Sycamore Shoals (1775), 29, 138
Trist, Nicholas, 223
Troup, George M., 146, 147
Tryon, William, 5, 19
Turner, Frederick Jackson, 16

Tyler, John: and election of 1840, 196; and Texas annexation, 197, 198–99, 210, 211

University of North Carolina, 7, 24–25
Upshur, Abel, 197, 198
Utah, as free state, 256

Vallé, Francois, 62
Van Buren, John, 227
Van Buren, Martin: Benton's relationship with, 96, 121; and Democratic Party, 12, 121; and election of 1844, 202; and election of 1848, 226–27, 229; and electoral reform, 276n23; and factory system, 100; and master race democracy, 128; and nationalist economic program, 110; and Panama Congress debates, 125; and Polk administration, 212; and public domain land sales, 151, 154, 166; and slavery in territories, 278n46; and Texas annexation, 196, 199, 200, 208
Vaudreuil, Pierre Rigaud de, 73–74
Vessey, Denmark, 127, 159
Voting rights, 88

Walker, Robert J., 202, 211, 218, 220
War Hawks, 39, 50, 123
War of 1812: Benton's involvement in, 42–53; causes of, 38–39; currency regulation during, 180; Jackson's campaigns in, 38, 42, 52–53; and Native Americans, 50–51, 52, 142–43
Wash, Robert, 181, 271n29
Watauga Purchase, 21. *See also* Sycamore Shoals Treaty (1775)
Weatherford, William, 50, 51

Webster, Daniel, 2, 8, 117, 155–59, 161, 197, 239
Wentworth, John, 250
Whiskey Rebellion (1791), 11
Whiteside, Jenkin, 37
White supremacy. *See* Master race democracy
Whitman, Walt, 227
Wiebe, Robert, 39
Wiener, Alan S., 114
Wilentz, Sean, 11–12, 118, 278n46, 283n61
Wilkinson, James: and separatist plots, 28, 36, 40–41, 43, 266n49; and Spanish land grants, 60
Williams, Abraham, 129
Williams, John, 92
Wilmot, David, 218, 227–28
Wilmot Proviso, 218, 220, 226, 227, 230, 240
Winchester, James, 273n64
Winchester, Marcus, 83, 273n64
Wirt, William, 170, 171
Wise, Henry A., 234
Worcester, Samuel A., 171
Worcester v. Georgia (1832), 171, 283n70
Wright, Silas, 198, 202, 208, 217, 220, 226, 228
Wyatt-Brown, Bertram, 68, 83

www.ingramcontent.com/pod-product-compliance
Lightning Source LLC
Chambersburg PA
CBHW030434300426
44112CB00009B/991